CREATING SPACE FOR DEMOCRACY

CREATING SPACE FOR DEMOCRACY

A Primer on Dialogue and Deliberation in Higher Education

Edited by

Nicholas V. Longo and Timothy J. Shaffer

Published in association with
Association of American Colleges and Universities

Campus Compact

Routledge
Taylor & Francis Group
NEW YORK AND LONDON

First published 2019 by Stylus Publishing, LLC

First Edition, 2019

Published 2023 by Routledge
605 Third Avenue, New York, NY 10017
4 Park Square, Milton Park, Abingdon, Oxon OX14 4RN

*Routledge is an imprint of the Taylor & Francis Group,
an informa business*

Copyright © 2019 by Taylor & Francis Group

CHAPTER 17 COPYRIGHT © NANCY KRANICH

All rights reserved. No part of this book may be reprinted or reproduced or utilised in any form or by any electronic, mechanical, or other means, now known or hereafter invented, including photocopying and recording, or in any information storage or retrieval system, without permission in writing from the publishers.

Notice:
Product or corporate names may be trademarks or registered trademarks, and are used only for identification and explanation without intent to infringe.

Library of Congress Cataloging-in-Publication Data
The CIP for this text has been applied for.

ISBN 13: 978-1-62036-927-2 (pbk)
ISBN 13: 978-1-62036-926-5 (hbk)
ISBN 13: 978-1-00-344381-0 (ebk)

DOI: 10.4324/9781003443810

To Aleida, grateful for your creativity, passion, and inspiration; and for inviting democratic possibility in everyday life with Maya and Noah.—N.L.

To Ellen. A thoughtful, reflective, and provocative partner in conversations about important topics—even while we have a home full of children! Your support makes this work possible. Thank you.—T.S.

CONTENTS

INTRODUCTION   1
Dialogue and Deliberation in Higher Education
    Nicholas V. Longo and Timothy J. Shaffer

1 DISCUSSING DEMOCRACY
Learning to Talk Together   13
    Nicholas V. Longo and Timothy J. Shaffer

PART ONE: CONCEPTS AND THEORIES

2 READINESS FOR DISCUSSING DEMOCRACY IN
SUPERCHARGED POLITICAL TIMES   41
    Nancy Thomas

3 DELIBERATIVE CIVIC ENGAGEMENT
Toward a Public Politics in Higher Education   57
    Derek W.M. Barker

4 CULTIVATING DIALOGUE AND DELIBERATION
THROUGH SPEECH, SILENCE, AND SYNTHESIS   69
    Sara A. Mehltretter Drury

PART TWO: METHODS OF DIALOGUE AND DELIBERATION

5 CREATING CULTURES OF DIALOGUE IN HIGHER EDUCATION   85
Stories and Lessons From Essential Partners
    John Sarrouf and Katie Hyten

6 BUILDING CAPACITY IN COMMUNITIES
Everyday Democracy's Dialogue to Change Approach   97
    Martha L. McCoy and Sandy Heierbacher

7 SUSTAINED DIALOGUE CAMPUS NETWORK   110
    *Elizabeth Wuerz, Rhonda Fitzgerald, Michaela Grenier,
    and Ottavia Lezzi*

8 EDUCATIONAL JUSTICE USING INTERGROUP DIALOGUE   119
   Stephanie Hicks and Hamida Bhagirathy

9 THE FREE SOUTHERN THEATER'S STORY CIRCLE PROCESS   128
   Lizzy Cooper Davis

10 THE NATIONAL ISSUES FORUMS
   "Choicework" as an Indispensable Civic Skill   140
   Jean Johnson and Keith Melville

11 WHAT IF?
   The Interactivity Foundation and
   Student-Facilitated Discussion Teams   147
   Jeff Prudhomme and Shannon Wheatley Hartman

PART THREE: DIALOGUE AND DELIBERATION IN THE CURRICULUM

12 THE STUDENT AS LOCAL DELIBERATIVE CATALYST
   The CSU Center for Public Deliberation   161
   Martín Carcasson

13 DIALOGUE AS A TEACHING TOOL FOR DEMOCRATIZING HIGHER EDUCATION
   The Simon Fraser University Semester in Dialogue   168
   Janet Moore and Mark L. Winston

14 CONVERSATIONS THAT MATTER   176
   Spoma Jovanovic

15 TALKING DEMOCRACY   184
   David Hoffman and Romy Hübler

PART FOUR: DIALOGUE AND DELIBERATION USING CAMPUS SPACES

16 DEMOCRACY PLAZA AT IUPUI   193
   Amanda L. Bonilla and Lorrie A. Brown

17 ACADEMIC LIBRARIES AS CIVIC AGENTS   199
   Nancy Kranich

CONTENTS   ix

18 RESIDENCE HALLS AS SITES OF DEMOCRATIC PRACTICE   209
    Laurel B. Kennedy

PART FIVE: DIALOGUE AND DELIBERATION IN THE COMMUNITY

19 PROVIDENCE COLLEGE/SMITH HILL ANNEX   219
    Keith Morton and Leslie Hernandez

20 LESSONS FROM THE FRONT PORCH
    Fostering Strengthened Community Partnerships Through Dialogue   228
    Suchitra V. Gururaj and Virginia A. Cumberbatch

21 LOCAL PARTICIPATION AND LIVED EXPERIENCE
    Dialogue and Deliberation Through Participatory Processes in
    Landscape Architecture   238
    Katie Kingery-Page

22 "GIVE LIGHT AND THE PEOPLE WILL FIND A WAY"
    Democratic Deliberation and Public Achievement at Colorado College   249
    Anthony C. Siracusa and Nan Elpers

PART SIX: DIALOGUE AND DELIBERATION NETWORKS

23 NEW HAMPSHIRE LISTENS
    Fulfilling the Land-Grant Mission While Strengthening Democratic Practice   259
    Bruce L. Mallory, Michele Holt-Shannon, and Quixada Moore-Vissing

24 START TALKING, STOP TALKING, AND TOXIC TALKING
    Resources for Engaging Difficult Dialogues in Higher Education   269
    Libby Roderick

25 ENACTING DEMOCRACY IN "DEMOCRACY'S COLLEGES"   275
    Carrie B. Kisker, John J. Theis, and Alberto Olivas

    CONCLUSION
    Sources of Democratic Professionalism in the University   285
    Albert Dzur

    RESOURCES   295

    EDITORS AND CONTRIBUTORS   301

    INDEX   321

INTRODUCTION

Dialogue and Deliberation in Higher Education

Nicholas V. Longo and Timothy J. Shaffer

"This is the penalty of democracy," Jane Addams (1902/2002) wrote in *Democracy and Social Ethics*, "that we are bound to move forward or retrograde together. None of us can stand aside" (p. 112). The words of this prominent social reformer at the turn of the twentieth century could not be more prophetic of our contemporary public life. As it becomes increasingly apparent that democracy is in crisis, it also becomes clear that the response to this challenge requires deeper and more robust public participation. We live in divisive and polarizing times, often remaining in comfortable social bubbles and experiencing few genuine interactions with people who are different or with whom we disagree. Stepping out and turning to one another is difficult but necessary. We can't leave the work of democracy to politicians or to specialized experts. To thrive, democracy must involve the full participation (Strum, Eatman, Saltmarsh, & Bush, 2011) of all of us. We need to learn to listen, think, and act with others to solve public problems. This collaborative task begins with creating space for democracy. This book provides a guide for doing so on campus.

Creating Space for Democracy is itself a collaborative work. The contributors provide diverse models and perspectives on dialogue and deliberation for audiences interested in using higher education to revitalize democracy. It is based on our collective experiences in experimenting with participatory practices through engaged teaching and scholarship. These efforts have shown us the importance of working across differences, as well as the vital role of colleges and universities in promoting actual experiences with democratic citizenship and addressing public problems. Our insights into civic education have been informed by our collaboration with the Kettering Foundation, a research foundation in Dayton, Ohio, where we have worked with Vice President Maxine Thomas since 2011 on what we have termed *deliberative pedagogy* with faculty members from around the world. Through this research, we connected with a network of scholars and practitioners interested in developing new approaches to politics, education, and engagement. We came to imagine a future where the development of knowledge is a cocreative process. In working together, we learned the importance of a collaborative, asset-based orientation, where 1 + 1 becomes greater than 2. In short, we have come to see participatory and collaborative approaches among a diverse mix of people as the touchstones for the future of democratic engagement.

The idea for this book was further developed through workshops and presentations following the publication of *Deliberative Pedagogy: Teaching and Learning for Democratic Engagement* (Shaffer, Longo, Manosevitch, & Thomas, 2017). These included several gatherings sponsored by Campus Compact, most notably at the plenary of the 2018 national conference in Indianapolis, Indiana, during which our collaborations with Leslie Garvin from North Carolina Campus Compact, Katie Hyten from Essential Partners, Rhonda Fitzgerald from the Sustained Dialogue Campus Network, and other leaders in the field created a platform to offer what they termed a *guide for the perplexed* on how to use dialogue to build a stronger democracy. These gatherings shaped our understanding of the value of creating space for participatory, democratic methods of engagement in colleges and universities. They also helped us see the diversity of civic experiments taking place across college campuses and the need to share the lessons and wisdom of these efforts. Thus, we set out with this book to work with innovators in the field of dialogue and deliberation to continue the conversation about what works to engage citizens in public life through serious and significant talk—which, when done well, is aligned with productive and public action. Colleges and universities have a vital role to play as sites where students can practice democracy on a human scale.

A Resource for Educating for Democracy

We encourage you to use this book as an organizing tool to democratize your institution, both on and off campus. Build a diverse leadership team of stakeholders who want to create positive changes in campus culture. Take time to develop a shared vision that commits to a transparent and democratic process, even if you don't know where this road may ultimately lead. Honor the unique stories and diverse voices of your campus community, while acknowledging that participants will come with different backgrounds, experiences, and communication styles. Make listening a celebrated civic practice. And then use the art of listening to facilitate leadership that recognizes the value of shared ownership and cocreation.

David Mathews (2009), president of the Kettering Foundation and a former U.S. cabinet secretary responsible for overseeing education policy, writes, "Deliberative democracy challenges academic institutions at every level: from the nature of teaching and the character of the extracurricular program to the very meaning of scholarship" (p. 13). Thus, we envision this book being useful for integrating dialogue and deliberation not only into courses in fields such as communication studies, education, and political science but also into other areas of academic and campus life. It is a resource for centers for teaching and learning, with application throughout the curriculum. It can be a catalyst for offices of diversity, multicultural affairs, or other campus centers hoping to start difficult conversations on issues of race, class, gender, sexuality, and gender identity. It is a wellspring of information for student life on campus, with tools for dialogue and deliberation in spaces like residence halls, libraries, and student clubs. Finally, it is a tool that offices of community engagement can use to incorporate dialogue and deliberation into reflections on service-learning and to promote civic engagement more broadly.

Ultimately, this book is about fostering a more democratic and participatory culture in higher education by providing ideas and practices that create space for dialogue and deliberation to flourish. To accomplish this goal, this book is designed to help bring together areas that are typically isolated. Engagement efforts are often "ships passing in the night" (Mathews, 2009), with various parts of the campus working separately rather than in coordination. This happens on all campuses, large and small. Dialogue and deliberation are meant to bring "islands of engagement" together. Creating space for democracy means talking to one another and finding solutions together.

Book Outline: A Guide to *Creating Space for Democracy*

Together, this book's contributors illuminate the importance of democratizing higher education using dialogue and deliberation. This process requires a long-term commitment. The chapters here offer tools and practices not only for promoting democratic dialogue but also for sustaining a culture in which these practices can continue to grow.

Part One of this book provides a conceptual framework, with leading voices in the dialogue and deliberation field providing insights on issues pertinent to college campuses, from free speech and academic freedom to neutrality and the role of deliberation in civic engagement. Our opening chapter, provides an introduction to the field of dialogue and deliberation, including the origins, concepts, and practices of this method of civic education. As such, it offers the promise of developing more collaborative and participatory practices that connect higher education with efforts to build a stronger democracy.

Drawing on data to stress the ways in which American society has become more polarized, Nancy Thomas provides a clarion call for "readiness" to embark on dialogue and deliberation. Thomas examines the political context on campuses, including extreme polarization and controversies around issues such as free speech, which has implications for learning. She also questions the feasibility of remaining neutral as a discussion leader, while offering concrete suggestions for skills campuses must help students develop as civic leaders, such as learning to build trust, establish group norms, listen, and learn from other perspectives.

Next, Derek W.M. Barker, a political theorist and program officer at the Kettering Foundation, locates deliberative democracy within the contemporary civic engagement movement in higher education. Barker's conceptual genealogy illustrates how what he terms *deliberative civic engagement*—which involves constructively engaging students in deliberating on controversial public issues, leading to enhanced understanding across political divides—provides an alternative to both adversary and unitary forms of democracy. Thus, he notes, the kinds of deliberative practices highlighted in this book can be "more public than nonpolitical service projects, yet less polarizing than 'politics as usual'" (p. 65, this volume).

Sara A. Mehltretter Drury's timely chapter frames the contemporary struggles around free speech on college campuses and offers a response to these challenges drawn from her work in communication studies—namely, a commitment to deliberative practices of free speech, reflective silence, and critical synthesis. According to Drury, these practices, seen in many of the chapters that follow, demonstrate how "dialogue and deliberation [can teach] and promote the rights of free speech as well as the responsibilities of those rights" (p. 69, this volume).

Part Two offers methods of dialogue and deliberation from groups that have developed and sustained deliberative practices. Chapters describe models from Essential Partners, Everyday Democracy, the Interactivity Foundation, Junebug Productions, the National Issues Forums Institute, the Program on Intergroup Relations, and the Sustained Dialogue Campus Network, with insight from leading scholars and practitioners in the field representing organizations such as the Kettering Foundation, the National Coalition for Dialogue and Deliberation, and the Deliberative Democracy Consortium. The contributors to Part Two introduce readers to several distinct models of dialogue and deliberation:

- *Reflective Structured Dialogue* (Essential Partners). According to John Sarrouf and Katie Hyten, Reflective Structured Dialogue is designed to help people talk about difficult topics, drawing on strategies developed by family therapists to determine "whether interventions pioneered by narrative therapy, family systems thinking, and communications theory could shift 'stuck' public conversations" (p. 86, this volume) about contentious issues. This work helps people with fundamental disagreements over divisive issues develop the mutual understanding and trust essential for strong communities and positive action.
- *Dialogue to Change* (Everyday Democracy). Whereas some models can take place as one-time events, dialogue to change is based on a commitment to bringing diverse groups of people together to meet over several weeks. As Martha L. McCoy and Sandy Heierbacher describe it, Everyday Democracy moved from referring solely to the dialogue part of its work—"study circles"—to emphasizing the importance of the larger process of dialogue to change and embedding democratic principles into the culture and shared governance of communities through "regular, structured opportunities," opportunities to "learn how to share knowledge, resources, and power for the common good" and "build relationships . . . strengthen[ing] each other's vision and practices, find[ing] ways to sustain their work across generations" (pp. 101–102, this volume).
- *Sustained Dialogue* (Sustained Dialogue Campus Network). Sustained Dialogue is a process for transforming and building the relationships that are essential to democratic political and economic practice. As Elizabeth Wuerz, Rhonda Fitzgerald, Michaela Grenier, and Ottavia Lezzi note, "Rather than 'focusing first on the problem, we focus on the people within the community affected by or contributing to the problem'" (p. 113, this volume). Sustained Dialogue is not a problem-solving workshop; rather, it is a sustained interaction to transform and build relationships among members of deeply conflicted groups so they can deal effectively with practical problems.
- *Intergroup Dialogue* (Program on Intergroup Dialogue). Intergroup dialogues are face-to-face meetings of people from two or more different social identity groups. They are designed to offer an open and inclusive space where participants can foster a deeper understanding of diversity and justice issues through experiential activities, individual and small-group reflections, and dialogues. Stephanie Hicks and Hamida Bhagirathy describe how this model is "rooted in the assumption that intergroup and interpersonal relationships are affected by the histories and current realities of intergroup contact

in the United States and that this conflict can be explored through dialogue" (p. 119, this volume). Intergroup dialogue strives to create new levels of understanding, relating, and action.

- *Story Circles* (Junebug Productions). The story circle model involves a group of people sitting together and sharing stories about their experience on a given topic or theme. It is a simple, yet radical, practice. According to Lizzy Cooper Davis, "Story circles encourage us to embrace dialogue over debate and to value the nuances of experience over even the best-structured arguments" (p. 128, this volume). The story circle may be used to build community within a group, to examine differences across lines of race or class, to explore social challenges that people are facing in their own lives, or for other purposes.
- *National Issues Forums* (National Issues Forums Institute). As Jean Johnson and Keith Melville describe them, National Issues Forums offer citizens the opportunity to join together to deliberate, to make choices with others about ways to approach difficult issues, and to work toward creating reasoned public judgment. Describing the work, they note, "Perhaps most importantly, at a time when many public exchanges are acrimonious, these forums are not occasions for partisan slugfests. They focus on issues, not personalities or partisan divisions" (pp. 142–143, this volume). By dealing with tensions and tradeoffs of different options, citizens engage in decision-making that can help them agree on what should be done about complex public problems.
- *Exploratory Discussion* (Interactivity Foundation). Exploratory discussion engages groups of people in examining public policy issues that require a choice through open discussion about possible ideas and solutions. Jeff Prudhomme and Shannon Wheatley Hartman explain how thinking about and discussing public policy through a democratic exploration of issues can encourage expanding rather than foreclosing possibilities. Significantly, participants engage in sanctuary discussions. These refer to the act of providing a "space protected from the rush toward evaluation and decision-making, protected from the need for achieving social approval (e.g., judgments about what might be politically or economically feasible), and protected from the constraints of the status quo or past conventions" (pp. 148–149, this volume).

Collectively, these chapters provide historical and organizational context for dialogue and deliberation models, while offering lessons and practiced wisdom from leading scholars. Part Two situates models within the broader field of civic education while providing principles, practices, and examples of deliberative democracy within higher education settings.

It is important to acknowledge the breadth of discussion approaches to citizen-centered politics across institutional and community settings. Parts Three through Six offer case studies of dialogue and deliberation in practice. The chapters illustrate the creative ways that dialogue and deliberation can be infused into the civic life of higher education through the curriculum, campus spaces, campus-community partnerships, and broader deliberative networks.

Part Three focuses on curricular integration, beginning with a chapter from Martín Carcasson, a leading voice for deliberative democracy in communication studies and beyond. Carcasson introduces principles and practices, successes and challenges, and recommendations and resources from the Center for Public Deliberation (CPD) at Colorado State University. One of the earliest centers of its kind, the CPD was founded in 2006 on the principle that "democracy requires high-quality communication" (p. 165, this volume). The CPD's signature student associate program offers dedicated coursework on facilitation in deliberative techniques to allow students to facilitate dialogues on community-identified local projects.

In what is perhaps the most immersive dialogue experience offered on any campus, the Simon Fraser University Semester in Dialogue Program enables students to take a full semester of courses related to dialogue. The university has offered the program since 2002 through its well-resourced Morris J. Wosk Centre for Dialogue. As Janet Moore and Mark L. Winston describe, each academic term a team of two to four faculty members coteach a course on a timely topic such as Governance for the Twenty-First Century, Leading Social Change, or Sustainable Food Systems. The chapter provides a grounding in the importance of dialogical approaches to teaching, along with practical assignments.

The contributors of the next two chapters reflect on innovative courses on dialogue and deliberation at civically engaged universities: Conversations That Matter at the University of North Carolina (UNC) at Greensboro, taught by Spoma Jovanovic, and Talking Democracy at the University of Maryland, Baltimore County (UMBC), taught by David Hoffman and Romy Hübler. The concepts and themes of these stand-alone courses, in communication studies and honors, respectively, serve as models for utilizing deliberative pedagogies in other areas. As Jovanovic remarks, "Engaging conversations that matter in the world can find resonance in diverse disciplines" (p. 182, this volume). The chapters offer lessons on how courses on dialogue and deliberation can be part of a larger culture of civic engagement, with examples including the development of "pop-up dialogues" throughout the campus at UNC Greensboro or the creation of the Center for Democracy and Civic Life at UMBC to foster cultures of deep engagement, full participation, and effective democratic communication.

Part Four offers three cases of deliberative practices in campus spaces. These chapters reimagine how campuses can create "free spaces" (Evans & Boyte, 1992) for dialogue and civic action by using areas such as student centers, academic libraries, and residence halls. Amanda L. Bonilla and Lorrie A. Brown provide an overview of the origins, development, and lessons from Democracy Plaza, a student-led effort at IUPUI that began in 2004 to provide physical spaces on campus for civil discourse and social issue programming. IUPUI illustrates how campuses can create "democracy walls" for visible and inclusive dialogues using timely and well-crafted questions, along with a student leadership model that provides scholarship funds to support student Social Justice Scholars who connect public spaces with programming on pressing social justice issues.

Nancy Kranich, a scholar on the role of libraries in democracy, introduces the ways that academic libraries can serve as civic agents. Drawing on her work at Rutgers University and other campus and public libraries, Kranich argues that academic libraries provide "comfortable, inviting, neutral, safe spaces conducive to democratic discourse" (p. 201, this volume). Laurel B. Kennedy similarly addresses how residence halls can be sites of democratic practice, outlining Denison University's rethinking of student life under the presidential leadership of Adam Weinberg, who has drawn from his earlier experience with democratic skill-building in residential education (Weinberg, 2005). Kennedy describes how student staff—renamed community advisers—are trained to engage in relational work and facilitate "civic deliberations" in the residence halls. These efforts enable residence halls, like democracy plazas and academic libraries, among other spaces, to "function as design studios for acquiring the skills for democratic living" (p. 210, this volume).

Part Five moves beyond the boundaries of the campus and into the community. Keith Morton and Leslie Hernandez describe the development of a "'third' space" (p. 225, this volume) for mutually beneficial relationships and dialogue between campus and community in their chapter on the Providence College/Smith Hill Annex. The chapter offers historical and philosophical foundations for dialogue in community-based spaces, along with practical advice for creating and maintaining hospitable spaces for meaningful conversations.

Suchitra V. Gururaj and Virginia A. Cumberbatch describe how dialogue and deliberation can create synergies between the aims of diversity and community engagement work. They relate the process of developing and then reenvisioning a series of dialogues—which they call "front porch conversations"—in creating effective and reciprocal community engagement initiatives through the University of Texas at Austin's Division of Diversity and Community Engagement (DDCE). Offering lessons on the importance of acknowledging "the power dynamic between the university and its communities" (p. 234, this volume), they describe how the DDCE seeks to develop inclusive and participatory processes in the community.

Katie Kingery-Page provides insight into how professional fields such as landscape architecture use participatory design and codesign processes. She explores how dialogue and deliberation can be incorporated into community-based engagement and research projects, such as those conducted by Kansas State University faculty and graduate students. This work helps to nurture the next generation of scholars and practitioners in embedding democratic practices within their work.

Anthony C. Siracusa and Nan Elpers describe how Colorado College has spent the past decade implementing Public Achievement, an international youth civic education program inspired by the civil rights movement, through which undergraduates serve as civic mentors for primary and secondary school students. The chapter offers an in-depth case study on the relationship between deliberative group processes and collective civic action.

The contributors in Part Six explore the larger landscape of higher education by describing a rich array of civic networks that promote dialogue and deliberation. Bruce L. Mallory, Michele Holt-Shannon, and Quixada Moore-Vissing provide a statewide model with New Hampshire Listens, a network housed at the Carsey School of Public Policy at the University of New Hampshire. Offering an overview of the evolution of the network and a detailed case study, the chapter explores how New Hampshire Listens works on campus and in communities throughout the state to build civic infrastructure, design and facilitate inclusive deliberative processes, and engage in research and assessment to improve overall civic health.

Libby Roderick of the University of Alaska at Anchorage details the work of the Difficult Dialogues Initiative, which has created a campus culture rooted in dialogue. This chapter demonstrates how funding from a national foundation can catalyze dialogue and deliberation on campuses, in this case through a network that continues to offer a multifaceted approach to facilitating "difficult dialogues" in safe and productive ways, including incorporating Indigenous practices.

Carrie B. Kisker, John J. Theis, and Alberto Olivas offer the promise of community colleges becoming "Democracy's Colleges"—an important vehicle in educating for democracy, as these institutions educate two-thirds of all U.S. students enrolled in higher education. The contributors describe a multicampus project in which 11 community colleges collaborate with the

Center for the Study of Community Colleges, the Democracy Commitment, and the Kettering Foundation to "establish deliberation as an essential practice within the community college sector as a whole" (p. 277, this volume). They argue that by participating in and moderating deliberative dialogues, students "realize that they have the ability—through listening, empathizing, and seeking common ground—to facilitate [the] enactment of democracy" (p. 283, this volume).

In the concluding chapter of this book, Albert Dzur lays out the major civic aim of campus dialogue and deliberation: educating democratic professionals. Although our hope is that this book offers a roadmap for cultivating future professionals with civic skills, values, and knowledge to engage with the public to solve problems, Dzur's research illustrates the importance of rethinking the roles of faculty, student affairs professionals, and other campus leaders to make this goal a reality. As he notes, it is essential to recognize the costs of "business as usual" and for institutions of higher education to "convey through their own practices that institutions can change" (p. 289, this volume). This includes making space for active listening and learning through deliberative processes to incorporate some of the lessons from the models in this book to bring "new democratic practice into higher education" (p. 291, this volume).

Moving Forward: A New Generation of Democratic Professionals

The practices of dialogue and deliberation are fundamental to this call to educate future democratic professionals. Dialogue and deliberation are methods of civic education that help us rethink how we deal with the complex issues that permeate our public life. But more than simply rethinking civic life, these chapters offer practical lessons for acting in public. Colleges and universities have an opportunity to be sites for democratic engagement, while preparing students to step into future roles and communities as democratic professionals. To do that, they need to be prepared for discussing democracy, as Nancy Thomas argues in chapter 2. But we also need to get started. This requires faculty, staff, and administrators to view themselves as civic agents with capacity to reconceptualize their work and create democratic spaces that can help foster a larger democratic movement.

Andrew Seligsohn, president of Campus Compact, put it best when he said that going forward, the civic engagement movement in higher education needs to focus on "how to hold public dialogues and teach deliberative practices, get students thinking through issues, teaching them how to value democracy" (quoted in Anft, 2018, para. 12). If we really want the next generation to value democracy, we need more opportunities for them to practice democracy. College and university campuses are important sites for this civic work. We hope this book will help teach us how.

References

Addams, J. (2002). *Democracy and social ethics.* Chicago: University of Illinois Press. (Original work published 1902).

Anft, M. (2018, January 7). How colleges ignite civic engagement. *Chronicle of Higher Education.* Retrieved from https://www-chronicle-com.providence.idm.oclc.org/article/How-Colleges-Ignite-Civic/242164

Evans, S. M., & Boyte, H. C. (1992). *Free spaces: The sources of democratic change in America.* Chicago, IL: University of Chicago Press.

Mathews, D. (2009). Ships passing in the night? *Journal of Higher Education Outreach and Engagement, 13*(3), 5–16.

Shaffer, T. J., Longo, N. V., Manosevitch, I., & Thomas, M. S. (Eds.). (2017). *Deliberative pedagogy: Teaching and learning for democratic engagement.* East Lansing: Michigan State University Press.

Strum, S., Eatman, T., Saltmarsh, J., & Bush, A. (2011). Full participation: Building the architecture for diversity and community engagement in higher education. *Imagining America, 17.* Retrieved from https://surface.syr.edu/ia/17

Weinberg, A. (2005). Residential education for democracy. *Learning for Democracy, 1,* 29–46.

I

DISCUSSING DEMOCRACY

Learning to Talk Together

Nicholas V. Longo and Timothy J. Shaffer

"You can't solve a problem if you can't talk about it," observes Beverly Tatum, former president of Spelman College, in reflecting on the 20th anniversary edition of her bestselling book, *Why Are All the Black Kids Sitting Together in the Cafeteria?* (Kenney, 2017). The inability to discuss complex and divisive issues such as racism and segregation permeates our public life. We might shy away because we don't want to offend people or say the wrong thing. Or we might be concerned that we don't have "all the facts," so we feel unprepared or uninformed. For many, it can be exhausting to face the constant need to explain a part of one's identity or beliefs that might be marginalized or go against the norm. Even when we want to engage in these conversations, it's difficult to know how to get the "right people" in the room or how to structure deliberative processes when we have so little practice in talking across differences. The resulting failure to engage in meaningful dialogue or sustained collaborative work means that public challenges go unaddressed.

This has to change. Rather than feeling powerless, we need to learn how to organize genuine dialogues that lead to productive action. As Peter Levine (2013) notes, to answer the fundamental question of civic studies—What should we do?—we need to work collectively to consider facts, values, and strategies. Facts are important because "we should not try to do something that is impossible, or redundant, or that has harmful but unintended consequences" (p. 25). We need values to distinguish between effective action that is "good" (e.g., the civil rights movement) and "bad" (e.g., fascist movements). Finally, Levine concludes, we need strategies: "It is insufficient to wish for better outcomes and determine that those outcomes are possible. We need a path to the desirable results" (p. 25). In short, we need to start talking with one another, and then turn these conversations into collective action. This book is about taking those first steps in order to make this happen on college campuses.

With the fraying of public life and the loss of community over the past decades, this collaborative engagement can't happen soon enough. Confidence in major institutions has reached historic lows, while we face a growing number of intractable public problems—such as inequality, racism, climate change, and gun violence—that cannot be solved with technical fixes. Historically fringe voices are gaining strength and becoming more visible, while the engaged, democratic citizens[1] most needed to address problems are sidelined with diminished roles and expectations because of the professionalization of public life, among other factors (Dzur, 2017; McKnight, 1995).

Engagement among citizens, it should be noted, also too often contributes to the polarization threatening American democracy as echo chambers provide content that reinforces existing beliefs, isolating us even further from contrasting views. And, according to a recent Pew Research Center (2018) study, a growing majority of Americans (53% in 2018 versus 46% in 2016) now say that "talking about politics with people they disagree with" is generally "stressful and frustrating," whereas a decreasing number (45% in 2018 versus 51% in 2016) say such conversations are usually "interesting and informative." Given this context, it is difficult even to engage in civil discourse about issues that matter (Boatright, Shaffer, Sobieraj, & Young, 2019).

Higher education is not immune to these challenges. Colleges and universities serve as microcosms for democratic life and its discontents. It should come as no surprise that the fall 2016 entering cohort of first-time, full-time college students had the "distinction of being the most polarized cohort in the 51-year history" (Eagan et al., 2017, p. 4) of student surveys by the Higher Education Research Institute. Once a beacon of achievement, higher education is also increasingly seen with scorn; 61% of Americans say the U.S. higher education system is going in the wrong direction, according to a new Pew Research Center survey (Brown, 2018).

There is also a deep partisan divide around most issues connected with higher education, with a sharp rise—from 37% to 58% in just two years—in the number of Republicans saying that "colleges and universities have a negative effect on the way things are going in the country" (Fingerhut,

---

1. When we refer to *citizens*, we use the term inclusively of individuals who are community members, broadly defined. We do not use the term to refer to legal status, but instead point to the idea of citizenship being an "office, a responsibility, a burden proudly assumed" (Walzer, 1989, p. 216).

2017). By comparison, a wide majority of Democrats (72%) continue to view colleges and universities as having a positive effect (Fingerhut, 2017). Although there is some consensus about issues such as the negative impact of the high costs of college and the need for greater development of workforce skills, issues involving political discourse elicit wide partisan disagreement. For example, views on professors bringing their political and social views into the classroom diverge sharply, with 79% of Republicans saying it has a negative impact, compared with just 17% of Democrats. Similarly, 75% of Republicans see too much concern about protecting students from views they might find offensive, compared with 31% of Democrats (Brown, 2018). In this context, tensions around free speech and diversity and inclusion abound (Knight Foundation, 2019). With controversial speakers and counterprotests being stoked by national leaders and garnering a disproportionate amount of media attention, it can seem like our campuses are ground zero for polarization and the partisan culture wars. Yet these tensions are also missed opportunities for civic learning, which can be catalyzed through participatory, democratic processes such as dialogue and deliberation.

To feel safe to take risks and speak genuinely, people need to have the opportunity to participate in shared life in educative spaces that are humanizing, authentic, and productive. As the authors of *Free Spaces* (Evans & Boyte, 1992), *The Great Good Places* (Oldenburg, 1999), and *Palaces for the People* (Klinenberg, 2018) argue in unique but interrelated ways, places we might not first think of as sites for democratic discussion are essential to community life and social change. When describing what they call *free space*, *third spaces*, or *social infrastructure*, these scholars point to the importance of creating spaces in which ordinary people can share experiences, associate and organize, participate in public decision-making, and plan for collaborative action. Sometimes this process involves reconceptualizing familiar locations—such as libraries or barbershops—as civic spaces. Other times it utilizes locations away from everyday life, such as retreat centers and folk schools. Regardless, these types of spaces are essential to the healthy functioning of any society (Malena, 2015). Throughout history, free spaces have served as "seedbeds of democratic change in education and beyond" (Boyte, 2017), which then serve as training grounds for developing civic leadership among diverse groups of people working collectively to solve problems.

Using free spaces to cocreate knowledge offers an alternative to the dominant expertise paradigm of the academy. Much of the framework for teaching and learning is situated within a context in which the narrow technical expertise of a professor provides the sole basis for instruction. Dialogue and deliberation, however, build on the change from an instructional to a learning paradigm—an important conceptual shift in higher education that Robert

Barr and John Tagg (1995) flagged almost 25 years ago. With this shift, colleges recognized their responsibility to "create environments and experiences that allow students to discover and construct knowledge for themselves and to become members of communities of learning that make discoveries and solve problems" (Barr & Tagg, 1995, p. 15). Since then, more active educational practices—what George Kuh (2008) refers to as "high-impact practices"—have grown through curricular interventions (e.g., first-year seminars, capstone courses, global learning) and classroom practices (intensive writing, undergraduate research, collaborative assignments), as well as through student life experiences (common intellectual experiences, learning communities) and off-campus engagement (internships, service-learning courses).

These are spaces where people interact with one another in ways that value the uniqueness and diversity of each other's stories, experiences, and ideas. These spaces become invitations to "listen eloquently" to people with different backgrounds and views, to use a phrase from educator Herman Blake (1996, 2014), and then turn these stories into not only meaningful learning experiences but also sustained common work. This type of cocreative, asset-based learning process is empowering; it needs to be the touchstone for learning in our networked society, where information is no longer the exclusive purview of experts and gatekeepers. We all have something to contribute. This means that learning and knowledge creation take place within an ecosystem that extends beyond the professor and students to include those in the larger community affected by an issue. Most significantly, through these participatory processes, learning becomes the foundation for a democratic society.

This work is important because strong evidence is amassing that democracy is in crisis. In the *Journal of Democracy*, Larry Diamond (2015) referred to a global democratic recession. Although we live in an era when more than half of the world's countries qualify as democratic, "more democracies than ever before are in decline" (p. 144), according to researchers at the Varieties of Democracy Institute. In the United States, and around the world in nations as diverse as Brazil, India, Russia, Turkey, and Venezuela, we see a rise in *autocratization* even in countries that have been heralded as exemplary democracies (Lührmann et al., 2018). The Kettering Foundation has been researching what it takes to make democracy work for several decades and recently remarked on the dangers of becoming "a citizenless democracy" (Mathews, 2010, p. iv), because ordinary citizens are being pushed to the sidelines, making it harder to work together to solve public problems or even to feel empowered to try. But more than simply noting these global trends, there are opportunities to think about democracy and its challenges in our own lived experience—especially on college campuses.

Civic Purposes of Colleges and Universities

Colleges and universities were founded with civic purposes. The missions of higher education institutions of every type still call upon campuses to "serve a larger purpose" (Saltmarsh & Hartley, 2011). But "democracy" often shows up only in the lofty rhetoric of administrators or as the subject of study in survey courses reviewing historical events or legislators in faraway capitals. Higher education itself has little experience with the actual work of democracy, especially as part of the student experience. The growth in community engagement and service-learning has led to an abundance of opportunities for structuring "good deeds," often through short-term volunteering. Yet the framing and practicing of engaged learning and civic engagement on college campuses remain thin. As Harry Boyte (2015) notes, "The fate of higher education and the larger democracy itself is inextricably tied *to the way* those of us in higher education understand citizenship, practice civic education, and convey our purposes to the larger society" (p. 1).

This insight emerged from extensive research and conversations about civic education in higher education with a diverse group of faculty members from campuses across the globe. Over the past decade, this group of scholars participated in a series of workshops known as "learning exchanges," hosted by the Kettering Foundation and led by Maxine Thomas, which led to the publication of *Deliberative Pedagogy: Teaching and Learning for Democratic Engagement* (Shaffer, Longo, Manosevitch, & Thomas, 2017). One central finding from this research is that *public deliberation must be part of the next generation of democratic engagement for colleges and universities to realize their public purposes.*

Myles Horton, cofounder of the Highlander Folk School in Tennessee, reflected: "When you believe in a democratic society, you create spaces for education that are democratic" (Horton, Kohl, & Kohl, 1998, p. 68). This is a simple yet profound idea about the connection between education and democracy from a savvy educator who found ways to put this idea into practice during the labor and civil rights movements. Yet making this connection today is particularly challenging in our colleges and universities. Despite putting in place mission statements and pronouncements about the importance of educating democratic citizens (Morphew & Hartley, 2006), higher education institutions do too little to put these lofty democratic ideals into practice in classrooms or beyond. We have seen this firsthand on campuses we've collaborated with across the country, and we've seen the results: College students learn most about democracy by how it is practiced—or, more often, not practiced—on campus.

The Kettering Foundation's research on this topic over a period of decades has come to similar conclusions about the need for campuses to empower students with real opportunities for democratic engagement (Harwood Group, 1993; Kiesa et al., 2007). This research also found students "eager for opportunities to talk about issues with a diverse group of people in open and authentic ways" (Kiesa et al., 2007, p. 5). If we care about the future of democracy, we can't just give lectures or research it as an abstract idea; we need to put it into practice. This book offers a blueprint for doing so by incorporating dialogue and deliberation into learning at colleges and universities. We hope to help readers understand, build, and strengthen an ecosystem of democracy, with citizen-centered practices acting as a sort of lifeblood flowing through the system. Connecting this lifeblood to the multitude of educative spaces—both formal and informal, on campus and in the community—is vital work for higher education.

Colleges and universities have the opportunity to create spaces where students—along with faculty and staff—can learn to be democratic citizens. This involves discussing important topics and divisive issues while also charting paths forward to address collective challenges.

Efforts to cultivate informed civil discourse through dialogue and deliberation have flourished on campuses across the United States and beyond (Carcasson, 2013; Dedrick, Grattan, & Dienstfrey, 2008; London, 2010; Shaffer, 2014; Shaffer et al., 2017; Thomas, 2010). Although public dialogue is increasingly being embedded within offices of institutional diversity or centers for community engagement, there are many more places on campus where such discussions aren't occurring. For faculty members and staff who are not comfortable leading conversations about contentious civic issues, avoiding such discussions is the safe and preferred path. Campus leaders may recognize the importance of helping students understand significant public issues but be hampered by uncertainty about what is possible or appropriate, or feel unqualified to facilitate discussions about contentious issues (Lukianoff & Haidt, 2018).

These are missed opportunities. Our campuses—and our broader society—will benefit from democratically structured communication and education processes with the creation of space where diverse voices can speak and be heard. Such efforts respond to concerns about viewpoint diversity, so that students are able to gain awareness of their views and those of other stakeholders, while also modeling constructive discourse.[2] Ultimately,

---

2. Visit the Heterodox Academy website at heterodoxacademy.org for more information on the importance of viewpoint diversity and efforts to create conditions for awareness of one's own views and the importance of understanding others.

democratic discourse creates space for a wider range of perspectives to listen to, engage with, and build trust and respect for—an anomaly to our more familiar existences within information bubbles and like-minded social circles. If this doesn't happen in institutions of higher learning, where else will it happen in our society?

Engaged learning has taken up these issues as educators realize the importance of bridging political and cultural divides. The diverse interactions of everyday life—when students are more likely to build relationships—may offer even more promise than more formal settings (Conover & Miller, 2018). On college and university campuses, opportunities to take part in structured discussions are growing, but there are also many settings, such as residence and dining halls, in which informal conversations can transform into more substantive discussions. This transformation requires proper support and training. Although this type of professional development must take place as part of the core work of teaching and learning (Shaffer et al., 2017), many other opportunities for discussion, dialogue, and deliberation exist to create space for civic education.

What has struck us in our conversations with colleagues and others since the publication of *Deliberative Pedagogy* has been the desire on the part of many within higher education to utilize discussion-based approaches in their work. The challenge has often been that they are not sure how to go about it.

For those with experience in service-learning and other community engagement settings, discussion has long been part of the reflection on experiential learning, as well as a needed vehicle to hear underrepresented voices in community settings (Stoecker, Tryon, & Hilgendorf, 2009). Developmental, cohort programs like the Bonner Program, which provides scholarships for students engaged in meaningful community work, have integrated dialogue into multiyear student experiences. This approach acknowledges that being able to engage in critical discussion about issues can lead to desired social change, or at least better understanding of what challenges exist and why.

More broadly, in diversity affairs and ethnic studies, creating opportunities for dialogues about social identities such as race, class, gender, sexual orientation, and gender identity is seen as foundational to equity work on campus. Grounded in theories and practices of equity and critical pedagogy (Freire, 1974, 2000; Shor & Freire, 1987), deliberative practices in these settings become integrated with efforts to decolonize the university. Issues of power—too often overlooked in the broader field of dialogue and deliberation—become more prominent. As a result, centers for multicultural education often catalyze dialogue and deliberation to build bridges between social and cultural identities on and off campus. Processes such as intergroup dialogue recognize the importance of social identity and focus on facilitating dialogue about group differences (Zúñiga, Nagda, Chesler, & Cytron-Walker, 2007).

Student affairs offices are also working to empower students to work through problems using respectful and civil conversations (Magolda, Magolda, & Carducci, 2019). For instance, in recognizing the efforts of sustained dialogue, deliberative dialogue, and intergroup dialogue as models used by student affairs professionals, one student affairs leader noted,

> While the challenges are real, there is no better place to do this work than on a college campus, the place in our society most likely to be made up of diverse individuals, full of open minds, and characterized by the spirit of inquiry. (Rue, 2019, p. 13)

The work of dialogue and deliberation is an especially useful skill set for residence assistants and student leaders of clubs on campus, where facilitation of conversations, leadership, and conflict resolution are paramount. Other areas that work toward conflict resolution, such as the office of the ombuds—where students bring concerns and complaints about the university—are also potential sites for dialogical and deliberative practice.

Nevertheless, thinking about the use of dialogue and deliberation processes, especially with models that utilize facilitators as neutral voices in the midst of divergent and sometimes discordant perspectives and positions, is still outside the comfort zone of many educators. This book is designed to expand this comfort zone by providing models for the many settings in which faculty, staff, administrators, and students might choose to use dialogue and deliberation to frame and enhance educative experiences. Our hope is that all educators who are concerned about democracy and who recognize the power and impact of public talk will be able to pick up this book, learn from the contributors' insights and experiences, and feel prepared to adopt or adapt these models in their own settings.

A Deliberative Turn

Communities can make significant progress on complex problems when citizens—as opposed to experts—are at the center of decision-making. This has led a growing number of public officials, school administrators, and other traditional decision-makers to realize that public problems are too complex for them to resolve alone. That's why they are increasingly reaching out and convening diverse groups of community residents and organizations to identify issues and develop and implement strategies to address them. Over the past few decades (building on traditions from much earlier), public deliberation has become more integral in domains such as public policy and the political sphere, with practices such as participatory budgeting getting more recognition for including diverse voices as well as for their tangible impact on communities.

This kind of engagement goes beyond simply asking residents for input or involving only select groups of people in decision-making processes. Instead, it is intentional about seeing residents as active and equal partners in all facets of planning, implementing, assessing, and improving efforts to strengthen communities. It is an approach that melds "top-down" and "bottom-up" strategies for decision-making, and it is inherently democratic.

Right now, a growing number of urban planning, civic, political, environmental, and educational groups are exploring and advocating citizen-centered approaches to a wide range of public problems, from community revitalization to clean air campaigns. In several states, groups have convened citizen-led deliberations that have produced a set of public priorities that local communities are now taking steps to enact. In New York City, every public high school uses a participatory budgeting process to make decisions on the use of funds (Lerner, 2018). Leading funders, such as the Ford Foundation, have even begun to develop deliberative processes to involve citizens and stakeholders in every aspect of funding decisions (Gibson, 2017). At the local level, cities and towns are opening the doors of their libraries and school gyms to bring people together to negotiate diverse interests, identify common ground, and make collective decisions (Longo & Gibson, 2017). These kinds of efforts—which are broadly understood as *dialogue* and *deliberation*—have also been occurring in colleges and universities around the world. These processes not only help solve problems by getting more voices into the conversation but also teach democratic citizenship.

Defining Dialogue *and* Deliberation

Given the significance of this work, it is essential to offer some clarity about what we mean by key terms. Fortunately, many scholars in this field offer definitions to clarify what can otherwise be muddied and confusing terminology for these concepts (Escobar, 2011).

At the most basic level, *dialogue* is not about trying to win an argument (the realm of debate); rather, it is a collaborative and relational process to engage with others and cocreate meaning. At the ontological level, in the words of philosopher Martin Buber (1947), "the basic movement of the life of dialogue is the turning towards the other" (p. 22). Educators like bell hooks, Paulo Freire, Meg Wheatley, and Myles Horton have since expanded these ideas to make dialogue a fundamental vehicle for understanding issues and making social change.

With echoes of the seminal writings of Martin Buber and scholarly work in the area of communication studies, Laura Black (2015) describes dialogue as "communication that involves a moment of full mutuality between people" (p. 365). She notes further that dialogue is "a way of speaking and relating in which both parties are fully present, open about their ideas, and accepting of the other people involved, even while engaging in disagreement" (pp. 365–366). Dialogue in this sense is a way of being as well as a way of communicating between people or groups.

Deliberation adds another dimension, often coming after or intersecting with dialogue. Specifically, *deliberation* is a process in which a diverse group of people moves toward making a collective decision on a difficult public issue. Best known as part of the jury system in the United States, deliberation involves weighing tradeoffs and tensions, recognizing competing values and interests, and coming to what has been termed *public judgment* (Yankelovich & Friedman, 2010). Public deliberation, according to David Mathews (2014) of the Kettering Foundation, is used in situations "when there are competing imperatives about what is worth most to us and our collective well-being" (p. 75).

Even within seemingly defined models, some fluidity exists. Definitions in the field overlap and form concentric circles. It is helpful to distinguish and clarify differences, however slight, in order to understand how models and approaches might be useful in different settings. Table 1.1 provides some context by depicting the linguistic roots and meanings of common terms.

Together, dialogue and deliberation have the potential for transformative work through relational engagement and robust discussion. Nearly 100 years ago, Mary Parker Follett (1924) recognized this potential, writing that in human relations, "It is I-plus-you reacting to you-plus-me." She explains, "'I' can never influence 'you' because you have already influenced me; that is, in the very process of meeting, by the very process of meeting, we both become something different" (pp. 62–63). It is this acknowledgment that we learn and cocreate knowledge when we enter into relationships, however fleeting, that reminds us of the importance of making those interactions as beneficial, constructive, and respectful as possible.

Naming and Framing Wicked Problems

Most complex social and public policy issues are best understood as *wicked problems* (Rittel & Webber, 1973). These challenges cannot be solved with technical fixes or the usual way of doing business. They involve complex

TABLE 1.1
Roots and Meanings

Debate	*De* = "down," "completely" *Batre* = "to beat" *Debate* = "to fight," "to resolve by beating down"
Discussion	*Dis* = "apart" *Quatere* = "to shake" *Discussion* = "to shake apart," "to break apart" Same roots as *concussion* and *percussion*
Conversation	*Com* = "with" *Vertare* = "to turn" *Conversation* = "turn about with," "keep company with," "act of living with," "having dealings with others"; "manner of conducting oneself in the world"
Dialogue	*Dia* = "through," "between," "across" *Logos* = "word," "speech," "meaning," "reason," "to gather together" *Dialogue* = "flow of meaning," "meaning flowing"
Deliberation	*De* = "entirely," "completely" *Librare* = "to balance, weigh" (from *libra:* "scale") *Deliberare* = "weigh, consider well"

Source: Escobar (2011).

issues with competing values, multiple perspectives, and tough tradeoffs. As Martín Carcasson (2017) notes, wicked problems "call for ongoing communicative processes of broad engagement to address underlying competing values and tensions" (p. 3). As a response, he offers that a "deliberative mindset [can help] develop mutual understanding across perspectives, negotiate the underlying competing values, and invent, support, and constantly adapt collaborative actions" (p. 3).

A critical step for taking action is being able to discuss problems and approaches for addressing them with others in the school, neighborhood, or community. To put it another way, it is about naming and framing an issue in public ways (Rourke, 2014).[3] *Naming* wicked problems is a fundamental step for addressing them because it identifies the specific issue that we need to talk about in a public way. People name problems in conversations all the

---

3. Rourke (2014) is a useful resource for groups trying to develop their own materials for deliberation. It offers step-by-step suggestions in a brief, accessible format for how to develop materials for deliberative forums.

time, a process that helps them capture their experiences and concerns. David Mathews (2016) explains that these conversations revolve around ordinary questions, such as the following: What's bothering you? Why do you care? How are you going to be affected? When people respond to these questions, they are identifying what is valuable to them. This is the first step toward being engaged—that is, "more likely to participate in making decisions and to see that . . . [citizens] have power to affect their future" (Rourke, 2014, p. 3).

This is a political, and sometimes defiant, act because professionals often name problems in different ways from the people and communities affected by a problem. For instance, professional stakeholders in education, such as school administrators, will often name problems differently from parents or students. This can be seen with an issue such as a chronically absent student who is forced to move during the school year: The challenge for families might be homelessness and housing insecurity, whereas school officials seemingly name the problem as "truancy." In higher education, provocative free expression or even discriminatory language can be named as "free speech" by advocates of academic freedom, but "hate speech" by vulnerable groups who feel harmed by this speech. How do we approach such issues? Is there a correct option or choice for how to name the problem? Who decides?

People often name problems differently depending on their own backgrounds, experiences, and positionalities. These examples are meant to demonstrate that it is vital for people with direct experience with an issue to be involved in the initial naming of the topic—and that this work not be left to experts or outsiders. Encouraging participants to name problems on their own terms in a public way is empowering and helps to make sure subsequent dialogues are relevant. Ultimately, an inclusive and deliberative process of naming issues affords a greater sense of ownership, allowing ordinary people to reclaim a civic identity and responsibility that is too often relinquished to experts in their professional capacities.

Framing wicked problems is also an essential aspect of democratic public talk, both in dialogue and in deliberation. With dialogue work, framing the right questions is important for inviting the type of participation you most want to cultivate. According to Juanita Brown and her colleagues (Brown, Issacs, Vogt, & Margulies, 2002), "When people frame their strategic explorations as questions rather than as concerns or problems . . . a conversation begins where everyone can learn something new together, rather than having the normal stale debates" (p. 2). Building on the wisdom of the Public Conversations Project (now Essential Partners), the following is a helpful guide for framing questions:

- Is this question relevant to the real life and real work of the people who will be exploring it?
- Is this a genuine question—a question to which I/we really don't know the answer?
- What "work" do I want this question to do? That is, what kind of conversation, meaning, and feelings do I imagine this question will evoke in those who will be exploring it?
- Is this question likely to invite fresh thinking/feeling? Is it familiar enough to be recognizable and relevant—and different enough to call forward new responses?
- What assumptions or beliefs are embedded in the way this question is constructed?
- Is this question likely to generate hope, imagination, engagement, creative action, and new possibilities, or is it likely to increase a focus on past problems and obstacles?
- Does this question leave room for new and different questions to be raised as the initial question is explored? (Brown et al., 2002, p. 4)

Similarly, framing is a key practice for the choicework involved in deliberation. This is the process by which groups critically discuss various options—including positive aspects, along with drawbacks—for deciding what to do about a problem. David Mathews (2014) writes, "Framing issues, like naming problems, goes on as people deliberate to reach some common ground for action" (p. 92). A key element of framing is that it should not prompt the usual conversations; in fact, ideally it disrupts old patterns of public talk and opens up new conversations. This process, in Mathews's words, "should not replicate the prevailing academic, professional, or partisan framework. It must reflect where citizens are in thinking about an issue, wherever that may be; it should start where people start" (p. 93).

Naming and framing an issue creates an environment for shared learning by acknowledging the complexity and scope of the issue, ways to invite dialogue about the topic, and the various ways to address the issue. As Mathews (2014) notes, "Deliberative frameworks or issue books that serve as guides to deliberation aren't created to simplify complex issues but rather to underscore the perplexity that is generated by tensions among and within options, and by the need to make difficult trade-offs" (p. 93). Naming and framing issues in ways that highlight the aspects causing perplexity serve as a kind of agitation, prompting learning that informs actions. This kind of public talk is fundamentally rooted in learning and essential for exploring the interwoven roots of democratic practice and civic education.

Democratic Roots and Aspirations

Dialogue and deliberation are not new. This process for coming to public judgment about difficult issues has been "part of the ongoing development of democracy" (Leighninger, 2012, p. 19) and has for many centuries been at the core of what makes communities work (Nabatchi, Gastil, Weiksner, & Leighninger, 2012). Public deliberation was used from the time of the ancient Greeks as a basis for democratic decision-making, and more recently in American history in the labor, women's, and civil rights movements, along with settlement houses, social centers, citizenship schools, and countless other civic engagement projects across the globe (Barker, McAfee, & McIvor, 2012; Dedrick et al., 2008).

The contemporary deliberative turn in political theory occurred in the 1990s and early 2000s as scholars shifted their focus to citizen-centered models of democratic life (Dryzek, 2000). Yet education has had a role in civic life since the founding of the United States, including as a vehicle for democratic renewal in formal and informal learning environments (Cremin, 1990). "Democracy has to be born anew every generation," John Dewey (1916/1993) famously wrote, "and education is its midwife" (p. 122).

The interest in participatory democracy gave birth to the deliberative democracy movement as an alternative to institution-centric models of democracy (Held, 2006). As calls for greater civic participation by ordinary people animated participatory democracy from the 1960s on, efforts to rethink the purpose and promise of higher education offered a tangible way to approach democracy as a way of being rather than simply as something to be studied (Loss, 2012). With the establishment of national networks such as Campus Compact in 1985, followed by and later Imagining America, the American Democracy Project, and many others, we've seen a growing commitment to the civic mission of higher education (Saltmarsh & Hartley, 2011). Aligned with institutional commitments, we've also seen the movement toward engaged scholarship (Boyer, 1996; Post, Ward, Longo, & Saltmarsh, 2016) become more widespread, affording the opportunity for educators to make a commitment to engaging public stakeholders in increasingly diverse and democratic ways.

These educators serve as democratic leaders—not necessarily through the traditional means of advocating for a specific cause, but rather by embracing the role of facilitator, mobilizing others to be civically engaged. They embody what Stephen Preskill and Stephen D. Brookfield (2009) term *organic leadership*, in which the leader is more concerned with "helping members of the organization, movement, or community realize what talents, knowledge, and skills they can contribute to a vision they themselves have generated" (p. ix). In many ways, the dialogue and deliberation field calls on educators to act as democratic professionals, which means developing a new set of skills so they can create space for learning and collaborative action.

This conception of learning and leadership necessitates the practice of openness, the "willingness to entertain a variety of alternative perspectives . . . and create dialogic open spaces—multiple opportunities for diverse voices and opinions to be heard" (Preskill & Brookfield, 2009, p. 21). Facilitators who show a passionate impartiality—that is, a deep commitment to democratic processes rooted in neutrality on the topic being discussed—give us an alternative model for democratic leadership (Sprain & Carcasson, 2013). This work needs educators with "skills in coaching without directing, listening without coddling or condescending, and challenging and energizing without dominating" (Boyte, 2017).

Engagement Streams in a Growing Field

Dialogue and deliberation are high-impact practices that attempt to create spaces for authentic and productive conversations. Grounded in real-world experiences, these democratic discussions and interactions can open up new understanding of issues and point us to action; ultimately, they can be not only educational but also transformative.

A multiplicity of approaches and spaces can help people engage one another in public talk that elicits insights and encourages action if a collective agreement can be reached about a path forward (see Levine, 2013). This book identifies some of the many ways in which people are using dialogue and deliberation in curricular, cocurricular, and community spaces. The chapters offer an introduction not only to what is happening now but also to what is possible for dialogue and deliberation in higher education to achieve in the future. This is not meant to be an exhaustive list or the final word on a robust and growing field; rather, we provide a range of models and approaches to demonstrate the depth and breadth of civic practices available.

On college campuses, dialogue and deliberation has grown as a form of civic education in recent years. To illustrate, 76% of colleges and universities hosted and/or funded public dialogues on current issues in 2015, according to a survey by Campus Compact (2015). Many disciplines, including education and communication studies, have long included dialogue and deliberation in pedagogical approaches and educational goals (Longo, 2007; Shaffer, 2017a, 2017b). These areas sprouted research on topics such as small-group communication (Follett, 1924; Gastil & Keith, 2005; Keith, 2007) and the scholarship of teaching and learning (Shaffer et al., 2017). Further, there is a growing infrastructure on college campuses for dialogue and deliberation—mirroring the capacity for other engaged pedagogies, such as service-learning and multicultural education.

Support structures for this work are varied and growing. Multiple consortiums promote dialogue and deliberation, including the Deliberative Democracy Consortium and the National Coalition for Dialogue and Deliberation (NCDD). Endowed institutions such as the Kettering Foundation and Everyday Democracy support research and practice. Academic journals such as the *Journal of Public Deliberation* offer venues for sharing the research, projects, experiments, and experiences of academics and practitioners in the multidisciplinary field of deliberative democracy. Finally, a multitude of practices in higher education are emerging from organizations such as the National Issues Forums Institute, the Sustained Dialogue Network, the Difficult Dialogues Initiative, Essential Partners, and the Program on Intergroup Relations, among others. This book features many of these practices and offers a detailed list of resources on dialogue and deliberation.

One common element to all of this work is the importance of establishing ground rules as a first step in the process. This is best done as a cocreative process with participants, but it can help to start by considering some general guidelines such as those developed by the Institute for Civic Discourse and Democracy at Kansas State University (Figure 1.1).

Another helpful resource for thinking about different ways of engaging through dialogue and deliberation comes from the NCDD. The NCDD's (2014) Engagement Streams Framework was designed to help navigate the range of approaches available by offering a simple-to-use reference guide outlining which process models might be useful for different types of groups, time commitments, and facilitator capabilities (Figure 1.2). Distinguishing among "Exploration," "Conflict Transformation," "Decision Making," and "Collaborative Action," the guide offers a glimpse into the distinct yet interrelated models that comprise dialogue and deliberation.

This book offers detailed descriptions and examples of many of these models in practice within higher education. Whether one is just coming into this field or is a seasoned practitioner, the Engagement Streams Framework is a tremendously useful tool when considering factors such as the number of people involved in a dialogue and deliberation effort, the way those people are invited or selected to participate, and the type of session envisioned (e.g., a one-day event or multimonth project). These considerations are significant, especially if what you are trying to accomplish really asks for a different process model from the one you may have chosen based on your previous experience or exposure. Nevertheless, these distinctions are often messy—like the work of dialogue and deliberation itself. Many people blend models once they become more familiar and comfortable with processes, recognizing the strengths and weaknesses of various options for their context. In Table 1.2,

DISCUSSING DEMOCRACY   29

Figure 1.1. Ground rules for public discussion.

- Seek understanding and common ground
- Expect and explore conflicting viewpoints
- Give everyone an opportunity to speak
- Listen respectfully and thoughtfully
- Offer and examine support for claims
- Appreciate communication differences
- Stay focused on issues
- Respect time limits

Source: Institute for Civic Discourse and Democracy, Kansas State University. Retrieved from www.k-state.edu/icdd/images/ICDD%20Ground%20Rules%20poster.pdf

Figure 1.2. Engagement Streams Framework.

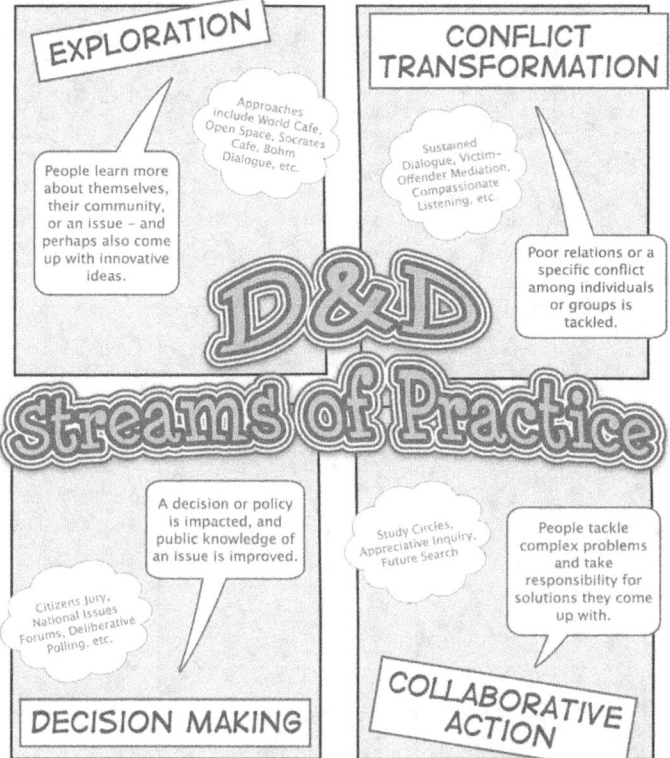

Note. This is a snapshot of the Engagement Streams Framework developed by Sandy Heierbacher and members of the NCDD in 2005. The framework helps people decide which methods of dialogue and deliberation best fit their goals and resources. Visit ncdd.org/streams for the full framework.

TABLE 1.2
Engagement Streams Dialogue and Deliberation Practices*

Processes	Exploration	Conflict Resolution	Decision-Making	Collaborative Action	Role of Facilitator	Size of Group	Type of Session	Participant Selection
Reflective Structured Dialogue (Essential Partners)	√√	√			Works collaboratively to design a process and prepare participants, de-centered from the conversation	Single or multiple circles of 4 to 12	Multiple or single 1.5- to 2.5-hour sessions, but could be shortened	Preexisting groups in conflict or a dynamic of silence or avoidance
Dialogue to Change (Everyday Democracy)	√		√	√√	Diverse local facilitators guide community members through dialogue, deliberation, and action with a racial equity lens	Up to hundreds meeting in separate small groups of 8 to 12; all come together later for Action Forum	Four to six 2-hour sessions	Open; recruit for representativeness
Sustained Dialogue (Sustained Dialogue Institute)	√	√		√√	Leads group through committing to talk openly, relationship-building, brainstorming, and action planning	Eight to 15	Series of at least seven 1-hour or longer sessions	Open to people able to commit to ongoing process over a span of weeks or months

Intergroup Dialogue (The Program on Intergroup Relations)	✓	✓✓		✓	Peer cofacilitators lead the group through the 4-stage dialogue model over the course of the semester; lead activities, respond to journals, help surface and process conflict in the group, and model dialogic inquiry for their peer participants	Twelve to 16 student participants divided into 2 groups, each representing a privileged or marginalized social identity category; two student cofacilitators, each representing one group in the dialogue	One 3-hour session per week for 12 to 14 weeks	Student participants in course rank three dialogue topics (e.g. gender, race, educational justice); Intergroup Relations then sorts students into dialogues based upon interest and availability of facilitators
Story Circles (Junebug Productions)	✓✓		✓		Introduces and guides the process, offers prompt for stories, shares story as well, ensures adherence to values and agreements	Circle is best with 4 to 8; can do any number of circles	Thirty to 40 minutes in smaller circles, and then 30 to 40 for processing discussion	Open

(Continues)

TABLE 1.2. (Continued)

Processes	Exploration	Conflict Resolution	Decision-Making	Collaborative Action	Role of Facilitator	Size of Group	Type of Session	Participant Selection
Deliberative Forum (National Issues Forums)	√	√	√√√		Leads participants through discussion guide and reflections	Twelve to 30; smaller meetings with breakout groups	Two hours or series of shorter sessions	Open or among preexisting group
Exploratory Discussion (Interactivity Foundation)	√√		√		Organizes the discussion event, introduces the topic and process, offers discussion prompts, guides discussants through exploration of topic and guidebook; encourages agreed-upon discussion guidelines	Six to 8 people; can be adjusted to accommodate larger or smaller groups	Multiple or single 1.5- to 2.5-hour sessions, but can be modified	Open

Source: Adapted from NCDD. (2014). Engagement Streams Framework. Retrieved from www.ncdd.org/files/rc/2014_Engagement_Streams_Guide_Web.pdf

*Three checks indicates the particular practice focuses significantly on that aspect. One check indicates secondary foci for that practice.

we have adapted the Engagement Streams Framework to help readers navigate the multiple models and approaches presented in Part Two of this book. These processes serve as vital tools and resources for educating for democracy on college campuses.

Conclusion

Creating space for democracy is critical for shifting the dominant paradigm in higher education, which asks students to be passive consumers of knowledge. Faculty confront—and contribute to—this paradigm in classrooms where students have been asked to defer by sitting in rows of chairs behind desks and regurgitating information. Students are further removed from decision-making in other areas of campus life, from curricular matters to campus housing to broader policy decisions about topics such as tuition increases, endowment investment, and relations with local neighborhoods. The disempowerment of young people is even more pronounced in the wider world of politics and public policy, where the voices of students are among the most marginalized.

The work of dialogue and deliberation is about changing this paradigm by making conversation, connection, and collaboration the center of public life. This book is meant to empower educators to facilitate this change, with concrete examples of how we can rethink learning environments. This includes developing curricula that focus on discussing issues that matter in a way that values the stories and experiences of students; creating spaces on campus, such as democracy walls and engaged libraries and residence halls, that foster public conversation; developing reciprocal partnerships in the community through third spaces and participatory research methods; and building networks that enable civic work to go beyond a single course or campus experience.

The field of dialogue and deliberation is developing and ever-changing, but we have a strong foundation for what works to engage citizens in public life. Much of this wisdom is in the chapters that follow. The contributors invite us to think and act in new ways in educating for democracy. When we create space to talk with one another about this great task, students become cocreators of their education, opening up possibilities for solving problems, together.

References

Barker, D., McAfee, N., & McIvor, D. (Eds.). (2012). *Democratizing deliberation: A political theory anthology.* Dayton, OH: Kettering Foundation Press.

Barr, R., & Tagg, J. (1995, November/December). From teaching to learning. *Change.* Retrieved from https://www.esf.edu/openacademy/tlc/documents/FromTeachingToLearningANewParadigmforUndergraduateEducation.pdf

Black, L. W. (2015). Dialogue. In K. Tracy, C. Ilie, & T. Sandel (Eds.), *The international encyclopedia of language and social interaction* (pp. 364–372). Malden, MA: Wiley.

Blake, H. (1996). Keynote speech at Invisible College, Indianapolis, IN.

Blake, H. (2014). "Look 'n M' face and hear M' story": An oral history with Professor J. Herman Blake. Retrieved from https://escholarship.org/uc/item/4m01p3bz

Boatright, R. G., Shaffer, T. J., Sobieraj, S., & Young, D. G. (Eds.). (2019). *A crisis of civility? Political discourse and its discontents.* New York, NY: Routledge.

Boyer, E. L. (1996). The scholarship of engagement. *Journal of Public Service and Outreach, 1*(1), 11–20.

Boyte, H. C. (2015). Reinventing citizenship as public work. In H. C. Boyte (Ed.), *Democracy's education: Public work, citizenship, and the future of colleges and universities* (pp. 1–33). Nashville, TN: Vanderbilt University Press.

Boyte, H. (2017, February 2). Free spaces in schools and colleges. *Huffington Post.* Retrieved from https://www.huffpost.com/entry/free-spaces-in-schools-and_b_9138744

Brown, A. (2018, July 26). *Most Americans say higher ed is heading in wrong direction, but partisans disagree on why.* Retrieved from https://www.pewresearch.org/fact-tank/2018/07/26/most-americans-say-higher-ed-is-heading-in-wrong-direction-but-partisans-disagree-on-why/

Brown, J., Isaacs, D., Vogt, E., & Margulies, N. (2002). Strategic questioning: Engaging people's best thinking. *The Systems Thinker, 13*(9), 2–6.

Buber, M. (1947). *Between man and man.* London, UK: Routledge and Kegan Paul.

Campus Compact. (2015). *Preparing to accelerate change: Understanding our starting line* (2015 Annual Member Survey). Retrieved from https://compact.org/resource-posts/2015-member-survey-executive-summary/

Carcasson, M. (2013). *Rethinking civic engagement on campus: The overarching potential of deliberative practice* (pp. 37–48). Retrieved from https://cpd.colostate.edu/wp-content/uploads/sites/4/2016/07/carcasson-rethinking-civic-engagement-on-campus-hex-version.pdf

Carcasson, M. (2017). Deliberative pedagogy as critical connective: Building democratic mind-sets and skill sets for addressing wicked problems. In T. J. Shaffer, N. V. Longo, I. Manosevitch, & M. S. Thomas (Eds.), *Deliberative pedagogy: Teaching and learning for democratic engagement* (pp. 3–20). East Lansing: Michigan State University Press.

Conover, P. J., & Miller, P. R. (2018). Taking everyday political talk seriously. In A. Bächtiger, J. S. Dryzek, J. Mansbridge, & M. Warren (Eds.), *The Oxford* handbook of deliberative democracy (pp. 378–391). New York, NY: Oxford University Press.

Cremin, L. A. (1990). *Popular education and its discontents*. New York, NY: Harper & Row.

Dedrick, J. R., Grattan, L., & Dienstfrey, H. (Eds.). (2008). *Deliberation and the work of higher education: Innovations for the classroom, the campus, and the community*. Dayton, OH: Kettering Foundation Press.

Dewey, J. (1916/1993). The need of an industrial education in an industrial democracy. In D. Morris & I. Shapiro (Eds.), *The political writings* (pp. 121–124). Cambridge, MA: Hackett.

Diamond, L. (2015). Facing up to the democratic recession. *Journal of Democracy*, *26*(1), 141–155.

Dryzek, J. S. (2000). *Deliberative democracy and beyond: Liberals, critics, contestations*. New York, NY: Oxford University Press.

Dzur, A. W. (2017). *Rebuilding public institutions together: Professionals and citizens in a participatory democracy*. Ithaca, NY: Cornell University Press.

Eagan, M. K., Stolzenberg, E. B., Zimmerman, H. B., Aragon, M. C., Whang Sayson, H., & Rios-Aguilar, C. (2017). *The American freshman: National norms fall 2016*. Los Angeles, CA: Higher Education Research Institute, UCLA. Retrieved from https://www.heri.ucla.edu/monographs/TheAmericanFreshman2016.pdf

Escobar, O. (2011). *Public dialogue and deliberation: A communication perspective for public engagement practitioners*. Edinburgh, UK: Edinburgh Beltane.

Evans, S., & Boyte, H. (1992). *Free spaces: The sources of democratic change in America*. Chicago, IL: University of Chicago Press.

Fingerhut, H. (2017, July 20). *Republicans skeptical of colleges' impact on U.S., but most see benefits for workforce preparation*. Retrieved from https://www.pewresearch.org/fact-tank/2017/07/20/republicans-skeptical-of-colleges-impact-on-u-s-but-most-see-benefits-for-workforce-preparation/

Follett, M. P. (1924). *Creative experience*. New York, NY: Longmans, Green.

Freire, P. (1974). *Education for critical consciousness*. New York, NY: Continuum.

Freire, P. (2000). *Pedagogy of the oppressed* (30th Anniversary ed., M. B. Ramos, Trans.). New York, NY: Continuum.

Gastil, J., & Keith, W. M. (2005). A nation that (sometimes) likes to talk. In J. Gastil & P. Levine (Eds.), *The deliberative democracy handbook: Strategies for effective civic engagement in the twenty-first century* (pp. 3–19). San Francisco, CA: Jossey-Bass.

Gibson, C. (2017). *Particpatory grantmaking: Has its time come?* New York, NY: Ford Foundation.

Harwood Group. (1993). *College students talk politics*. Dayton, OH: Kettering Foundation.

Held, D. (2006). *Models of democracy* (3rd ed.). Stanford, CA: Stanford University Press.

Horton, M., Kohl, J., & Kohl, H. (1998). *The long haul: An autobiography*. New York, NY: Teachers College Press.

Keith, W. M. (2007). *Democracy as discussion: Civic education and the American forum movement*. Lanham, MD: Lexington Books.

Kenney, L. (2017, August 1). You can't solve a problem unless you talk about it: A conversation about race with Beverly Daniel Tatum '75. *Wesleyan University Magazine*. Retrieved from http://magazine.blogs.wesleyan.edu/2017/08/01/you-cant-solve-a-problem-unless-you-talk-about-it-a-conversation-about-race-with-beverly-daniel-tatum-75/

Kiesa, A., Orlowski, A. P., Levine, P., Both, D., Kirby, E. H., Lopez, M. H., & Marcelo, K. B. (2007). *Millennials talk politics: A study of college student political engagement*. College Park, MD: The Center for Information & Research on Civic Learning & Engagement.

Klinenberg, E. (2018). *Palaces for the people: How social infrastructure can help fight inequality, polarization, and the decline of civic life*. New York, NY: Crown.

Knight Foundation. (2019, May 13). *Free expression on campuses: A college pulse study commissioned by the Knight Foundation*. Retrieved from https://knightfoundation.org/reports/free-expression-college-campuses

Kuh, G. D. (2008). *High-impact educational practices: What they are, who has access to them, and why they matter*. Washington DC: Association of American Colleges & Universities.

Leighninger, M. (2012). Mapping deliberative civic engagement: Pictures from a (r)evolution. In T. Nabatchi, J. Gastil, M. Leighninger, & G. M. Weiksner (Eds.), *Democracy in motion: Evaluating the practice and impact of deliberative civic engagement* (pp. 19–39). New York, NY: Oxford University Press.

Lerner, J. (2018, February 14). Mayor launches participatory budgeting in all NYC high schools. Retrieved from https://www.participatorybudgeting.org/mayor-launches-participatory-budgeting-nyc-high-schools/

Levine, P. (2013). *We are the ones we have been waiting for: The promise of civic renewal in America*. New York, NY: Oxford University Press.

London, S. (2010). *Doing democracy: How a network of grassroots organizations is strengthening community, building capacity, and shaping a new kind of civic education*. Dayton, OH: Kettering Foundation.

Longo, N. V. (2007). *Why community matters: Connecting education with civic life*. Albany, NY: State University of New York Press.

Longo, N. V., & Gibson, C. (2017). Thinking out of school: Using deliberative pedagogy to connect campus and community. In T. J. Shaffer, N. V. Longo, I. Manosevitch, & M. S. Thomas (Eds.), *Deliberative pedagogy: Teaching and learning for democratic engagement* (pp. 37–48). East Lansing: Michigan State University Press.

Longo, N. V., Manosevitch, I., & Shaffer, T. J. (2017). Introduction. In T. J. Shaffer, N. V. Longo, I. Manosevitch, & M. S. Thomas (Eds.), *Deliberative pedagogy: Teaching and learning for democratic engagement* (pp. xix–xxxv). East Lansing: Michigan State University Press.

Loss, C. P. (2012). *Between citizens and the state: The politics of American higher education in the 20th century*. Princeton, NJ: Princeton University Press.

Lührmann, A., Dahlum, S., Lindberg, S. I., Maxwell, L., Mechkova, V., Olin, M., & Stepanova, N. (2018). *Democracy for all? V-Dem annual democracy report 2018* (May 2018 ed.). Gothenberg, Sweden: V-Dem Institute.

Lukianoff, G., & Haidt, J. (2018). *The coddling of the American mind: How good intentions and bad ideas are setting up a generation for failure.* New York, NY: Penguin Press.

Magolda, P. M., Magolda, M. B. B., & Carducci, R. (Eds.). (2019). *Contested isues in troubled times: Student affairs dialogues on equity, civility, and safety.* Sterling, VA: Stylus.

Malena, C. (2015). *Improving the measurement of civic space.* London, UK: Open Society Foundation.

Mathews, D. (2014). *The ecology of democracy: Finding ways to have a stronger hand in shaping our future.* Dayton, OH: Kettering Foundation Press.

Mathews, D. (2010). Preface. In S. London, *Doing democracy: How a network of grassroots organizations is strengthening community, building capacity, and shaping a new kind of civic education.* Dayton, OH: Kettering Foundation.

Mathews, D. (2016). *Naming and framing difficult issues to make sound decisions.* Dayton, OH: Kettering Foundation.

McKnight, J. (1995). *The careless society: Community and its counterfeits.* New York, NY: Basic Books.

Morphew, C. C., & Hartley, M. (2006). Mission statements: A thematic analysis of rhetoric across institutional type. *Journal of Higher Education, 77*(3), 456–471.

Nabatchi, T., Gastil, J., Weiksner, G. M., & Leighninger, M. (Eds.). (2012). *Democracy in motion: Evaluating the practice and impact of deliberative civic engagement.* New York, NY: Oxford University Press.

National Coalition for Dialogue and Deliberation (NCDD). (2014). *Engagement Streams Framework.* Retrieved from http://www.ncdd.org/files/rc/2014_Engagement_Streams_Guide_Web.pdf

Oldenburg, R. (1999). *The great good place: Cafes, coffee shops, bookstores, bars, hair salons and other hangouts at the heart of a community.* Cambridge, MA: Da Capo Press.

Pew Research Center. (2018, November). *More now say it's stressful to discuss politics with people they disagree with.* Retrieved from https://www.people-press.org/2018/11/05/more-now-say-its-stressful-to-discuss-politics-with-people-they-disagree-with/

Post, M., Ward, E., Longo, N., & Saltmarsh, J. (Eds.). (2016). *Publicly engaged scholars: Next generation engagement and the future of higher education.* Sterling, VA: Stylus.

Preskill, S., & Brookfield, S. D. (2009). *Learning as a way of leading: Lessons from the struggle for social justice.* San Francisco, CA: Jossey-Bass.

Rittel, H. W. J., & Webber, M. M. (1973). Dilemmas in a general theory of planning. *Policy Sciences, 4*(2), 155–169.

Rourke, B. (2014). *Developing materials for deliberative forums.* Dayton, OH: Kettering Foundation.

Rue, P. (2019). Why is it so hard for the student affairs profession to foster inclusive environments for learning? In P. M. Magolda, M. B. B. Magolda, & R. Carducci (Eds.), *Contested issues in troubled times: Student affairs dialogues on equity, civility, and safety* (pp. 3–28). Sterling, VA: Stylus.

Saltmarsh, J., & Hartley, M. (Eds.). (2011). *To serve a larger purpose: Engagement for democracy and the transformation of higher education.* Philadelphia, PA: Temple University Press.

Shaffer, T. J. (2014). Deliberation in and through higher education. *Journal of Public Deliberation, 10*(1), article 10. Retrieved from http://www.publicdeliberation.net/jpd/vol10/iss11/art10

Shaffer, T. J. (2017a). Democracy and education: Historical roots of deliberative pedagogy. In T. J. Shaffer, N. V. Longo, I. Manosevitch, & M. S. Thomas (Eds.), *Deliberative pedagogy: Teaching and learning for democratic engagement* (pp. 21–36). East Lansing: Michigan State University Press.

Shaffer, T. J. (2017b). Institutions supporting democratic communication among citizens. *National Civic Review, 106*(1), 32–41.

Shaffer, T. J., Longo, N. V., Manosevitch, I., & Thomas, M. S. (Eds.). (2017). *Deliberative pedagogy: Teaching and learning for democratic engagement.* East Lansing: Michigan State University Press.

Shor, I., & Freire, P. (1987). *A pedagogy for liberation: Dialogues on transforming education.* South Hadley, MA: Bergin & Garvey.

Sprain, L., & Carcasson, M. (2013). Democratic engagement through the ethic of passionate impartiality. *Tamara Journal of Critical Organisation Inquiry, 11*(4), 13–26.

Stoecker, R., Tryon, E. A., & Hilgendorf, A. (Eds.). (2009). *The unheard voices: Community organizations and service learning.* Philadelphia, PA: Temple University Press.

Thomas, N. L. (Ed.). (2010). *Educating for deliberative democracy* (New Directions for Higher Education, No. 152). San Francisco, CA: Jossey-Bass.

Walzer, M. (1989). Citizenship. In T. Ball, J. Farr, & R. L. Hanson (Eds.), *Political innovation and conceptual change* (pp. 211–219). New York, NY: Cambridge University Press.

Yankelovich, D., & Friedman, W. (Eds.). (2010). *Toward wiser public judgment.* Nashville, TN: Vanderbilt University Press.

Zúñiga, X., Nadga, B. A., Chesler, M., & Cytron-Walker, A. (2007). Intergroup dialogue in higher education: Meaningful learning about social justice [monograph]. *ASHE Higher Education Report, 32*(4), 1–128.

PART ONE
CONCEPTS AND THEORIES

2

READINESS FOR DISCUSSING DEMOCRACY IN SUPERCHARGED POLITICAL TIMES

Nancy Thomas

Creating Space for Democracy challenges college and university educators to teach students their responsibilities for the health and future of democracy by *practicing* democracy. The aim is a more ideal version of democracy, referring to both a system of governance and a culture, a way that people interact and work together to improve society. Currently, Americans rely heavily on voting to make public decisions. Although our representative system and the electoral process cry for public oversight, this book concerns a different approach.

This ideal is perhaps best articulated by a framing paper for The Democracy Imperative (TDI), a national network of scholars and civic leaders committed to strengthening democracy through higher education.[1] That statement described the work this way:

> Modern deliberative democratic initiatives include study circles, intergroup dialogues, issue forums, public conversations, e-democracy, and more. This movement toward greater deliberation reflects a convergence of two forces

---

1. I served as the founding director of TDI from its launch in 2007 at the University of New Hampshire. Members continue to convene at Tufts University's Frontiers of Democracy conference annually. Some of TDI's work continues through the work of the Institute for Democracy & Higher Education, which I direct, also at Tufts University. Tim Shaffer, coeditor of this book, also served as codirector of TDI, and many of the contributors in this book were members of TDI.

in our aspirational democracy—cyclical efforts to engage citizens in public life and ongoing efforts to promote equity and justice. Together, these projects aim to make our social and political systems inclusive, fair, accessible, and effective, and we believe they can be powerful antidotes to exclusion, inequality, disengagement, polarization, and incivility. (Thomas, 2010, p. 2)

College and university students should graduate with the knowledge and skills they need to discuss issues across differences of identity and ideology, affirm democratic principles and responsibilities, manage conflict, compromise, and engage in collaborative action for the common good. These desired outcomes sound easy enough, but they are not. The current political context for deliberative democracy makes the task even more difficult—and more urgent. There is too much at stake to improvise.

This chapter concerns readiness—what it takes for higher education professionals to be *ready* to engage students in discussions about the state of and controversial issues in democracy. At a minimum, discussion leaders and teachers need the *skills* to frame, organize, and manage discussions. Beyond basic facilitation skills, however, readiness also calls for reflection and conscious decisions about anticipated pedagogical choices in a discussion process, decision points best considered before a discussion begins. Should all perspectives get a fair hearing, even if they reflect ideas antithetical to learning goals or institutional values? Should beliefs that contradict established science or evidence get a full hearing? Do feelings belong in a deliberation? Should discussion leaders and teachers aspire to be "neutral," and if so, what does that mean? Answers to these and similar questions are particularly hard in today's hyperpartisan and divisive political climate.

The Political Context

Much has been written about the political climate and deep partisan divides in American society. Partisanship often falls along fault lines of gender, race and ethnicity, geography, educational attainment, wealth and class, and religion. Each identity brings unique experiential knowledge, vocabularies, values, frameworks, and political perspectives, making controversial-issues discussions difficult. Americans also face greater social isolation because they increasingly live alone, lack social support and a network of friends, and do not belong to community organizations (Atwell, Bridgeland, & Levine, 2017).

According to the Pew Research Center (2017), Republicans and Democrats have held "mostly negative" (as opposed to "very unfavorable") opinions of the other party for decades, but mutual animosity has increased significantly. In 1994, 17% of Republicans (and "Republican leaners") viewed the Democratic Party "very unfavorably." That number increased to 45% in 2017. Similarly, very unfavorable views of Democrats toward Republicans jumped from 16% in 1994 to 57% in 2017. Reciprocal partisan contempt is so strong that it affects who people choose to marry, how they raise their children, and attitudes toward their children's choices in a partner (Iyengar, Konitzer, & Tedin, 2018).

Perhaps most disconcerting is the fact that Republicans and Democrats disagree about which public issues deserve legislative attention. According to the Pew Research Center (2018), Republicans view illegal immigration as the most significant problem facing the nation, followed by drug addiction and the federal budget deficit. For Democrats, the nation's most significant problems are the affordability of health care, gun violence, ethics in government, and the gap between rich and poor. The widest disparities concern criminal justice reform, climate change, and gun violence. Most Democrats (71%) view the way racial and ethnic minorities are treated by the criminal justice system as a serious problem, compared with only 10% of Republicans. There are similar gaps over climate change and gun violence. When partisans do not even agree about the seriousness of issues plaguing the United States, it's difficult to get them to the table to talk. This dynamic can affect student interactions, with fewer students than ever before (42.3%) characterizing their political views as "middle of the road" (Eagan et al., 2017).

External Influences Affecting Student Learning and Discourse on Campuses

Partisanship is also driving efforts to police speech on campus. On March 21, 2019, President Trump signed an executive order holding institutional administrators accountable for ensuring "free inquiry" (Exec. Order, 2019). This follows several years of state legislation to "restore" free speech at public colleges and universities. The laws vary, but most of them nullify speech codes and prohibit institutions from withdrawing invitations to controversial speakers. Some allow disinvited speakers to seek money damages from institutions where they are unable to speak. Some mandate that students who interrupt speakers and prevent them from speaking face disciplinary action. Other laws eliminate "free speech zones." A few even require institutions to remain "neutral" on public issues. In North Carolina, for example, the law requires boards of trustees to document "a description of substantial difficulties, controversies, or successes in maintaining a posture of administrative and institutional neutrality with regard to political or social issues" (Act to Restore and Preserve Free Speech, 2017). Similar provisions have been enacted or proposed in Arizona, California, Georgia, Missouri, South Carolina, West Virginia, and Wisconsin.

At the same time, many students and others question the application of the First Amendment to the university setting. In a 2018 survey, the Knight Foundation and Gallup found that most students (56%) want to protect free speech and most students (52%) want to protect diversity and inclusion, but when asked which is more important, students chose inclusion over speech, 53% to 46% (Gill, 2018). Women, blacks, and Democrats were more likely than their counterparts to choose inclusion over speech ("8 Ways," 2018). The decline in unfettered support for expressive freedoms alarms many who view free expression as inviolable.

Should educators draw the line, however, at speakers who traffic hate or speech that is antithetical to institutional values? Organizations like the Anti-Defamation League and Facing History track the exponential rise of hate groups in the United States. In March 2019, Amy Sherman reported in a thoroughly cited article in *Politifact* that although documenting incidents of white nationalism can be challenging, "data from multiple sources suggest extremist attacks associated with white nationalism and far-right ideology is [sic] on the rise" (Sherman, 2019). The number of hate groups in the United States has reached a record high number—totaling 1,020, in the fourth straight year of hate group growth following 3 consecutive years of decline near the end of the Obama administration. These hate groups include neo-Nazis, the Ku Klux Klan, racist skinheads, and white nationalists who adhere to some form of white supremacy or separatist views, but the list also includes black nationalist groups (Beirich, 2019). Unfortunately, many of these groups or individuals target colleges and universities. In February 2019, a Leadership, Equity, Access, and Diversity (LEAD) Fund report indicated that a majority of surveyed educators reported incidents over the past 2 years of bias—symbols, leafleting, social media, speakers (68%); hate speech—offensive speech based on race, religion, and other traits (54%); or incivility—bullying, offensive conduct not motivated by bias (54%). Nearly 20% of the respondents reported incidents of hate crimes (Jones & Baker, 2019). When discrimination and exclusion become more mainstream, people become emboldened to say things they may not have said before. The challenge for the discussion leader and teacher is to know whether and when to draw a line. Yes, the free exchange of ideas is critical to student learning, but so is a commitment to standards and integrity and to providing equal learning environments for all students.

These political forces have implications for learning. Extreme polarization can foster distrust of someone with a different perspective, party affiliation, or lived experience. Polarization can erode trust, making it even harder for discussion organizers and teachers to design a process or build relationships. Professors might avoid controversial issue discussions for the sake of harmony in the classroom. Students might decline invitations to engage in political discussions out of fear of saying the wrong thing or the belief that their perspectives will be met with hostility. Ironically, partisan efforts to promote free speech may be resulting in chilled speech and learning.

Misunderstandings about whether higher education professionals teach versus indoctrinate may be less about disinviting controversial speakers and more about seemingly small pedagogical decisions educators make daily. Educators can prepare by anticipating the challenges and developing strategies in advance for managing them. Not all challenges can (or even should) be avoided, and with some creative thinking and planning on a campus, conflicts can become opportunities for learning.

Preparation

Readiness approaches might include pursuing facilitation training, finding colleagues and creating a community of practice for sharing teaching or facilitation tips, and practicing. Strong facilitation skills include community and trust-building and sharing responsibility for the success of the discussion; establishing group agreements; inquiry and asking "good" questions; using silence and listening strategically; drawing out perspectives; and being proactive about decision points in a discussion.

Community, Trust-Building, and Sharing Responsibility

Discussion groups and classes often consist of people who do not know each other well, if at all. In classroom settings, they may view each other as competitors for grades or attention from the professor or each other. In any discussion, students may engage in ways that reinforce rather than break down barriers sometimes based on social identity, political ideology, or lived experiences, particularly if the group dynamic is disrespectful, dismissive, or antagonistic. It's important to establish expectations of cooperation and shared responsibility.

A good place to start is with finding common experiences or traits. Class or group participants probably have an automatic connection to each other because of their interest in the course or topic. It's still important, however, to carve out time in the group or outside of class, perhaps through an assignment, for students to explore what they have in common. Students can work in pairs or small groups to find out why each chose to take this course or participate in this issue forum. For group projects, ask the students to complete the assignment (a paper, a presentation) *and* write a short reflection paper on how the group worked together.

In graduate school, I took a course in which the professor asked each student to send him a letter before the semester started, telling him our "itches and ouches," with no guidance beyond that vague request. Throughout the semester, he would then refer to our letters, pointing to our common experiences, interests, or connections. Through his masterful facilitation, we learned things about each other that then served as a foundation for cooperation.

If planned well, the classroom or discussion group can come to view themselves as members of a learning community of students who collaborate and share responsibility for each other's learning and success. Students in learning communities develop a sense of common purpose and group identity. A successful learning community helps students overcome feelings of isolation from each other and builds relationships.

Trust is not automatic; it's earned. The sections that follow about establishing group agreements, framing questions, perspective-taking, and anticipating political and facilitation challenges should help.

Establishing Group Agreements

Good discussion leaders establish reciprocal agreements or "ground rules" with students before a class or discussion begins. These are critical to the success of a group, yet in my experience, not enough professors take the time to cocreate and discuss them with a class. Agreements are reciprocal because discussion leaders and teachers should model the kinds of behaviors they expect.

Agreements are important. They shape the climate for a discussion by setting limits about behavior, encouraging some forms of participation and discouraging others, and even identifying speech that is appropriate and inappropriate. The idea behind agreements is that they will prevent personal attacks or intimidation. They are also supposed to encourage behaviors such as preparing, risk-taking, listening, and open-mindedness.

Sometimes agreements clash; for example, an agreement that "all viewpoints matter equally" can contradict an expectation of "respect." For this reason, it is important for groups to propose agreements and discuss their pros and cons in advance. The goal of establishing agreements is not consensus but rather exploration and reasoning. Setting agreements is one way to exchange perspectives and explore *why* a particular agreement might work for one person and not another. Setting agreements can also be a relatively low-stakes way of encouraging active participation.

If not clarified or thought through carefully, agreements can become tools for shutting down discussions. I was once asked to facilitate a session with a group that had already established a set of agreements, including one that read, "This is a safe space." Unfortunately, some members of the group used this agreement to shut down discussions. At one point, a student expressed a controversial but not intimidating viewpoint about a policy matter, and another student stood up and walked out, stating loudly, "This is not a safe space for me," not because the viewpoint was demeaning but because the exiting student simply disagreed.

Typical agreements include the following:

- Listen for understanding.
- Assume goodwill.
- If you are offended, say so and say why.
- You can disagree, but don't personalize.
- Speak for yourself, not others.
- Step up, step back, *or* share "air time."
- Silence is okay (discussed more in a following section).
- Share responsibility for the quality of the discussion.
- Confidentiality: It's okay to share ideas and themes, but not what individuals say.
- Prepare.
- Be present. Turn off cell phones.

I view two agreements as critical: Assume good will and share responsibility for the quality of the discussion. Consider the previous example involving the student who stormed out, proclaiming the discussion unsafe. In that case, the student would have violated an agreement about assuming goodwill. The student could have stated what caused the offense, the group could have talked it through, and the discussion could have continued. As facilitator, I also could have asked the group for advice on keeping the discussion going and working through conflict as a group, per a "share responsibility" agreement. Because neither agreement was in place, I could not draw on them to correct the malfunction.

Should civility be a ground rule for discussions? To many, it means courtesy or politeness. A civil society, if based on principles of a diverse democracy, can make it possible for people with opposing viewpoints to express and talk through their differences. But excessive politeness can mask power dynamics and oppression. Activists, for example, may protest in ways viewed as uncivil by those who do not want to change the status quo. When setting group agreements, it is important to consider whose definition of *civility* would be supported, who makes the rules about what is civil. In my view, students should learn *about* different perspectives on civility, not how to *be* civil.

It is also important for groups to revisit and, if necessary, amend group agreements periodically. By doing this, discussion participants may feel more responsibility for the success of the group, and behavioral challenges can be exposed and addressed.

Inquiry and "Good" Questions

Questions can be used by the discussion teacher or leader to maintain or share power and authority. They can be asked in ways that foster or shut down curiosity and learning. They can encourage or discourage rigor. They can build a climate of cooperation or competition. Because, ideally, discussions are lively and fast-paced, good questions might be more intuitive than planned. Recall my previously mentioned professor who requested a letter from each class member about their itches and ouches. That same professor told us that for every hour of discussion/teaching, he prepared for three hours. Although he undoubtedly revisited the content goals for the class and opportunities to connect student experiences, he also spent time preparing his questions. Inquiry is at the heart of a robust discussion.

Good questions add clarity about definitions and terms. (What language do you use to describe this situation? How do you interpret that language? What do you mean by that term?) The goal is not consensus about a term or language choice but an exploration and shared understanding of different terms.

Good questions help people think critically and analytically. (What do we know about this topic? What are the facts? What evidence do you have to support your statement? What are the consequences of this approach?) In Institute for Democracy & Higher Education (IDHE) research[2] on politically engaged campuses, we found that professors anticipated their responses to beliefs or viewpoints and were transparent in the course syllabus about standards of evidence. Beliefs had to be factually verifiable. In our focus groups with students, some would complain that professors would "pick on

---

2. Throughout this chapter, I refer to "our research." IDHE studies political learning and campus climates, and findings are reported in the book chapters, journals, and magazines listed under "Politics 365 Resources" at the end of the chapter.

them" by forcing them to back up their opinions with evidence, but most felt that standards and a commitment to accuracy preserved the integrity of the process. In 2017, the U.S. Tenth Circuit affirmed the right of professors to insist that viewpoints be factually supported, even partisan preferences (Thomas, 2017).

Good questions help people reason together. (How did you reach that conclusion? How does your idea overlap with those of others in the group? Can we combine these perspectives in creative, new ways?) Good questions can build relationships that, in turn, empower groups to take ownership of solutions.

Good questions can foster open-mindedness, a willingness to understand and even change positions. (Do you think that a different approach might work? What information do you need to accept a different perspective?) The aim is to challenge assumptions and encourage new thinking.

The goal, of course, is never to indoctrinate. In 2017, 58% of Republicans responded to a Pew Research Center survey that colleges and universities have a *negative* effect on "the way things are going in this country" (Fingerhut, 2017). Also in 2017, Gallup found that 67% of Republicans have "some" or "very little" confidence in colleges and universities because they view them as "too liberal" and that professors "push their own agendas" and "don't allow students to think for themselves" (Gallup, 2019). Although important to know, these partisan attitudes are not supported by evidence. It is simply inaccurate to suggest that college students can be easily indoctrinated. Studies repeatedly demonstrate that students do not change their political leanings while in college (Mariani & Hewitt, 2008; Woessner & Kelly-Woessner, 2009). In a national study of more than 7,000 undergraduates at 120 colleges, Mayhew, Rockenbach, Selznick, and Zagorsky (2018) concluded that after the first year of college, 48% of students viewed liberals more favorably than when they arrived on campus and 50% of students viewed conservatives more favorably. The most deeply entrenched students demonstrated the most open-mindedness. The researchers concluded that "college attendance is associated, on average, with gains in appreciating political viewpoints across the spectrum, not just favoring liberals" (Mayhew et al., 2018). These findings were consistent with IDHE's research that skilled facilitation in classroom discussions created the conditions for increased understanding across political viewpoints.

Good questions do not necessarily lead to one correct answer. For example, in a discussion about the right size of government, the correct answer is most likely "It depends." In this case, the goals are to understand the facts, examine the topic from multiple perspectives, explore reasons, and weigh the pros and cons of solutions.

Finally, gestures, tone, and inflection by both the discussion leaders/teachers and the participants/students can distinguish good questions from bad questions. Asking someone, "Why do you think that?" can be said with different emphases and body language, suggesting genuine curiosity or conversely implying disdain. Discussion leaders and teachers need to teach students how to ask questions of each other, in addition to modeling good questioning. It's okay to pause a discussion to say, "I wonder if there is a better way to ask that question?"

Silence, Listening, and Perspective-Taking

To some, fast-paced discussions are fun; to others, the experience can be uncomfortable. I often include in group agreements the statement "As a discussion leader, I am okay with silence." I often half-jokingly say, "Silence is un-American." Silence is awkward. Some people want to fill the space regardless of the quality of the comment. Giving students permission to be silent is a respectful way to acknowledge those who like to reflect and collect their thoughts before speaking. It also demonstrates respect for diversity in how people learn and communicate, particularly when learning and communication styles align with cultural or gender norms.

Silence also encourages listening, a core ingredient to learning and to understanding and integrating the perspectives of others. We've all worked with groups of students in which some are quick-witted, easy contributors and others are more reflective and measured. A fast-paced discussion is exciting, but are the ideas merely presented or are they being understood, discussed, and sharpened?

In IDHE's research on politically engaged campuses, students expressed concerns about failures in listening—professors who shut down a conversation because of a conflict, premature endings to a discussion because of time constraints, students who make their point as if it is the final word, students who roll their eyes because they have heard it all before or they don't want to hear it, and professors who approve or let all comments go without any guidance or interception. These dysfunctions derail good discussions. Teaching students the arts of discussion provides an ideal opportunity to review the pros and cons around the pace of a discussion and the need for comprehensive listening as fundamental to the learning process.

Discussion leaders and teachers control content by making judgments about which perspectives on an issue get a fair hearing. In IDHE's research, we found that students respected professors who played devil's advocate and who probed critically into all perspectives. Many professors told us that they assign students papers requiring they advocate for a perspective they do not have. Students and faculty alike valued learning about these tensions rather than being told right and wrong answers.

That said, nearly all focus group participants in our research drew lines at giving fair hearings for perspectives that were inaccurate, hateful, discriminatory, or that promoted inequality. Clearly, if a student said, "The Earth is flat" or "The Holocaust never happened," the statement should be challenged. Facts, evidence, and standards on a college campus matter and should not go unchallenged (unless they are small or silly). There are multiple ways to do that—for example, by asking the group members what they think about that statement ("Does anyone want to make the case for another position?") or challenging it outright ("What evidence can you give me, because I am unaware of any credible evidence to support that position?").

Facilitating difficult discussions is an art, not a science, and there are many considerations, such as right-size grouping, drawing out reticent speakers, setting up small groups, and planning a discussion sequence.

If discussion leaders or teachers master the art of discussion among diverse groups, will the discussion achieve the goals of enhancing student learning, building relationships, and modeling an exemplary process? Unfortunately, given the political context, it is not enough to "trust the process." Readiness also includes reflection and advance thinking regarding tough choices about speech, neutrality, and educational goals.

The Neutrality Challenge

Discussion teachers and leaders inescapably face choices that can have consequences for the success of the discussion: goal-setting, reading selections, sequencing of how ideas are presented, whom to call on, how to correct false statements, and how to manage personal viewpoints. Some can be anticipated and managed through the facilitation techniques suggested previously, but many require seemingly small, in-the-moment decisions. In discussion leadership, the following axiom holds: The devil is in the details. These challenges concern objectivity, fairness, and judgment, which I place in an umbrella category of the *neutrality challenge*.

Sharing Personal Perspectives

Fundamentally, discussion teachers and leaders need to decide whether they will share personal perspectives with their students. In IDHE's research, most professors chose to withhold their personal viewpoints and some even kept the students guessing throughout the semester or process. They remained steadfastly mysterious about their party affiliation, the news stations they watched, and their positions on issues. Others felt that this approach was disingenuous. Instead, they shared their perspectives and invited the students to offer alternative arguments and to check their bias in real time. Many students enjoyed the mysterious approach, but others expressed the view that they could see through it. To those students, transparency with permission to dissent invited more candid perspectives and risk-taking. There is no consensus on this question, but it is important for discussion teachers and leaders to decide in advance which approach to take.

Advocacy or Objectivity Around Democracy, Equity, and Inclusion

Currently, career preparation and economic security are viewed as one of higher education's primary purposes, and that mission has long been interpreted to include educating for social and economic mobility. Higher education's social justice or equity mission includes ensuring individuals equal opportunity in access to political, economic, and social systems; protections of civil rights; and fair and equitable outcomes. The equity mission is, in fact, part of higher education's role in democracy. Perhaps the clearest statement of higher education's purpose occurred after World War II when U.S. leaders reacted to the madness and horror of Nazi Germany. The Truman Commission on Higher Education (1947) identified education as necessary to a "fuller realization of democracy in every phase of living." The commission articulated higher education's responsibility to cultivate in students the "creative imagination and trained intelligence to the solution of social problems and to the administration of public affairs" (p. 285). Higher education's civic and equity missions are deeply connected.

Universally, educators would say that the desired outcomes of a college education include critical thinking, independent judgment, open-mindedness, curiosity, and reasoning. As mentioned previously, leaving misstatements uncorrected may damage the learning of others in the group. But that's the easy case. Arguably, the role of higher educators includes encouraging students to become advocates for a more equitable and just society. To take a neutral stance in the face of injustice can be interpreted as tacit acceptance of an inequitable status quo.

Discussion leaders need to consider whether social justice is a desired outcome of a process or course and how that might affect a discussion process. Is it enough to ensure an equitable process, or should a discussion include a critical assessment of every issue from the perspective of those most marginalized by social, political, and economic systems, with a goal of increased empathy and a commitment to equality and justice? I noted previously that partisans do not agree on the seriousness of public issues such as racial discrimination. It's tricky to facilitate a discussion involving diverse perspectives if some people do not even view the issue as being worthy of discussion.

Some viewpoints are not simply misinformed; they may be antithetical to the institution's values and goals. Should hateful, misogynistic, homophobic, xenophobic, anti-Semitic or anti-Muslim, white or black nationalist, and similar perspectives get a fair hearing in a discussion? To some, allowing speech of this nature is a way to shine a light on it, and as Supreme Court justice Louis Brandeis famously said, sunlight is said to be the best disinfectant. To others, it alienates people and shuts down speech, probably as it was intended to do. I do not agree with censoring or sanctioning speech, but I also disagree that speech that disrupts learning, creates toxic learning environments for students from historically marginalized groups, or perpetuates misinformation should go unchallenged. To the contrary, educators have the academic freedom to control the learning environment and determine on academic grounds what is taught (*Sweezy v. New Hampshire*, 1957). In other words, decisions about speech in a learning environment present the discussion leader and teacher with choices, and it's important to think through those choices before they become conflicts.

Such situations present neutrality challenges. Clearly educators have a responsibility to use their expertise and platform to take a stand against misinformation, falsehoods, mistakes, and flawed reasoning, but what is their obligation against undemocratic forces in society? Are there some perspectives that simply do not deserve a fair hearing? Harboring one leaning over the other will undoubtedly shape the way an issue is framed, the required readings, whose viewpoints get more consideration, and which viewpoints provoke the most critique.

What worries me the most, however, is when the desire to remain neutral, either institutionally or from the perspective of a discussion leader/teacher, is used as an excuse to avoid wrestling with controversial issues. Educators who are ready to lead discussions are less likely to avoid their obligations to educate for their field and for the health and future of democracy.

Institutional Readiness for Discussion Leadership and Teaching

Engaging in the pedagogical approaches described previously benefits from having institutional support. Institutional climate can either support or stifle political discussions. An institutional readiness checklist might include identifying an institutional leader with positional authority to catalyze change, establishing a coalition of diverse constituents on campus who will help with outreach and design, setting goals, identifying existing programs and assets (e.g., trained facilitators), finding and/or pursuing funding sources and incentives, planning kick-off and action groups, and evaluating and documenting the process. Having a supportive institutional environment can make clear to supporters or detractors the commitment a college or university has to engaging contentious topics in classrooms and other educational spaces.

In IDHE's research, we were surprised to learn that four of the seven highly politically engaged campuses embedded dialogue and discussion skills in a required course. In some cases, learning to frame, debate, discuss, and advocate for positions was embedded into for-credit courses on rhetoric or an English 101 class. In others, students spent a semester on a public issue (or multiple issues), learning the art of discussion while learning about the subject. Professors at those institutions appreciated that readiness on the part of students.

Conclusion

The simple message of this chapter is to reflect and plan ahead for inevitable pedagogical choices. Quality discussions of controversial issues are inherently political and, given today's political context, partisan. The circumstances make discussions difficult to facilitate, but it does get easier. With practice, discussion leaders and teachers learn how to read faces, gauge levels of tension, and diffuse conflict. There are ways to build trust, such as recognizing and rewarding well-reasoned arguments (even if they reflect unpopular or dissenting views) and balancing objectivity with the desire to advance democratic principles and practices. Most importantly, teachers and leaders can learn to share with the group responsibility for the success of the discussion. Sharing responsibility involves relinquishing some control, but if everyone around the table believes they are part of making a discussion work, they may voluntarily curb behaviors that add no value, without inhibiting the robust exchange of ideas.

Politics 365 Resources

Thomas, N., & Brower, M. (2017). The politically engaged classroom. In E. Matto, A. R. M. McCartney, E. Bennion, & D. Simpson (Eds.), *Teaching civic engagement across the disciplines* (pp. 21–33). Washington DC: American Political Science Association. Retrieved from https://idhe.tufts.edu/resource/book-chapter-politically-engaged-classroom

Thomas, N., & Brower, M. (2017). Politics 365: Fostering campus climates for student political learning and engagement. In E. Matto, A. R. M. McCartney, E. Bennion, & D. Simpson (Eds.), *Teaching civic engagement across the disciplines* (pp. 361–364). Washington DC: American Political Science Association. Retrieved from http://web.apsanet.org/teachingcivicengagement/wp-content/uploads/sites/9/2016/10/Teaching-Civic-Engagement-Across-the-Disciplines_opt.pdf#page=376

Thomas, N., & Brower, M. (2018). Conceptualizing and assessing campus climates for political learning and engagement in democracy. *Journal of College and Character, 19*(4). Retrieved from https://www.tandfonline.com/doi/full/10.1080/2194587X.2018.1517651

Thomas, N., & Brower, M. (2018). Promising practices to facilitate politically robust campus climates. *Change: The Magazine of Higher Learning, 50*(6), 24–29. Retrieved from https://www.tandfonline.com/doi/abs/10.1080/00091383.2018.1540818

Thomas, N., Brower, M., Casellas-Connors, I., Gismondi, A., & Upchurch, K. (2018). *Election imperatives: Ten recommendations to increase college student voting and improve political learning and engagement in democracy.* Retrieved from https://idhe.tufts.edu/electionimperatives

References

8 ways college student views on free speech are evolving. (2018, March 11). *The Medium.* Retrieved from https://medium.com/informed-and-engaged/8-ways-college-student-views-on-free-speech-are-evolving-963334babe40

Act to Restore and Preserve Free Speech on the Campuses of the Constituent Institutions of the University of North Carolina. (2017). Session Law 2017-196, House Bill 527. Retrieved from https://www.ncleg.net/Sessions/2017/Bills/House/PDF/H527v6.pdf

Atwell, M. N., Bridgeland, J., & Levine, P. (2017). *Civic deserts: America's civic health challenge.* National Conference on Citizenship.

Beirich, H. (2019, Spring). Rage against change. *Intelligence Report*, no. 166, 31–61.

Eagan, M. K., Stolzenberg, E. B., Zimmerman, H. B., Aragon, M. C., Whang Sayson, H., & Rios-Aguilar, C. (2017). *The American freshman: National norms fall 2016.* Los Angeles, CA: Higher Education Research Institute, UCLA. Retrieved from https://www.heri.ucla.edu/monographs/TheAmericanFreshman2016.pdf

Exec. Order. (2019, March 21). *Improving free inquiry, transparency, and accountability at colleges and universities.* Retrieved from https://www.insidehighered.com/sites/default/server_files/media/White%20House%20Executive%20Order.pdf

Fingerhut, H. (2017). Republicans skeptical of colleges' impact on U.S. but most see benefits for workforce preparation. Retrieved from http://www.pewresearch.org/fact-tank/2017/07/20/republicans-skeptical-of-colleges-impact-on-u-s-but-most-see-benefits-for-workforce-preparation/

Gallup. (2019). *Party affiliation*. Retrieved from https://news.gallup.com/poll/15370/party-affiliation.aspx

Gill, S. (2018). Free speech on campus: New perspectives emerge from Gallup/Knight student survey. Retrieved from https://knightfoundation.org/articles/free-speech-on-campus-new-perspectives-emerge-from-gallup-knight-student-survey

Iyengar, S., Konitzer, T., & Tedin, K. (2018). The home as a political fortress: Family agreement in an era of polarization. *The Journal of Politics, 80*(4), 1326–1338.

Jones, C. J., & Baker, R. A. (2019). *Report on the uncivil, hate and bias incidents on campus survey*. Retrieved from https://www.aaaed.org/images/aaaed/LEAD_Fund/LEAD-Fund-Report-UHBIOC-Report.pdf

Mariani, M. D., & Hewitt, G. J. (2008). Indoctrination U.? Faculty ideology and changes in student political orientation. *Political Science and Politics, 41*(4), 773–783.

Mayhew, M., Rockenbach, A., Selznick, B., & Zagorsky, J. (2018, February 2). Does college turn people into liberals? *The Conversation*. Retrieved from https://theconversation.com/does-college-turn-people-into-liberals-90905

Pew Research Center. (2017, October 5). *The partisan divide on political values grows even wider*. Retrieved from https://www.people-press.org/2017/10/05/the-partisan-divide-on-political-values-grows-even-wider/

Pew Research Center. (2018, October 15). *Little partisan agreement on the pressing problems facing the U.S.* Retrieved from http://www.people-press.org/2018/10/15/little-partisan-agreement-on-the-pressing-problems-facing-the-u-s/

Sherman, A. (2019, March 20). Donald Trump doesn't think white nationalism is on the rise. Data show otherwise. *Politifact*. Retrieved from https://www.politifact.com/truth-o-meter/article/2019/mar/20/donald-trump-doesnt-think-white-nationalism-rise-d/

Sweezy v. New Hampshire, 354 U.S. 234 (1957).

Thomas, N. L. (Ed.) (2010). Why it is imperative to strengthen American democracy through study, dialogue and change in higher education" *Journal of Public Deliberation, 6*(1), article 10. Retrieved from https://www.publicdeliberation.net/jpd/vol6/iss1/art10

Thomas, N. (2017). A case for academic freedom: Student opinions, faculty standards. *Dean & Provost (19)*12, 1–5. Retrieved from https://onlinelibrary.wiley.com/doi/full/10.1002/dap.30352

Truman Commission on Higher Education. (1947). *Report of the Truman Commission on Higher Education* (Vol. 1). Retrieved from https://archive.org/details/in.ernet.dli.2015.89917/page/n7

Woessner, M., & Kelly-Woessner, A. (2009). "I think my professor is a Democrat": Considering whether students recognize and react to faculty politics. *Political Science and Politics, 42*(2), 343–352.

3

DELIBERATIVE CIVIC ENGAGEMENT

Toward a Public Politics in Higher Education

Derek W.M. Barker

In recent years, significant efforts have emerged within higher education to position the university as a leading institution in the practice and advancement of deliberative democracy. In the context of an electoral system prone to periods of polarization and divisiveness, higher education may have once sought to distance itself from politics. As these problems have intensified, however, campuses are emerging as important sites for playing neutral and facilitative roles in modeling a deliberative approach to politics for the next generation. This chapter presents a conceptual genealogy of deliberative democracy in higher education, including an overview of deliberative democracy's conceptual origins in the political theory literature as an alternative to both adversary and unitary forms of democracy; how deliberative democracy does and does not fit within the core purposes of higher education; how it builds on, and fills important gaps within, the civic engagement movement in higher education; and, finally, how deliberative democracy is emerging as a distinct mode or practice of civic engagement.

Deliberative Democracy: A Different Kind of Politics

Although *deliberative democracy* has antecedents in political theory dating at least to Aristotle, the term was first coined in 1980 (Bessette, 1980). At the time, political theory was largely characterized by an impasse between liberalism and communitarianism. Liberalism was premised on an individualistic view of human nature and a rejection of the common good. Liberalism also had a strong affinity with pluralist tradition in political science. With roots dating back to the *Federalist Papers*, this tradition argues that democracy is best understood as a healthy competition, aiming at a balance of power among diverse competing factions (Madison, Hamilton, & Jay, 1788/1987). Thus, the dominant understanding of democracy emphasized electoral politics and the proper design of electoral systems to prevent the dominance of any single faction or enduring coalition.

However, in the absence of any common good, some saw the need for a corrective to periods of excessive polarization and declining confidence in government. The most common alternatives turned liberalism on its head. Critics of the liberal-pluralist paradigm began arguing for more social understandings of human nature. Instead of a competition for power, these communitarian thinkers saw politics as a process of socialization toward a sovereign collective actor, unified by a thick consensus on the common good (Sandel, 1996). Although offering an important alternative vision, communitarianism was critiqued as normatively undesirable for suppressing difference, as well as empirically unrealistic in its aspirations for political unity. As a result of dissatisfaction with these alternatives, Jane Mansbridge (1983) and others articulated the need for a middle ground between adversarial and unitary politics.

With its notion of public reasoning across differences, deliberative democracy has filled this gap. Deliberative democracy holds that the essence of democracy is not voting in itself, but rather the public discourse systems and processes that lend legitimacy to any outcome. As Simone Chambers (2003) has suggested, deliberative democracy is *talk centric* rather than *voting centric* in its understanding of democracy. Deliberative democracy is perhaps most credited to the philosopher and social theorist Jürgen Habermas. Building on his earlier study (Habermas, 1989) of the public sphere in modern Europe, *Between Facts and Norms* (Habermas, 1996) worked out Habermas's conception of *deliberative democracy* and helped launch the field. Shortly thereafter, John Rawls, previously known as the preeminent philosopher of American liberalism, endorsed Habermas's core principles, while offering his own conception of *public reasoning* (Rawls, 1993). Subsequently, the term was adopted and refined by numerous scholars across several fields (Benhabib, 1996; Dryzek, 2000).

Fundamentally, deliberative democracy remains within the liberal paradigm in that it values disagreement and acknowledges the need for adversarial elections. However, deliberative democracy also recognizes the inherent tendency within adversarial systems toward excesses of polarization and conflict. From this perspective, a mere balance of power among competing groups is insufficient. Thus, it proposes a fair process of public reasoning to ensure a sense of legitimacy in the outcomes of political decisions.

This kind of public reasoning process is only possible with a certain image of society in mind—namely, deliberative democracy sees enough commonality among citizens that they can engage in communication with one another. At the same time, the sense of legitimacy created by the deliberative process is much weaker than the solidarity envisioned by communitarians. Citizens can remain in deep disagreement, without any sense of a thick or substantive common good, so long as they acknowledge the legitimacy of public reasons and the fairness of the deliberative process. In this way, deliberative politics is more integrative than adversarial elections and debates but more open to conflict and disagreement than the communitarian model.[1] Rather than seeing society as a homogenous union or a collection of atomized individuals, deliberative democracy is based on an image of society as a union of differences, a public that is fundamentally in disagreement with itself, yet capable of constructive communication. Deliberative democracy can thus be contrasted with adversarial and unitary political theories, as shown in Table 3.1.

TABLE 3.1.
Three Concepts of Democratic Politics

	Adversarial	*Deliberative*	*Communitarian*
Level/type of unity	None	Thin/procedural	Thick/substantive
Goal of politics	Balance of power, healthy competition	Legitimacy	Consensus
Mode of politics	Voting, competition	Talk, public reasoning	Socialization
Image of the citizenry	Atomized individuals	Public	Sovereign actor ("the people")

---

1. As Habermas (1996) puts it, "Discourse theory invests the democratic process with normative connotations stronger than those found in the liberal model, but weaker than those found in the republican model. Once again, it takes elements from both sides and puts them together in a new way. . . . According to discourse theory, the success of deliberative politics depends not on a collectively acting citizenry but on the institutionalization of the corresponding procedures and conditions of communication. . . . This concept of democracy no longer has to operate with the notion of a social whole centered in the state. . . . Nor does it represent the whole in a system of constitutional norms mechanically regulating the balance of power and interests" (p. 298).

Despite broad agreement among deliberative theorists, several questions remain contested and unresolved. Habermas and Rawls originally conceived deliberation as a deontological (rules-based) process of reasoning according to certain rules or procedures. However, this view has been challenged for being too narrowly rationalistic and exclusive of other noncoercive forms of communication (Young, 2001). As a result, some have proposed including other communicative practices within a broader concept of deliberation or public discourse, such as emotion and narrative (Dryzek, 2000; Krause, 2008). Similarly, others have drawn upon virtue ethics and other philosophical traditions to understand deliberative democracy in terms of habits of character rather than a narrowly defined form of reason (Barker, 2017; Bickford, 1996). Some conceive deliberative democracy purely in terms of legitimacy, whereas others propose additional epistemic benefits, such as that deliberation yields more informed and objectively "better" decisions (Landemore, 2017). Despite these disagreements, deliberative theorists broadly hold that politics cannot be defined simply as a competitive struggle for power. Between the extremes of adversarial and unitary democracy, deliberative democracy offers a different kind of politics and a corrective to the dysfunctions of division and polarization.

A Challenge for Higher Education

One would think that higher education—as a public-sphere institution charged with the production and dissemination of knowledge—would play a key role in strengthening the facilitation of public deliberation. As an inherently communicative institution, higher education figures prominently in our public sphere, educating future citizens and ensuring that public discourse is informed by academic research. Moreover, as an institution that needs to be seen as strictly neutral in order to ensure its legitimacy, higher education could potentially play an important role in moderating political conflicts. Nevertheless, deliberation per se is not the primary focus of the university. Rather, the organizing principle of the university is the pursuit of academic knowledge. That is, the university sees itself primarily as an epistemic institution rather than a civic institution. To the extent that the university has a core democratic mission, it is to inform the public rather than to create or strengthen the public.

It is worth thinking through how deliberation may or may not fit within the university's overarching epistemic framework. Knowledge is neither subject to deliberation nor to be confused with deliberation itself.

Information is readily accessible with the spread of the Internet, yet our public life remains polarized and divisive. Although higher education may be highly effective at producing and disseminating information, that does not necessarily mean that it has a role to play in making our democracy more deliberative. The motto of Harvard University is, famously, the simple word *Veritas* ("truth"). Truth may be conceived as scientific knowledge, logical truths, or the broader truths explored (and subjected to critique) in the liberal arts, but all types of truth must be universally recognized according to valid, rational procedures. Although universities often refer to educating the next generation of citizens and leaders, they primarily mean in their academic knowledge in one of these senses. However, deliberation concerns political questions, matters that are inherently value laden as well as uncertain and subject to legitimate disagreements (Barber, 1984). Questions subject to deliberation are also referred to in the policy literature as *wicked problems* (Rittel & Webber, 1973). If anything, appeals to expertise can shut down deliberation while attempting to inform it (Brown, 2014).

Moreover, deliberative democracy fits uneasily within an institution that aspires to be free from politics. The notion of academic freedom at the heart of the university implicitly requires that the university strictly refrain from privileging some views over others, and the public investments in higher education rest on a perception that the university serve the interest of the whole society rather than this or that partisan interest. At least in a system that is predominantly adversarial, politics takes on an ideological character that is understandably at odds with higher education's mission to produce and disseminate knowledge. Any attempt to engage in politics, even as a neutral facilitator of deliberation, could be perceived as partisan, especially in the current climate.

That said, higher education may have a self-interest in playing a more active role in facilitating public deliberation. As divisions within the nation intensify and the very notion of a public good appears to be unraveling, it is only natural that the consensus supporting higher education as a public institution would suffer. In the current climate, despite its best intentions, higher education has increasingly become perceived as a partisan institution, with a majority of Republicans recently reporting that they view higher education as harmful to the country (Busteed, 2017). Expert knowledge itself has similarly been delegitimized in charged public debates on topics such as climate change, where "facts" are seen as partisan. As a result, the more common reaction appears to be a defensive mode, in which higher education attempts to maintain its image as an impartial institution, serving the public by producing and disseminating expert knowledge, without playing a more active bridging role in facilitating dialogue across value differences.

A visible role in strengthening public deliberation could offer higher education a more proactive way of demonstrating its public value. However, doing so would take higher education into unfamiliar territory, forcing it to enlarge its conception of itself as a genuinely civic institution rather than a merely epistemic one. Fortunately, a robust civic engagement movement has laid the groundwork for such a transformation to take place.

Higher Education and the Civic Engagement Movement

While deliberative democracy was taking root in political theory and other disciplines, higher education saw growing interest in renewing and expanding its civic role. Programs using civic engagement terminology and related frameworks are now widespread across campuses, providing an opening for developing practices based on deliberative democracy. However, the relationship between deliberative democracy and civic engagement is complex and somewhat contested. Nevertheless, in addition to deliberative theory, the civic engagement movement constitutes another important background factor informing the use of deliberation in higher education.

Following the collapse of the Soviet Union, interest in democracy and civil society spiked around the world and across partisan lines. Community service grew in popularity as a way of accomplishing progressive goals independent of government programs. In this climate, for example, both the George H.W. Bush and Clinton administrations sponsored influential community service initiatives. Higher education responded to these calls by rapidly expanding and institutionalizing community service programs on campuses around the nation, and service-learning became an academic field in its own right, with its own academic associations and literature.

However, a key issue emerged within the service-learning community in the 1990s. Service-learning originally developed within a paradigm of academic neutrality, which traditionally meant that it had to be kept strictly apolitical. For some, however, the language of service seemed unsatisfactory, with connotations of voluntaristic, largely individual activities. Although careful to avoid specific partisan commitments, they sought to connect higher education to larger civic and democratic outcomes. Building on the service-learning infrastructure, language began to shift toward civic engagement. The late Ernest Boyer introduced the term *scholarship of engagement* to further capture how civic engagement could be incorporated into the core functions of the university, including not only teaching and learning but also research and application (Boyer, 1996). The tension between service and engagement surfaced in the 1999 *Wingspread Declaration on the Civic Responsibilities of Research Universities*, authored by Harry Boyte and the late Elizabeth Hollander, then executive director of Campus Compact, which endorsed this more expansive vision, including themes of not only service but also "participation in public affairs," "stirrings of democracy," and "active citizenship" (Boyte & Hollander, 1999, p. 1). The document reflected a growing consensus that higher education need not be limited to academic outcomes and the dissemination of expert knowledge (Checkoway, 2000). Rather, it proposed a larger vision of civic engagement, understood as a different kind of politics rather than an alternative to politics.

Since that time, *civic engagement* has become a widely used term. It has seemed both inclusive of service-learning and suggestive of other aspects of civic education that higher education must take on as it expanded its civic mission. In the following decade, civic engagement became a rallying cry, such that it was often referred to as a "movement"—again, with not only its own set of journals and conferences but also a larger vision and set of practices for civic renewal. A 2012 report, *A Crucible Moment*, representing a coalition of leading higher education associations and organizations, affirmed this shift, calling for a national commitment to *civic learning* and *democratic engagement*, as well as more comprehensive understandings of these terms (although the report apparently also considered service-learning to constitute a form of democratic engagement) (National Task Force on Civic Learning and Democratic Engagement, 2012).

Nevertheless, important ambiguities within this emerging paradigm remain unresolved. With a both-and approach to service-learning, the extent to which the content of civic engagement programs has actually changed is unclear. Although the civic engagement movement has embraced new terminology, service-learning still has an infrastructure in place, along with a network of adherents, and there is much overlap between the old service-learning and the new civic engagement. Indeed, as early as 2008, proponents of this civic engagement movement began to express frustration that the shift had not accomplished its democratic aims and that the movement was conceptually stalled, even as it continued to gain popularity (Hartley, Saltmarsh, & Clayton, 2010; Saltmarsh & Hartley, 2011). As they argued, *civic engagement* had become defined by "activity and place," referring merely to programs that happen to occur outside of the classroom, rather than to any substantive conception of democracy or higher education's civic role (Saltmarsh & Hartley, 2011, pp. 18–19).

Moreover, the language of civic engagement is also ambiguous not only regarding its democratic aims in general but also regarding the specific type(s) of democracy that it represents. As I have suggested previously, democracy can be understood as adversarial, unitary, or something in between. However, the emerging civic engagement literature at times appears to conflate substantively different practices under a common umbrella, despite intentions to address very different aspects of democracy. As I have suggested, the conventional service-learning approach fits with a communitarian frame by focusing on voluntary activities, setting controversial political issues to the side. At the same time, *A Crucible Moment* calls for cross-partisan dialogue and deliberation in general, but also for higher education to actively promote action toward specific progressive goals such as sustainability and the reduction of racial and global inequalities (National Task Force on Civic Learning and Democratic Engagement, 2012). Similarly, proponents of "critical" service-learning also advocate experiences explicitly committed to social justice and engaging students in social transformation (Mitchell, 2008). Although such language does not explicitly embrace adversarial politics, it at least suggests an adversarial attitude toward social injustice and inequality rather than a commitment to dialogue *about* social injustice and inequality, for example. This suggests that the civic engagement movement may be at least incoherent, or perhaps even fundamentally contradictory, in its democratic aspirations.

In any case, the civic engagement movement has contributed an important infrastructure for expanding higher education's civic role beyond academic learning, and even some conceptual precedents for moving beyond the service-learning framework to more political or democratic outcomes. Nevertheless, the most common approaches to community engagement either seek to avoid politics and democracy altogether (the communitarian frame) or unwittingly reinforce conventional adversarial notions of politics and democracy (the adversarial frame). At least until recently, approaches specifically informed by a deliberative conception of democracy have largely been left out of the civic engagement conversation. If higher education is to make a concerted effort to address problems of polarization and division, another approach to civic engagement is needed.

Deliberative Civic Engagement

Fortunately, as the contributions to this volume suggest, new approaches to civic engagement are beginning to emerge in higher education to fill this gap. I will use the term *deliberative civic engagement* to refer to civic engagement practices that incorporate a specifically deliberative concept of democracy.[2] Building on the democratic aspirations of the civic engagement movement, as well as its practical and concrete orientation, deliberative approaches provide a constructive way to address controversial issues, and an alternative to adversarial democracy.[3] Deliberative civic engagement is more public than nonpolitical service projects, yet less polarizing than "politics as usual." Rather, deliberative civic engagement involves students in controversial public issues in a way that can feel constructive and result in enhanced understanding across political divides.

Deliberative civic engagement can take many forms while accomplishing these core objectives. Most approaches use a discussion-centered format with a neutral moderator to facilitate the dialogue. Unlike debate formats, which consist of adversarial argumentation for one side versus the other, deliberation emphasizes constructive exchanges and a nonadversarial tone, with the assumption that various perspectives add value to the dialogue. Careful effort is made to ensure a safe, welcoming space for the discussion of the issue, with the moderator ensuring that each perspective is equally recognized and included.

National Issues Forums (NIF), the approach with which I am most familiar, is a flagship approach to deliberative civic engagement (see chapter 10 of this volume). NIF dialogues are informed by background materials (called *issue guides*) that address controversial, highly polarized national issues, but they do so in a way that reframes the issue such that constructive dialogue can take place. NIF guides typically replace a conventional liberal-versus-conservative dichotomy with a more complex structure. The guides include at least three options, making the best case for each option while also considering inherent tensions and tradeoffs for each one. The moderator facilitates a discussion in which all the options are discussed roughly equally. Rather than a consensus decision or vote, the outcome is simply collectively enhanced understanding of each perspective and the complexity of the issue as a whole.

Through the use of NIF issues guides, or other approaches, deliberative civic engagement has also been applied in numerous higher education contexts. Deliberation is perhaps most commonly used within the classroom but has also been applied in campus activities as well as in participatory research and community partnership contexts (Dedrick, Grattan, & Dientsfrey, 2008).

---

2. The term *deliberative civic engagement* has also been used by Lorlene Hoyt to describe the research collaboration of the Kettering Foundation and the Talloires Network (Talloires Network, n.d.).

3. One question within this literature is how *dialogue* and other related practices fit within deliberative civic engagement. I use the term broadly to include any nonadversarial and noncoercive communicative practices, similar to some political theorists' use of the broader term *discursive democracy* to include nondeliberative discourse that might have deliberative effects (Dryzek, 2000).

Deliberation helps achieve liberal education (in the classical sense) outcomes beyond technical knowledge, such as critical thinking and social skills. Recently, deliberation has been conceived as a distinctive pedagogy, effective in teaching academic content and achieving positive academic outcomes, analogous to seminar or lecture, but repositioning the teacher as a facilitator rather than expert (Shaffer, Longo, Manosevitch, & Thomas, 2017). In this way, even in narrowly academic terms, deliberation fits within the purview of higher education.

From the perspective of a commitment to educating for democracy, deliberation is perhaps most valuable as a civic education device, in the development of civic skills and habits of character that citizens need within an adversarial system. Traditionally associated with the subfield of philosophy known as *virtue ethics*, such skills and habits are not reducible to technical knowledge (Barker, 2017). Ultimately, whether deliberation takes root across the university probably depends on the extent to which these civic virtues are prioritized as a central aim of higher education.

I do not claim that deliberation is the best or only form of civic engagement. Neither is it a cure-all for everything that ails our democracy. Rather, deliberation is a specific form of civic engagement, informed by a distinctive conception of democracy. Deliberation thus fills an important gap within the civic engagement movement and higher education as a whole. Civic engagement proponents and practitioners should be critically aware of its strengths and weaknesses. However, this is also not to say that all forms of civic engagement are well and good. Different approaches to civic engagement could very well work at cross-purposes with one another, so civic engagement proponents and practitioners should be aware of the potential tensions between deliberation and approaches reflecting other conceptions of democracy. As the civic engagement movement matures, rather than attempt a perfect synthesis, it should think critically and carefully about the type of democracy it aspires toward, the problems of democracy that are most urgent, and the various forms of civic engagement that can help achieve these civic outcomes. If higher education is to play an active role in bridging divides and building public understanding across differences, deliberative civic engagement should be given strong consideration.

References

Barber, B. (1984). *Strong democracy: Participatory politics for a new age*. Berkeley: University of California Press.

Barker, D. W. M. (2017). Deliberative justice and collective identity: A virtues-centered perspective. *Political Theory, 45*(1), 116–136.

Benhabib, S. (1996). Toward a deliberative model of democratic legitimacy. In *Democracy and difference: Contesting the boundaries of the political* (pp. 67–94). Princeton, NJ: Princeton University Press.

Bessette, J. (1980). Deliberative democracy: The majority principle in republican government. In R. A. Goldwin & W. A. Schambra (Eds.), *How democratic is the Constitution* (pp. 102–116). Washington DC: American Enterprise Institute Press.

Bickford, S. (1996). Beyond friendship: Aristotle on conflict, deliberation, and attention. *Journal of Politics, 58*(2), 398–421.

Boyer, E. (1996). The scholarship of engagement. *Journal of Public Service and Outreach, 1*(1), 11–20.

Boyte, H., & Hollander, E. (1999). *Wingspread declaration on renewing the civic mission of the American research university*. Retrieved from http://www.compact.org/civic/Wingspread/Wingspread.html

Brown, M. B. (2014). Expertise and deliberative democracy. In S. Elstub & P. McLaverty (Eds.), *Deliberative democracy: Issues and cases* (pp. 50–68). Edinburgh, UK: Edinburgh University Press.

Busteed, B. (2017, December 12). The political divide over higher education in America. *Gallup Blog*. Retrieved from https://news.gallup.com/opinion/gallup/223451/political-divide-higher-education-america.aspx

Chambers, S. (2003). Deliberative democratic theory. *Annual Review of Political Science, 6*, 307–326.

Checkoway, B. (2000). Renewing the civic mission of the American research university. *Journal of Higher Education, 72*(2), 125–147.

Dedrick, J., Grattan, L., & Dientsfrey, H. (Eds.). (2008). *Deliberation and the work of higher education*. Dayton, OH: Kettering Foundation Press.

Dryzek, J. (2000). *Deliberative democracy and beyond: Liberals, critics, and contestations*. Oxford, UK: Oxford University Press.

Habermas, J. (1989). *The structural transformation of the public sphere*. Cambridge, MA: MIT Press.

Habermas, J. (1996). *Between facts and norms: Contributions to a discourse theory of law and democracy*. Cambridge, MA: MIT Press.

Hartley, M., Saltmarsh, J., & Clayton, P. (2010). Is the civic engagement movement changing higher education? *British Journal of Educational Studies, 58*(4), 319–406.

Landemore, H. (2017). Beyond the fact of disagreement? The epistemic turn in deliberative democracy. *Social Epistemology, 31*(3), 277–295.

Krause, S. (2008). *Civil passions: Moral sentiment and democratic deliberation*. Princeton, NJ: Princeton University Press.

Madison, J., Hamilton, A., & Jay, J. (1788/1987). *The Federalist papers*. New York, NY: Penguin.

Mansbridge, J. J. (1983). *Beyond adversary democracy.* Chicago, IL: University of Chicago Press.

Mitchell, T. D. (2008). Traditional vs. critical service-learning: Engaging the literature to differentiate two models. *Michigan Journal of Community Service Learning, 14*(2), 50–65.

National Task Force on Civic Learning and Democratic Engagement. (2012). *A crucible moment: College learning and democracy's future.* Washington DC: Association of American Colleges & Universities.

Rawls, J. (1993). *Political liberalism.* New York, NY: Columbia University Press.

Rittel, H. W. J., & Webber, M. M. (1973). Dilemmas in a general theory of planning. *Policy Sciences, 4,* 155–169.

Saltmarsh, J., & Hartley, M. (2011). *"To serve a larger purpose": Engagement for democracy and the transformation of higher education.* Philadelphia, PA: Temple University Press. Retrieved from http://public.eblib.com/EBLPublic/PublicView.do?ptiID=692509

Sandel, M. J. (1996). *Democracy's discontent: America in search of a public philosophy.* Cambridge, MA: Belknap Press.

Shaffer, T. J., Longo, N. V., Manosevitch, I., & Thomas, M. S. (2017). *Deliberative pedagogy: Teaching and learning for democratic engagement.* East Lansing: Michigan State University Press.

Talloires Network. (n.d.). *Deliberative civic engagement.* Retrieved from https://talloiresnetwork.tufts.edu/deliberative-civic-engagement/

Young, I. M. (2001). Activist challenges to deliberative democracy. *Political Theory, 29*(5), 670–690.

4

CULTIVATING DIALOGUE AND DELIBERATION THROUGH SPEECH, SILENCE, AND SYNTHESIS

Sara A. Mehltretter Drury

Institutions of higher education have long traditions of creating a fertile field for open expression. This rich soil of critical ideas from history can combine with seeds of innovative research, teaching, and student experiences to grow new insights and diverse understandings. Still, the last few years have demonstrated that this vision of higher education is not inevitable. Fostering free and open discussion on campuses is a critical, yet challenging, mission for higher education. Although this struggle is not new (Springer, 2006), it has increased importance in today's civic landscape. Dialogue and deliberation provide an opportunity to teach and promote the rights of free speech as well as the responsibilities of those rights. Speaking directly to this struggle, dialogue and deliberation offer pathways for teaching robust and productive communication habits, foundations of democracy, empathetic listening, and critical thinking (Drury, Brammer, & Doherty, 2017).

One perspective on free speech says that institutions of higher education face threats to freedom of expression from outside and from within. From outside, concerned citizens and lawmakers have raised queries about the political neutrality of curricula and the professoriate (Flaherty, 2017;

Drury delivered a version of this chapter as a Wabash College Chapel Talk, on September 6, 2018, entitled "Speech, Silence, and Synthesis."

Hiltzik, 2018; Mangan, 2018). Some campuses have begun or continued to section off political speech to free speech zones, isolating potentially provocative debate (Bauer-Wolf, 2018; Kolowich, 2018). Institutions of higher education are struggling to determine how to handle divisive speakers, legacies of slavery and oppression in institutional history, and protests. Additionally, some argue that there is a growing wariness of free speech if it means encountering ideas contrary to held views. Greg Lukianoff and Jonathan Haidt (2015) first drew attention to this trend in an article in *The Atlantic*, writing that the current restrictions on free speech are less about politics and more about "emotional well-being," turning the campus into "'safe spaces' where young adults are shielded from words and ideas that make anyone uncomfortable" (p. 5). Lukianoff and Haidt (2018) followed their article with a more comprehensive book that argued the case that the *post-Millennial generation*—loosely defined as students born 1997–2012 by the Pew Research Center (Fry & Parker, 2018)—is entering college with more desire to protect themselves from potential harm, less willingness to engage ideas different from their own, and less resilience to overcome struggle.

A critique of absolute free speech suggests that an absolute commitment to free speech necessarily privileges hegemonic, harmful, and oppressive views. In this view, the marketplace of ideas for free speech means that traditionally empowered groups have louder voices than marginalized communities (Strunk, 2018). As such, free speech may "protect the expression of biased views" and create "an unequal burden" (Ben-Porath, 2018, p. 10) on those who already face systemic racism, sexism, and oppression. Psychologist Lisa Feldman Barrett (2017) has argued that speech can be a form of violence, through the "constant, casual brutality" of insults and hate speech found in today's political climate. From this perspective, it seems problematic to offer absolute free speech protections for speech designed to provoke.

Within this contentious environment, the University of Chicago recently staked out a strong commitment to free speech in higher education. In 2015, for instance, the University of Chicago's Committee on Freedom of Expression (2015) released a report that offered a fervent defense of free speech:

> Because the University is committed to free and open inquiry in all matters, it guarantees all members of the University community the broadest possible latitude to speak, write, listen, challenge, and learn. Except insofar as limitations on that freedom are necessary to the functioning of the University, the University of Chicago fully respects and supports the freedom of all members of the University community "to discuss any problem that presents itself." (p. 2)

The report acknowledged the tension of protecting free speech on campus—namely, that individuals will encounter difficult ideas. Yet the committee argued that it was "not the proper role of the University to attempt to shield individuals from ideas and opinions they find unwelcome, disagreeable, or even deeply offensive" (p. 2). The solution to "deeply offensive" speech, according to the University of Chicago, is "openly and vigorously contesting the ideas that they oppose." Fostering such debate is seen as "essential" (p. 1) to the mission of the university. The so-called "Chicago principles" have now become a part of the debate over free speech on campus, provoking responses from multiple perspectives about the struggles and challenges of speech in educational settings.

Pragmatically, the Chicago principles' commitment to free expression comes with challenges, both intellectual and physical. The circumstances facing our institutions reflect the qualities and characteristics of U.S. political discourse at large. Communities struggle to productively engage diverse viewpoints on difficult issues. Various members of a public feel offended by others; in the best case, they cease conversation and civilly agree to disagree. In some cases, conversations devolve into screaming matches, name-calling, or even physical violence. Worse, the last few years have seen a rise in hate crimes, many of which are speech-based and some of which link speech to violence (De Avila, 2018). Others have argued that the extreme openness and free speech protection of the Internet gave "white supremacists a safe space to explore ideologies and intensify their hate without consequence" (Hatzipanagos, 2018, p. 7) and that the media has functioned to "catalyze the visibility of alt-right manipulators" (Phillips, 2018a, p. 5). However, the media's coverage (and possible amplification) is a double-edged sword because not amplifying could "inadvertently contribute to the process of radicalization" and would not "mean the issue, whatever it is, will go away" (Phillips, 2018b, p. 6).

Faced with these twin threats to free speech—feeling like speech is high-stakes, while recognizing the reemergence and amplification of racist and antagonistic discourse in our public sphere—it is no wonder that campuses struggle with how to respond. But these challenges are not insurmountable. Higher education must navigate these challenges while upholding a commitment to the First Amendment's free speech protections for individuals, marginalized voices, organizations, and the press. I contend that dialogue and deliberation are pathways toward that end.

Practicing Dialogue and Deliberation

Dialogue and deliberation offer a response that embraces the rights *and* the civic responsibilities of free speech—the letter of the law guaranteeing the right of free speech, along with expectations of considering the ethical impact and implications of speech. These practices provide a way to promote diverse speech and recognize different perspectives and experiences, all while incorporating evidence and sound reasoning. This is done, in part, through fostering robust speech alongside teaching active, engaged listening. Dialogue and deliberation also provide an opportunity to *use* free speech through individual and collective synthesis, which is the difficult discursive and mental task of weighing tradeoffs and tensions, prioritizing values, and finding a way forward to address significant social issues and concerns.

Protecting Free and Open Expression

The right of every citizen to free speech is enshrined in the First Amendment of the Constitution. In fact, James Madison's original proposed text for the First Amendment, given in a speech in his capacity as a representative in the House, centralized the public sphere and free expression: "The people shall not be deprived or abridged of their right to speak, to write, or to publish their sentiments; and the freedom of the press, as one of the great bulwarks of liberty, shall be inviolable"(as cited in Feldman, 2017, p. 269; see also Cogan, 2015). Committees of the House, and then the Senate, acted as editors, although unfortunately we have no record of why and how those changes were made (Lewis, 2007, pp. 9–10). Today our First Amendment contains the shortened clause "Congress shall make no law abridging the freedom of expression." Though the edited formation may have served us well legally because it identifies the actor (Congress) who shall not restrict speech, Madison's original emphasis on "the people" reminds us that it is *the people* who are empowered in democratic, republican government. Although this right was once historically restricted to white, landowning men, subsequent amendments and protections mean that today each citizen has the right to freedom of expression.

This notion of the people having the right to speak to promote the free and open exchange of ideas is critical for higher education's mission to educate students to be active, contributing members of public discourse. However, because productive public speech is rarely modeled by national political debates, college campuses should be sites for students to learn productive habits of engagement for public life. Writing for students in his public speaking and oral communication courses, Wabash College professor of speech W. Norwood Brigance (1952) advised students that free speech was critical for preserving the way of life in democracy:

> Why speak? To keep a free society free. To settle differences by talk instead of force. To alter and promote thought. To water and cultivate ideas, hopes,

sentiments and enthusiasms in a way and to a degree that cannot be done while we are separated one from another. (p. xvi)

Encouraging dialogue and deliberation means creating a classroom that promotes the cultivation of ideas in democracy's garden (Liu & Hanauer, 2011). Of critical importance to tending the gardens of democracy are cultivating robust, diverse rhetoric and protecting the rights of citizens to speak in myriad forms. Speech is important enough to our nation, to our form of government, and to our future preservation that it deserves its own focused consideration within the habits and practices of democratic life.

Just like a real garden, tending to the growth and flourishing of free speech requires a variety of different types of engagement—engagement taught through the processes of deliberation and dialogue. One student might propose an idea, and another might add evidence or credibility to the claim, fertilizing the concept. Another may counter the idea, offering a condition or evidence that alters the original premise, the way a gardener might prune away one part of a plant so that another part can grow. The challenge here is not to strike down an idea and "win," but rather to grow something stronger together. Still other deliberative processes might encourage strategic cross-cultivation, seeing how two ideas could combine to create something new, yet related to the strengths of the original seed.

This garden metaphor, although optimistic, provides a central grounding for the work that dialogue and deliberation do on campus. The cultivation of dialogue and deliberation helps them grapple with the trade-offs and tensions among competing values, a necessary step for reasoning and deciding public action (Longo, Manosevitch, & Shaffer, 2017). Deliberative practices work to *grow something new*. The fruit of a dialogue might be understanding, whereas deliberation's fruit is choicework when faced with wicked, difficult problems (Carcasson & Sprain, 2016; National Coalition for Dialogue and Deliberation, 2013). This is how we might view our efforts at fostering free speech through dialogue and deliberation on campus—we are in the process of growing fruits necessary for democracy, among them reason-giving, collaboration, and reflection (Drury, Andrews, Nguyen, & Sklar, 2017).

Dialogue and deliberation do the slow, hard work of coming to understand a public issue and its possible solutions from different perspectives, as seen in the case studies that follow in this book. This is also present in my own work through Wabash Democracy and Public Discourse (WDPD), an interdisciplinary undergraduate research and practice program. Founded on the rights of free and open expression, WDPD teaches students to research, design, and facilitate productive dialogues and deliberation processes to address urgent real-world problems (Wabash College, 2019). Undergraduate students in the program can take a course in deliberation, where they learn the history and theory of deliberative practices; then they can apply for an academic year fellow position within WDPD. Working collaboratively, students and staff create programs on and off campus for partners interested in having focused, diverse, and vigorous forums.

The work of WDPD on campus spans a variety of issues, from campus life to disciplinary content. For example, WDPD has held forums on mental health among first-year students, inspired by the "Let's Talk About It" and "Conversations in Your Community" initiatives ("Conversations in Your Community," 2019). The WDPD students undertook this project with careful partnership with and guidance from the campus counseling services, aiming to bring forth different mental health challenges that students might encounter in their peers and in themselves. This type of dialogue destigmatizes mental health, while also promoting greater understanding of campus resources. It also provides productive peer responses for mental health. WDPD students have partnered with faculty across the curriculum to develop deliberations that complement in-class content. In a nonmajors chemistry course, a deliberation on environmental contaminants connected with real-world crises such as Flint, Michigan's water supply and in the soil of East Chicago, Indiana (Drury et al., in press). This deliberation prompted students to discuss the logistics and tradeoffs of how to handle the immediate crisis, including who should be responsible for costs, while balancing the need for long-term environmental policy changes. Thus, deliberation brings forth robust speech designed to address problems; practicing the habits of deliberation also prepares students to approach politics from a new perspective.

Of course, there are times that call for advocacy against troubling, concerning, and offensive ideas. In response to such problematic and offensive ideas, we can be guided by the words of Justice Louis Brandeis (1927) in his famous concurring opinion to the *Whitney v. California* case. Warning that restrictions to speech must be limited, Brandeis wrote, "If there be time to expose through discussion the falsehood and fallacies, to avert the evil by processes of education, the remedy is more speech, not enforced silence" (p. 377). When encountering troubling or disagreeable ideas, the solution is not to eliminate that speech, but rather to *use* speech to propose counterarguments to those ideas, to expose their flaws, and to debate against them.

Embracing *better speech* to counter bad speech is congruent with the mission of higher education. This sort of speech can—and should—point out misleading or incorrect information, ask questions that lead toward unmasking fallacies, and protect and promote the voices of marginalized communities, and those left out of the conversation. For example, WDPD has sponsored campus programs in the "Free Speech Reading Group" series that focus on how citizens can use their speech rights to counter the negative impacts of false or misleading news—what Kathleen Hall Jamieson (2018) has termed *viral deception.*

Productive speech practices such as deliberation should consider the intended ends of communication. If meant to critique, speech should do so ethically and meaningfully. If meant to persuade others, the speech should recognize the concerns, ideas, and perspectives of diverse audience members. Speakers should consider the views of others, incorporating reasoning that would encourage them to listen, consider, and change their minds. Such a perspective is not oppositional to free speech but rather embraces the notion that the deliberative field expands beyond a single process, beyond a single classroom.

Silence and Responsible Speech

In addition to protecting free expression and encouraging diversity of thought, dialogue and deliberation also promote silence. An emphasis on silence may seem out of place in a defense of discussion and democratic practices. But teaching silence as a part of the exchange of ideas is just as important for deliberative pedagogy as protecting the right of free expression. Silence from a deliberative perspective is not about being passive or still. Rather, silence encourages citizens to pause from *their own* speech to make space for and listen to the speech of others. This allows for the consideration of new information and reflection on previously held understandings. In this setting, silence is an active pursuit of listening—engaged listening, with the intention to understand fully, rather than listening with the desire to immediately respond and counter-argue.

This type of silence is an intentional and active choice, and one that is desperately needed in our information-rich society. We are, in many ways, in a constant stream of speech. The news cycle is never-ending, and updates are pushed to personal devices continuously. Interaction among peers happens not just through one-to-one messaging, but through social media apps that are always with us. Furthermore, with the advent of digital transmission and information, there is more speech immediately accessible. Magazines that used to publish monthly now produce daily articles. Newspapers tweet out instant headlines before the paper goes to press. In this environment, intentional listening is needed to process messages, to find deeper information and think about it in a critical way, evaluating arguments and the relevance and reliability of evidence.

Deliberative practices embrace this silence of pausing judgment, of temporarily putting on hold the desire to push toward a clear conclusion. Doing so will enable us to better understand a fuller range of arguments and perspectives. In today's world of personal, curated media, we often are exposed to many views that agree with our general opinions—in fact, we can isolate ourselves from media, views, and ideas that do not meet our worldview with single clicks. In the 2016 election, the *Wall Street Journal* demonstrated the degree to which understandings of current events may differ through their "Blue Feed, Red Feed" interactive website, which brought together liberal and conservative media content around key public issues. The effects are stark, with the headlines and linked articles seeming to convey completely different views of the world (Keegan, 2016). New, personalized media is replicating this divide as new forms of communication, such as Snapchat, podcasts, and YouTube, curate messages toward our own beliefs. In so doing, we may listen or watch because we already know, or at least suspect, the judgment—we anticipate the view that is being advocated, and we know the conclusion. For instance, a recent study by Eytan Bakshy, Solomon Messing, and Lada Adamic (2015) suggests that individual choice is still a significant factor in cross-cutting ideological content: "The power to expose oneself to perspectives from the other side in social media lies first and foremost with individuals" (p. 1132). Instead of continuing to affirm our own beliefs, we need to pause judgment and undertake the work of silence to hear from others and reflect on their arguments.

Silence also creates space for others to speak. Dialogue and deliberation practices encourage us to listen *with* others, trying to understand their view, rather than listening to oppose and challenge them. At Wabash College, we have organized a number of dialogue events around racial inequalities and racial justice. One of the first was an event called "I Too Am Wabash." The development of this event reflects how dialogue can prompt students to consider speech and silence, with an underlying foundation of promoting critical thinking and understanding diverse perspectives. Two student leaders trained as facilitators conceived of the event idea after hearing about Tumblr accounts that were using pictures of students with whiteboard signs to share experiences of racism on university and college campuses (Butler, 2014). These students built upon this by developing a sequenced event, using a multimedia video of students with whiteboard descriptions, a facilitated panel of students of color sharing their experiences on campus, and then a facilitated dialogue in small groups. This event became a foundation for additional dialogue events about race, diversity, and justice on campus as well as an opportunity to reflect on trends and concerns in the broader society.

As a caution, speech and silence may not always be in equilibrium. Turn-taking may not be appropriate when confronting troubling speech. Deliberative practice should create space for the *rights* of free speech, including for robust, boisterous forms of speech designed to counter odious speech. Active, intentional silence can be an opportunity to promote the free speech rights for quieter or silenced voices in the public sphere (Young, 2000). Silence connects the *right* to express one's ideas with the *responsibility* of listening to others, leading to a diversity of ideas, perspectives, considerations, and concerns.

Synthesis for Public Life

The challenges of speech and silence require digging deeper and turning toward synthesis, bringing together ideas and critiques, and weighing possibilities and tradeoffs, all of which combine to create a conclusion. This conclusion may contain large amounts of the original idea, with small changes to address a concern or tradeoff, a cross-cultivation of multiple perspectives that mitigate tradeoffs, or perhaps even an entirely new innovation conceived out of the imaginative work of public deliberation. Synthesis through deliberative practices teaches that public policy need not be a winner-take-all system. Furthermore, given the democratic underpinnings of deliberation, the conclusions of synthesis should gesture toward "the community good," with the intention of improving the public issue from a communal, rather than individual, perspective (Drury et al., 2017, p. 195).

Synthesis can help us find unlikely common ground. This isn't easy, whether on campus or in the public sphere, because different things are important to diverse groups of people. For example, two factions in a community might disagree on taxes and government organization (one preferring lower taxes and fewer services, with the other preferring higher taxes and more services), but they might agree when funding is spent on education. There might be common ground that the community should look to new educational opportunities that meet the needs of twenty-first-century young people (Drury et al., 2015). Through discussion of different options and tradeoffs, the *value* of young people having opportunities was highly held enough to transcend more divisive issues.

Deliberation is not, however, inherently about consensus. There are times when synthesis also helps citizens move through difficult choicework when consensus does not exist. Someone may have to "lose," but carefully considering *all* perspectives may reveal how to make that loss a little less painful. Undertaking the work of deliberative pedagogy teaches students how to sort through competing perspectives. Endemic to choicework is the reality that in some situations, one group may not have their ideas come to fruition; something is given up by someone(s) for the public to move forward. Our political system would call this defeat, but the perspective of political theorist Danielle Allen suggests that we might instead think about such choices as the sacrifice necessary to sustain democracy. In her writings about sacrifice and citizenship, Allen (2004) explains that "an honest account of collective democratic action must begin by acknowledging that communal decisions inevitably benefit some citizens at the expense of others, even when the whole community generally benefits" (p. 28). But as Allen acknowledges, sacrifice has all too often come from the same groups of people in our society. She urges us to find new pathways, through rhetoric (speech) and listening (silence), to develop a connected form of political friendship amongst ideological strangers, honoring the sacrifices made in order to create a better future for all.

Synthesis is a challenging practice for classrooms and in public life. Trying to make decisions where some people sacrifice, while acknowledging past sacrifices as another contextual factor, and continuously evaluating the different perspectives and arguments is messy work. But such deliberative work is essential for finding ways to transcend polarized politics. In higher education classrooms, students can undertake deliberative practices to slow down the process of decision-making and learn more about the issue, absorb different perspectives, consider tradeoffs, and come to a better understanding of a public decision. Students might, for example, develop a stakeholder and value chart, mapping the values that are important and seeing the potential for common ground and conflict. We then might prompt students to ask whose perspective is missing and engage in dialogue about why that perspective might have been overlooked. Synthesis can take students through the process of evaluating the quality and forms of reasoning, alongside benefits and tradeoffs, while pausing to reflect on new possibilities.

Although dialogue and deliberation do not provide easy answers, protecting speech and promoting reflective silence bring forth difficult but important conversations, as opposed to pushing citizens to retreat to their own ideas and preferences. When we engage others, we are far better equipped to encounter, map, and understand—and move toward proposing a new pathway, action, or idea to address wicked problems.

Conclusion

The practices of speech, silence, and synthesis create a robust purpose for dialogue and deliberation in higher education, one that relates to higher education's need to promote and protect free speech. Although acknowledging the legal limits of speech as recognized by courts of the United States, higher education should foster free speech, creating a marketplace of ideas among students, faculty, and staff, as well as members of broader publics. Doing so will serve higher education's mission of creating a fertile ground for critical thinking, engaging with multiple perspectives, and developing new ideas and innovations.

A key strength of dialogue and deliberation is that its practices of free speech, reflective silence, and critical synthesis promote education for public life, for the engagement of difficult challenges in the fast-paced, ever-changing world. Free speech provides the constitutional and practical foundation for intellectual freedom and diversity of viewpoints. Reflective silence prompts community members to more fully consider the responsibilities of free speech—namely, how a shared commitment to free expression for all dovetails with the need for listening and engagement with other viewpoints. The interplay of speech and silence feeds critical synthesis, an evaluative process that brings together ideas to counter, condemn, balance, support, transcend, and otherwise engage in the creation of new conclusions, priorities, and decisions. The interactions of speech, silence, and synthesis work to water and feed; to nurture and cull; to develop, expand, and bear fruit from the gardens of democracy and in our shared public life.

References

Allen, D. S. (2004). *Talking to strangers: Anxieties of citizenship since* Brown v. Board of Education. Chicago, IL: University of Chicago Press.

Bakshy, E., Messing, S., & Adamic, L. A. (2015). Exposure to ideologically diverse news and opinion on Facebook. *Science, 348*(6239), 1130–1132. doi:10.1126/science.aaa1160

Bauer-Wolf, J. (2018, November 28). Civility at Berkeley. *Inside Higher Ed.* Retrieved from https://www.insidehighered.com/news/2018/11/28/new-policies-student-groups-change-culture-free-speech-berkeley

Ben-Porath, S. (2018, December 11). Against endorsing the Chicago Principles. *Inside Higher Ed.* Retrieved from https://www.insidehighered.com/views/2018/12/11/what-chicago-principles-miss-when-it-comes-free-speech-and-academic-freedom-opinion

Brandeis, L. (1927, May 16). Concurrence, *Whitney v. California.* 274 U.S. 357. Retrieved from https://www.law.cornell.edu/supremecourt/text/274/357#writing-USSC_CR_0274_0357_ZC

Brigance, W. N. (1952). *Speech: Its techniques and disciplines in a free society.* New York, NY: Appleton-Century-Crofts.

Butler, B. (2014, March 5). "I, too, am Harvard": Black students show why they belong. *Washington Post*. Retrieved from https://www.washingtonpost.com/blogs/she-the-people/wp/2014/03/05/i-too-am-harvard-black-students-show-they-belong/

Carcasson, M., & Sprain, L. (2016). Beyond problem solving: Reconceptualizing the work of public deliberation as deliberative inquiry. *Communication Theory, 26*, 41–63.

Cogan, N. H. (with Pret, A., Adams, D. L., & Harvey, T. L.). (2015). *The complete Bill of Rights: The drafts, debates, sources, and origins* (2nd ed.). New York, NY: Oxford University Press.

Conversations in your community. (2019). Retrieved from http://www.mentalhealth.gov/talk/community-conversation

De Avila, J. (2018, November 13). Anti-Semitic incidents fuel 17% rise in hate crimes, FBI says. *Wall Street Journal*. Retrieved from https://www.wsj.com/articles/anti-semitic-incidents-fuel-17-rise-in-hate-crimes-fbi-says-1542129814

Drury, S. A. M., Andrews, T., Nguyen, M., & Sklar, G. (2015). *The next Montgomery County: A community conversation about quality of place*. Retrieved from http://blog.wabash.edu/wabashdpd/2015/08/02/final-report-the-next-montgomery-county-spring-2015/

Drury, S. A. M., Brammer, L. R., & Doherty, J. (2017). Assessment through a deliberative pedagogy outcomes rubric. In T. J. Shaffer, N. V. Longo, I. Manosevitch, & M. S. Thomas (Eds.), *Deliberative pedagogy: Teaching and learning for democratic engagement* (pp. 191–201). East Lansing: Michigan State University Press.

Drury, S. A. M., Rush, R., Wilder, S., & Wysocki, L. (in press). Encouraging bridges: Connecting science students to public problem solving through science communication. In *Communication in Chemistry*. ACS Symposium Series.

Feldman, N. (2017). *The three lives of James Madison: Genius, partisan, president*. New York, NY: Random House.

Feldman Barrett, L. (2017, July 14). When is speech violence? *New York Times*. Retrieved from https://www.nytimes.com/2017/07/14/opinion/sunday/when-is-speech-violence.html

Flaherty, C. (2017, February 21). Iowa bill would force "partisan balance" in hiring. *Inside Higher Ed*. Retrieved from https://www.insidehighered.com/quicktakes/2017/02/21/iowa-bill-would-force-partisan-balance-hiring

Fry, R., & Parker, K. (2018, November). *Early benchmarks show "post-millennials" on track to be the most diverse, best-educated generation yet*. Retrieved from https://www.pewsocialtrends.org/2018/11/15/early-benchmarks-show-post-millennials-on-track-to-be-most-diverse-best-educated-generation-yet/

Hatzipanagos, R. (2018, November 30). How online hate turns into real violence. *Washington Post*. Retrieved from https://www.washingtonpost.com/nation/2018/11/30/how-online-hate-speech-is-fueling-real-life-violence/

Hiltzik, M. (2018, May 30). How a right-wing group's proposed "free speech" law aims to undermine free speech on campus. *Los Angeles Times*. Retrieved from https://www.latimes.com/business/hiltzik/la-fi-hiltzik-free-speech-20180530-story.html

Jamieson, K. H. (2018, November 25). *Kathleen Hall Jamieson on viral deception* [Video file]. Retrieved from https://www.youtube.com/watch?v=nGAZKkx-Khk

Keegan, J. (2016, May 18). Blue feed, red feed. *Wall Street Journal.* Retrieved from http://graphics.wsj.com/blue-feed-red-feed/

Kolowich, S. (2018, September 13). U. of Nebraska wondered whether conservative students were being silenced. Here's what it found out. *The Chronicle of Higher Education.* Retrieved from https://www.chronicle.com/article/U-of-Nebraska-Wondered/244517

Lewis, A. (2007). *Freedom for the thought we hate: A biography of the First Amendment.* New York, NY: Basic Books.

Liu, E., & Hanauer, N. (2011). *The gardens of democracy: A new American story of citizenship, the economy, and the role of government.* Seattle, WA: Sasquatch Books.

Longo, N. V., Manosevitch, I., & Shaffer, T. (2017). Introduction. In T. J. Shaffer, N. V. Longo, I. Manosevitch, & M. S. Thomas (Eds.), *Deliberative pedagogy: Teaching and learning for democratic engagement* (pp. xix–xxxv). East Lansing: Michigan State University Press.

Lukianoff, G., & Haidt, J. (2015, September). The coddling of the American mind. *The Atlantic.* Retrieved from https://www.theatlantic.com/magazine/archive/2015/09/the-coddling-of-the-american-mind/399356/

Lukianoff, G., & Haidt, J. (2018). *The coddling of the American mind: How good intentions and bad ideas are setting up a generation for failure.* New York, NY: Penguin Press.

Mangan, K. (2018, January 31). Texas lawmakers weigh the limits of free speech on campus. *The Chronicle of Higher Education.* Retrieved from https://www.chronicle.com/article/Texas-Lawmakers-Weigh-the/242405

National Coalition for Dialogue and Deliberation. (2013, July). *Engagement streams.* Retrieved from http://www.ncdd.org/files/NCDD2010_Engagement_Streams.pdf

Phillips, W. (2018a). The oxygen of amplification: Executive summary. *Data & Society.* Retrieved from https://datasociety.net/wp-content/uploads/2018/05/FULL-REPORT_Oxygen_of_Amplification_DS.pdf

Phillips, W. (2018b). The oxygen of amplification, part two: The ambivalence of journalistic amplification. *Data & Society.* Retrieved from https://datasociety.net/wp-content/uploads/2018/05/FULLREPORT_Oxygen_of_Amplification_DS.pdf

Springer, A. (2006). *Academic freedom of students and professors, and political discrimination.* Retrieved from https://www.aaup.org/academic-freedom-students-and-professors-and-political-discrimination

Strunk, K. K. (2018, September 21). Free speech for some, civility for others. *Inside Higher Ed.* Retrieved from https://www.insidehighered.com/advice/2018/09/21/colleges-and-politicians-promote-free-speech-some-insist-civility-others-opinion

University of Chicago, Committee on Freedom of Expression. (2015). *The Chicago Principles: Report of the Committee on Freedom of Expression.* Retrieved from https://provost.uchicago.edu/sites/default/files/documents/reports/FOECommitteeReport.pdf

Wabash College. (2019). *Liberal arts plus: Wabash democracy and public discourse.* Retrieved from https://wabash.edu/plus/democracy

Young, I. M. (2000). *Inclusion and democracy.* Oxford, UK: Oxford University Press.

PART TWO
METHODS OF DIALOGUE AND DELIBERATION

5

CREATING CULTURES OF DIALOGUE IN HIGHER EDUCATION

Stories and Lessons From Essential Partners

John Sarrouf and Katie Hyten

It was the fall of 2015, and the debate over whether to remove Confederate statues and other symbols of the Confederacy from public spaces was in full swing—no place more so than at this small college in the rural South. College administrators invited Essential Partners to facilitate a dialogue on the topic.

From the outset, tensions were high because students assumed the divisions were clear and fixed. As they began to talk, however, participants discovered that people on all sides felt stereotyped and misunderstood, and that all wanted to be known. Students took risks, and as a result their stories were revelatory. One young Latina woman from New York City always thought of the Confederate flag as a statement of hatred and anger, and she couldn't understand why some of her classmates would fly it. She spoke of feeling scared. A young man from the rural South talked about the flag as a symbol of pride of place, of self-sufficiency: It was his image of resilience. He was shocked and disturbed that this symbol, which meant so much to him and his family, was painful to someone else. They asked each other questions. "What do you mean by *resilience*—resilience around what?" "What symbols are important to you?" "What would you lose if we got rid of the flag?"

They did not come away ready to change their beliefs or the meaning of their experiences, although that may happen in time. They did come away feeling more clarity about their beliefs and more understanding of what the flag meant to others. They also came away with less fear of each other, a desire to keep talking to one another, and a deeper sense of belonging to each other and to the community. They felt committed to making space for more conversations across campus, not only about the flag but also about other issues.

About Essential Partners

Essential Partners (EP), what was then known as the Public Conversations Project, began as a conversation among a group of family therapists in the late 1980s. Listening to the public discourse at that time between pro-life and pro-choice advocates—which in some places had turned violent—the therapists heard patterns that they also encountered in their family and group therapy sessions. They became curious about whether interventions pioneered by narrative therapy, family systems thinking, and communications theory could shift "stuck" public conversations around abortion and other hotly contested topics to support constructive engagement. By employing therapeutic interventions on a larger scale, could they shift the public conversation, shift what was possible in communities? The therapists decided to undertake a decade-long study that became EP. Their groundbreaking approach has since been used to discuss some of the most polarizing issues of our time, including Israel-Palestine, sexuality in the Christian church, interfaith relations, immigration, race, gender dynamics, and the role of guns in communities.[1]

Although EP has roots in the early days of conflict resolution work, we now live at the intersection of conflict transformation and community engagement, embracing the idea that conflict is a natural part of human relationships and should be engaged for productive change and growth.[2] At its heart, our work is about managing strongly held and seemingly mutually exclusive convictions in communities where people either want to—or have to—live together in the tension of their differences. This is why colleges and universities have proved to be ideal settings for Reflective Structured Dialogue.

---

1. See the EP website (whatisessential.org) for details of these discussions, including videos from members of the Providence College community.

2. John Paul Lederach has discussed conflict transformation in depth; see, for example, *Conflict Transformation* (Lederach, 2003).

Our Method

Reflective Structured Dialogue (RSD) is a culturally adaptive approach to structuring conversations between people in a community. It intentionally interrupts old, destructive patterns of communication that have prevented a group from having the conversations it needs to have. RSD gives people the opportunity to cocreate a new communication culture explicitly and intentionally, so they can communicate constructively across difference in ways that invite full, authentic, and constructive engagement. By shifting away from stereotypes, accusations, and escalating patterns of conflict, RSD invites narrative, inquiry, and communal self-reflection, helping a community address its divisions, inaction, or structural inequities. In all of our work, EP aims to foster conversations meant "to enhance mutual understanding among people who differ deeply about treasured values, identities, and beliefs" (Stains, 2016, p. 1534), while working with communities to help them establish and accomplish their unique purposes for dialogue.

To change old patterns requires attention and intention—attentiveness to what needs to change and intentional choices to "foster the new" (Chasin et al., 1996, p. 332). Within RSD, every choice we make as facilitators and teachers invites one way of being together and discourages another, creating spaces where people are better able to speak openly, listen respectfully, and express the kind of curiosity that fosters engagement and deep knowledge, even when difference is present. RSD uses the elements in the following sections to support constructive conversations across differences.

Purpose and Preparation

When designing a dialogue, we begin by helping a campus community clarify its purpose—the larger hope for what it wants to accomplish—and prepare for a new kind of conversation. From the beginning, our goal is for communities to feel ownership and responsibility for the conversations they've helped create and prepare themselves to engage in ways that help them accomplish their stated purposes.

Facilitation

Facilitators in RSD hold the container that enables participants to avoid devolving back into patterns that threaten the cohesion and effectiveness of the community. Their role is to design a dialogue that meets the needs and cultural norms of the group and then to use agreements or ground rules to ensure participants hold to that design, even in difficult moments. In RSD, facilitators support constructive conversation within the group rather than direct the conversation or move it in a particular direction.[3]

Inquiry
RSD invites two new types of questions. First, we design dialogue questions that invite everyone to share personal narratives that break stereotypes, connect to values and convictions (rather than analysis), and nurture complexity in people's thinking (rather than reinforcing certainty). A good dialogue question asks people to move from what family therapists term *landscapes of action* to *landscapes of meaning* (Combs & Freedman, 2004), places where people probe values and motivations rather than offer simple responses. Second, we invite participants to ask questions of each other that reflect a genuine desire to understand, rather than to trap, convince, or judge, as demonstrated in Table 5.1.

Structured Speaking and Listening
For a dialogue to be successful, we work to break the old patterns of the same people speaking first in a meeting, dominating the space, interrupting others, or not speaking at all. These patterns are often well-established and hard to break, so RSD offers structures for speaking and listening—like timed speaking, go-arounds, communication agreements, and intentional pauses—that build new patterns of conversation.

Reflection
RSD draws its name from the centrality of reflective moments within the dialogue that help participants become curious, shift their internal responses, speak to be understood, and reflect deeply on their convictions and values. Dialogue relies heavily on taking moments to pause and reflect before responding to questions, between speakers, and when looking back on the conversation.

Where We Work and With Whom

EP works with any self-defined group of people who live, work, study, and/or worship together; generally, we work with those who must communicate across difference regularly, regardless of the outcome of a single conflict. At

---

3. For details about this process, see *Fostering Dialogue Across Divides* (Essential Partners, n.d.).

TABLE 5.1
Shifting the Questions

Trapping, Judgmental Questions	Open, Genuine Questions
Isn't it true that people who think that way don't understand anything about how people really live, or have never had to deal with this situation?	Help me understand how you came to your beliefs around this issue. What is your experience with this situation?
Isn't it hypocritical to say you believe [x] and then to do [y]?	I wonder how you make sense of believing [x] and doing [y]. For me, they seem to be in contradiction—could you help me understand?
Why is such a small thing such a big deal to you?	Could you say more about why this is an important issue to you?

the outset of our work together, *communities* are defined by project participants and are based on their goals for the process. In higher education, communities can be the entire campus, dorms, school-community relationships, staff teams, student clubs, faith groups, or other configurations. Because of our focus on customized design and purpose, each project in higher education has a different definition of *success*. For example, an institution might want to equip resident advisers to hold difficult conversations in their residence halls, or support interreligious conversations on Israel-Palestine. EP also works to enhance dialogue in the classroom and strengthen campus-wide engagement across difference on college campuses. Across all the projects we do, the communities must want to engage with the other side in more constructive ways, even in the midst of differences and disagreements, in order to move forward and create a preferred future together.

Once we have a clear sense of a dialogue's purpose and stakeholders, we pay attention both to those who will be primary decision-makers and to those who may be affected. In other words, RSD helps communities work toward more social cohesion and resilience, rather than focusing solely on agreement (which may or may not happen). Therefore, it must include (and truly represent) all stakeholders in a community. This also means that we need to include strong advocates representing all groups from the outset to ensure that our design does not exclude people from the process.

We also work to design conversations in a way that empowers people and allows them to take care of themselves in the conversation, to help bring people to the table in equitable ways. The tools and elements of RSD make it possible for all stakeholders in a community to fully enter into important conversations in their communities on their terms and in ways that have felt impossible before. This work of overcoming relational barriers makes it possible for communities to address important issues and structural change in new ways.

Dialogue at Bridgewater College: Five Years In

EP's work at Bridgewater College—a private, coed, liberal arts campus in Virginia—is grounded in the vision of a *dialogic campus* (i.e., one which has the ethos, experience, and capacity to turn to dialogue in moments of discernment, community-building, or crisis). In 2012, Bridgewater set about building a Quality Enhancement Plan centered on academic citizenship, including the principles of civil discourse, perspective-taking, public reasoning, and self-authorship. RSD emerged as the clearest pathway to these goals because it gives space for students to define their purpose for engagement, refine their public voice, and remain open to others.

Recognizing that student ownership of a dialogue project would be crucial in cultivating academic citizenship on campus, EP began by training students, who then formed a club to facilitate difficult conversations throughout the academic year around a "big question," a topic integral to the life of the college. Using their skills as RSD facilitators, students were also able to respond to crises of racial discrimination, navigate contentious elections, and support democratic engagement. This blend of planned and responsive dialogues built the foundation of academic citizenship.

Now, five years later, dialogic pedagogy is part of all first-year seminar teaching by faculty in every department across the college. RSD works well at Bridgewater because the project is supported at all levels—by student leaders, faculty, and administration. There is an institution-wide commitment to dialogic practices that President David Bushman articulated in his opening address to students at the start of the 2018–2019 academic year:

> When we are engaging in difficult dialogues that tap into our most central identities, whether those identities are tied to our gender, race, ethnicity, sexuality, faith, ethical stance, or political perspectives, we need to be courageous enough to listen, be intellectually curious, respect the humanity in others, collaborate and problem-solve creatively, and find our own voices. (D. Bushman, personal communication, September 5, 2018)

Dialogue at Tufts University: Building Momentum

At Tufts University in Massachusetts, dialogue began in a more decentralized way. At various points, EP worked with chaplains, student affairs staff in a graduate school, faculty members in the dental school, researchers working on civic engagement, and administrators to develop discrete programs. But student involvement and ownership remained elusive. So we shifted our strategy to focus on engaging students in the classroom. In courses like Science and Civic Action and Dialogue, Identity, and Civic Action, students dedicated specific blocks of time to developing dialogue skills and then decided together how to bring dialogue to the larger campus community. Students enrolled in Dialogue, Identity, and Civic Action also facilitated at least one dialogue on campus about an issue they care about; projects have focused on immigration, race, housing, Greek life, sexual assault, belonging on campus, and civic science. One student wrote about this process: "[Dialogue] helped me connect with others at Tufts and created a platform where I can hear a diversity of voices. Dialogue also helps lead us to solutions for issues on campus" (personal communication, May 2017). Another student added:

> One of the things I always think about is my willingness to listen. When I first came to college, my conversations were very reactionary. Now I have curiosity to hear other perspectives. In dialogue, you can hear diverse backgrounds, and I know there's value to those perspectives. (Personal communication, May 2017)

At Tufts, embedding dialogue in the curriculum has proved the most effective strategy for engaging diverse student voices in campus conversations across difference. It has also created a built-in resource for facilitation in other initiatives on campus. These efforts have also expanded to other areas of the university. For instance, EP has now equipped more than 30 faculty and staff members with the tools to use dialogue in their teaching and student-facing roles. In the summer of 2018, we trained 20 professional staff in residential life and all 100 first-year residential advisers, who, in turn, led the 1,546 incoming students in a dialogue on the last day of orientation. Thus, the RSD program at Tufts has a strong foundation of student ownership and administrative buy-in through curricular and cocurricular training and development in collaboration with EP.

The Impact of RSD in Communities

We know that our work supporting new conversations in diverse communities makes a difference because we employ a robust evaluation system that measures our impact in four domains.[4] We not only assess the efficacy of each training but also work with each community to collaboratively develop goals that we measure in surveys and phone interviews in the first year after an initial engagement.

First, we measure the degree to which participants feel they better understand others who are different and the degree to which they feel more understood themselves.

Second, we measure social cohesion—individuals' sense of belonging, their sense of community cohesiveness, the trust they feel across difference, and the number and healthiness of relationships across differences.[5]

Third, we measure the degree to which participants are more willing to engage across difference and the degree to which they have experienced personal transformation vis-à-vis the competence and confidence to engage constructively in difficult moments.

Fourth, we measure the degree to which participants have gained and applied skills both in accomplishing their own purposes and in building the resilience to respond constructively to community challenges. We define *resilience* as the capacity of community members to remain invested in one another in moments that threaten the identities of one or more groups.[6]

Our initial findings have been promising. In the past two years, we have found that communities experience increased cohesion and resilience after using the RSD approach. For example, the vast majority of people who train to be facilitators go on to use their dialogue skills with groups, working with an average of 50 people in the first year of applying their skills. And those with whom they work feel more understood, more cohesive, and more resilient. For example, although most participants, both before and after dialogue, feel that they understand others, almost 40% of participants before a dialogue do not feel understood by those different from themselves. This number falls to 10% after they participate in EP's approach to dialogue.[7]

---

4. Our unique evaluation system is available for adaptation, with attribution (see whatisessential.org/evaluation).

5. Our definition of *social cohesion* references, but deviates from, models established by Chan, To, and Chan (2006); Acket, Borsenberger, Dickes, and Sarracino (2011); and Jenson (2010).

6. This definition references, but deviates from, a model established by Frankenberger, Mueller, Spangler, and Alexander (2013).

7. These data are drawn from EP presurveys of almost 300 participants and postsurveys of almost 500 participants.

Emerging Opportunities and Challenges of RSD in Higher Education

As EP continues to work in the context of higher education, we face both opportunities and challenges for dialogue in campus communities.

Emerging Opportunity: Cultivating Dialogue in the Classroom

Following requests from faculty who reported challenging conversations arising in their classrooms after the 2016 election, we adapted our dialogue work to facilitation of classroom discussions. In a project with four institutions funded by the Templeton Foundation, we have studied the power of dialogic classrooms to develop conviction and intellectual humility in students. Over the past two years, we have developed a curriculum to train faculty to facilitate difficult conversations in their classrooms; Bridgewater College and Tufts University were among the institutions that took part in the pilot study. Our research has yielded strong evidence that dialogue engages more voices in the classroom and helps students reflect on and articulate their own convictions, while remaining open to and curious about others' perspectives. In dialogic classrooms, students report that dialogue helped them build trust, find their voice, achieve greater understanding of the material, and understand multiple perspectives with complexity and nuance.[8]

Challenges and Lessons From Applying RSD in Higher Education

In bringing RSD to higher education, we have faced some challenges that echo across schools and regions. In evaluating our work, we have found that people who train in dialogue as a team are almost twice as likely to use RSD successfully in their community as those who attend a training individually.[9] We also see that it takes time for communities to make progress on their plans; they often do not see shifts in the four evaluation domains for at least six months. These findings present challenges when developing dialogue in higher education. All too often, students, staff, and faculty alike feel overcommitted and unable to take on another project. Sustainability of campus

---

8. For more information about this research, contact principal investigator John Sarrouf (john@whatisessential.org).

9. Six months after training, 54% of participants who trained alone reported progress on plans or increased resilience, whereas 92% of those who attended training with a group in their community reported such progress. Only 24% of participants who trained alone reported improved cohesion after 5 months, whereas 54% of those who attended training with a group in their community reported improved cohesion.

dialogue efforts is increased by institutional buy-in, as when a representative group of committed and equipped leaders spearheads the dialogue across campus. Sustainability is also increased by creating multiple opportunities for formal and informal dialogue in classes, community forums, residential life, spiritual life, and interpersonal advising or mentorship. We also design projects in ways that integrate dialogic practices into preexisting spaces, to meet the unique needs of each community.

At the same time, our intention to meet the needs unique to each campus can encounter obstacles. For example, some campuses struggle to determine where to start or how to envision a way forward. In this situation, we encourage the campus to identify a starting place where there is both a network of committed people (or existing infrastructure) and a felt need or urgency to find new ways to communicate about difficult things. Financial investment, although not always necessary, can also reduce obstacles. For example, dedicated funding has enabled some campuses to host regular support lunches for faculty who are using dialogue or to provide ongoing training or coaching for tough moments.

Finally, we often face questions about the role RSD will play on campus, what it will allow, and what it will make space for. There are often suspicions behind these questions, including concerns that dialogue is intended to quell protest, delay action, or reinforce existing power structures. As students, faculty, and staff wrestle with power imbalances, identity, and inclusion, we try to meet them where they are and help them use dialogue as one of many tools to meet their needs and build resilient, cohesive campus communities. We see dialogue as a complement to other forms of engagement, including civil protest, advocacy, and education. In an interview with the Tufts University student newspaper, one student fellow reflected on this experience:

> I think that because everyone gets a chance to speak and a facilitator can intervene if someone starts to say something harmful, it creates a space where the sharing of that story might be held a little more carefully than it potentially would in other spaces. . . . Something I really appreciate is that this model isn't meant to silence activism and it isn't meant to replace activism, it's meant to be a complement to activism. . . . I actually think that activists and folks who care about engaging in change are able do their jobs better if they are more aware of how other people are thinking about these issues. (French, 2017)

Conclusion

EP's work has the capacity to shift how diverse communities engage across difference, particularly in tense moments. Today's campus communities are facing tremendous challenges as student bodies become more diverse and increasingly enter into difficult conversations. Dialogue is becoming critically important as institutions work to move from diversity to true inclusion of all community members and as students seek opportunities to be active and involved on their campuses. RSD can equip faculty to engage competently the conversations that come up in class; can help students, faculty, and administrators hear each other in difficult moments; and can support conversations that build an engaged and inclusive campus community.

References

Acket, S., Borsenberger, M., Dickes, P., & Sarracino, F. (2011, January). *Measuring and validating social cohesion: A bottom-up approach.* Working paper presented at the meeting of the International Conference on Social Cohesion and Development, Paris. Retrieved from https://www.oecd.org/dev/pgd/46839973.pdf

Chan, J., To, H., & Chan, E. (2006). Reconsidering social cohesion: Developing a definition and analytical framework for empirical research. *Social Indicators Research, 75*, 273–302. doi:10.107/s11205-05-2118-1

Chasin, R., Herzig, M., Roth, S., Chasin, L., Becker, C., & Stains, R. (1996). From diatribe to dialogue on divisive public issues: Approaches drawn from family therapy. *Mediation Quarterly, 13*(4), 323–344.

Combs, G., & Freedman, J. (2004). A poststructuralist approach to narrative work. In L. Angus & J. McLeod (Eds.), *The handbook of narrative and psychotherapy* (pp. 137–155). Thousand Oaks, CA: Sage.

Essential Partners. (n.d.) *Fostering Dialogue Across Divides.* Retrieved from https://whatisessential.org/fdad

Frankenberger, T., Mueller, M., Spangler, T., & Alexander, S. (2013). *Community resilience: Conceptual framework and measurement feed the future learning agenda.* Rockville, MD: Westat.

French, K. (2017, November 15). Inaugural cohort of Tisch dialogue fellows promotes critical discussion, lived experience, activism. *The Tufts Daily.* Retrieved from https://tuftsdaily.com/features/2017/11/15/dialogue-article/

Jenson, J. (2010). *Defining and measuring social cohesion.* Retrieved from http://www.unrisd.org/80256B3C005BCCF9/(httpAuxPages)/170C271B7168CC30C12577D0004BA206/$file/Jenson%20ebook.pdf

Lederach, J. P. (2003, October). *Conflict transformation.* Retrieved from https://www.beyondintractability.org/essay/transformation

Stains, R. (2016). Cultivating courageous communities through the practice and power of dialogue. *Mitchell Hamline Law Review*, *42*(5), article 5. Retrieved from https://open.mitchellhamline.edu/cgi/viewcontent.cgi?article=1053&context=mhlr

6

BUILDING CAPACITY IN COMMUNITIES

Everyday Democracy's Dialogue to Change Approach

Martha L. McCoy and Sandy Heierbacher

Wagner, South Dakota, is a small rural town in the southeastern part of the state, within the larger area of the Yankton Indian Reservation. As in many ethnically diverse places across the United States, there is a history of deep racial tensions, with few relationships among people from different backgrounds. Given that, it is unsurprising that over most of its history there has been little collaboration to address community concerns, even though people from every ethnic group—whether white, Native American, African American, Latino, or Asian American—have struggled to meet their basic needs.[1]

Wagner began to address these challenges when it became a part of the Horizons initiative sponsored by the Northwest Area Foundation. The goal of Horizons was to help small rural and reservation communities with fewer than 1,000 residents and a poverty rate of more than 10% to build their civic leadership and community capacity to address poverty and improve their economic well-being. In 2006, the Study Circles Resource Center (now Everyday Democracy) was invited by the foundation to be part of this project, which took place across 7 states in the northwestern United States.

---

1. At the time of the 2010 census, there were 1,566 people, 639 households, and 367 families residing in the town. The racial makeup of the town was 54.7% white, 0.2% African American, 40.5% Native American, 0.2% Asian American, 0.8% from other races, and 3.6% from 2 or more races. Hispanic or Latino of any race were 3.0% of the population.

Our charge was to help communities create welcoming opportunities for people from all backgrounds and income levels to have productive conversations about poverty and then work together to address it. As part of this process, Wagner residents began meeting with each other for structured dialogue (sometimes called study circles) about poverty in their community and what they could do to build prosperity. According to participants, this was the first time in the history of the town when people from Native and non-Native backgrounds were sitting down together, sharing their stories and experiences, and learning a more complete history of their community.

As we have done in hundreds of other communities, Everyday Democracy supported the dialogues as part of Horizons by creating dialogue materials, training dialogue facilitators, and providing coaching and training to organizers. What differed in this case was that instead of coaching community leaders in each small community, we trained staff members from South Dakota State University (SDSU) Extension and Sitting Bull College, who in turn trained community leaders in the rural communities and reservations that took part in the multiyear initiative. In this way, institutions of higher education became "coaching hubs" for democratic engagement aimed at reducing poverty.

Thriving Communities (Rourke, 2008), the guide we developed, provided a framework, for people from different cultures to explore what poverty meant to them in their own lives and community, as did *Organizing Rural and Reservation Communities for Dialogue and Change* (Everyday Democracy, 2008). During the study circle process we learned that for the people of Wagner, *poverty* meant more than a lack of adequate work opportunities. They also defined it as a lack of opportunities for good education, as being cut off from their culture or faith community, and as a lack of strong networks of friends and family. And just as importantly, their hopes for the future of Wagner went beyond the creation of economic opportunity to include the values they wanted their community to embody.

With a deeper understanding of each other and the issues they faced, the multiracial steering committee decided to organize another round of dialogues to address what had emerged as a primary issue in the dialogues on poverty: the structural racism at the root of the economic and cultural divide between white and Native American residents.

As a result of the dialogues on poverty and racism, residents worked together on the action ideas they had generated. Positive changes in relationships and culture sprang up throughout the town. Some American Indians invited white residents to attend traditional events and ceremonies; as white residents attended, they gained a new understanding of the impact of racism on the Native community and all of Wagner. New relationships between residents of different backgrounds formed and deepened. A movie theater with a European American owner began to display a "Thank you" sign in both English and Yankton Sioux. A local coffee shop began to display a Welcome sign in both languages, and American Indian patrons began to feel more welcome there.

Institutional changes also took place as a result of the dialogues and collective action, from the establishment of a small business incubator with equal governance among American Indian and white residents to a significant increase in high school graduation rates among American Indians. Further, the school system instituted study circles on racism that included administrators, teachers, and students. As a result, teachers became more intentional about creating more inclusive curricula. Native symbols and ceremonies were incorporated into school functions. And more American Indians began attending school events, such as prom, that had previously been predominantly white.

About Everyday Democracy

Everyday Democracy began as the Study Circles Resource Center in 1989, created by entrepreneur and philanthropist Paul Aicher. Aicher had a vision of a United States where people of all backgrounds and education levels would have regular, welcoming opportunities to connect with people different from themselves to learn about and work on public issues. He was drawn to the study circle idea (a model of peer-led, democratic dialogue) because of its roots in adult learning and community-building in the late nineteenth century (Bjerkaker, 2014). Aicher's participation in a peer-led discussion of public issues when he was a young engineer had transformed his life. It led to his first realization that his voice as an "ordinary citizen" was important and valid, and he wanted others to have a similar experience.

To help make our founder's vision a reality, we began to look for ways to bring highly diverse groups of people together to engage with one another on critical social and political issues. We learned the following important lessons in our first decade:

- There were few settings in society where people from different backgrounds felt welcome to meet together for any purpose, much less to discuss tough public issues. That led us to explore ways to create diverse and welcoming settings for public discourse.

- There were few models of productive conversations about public issues, especially among people from different experiences, backgrounds, and views. Given that, we began to explore public talk that was welcoming and accessible to all kinds of people.
- Productive conversation about pressing issues, as vital as it is, isn't enough in and of itself to draw most people into a discussion or sustain their engagement. Many dialogue efforts (past and present) fall short because they don't acknowledge what motivates people as community members and citizens. People need to be invited by those they know and trust, and they need to know that their participation will make a tangible difference in the community. This is especially true of those who are most affected by the issues, who often face additional barriers to participation in traditional kinds of public meetings.
- As we explored the kinds of issues that would draw a critical mass of people into dialogue and action with each other, we discovered that issues surrounding our country's racial history and ongoing racial tensions were compelling to a wide diversity of people. Even though the issue of racism was so difficult to talk about—and often completely avoided—it was persistent in its impact. Many people of all backgrounds wanted to be part of a productive, diverse dialogue about race *if it could lead to positive community change.* In addition, many community institutions—faith groups, nonprofits, businesses, local governments, and civil rights groups—wanted to create diverse public spaces for productive collective work on race.

All of these lessons gave us the impetus to develop processes and advice that could help cross-sector and grassroots community groups work in collaboration to organize inclusive dialogue that would lead to collective action and meaningful change—at individual, interpersonal, institutional, and policy levels. We began to adapt principles from community organizing, community development, and racial justice. We worked with traditional and nontraditional leaders, from all sectors and the grass roots, who understood that it was impossible to solve long-standing problems in their communities without the voices and participation of all kinds of people, working with each other and with public officials to create change. As we worked with a diversity of communities in every region of the country, on many kinds of issues, we created and adapted advice and tools.

One of our earliest innovations, now widely used in the field of dialogue and deliberation, was to develop and test a progression of dialogue sessions in which participants start with their own stories and personal experiences, explore the nature and root causes of an issue, consider a variety of possible approaches to making a difference, explore common ground for solutions, and set priorities for action and policy they can be part of implementing. We have created and tested many issue-specific guides and training materials to help communities structure and facilitate productive conversations aimed at action and change (McCoy & Scully, 2002).

Large-scale evaluation of our work on racism began to deepen our understanding of the place of democratic dialogue in community change (Roberts & Kay Inc., 2000). In the early 2000s, we recognized that we needed to better understand and address the impact of structural racism on all kinds of public issues (Young, 2000). We set out to "walk the talk" on racial equity, so that we could model multiracial, equitable practices in all our work. This journey has been critical to our work with community leaders and in our partnership with organizations to help build a movement for stronger, more equitable democracy (McCoy, 2014).

In 2008, we changed our name to Everyday Democracy to reflect our ultimate aim—to help create democracy that works for everyone, every day, and where processes that value voice and participation for all and where racial equity and shared power are a regular part of problem-solving and governance at all levels of society. We moved from referring solely to the dialogue part of our work—study circles—to emphasizing the importance of the larger process of dialogue to change and embedding democratic principles into the culture and shared governance of the community.

Today we are implementing strategies for large-scale expansion of the practice of dialogue to change with a racial equity lens and for influencing the emergent national movement for stronger democracy.

Our Approach to Community Change

As we have worked with people and institutions in places of every size, region, and demographic makeup, we have seen that equitable community change can happen

- when there are regular, structured opportunities for people from different backgrounds and views to share their experiences and concerns, listen to each other, consider the nature of the issues affecting them, and find solutions they can be part of;
- when decisions, practices, and policies reflect and are accountable to everyone's voice, particularly those who have been marginalized and excluded;

- when people, institutions, and government learn how to share knowledge, resources, and power for the common good;
- when there are regular opportunities for people, institutions, and government to work together to understand how structural racism has shaped communities, institutions, and the nation as a whole;
- when people, institutions, and government use their understanding of racial equity to create equitable opportunities and outcomes; and
- when grassroots, organizational, and public leaders connect to each other and to others across the country who are strengthening participatory democracy with an equity lens and who, as they build relationships, strengthen each other's vision and practices, find ways to sustain their work across generations, and help build a national infrastructure for participatory democracy.

For these practices to take root in communities or campuses, it is often necessary for coaches who are skilled in leadership development and democratic processes to work alongside local leaders to model equitable leadership and help them build their own capacity to engage the community. For this reason, over the past 20 years we have been cultivating a diverse network of coaches across the United States. In addition, our partnerships with national, regional, and state-level organizations and networks, including colleges and universities, are essential to cultivating democratic leadership and practices in communities.

Our work with institutions of higher education has spanned many applications of our approach and tools—including campus-wide dialogue on issues of common concern and campus-led initiatives that include the larger community. In many of our partner communities, institutions of higher education bring expertise to a larger dialogue that supports novel initiatives, recruitment, training, issue-specific tools, and/or evaluation.

One standout example of our work with colleges and universities is that of New Hampshire Listens, an initiative of the Carsey Institute at the University of New Hampshire. New Hampshire Listens has worked at local and state levels since 2010 to support civil, public deliberation of complex issues affecting New Hampshire residents' everyday lives—on campus and in conjunction with local partners across the state. It was one of Everyday Democracy's first anchor partners. Our anchor partners receive capacity-building support on democratic engagement; share their lessons with Everyday Democracy; become part of a learning community with other anchors; and engage in regional and national efforts to build a movement for strong, equitable democracy.

We are cultivating similar mutually supportive relationships with civic engagement centers at other colleges and universities across the United States. We are finding that our approach to community change and to building the capacity of institutions to coach, train, and model inclusive and equitable engagement aligns well with the mission and goals of many community colleges, colleges, and universities.

Horizons: Partnering With Extension to Expand and Deepen Democratic Capacity

Horizons' partnership with Extension demonstrated the potential of higher education to build communities' democratic capacities at a large scale. As we coached and trained Extension staff, they were able to work with local partners to support the engagement of 10,000 grassroots participants across 283 communities.

In fact, Extension's role was essential for not only scale but also deep and lasting effects on the communities it coached. The project demonstrated how dialogue work can build on the long history of Extension's role as a catalyst for community engagement and problem-solving. Extension was formalized in 1914, when Congress established the U.S. Department of Agriculture's partnership with land-grant universities to apply research and provide education in agriculture. As early as the 1930s and 1940s, Extension was playing a role in creating spaces for people to engage with each other on public issues. In recent decades, public deliberation about issues has become an even more significant part of Extension's work (Shaffer, 2017).

Impact on Communities' Democratic Capacity and on Issue-Specific Outcomes

In Horizons, SDSU Extension built on this historic mission in order to cultivate community engagement that led to meaningful and measurable changes. An external evaluation of Horizons, for instance, demonstrated important and widespread impact in strengthening communities' democratic capacities. Among those successes, new leaders emerged who had never before thought of themselves as leaders, existing leaders received training to strengthen their skills in inclusive engagement, and communities had new skills to mobilize community participation and civic engagement (Morehouse, 2010). One of the most common long-term effects of the dialogues was increased participation. More people have come out for local meetings, such as board and town/

city council meetings, and dialogue participants have run for elective office in over 35% of Horizons communities. One participant noted, "We have new leaders in the community because of what we are doing here" (Clark & Teachout, 2012, p. 151).

On the issue of poverty itself, evaluators noted a strong increase in community awareness that laid the foundation for action and change:

> All of our findings confirmed that the process of democratic dialogue experienced in the Study Circles process . . . was a very powerful experience. Many said that this was the first time they had thought about, much less discussed, poverty. Many had misconceptions and stereotypes about the rural poverty in their midst. Interviews confirmed that the dialogue was in many ways pivotal in building acknowledgement of the existence of poverty, and a new awareness of the complicated and multi-faceted nature of community poverty.
>
> Importantly, too, participants provided data indicating a sense of optimism about their collective ability both to make a positive difference in the community and to reduce community poverty. Clearly the Study Circles discussions change knowledge, attitudes, and create a sense of agency to address community poverty. (Morehouse, 2010, p. 10)

New knowledge and democratic capacity translated into specific impact related to poverty. The process of moving from dialogue to action enabled communities across the region to carry out a broad range of steps to address poverty and create more thriving communities, including (among others) the creation of nonprofit organizations that could receive much-needed grant funds for day care centers, after-school programs, community gardens, farmers' markets, financial planning courses, and youth centers (Hoelting, 2010).

Impact on Extensions in the Northwest and Beyond

Although the impact on communities' capacity to address poverty was the ultimate aim of Horizons, the initiative also had a significant, lasting impact on the ways in which the Extensions partner with communities. Project evaluators noted that

> in some cases, it has been transformative. . . . In virtually every Delivery Organization [the term used for Extensions in the initiative], those interviewed talked about how they had moved beyond the traditional expert delivery of information to selected audiences to learning how to work in partnership with the entirety of a community. This in particular has led them to include low-income community members. . . .

Interview responses emphasized that the role and mission of extension divisions, and of land grant universities, has typically included outreach and community involvement, but the Horizons model provided a more effective, proven and focused way to do this. In some cases, this has led to changes in how the institutions both conceptualize and practice outreach. (Morehouse, 2010, p. 49)

Thus, many of the state university Extension systems that took part in Horizons have continued their support for community engagement, albeit at a smaller scale because external funding for Horizons came to an end in 2011. Two of these Extension systems—at Montana State University and SDSU—have become anchor partners with Everyday Democracy to expand and deepen their coaching through a lens of racial and economic equity.

Horizons was also the catalyst for similar Extension work in rural communities across the Deep South. In 2009, the Southern Rural Development Center (SRDC), headquartered at Mississippi State University, began to replicate the essential elements of Horizons in a multiyear initiative called Turning the Tide on Poverty (Tide). Without the level of funding that enabled the large scale of Horizons, Tide was still carried out in 14 communities with levels of poverty higher than 20%. In the first year of the initiative, Everyday Democracy provided training and coaching to Extension professionals in Alabama, Georgia, Louisiana, Mississippi, and Oklahoma. As in Horizons, Extension agents served as community coaches (Monroe et al., 2016).

The evaluation of Tide, carried out in conjunction with the Kettering Foundation, indicated that the initiative led to significant strides in the building of civic capacity, particularly in severely poverty-stricken communities. Evaluators used ripple mapping and the community capitals framework to document and report the significant accomplishments that took place in Tide (Beaulieu & Welborn, 2012). As in Horizons, many of these Extensions are strengthening their role as colearners with the community rather than as one-way educators. As noted in the evaluation, "a shift from being in the 'driver's seat' to a more collaborative or capacity-building role seems to have taken hold" (Beaulieu & Welborn, 2012, p. 22). Because of this, many are continuing to develop their own capacities to coach communities in dialogue to change.

Limits and Challenges

One of the greatest challenges in the work of democratic dialogue for community change lies in sustaining the financial resources necessary for supporting the work. Although external evaluators of Horizons noted that relatively modest resources leveraged real changes in community capacity (Morehouse, 2010), those resources were essential. They made it possible for Extension professionals to spend their time in this community-dedicated way, for Extensions to add staffing where needed for community support, and for Everyday Democracy and the communities to take part. Even when practices of dialogue to change become embedded in the community, funding resources are critical to make it possible for local people to spend their time continuing to organize and facilitate change processes (Allen & Lachapelle, 2012).

Alongside this challenge is the complexity of the issue of poverty. A multiyear process, no matter how successful, can only begin to address an issue that reflects myriad historical and current-day systems and policies, many of which go beyond the local level. As noted in the evaluation report:

> Data over time have indicated that this is a kind of developmental process, requiring first awareness, second knowledge, third action, and only later focused action.... [In a pilot process in the second phase of Horizons,] we learned that communities were only now ready, after three years, to tackle the larger, longer-term and potentially more effective poverty reduction strategies. We have concluded ... that this process is a long-term one, and will take time to achieve measurable or hard results. We have also concluded that it is a difficult challenge for small, rural and under-resourced communities to tackle intractable issues, and we agree with them that they will need continuing assistance to do so. (Morehouse, 2010, pp. 10–11)

Another important realization for Extension that grew out of the work of Horizons and Tide was the need to address racism as fundamental to addressing other community issues and the need to build skills to do so into the coaching capacity of Extension.

That has led USDA's Cooperative Extension Service to work with others to sponsor and launch Coming Together for Racial Understanding, a national initiative to train and support Cooperative Extension staff to coach communities on dialogue on racial issues. At a train-the-trainer event in 2018, Everyday Democracy trained 60 Extension professionals from 20 states in dialogue to action on racial equity.

As a result, land-grant universities, tribal colleges, and historically black colleges and universities (HCBUs) are working together within state-based teams to train others. An early evaluation of this training demonstrates evidence of impact on Extension professionals—for example, in their comfort in organizing and facilitating racially diverse audiences in dialogues about race and in their commitment to work on civil dialogue on race as part of their Extension Service mission. The evaluation found that state Extension Services, tribal colleges, and HBCUs in 10 states have expressed interest in being part of the next cohort of this project (SRDC, 2018).

Looking to the Future

There is a critical need in our country for inclusive, diverse dialogue structured to lead to collective action. Practitioners and scholars who are dedicated to advancing participatory democracy have learned much about how to recognize and strengthen communities' democratic capacities to solve problems (Scully & Diebel, 2015). One of the greatest opportunities to take these lessons to scale is to prepare institutions' readiness to develop diverse leaders who can help guide democratic engagement and change at the local level. A growing number of institutions of higher education see it as essential to their mission to cultivate leaders who can model and transfer these practices both on their own campuses and in the larger communities of which they are part.

The most effective examples of democratic engagement supported by colleges and universities demonstrate mindfulness of the power dynamics that are present in every community-university partnership. Universities almost always have more financial resources and political clout than the communities in which they are embedded, and this power imbalance can make it challenging to collaborate with community partners effectively and authentically (White, 2010). In fact, the willingness to learn and model power sharing—something that is simply not the norm in most town-gown partnerships—is key to the success of institutions of higher education in cultivating the democratic capacities of communities.

Everyday Democracy encourages the communities and institutions that use the practice of dialogue to change to adopt a racial equity lens for just this reason. Differences in power and privilege cause tensions and power struggles between campuses and communities, just as they do between various community institutions and groups. The differences must be seen, acknowledged, and addressed for effective collaboration, true reciprocity, and long-term change to take hold.

Whether used in the classroom for civic learning, on campus to address campus-wide issues, or in partnership with the local community to address systemic problems like poverty and racism, the dialogue to change approach is consistent with higher education's civic mission. The dialogues' structure of beginning with personal concerns and experiences and valuing different forms of expression supports the development of trust and relationships across difference that make social change possible. The dialogues' exploration of root causes in the context of respect for different views and approaches to complex problems aligns with higher education's mandate to foster meaningful learning. And the connection of the dialogue to individual and collective action supports experiential learning and the development of civic leadership skills.

As Everyday Democracy and others highlighted in this book collaborate more intentionally and at greater scale with institutions of higher education, we are strengthening a nationwide infrastructure for democratic participation and community problem-solving that our country sorely needs. Our most complex and long-standing problems—including poverty and racial equity—require the unique strengths of higher education if we are to make meaningful progress in the long term.

References

Allen, R., & Lachapelle, P. R. (2012). Can leadership development act as a rural poverty alleviation strategy? *Journal of Community Development, 43*(1), 95–112.

Beaulieu, B., & Welborn, R. (2012). *Turning the tide on poverty: Measuring and predicting civic engagement success.* Report for the Southern Rural Development Center. Retrieved from http://srdc.msstate.edu/tide/files/turning_the_tide_on_poverty_report_2011_final.pdf

Bjerkaker, S. (2014). Changing communities: The study circle—for learning and democracy. *Procedia Social and Behavioral Sciences, 142,* 260–267.

Clark, S., & Teachout, W. (2012). *Slow democracy: Rediscovering community, bringing decision making back home.* White River Junction, VT: Chelsea Green Publishing.

Hoelting, J. (2010, April). Horizons program mobilizes communities to address rural poverty. Community Dividend. Retrieved from https://www.minneapolisfed.org/publications/community-dividend/horizons-program-mobilizes-communities-to-address-rural-poverty

McCoy, M. L. (2014, April 17). *7 key lessons for addressing racism in community change work.* Retrieved from https://www.everyday-democracy.org/news/7-key-lessons-25-years-addressing-racism-through-dialogue-and-community-change

McCoy, M. L., & Scully, P. L. (2002). Deliberative dialogue to expand civic engagement: What kind of talk does democracy need? *National Civic Review, 91*(2), 117–135.

Monroe, P. A., Tyler-Mackey, C., Hyjer Dyk, P., Welborn, R., Lokken Worthy, S., Lowe, C. H., & Pickett, N. J. (2016). Turning the tide on poverty: Sustainability of community engagement in economically distressed communities. *Journal of Community Development, 47*(3), 358–374.

Morehouse, D. (2010). *Northwest Area Foundation Horizons Program 2003–2010 final evaluation report.* Retrieved from http://msucommunitydevelopment.org/pubs/Report2010.pdf

Everyday Democracy. (2008). *Organizing rural and reservation communities for dialogue and change: A quick guide.* Retrieved from https://www.everyday-democracy.org/sites/default/files/attachments/Organizing-Rural-Reservation-Communities-Dialogue-Change_Everyday-Democracy.pdf

Roberts & Kay, Inc. (2000). Toward competent communities: Best practices for producing community-wide study circles. Retrieved from https://www.everyday-democracy.org/sites/default/files/attachments/Toward-Competent-Communities-Best-Practices_Everyday-Democracy.pdf

Rourke, B. (2008). *Thriving communities: Working together to move from poverty to prosperity for all.* Retrieved from https://www.everyday-democracy.org/resources/thriving-communities-working-together-move-poverty-prosperity-all

Scully, P. L., & Diebel, A. (2015). The essential and inherent democratic capacities of communities. *Community Development, 46*(3), 212–226.

Shaffer, T. (2017). Supporting the "Archstone of democracy": Cooperative Extension's experiment with deliberative group discussion. *Journal of Extension, 55*(5), 1–3.

Southern Rural Development Center (SRDC). (2018). Coming together for racial understanding training report. Retrieved from http://srdc.msstate.edu/civildialogue/coming-together-training-report-2018.pdf

White, B. (2010). Power, privilege, and the public: The dynamics of community-university collaboration. In N. L. Thomas (Ed.), *Educating for Deliberative Democracy* (New Directions for Higher Education, No. 152, pp. 67–74). San Francisco, CA: Jossey-Bass.

Young, I. M. (2000). *Inclusion and democracy.* New York, NY: Oxford University Press.

7

SUSTAINED DIALOGUE CAMPUS NETWORK

Elizabeth Wuerz, Rhonda Fitzgerald, Michaela Grenier, and Ottavia Lezzi

> *Dialogue is a process of genuine interaction through which human beings listen to each other deeply enough to be changed by what they learn.*
>
> —Harold Saunders (Founder of Sustained Dialogue Institute),
> *Sustained Dialogue in Conflicts*, 1999, p. 82

Organization and Model History

Sustained Dialogue (SD) is a patented peace process[1] developed not on a college campus but in the thick tensions of international diplomacy by Harold "Hal" Saunders, a pioneering U.S. diplomat who is credited with coining the phrase "peace process" to describe U.S. negotiation efforts in the Middle East. After over a decade serving as a member of the National Security Council as an adviser on Middle East policy, Saunders was appointed assistant secretary for the Near East and South Asia in 1974. He was intensively involved in the Arab-Israeli peace process and served as a key member of the small team of U.S. diplomats led by Secretary of State Henry Kissinger that mediated several agreements in the Middle East, including the Kissinger shuttle agreements between 1973 and 1975, the Camp David Accords of 1978, the Egyptian-Israeli Peace Treaty of 1979, and the

---

1. While SD is patented as a distinct dialogue process, the Sustained Dialogue Institute works in collaboration with many campuses and other organizations to adapt and use the model to suit the needs of each partner. The Sustained Dialogue Institute invites new partners interested in collaborating to connect.

release of the U.S. embassy staff held during the Iran hostage crisis in 1979. Following his departure from government in 1981, Saunders began writing the key lessons from his experience in what he called *disciplined perseverance* toward peace, which became the foundation of the SD model: (a) the power of continuous political process to change relationships, (b) the importance of recognizing the human dimension of conflictual relationships, and (c) the possibility of thinking in terms of relationships among whole bodies politic (Saunders, 2008).

Throughout the 1980s, Hal Saunders participated in a wide range of nonofficial dialogues, including coleading with Yevgeny Primakov, the future prime minister of Russia, the Task Force on Regional Conflicts within the Dartmouth Conference. This is the longest continuous dialogue between U.S. and Soviet citizens. From that decade of experience in citizen-led dialogue, in addition to his extensive work in international mediation in the 1970s, Saunders began to realize that these interactions evolved in a discernible progression. In 1993, he conceptualized his observations and experience as a five-stage process called SD, published alongside Gennady Chufrin in *Negotiation Journal*. Saunders implemented the SD approach in the Inter-Tajik Dialogue, a series of 35 dialogues between warring factions in the Tajik civil war (1993–2003) that is considered to have been a deeply impactful component to the resulting final peace (Saunders & Slim, 2001).

In 1999, a group of students at Princeton University approached administrators seeking resources to deal with tense race relations on campus. The group was referred to Saunders, who was then a member of Princeton University's Board of Trustees. These students collaborated with Saunders to adapt the SD process to their campus and even won a campus award for biggest contribution to campus life ("'Prince' Board Honors Sustained Dialogue," 2001). Within two years, with students from one campus traveling to train others in a grassroots style, the University of Virginia established an SD group on campus. In the fall of 2001, SD spread further to Dickinson College in Pennsylvania. The following year, the Sustained Dialogue Institute (SDI) was founded. With Saunders as president, SDI promoted the process of SD for transforming racial, ethnic, and other deep-rooted conflicts in the United States and abroad. In a surprise to Saunders, the original student colleagues who had adapted the process formed the Sustained Dialogue Campus Network (SDCN) in 2003 to continue spreading SD on college campuses as a part of the new institute (Saunders, 2011). SDCN has since supported the growth of more than 40 campus programs in the United States, as well as youth-led SD initiatives in Ethiopia, Sudan, and Kenya.

Core Pillars of SD

The SD model has two core pillars that distinguish it from other dialogue methods and conflict transformation processes. Our five-stage dialogue-to-action process is the first core pillar, guided by a conception of dialogue as a systemic process that helps participants develop new understandings of community conflicts. These are insights that could not have been reached by any single participant. When engaging in SD's five-stage dialogue-to-action process, a group meets over the span of several months (or potentially even years) and collectively moves from initial experience-sharing and issue identification to developing and implementing a shared action plan for addressing community issues. A key feature of the model is the *sustained* nature of the dialogue. Specifically, the same group of individuals meets regularly over an extended period of time and develops a cumulative agenda for meetings in which each dialogue session picks up where the last one left off. This structure allows for participants to engage deeply with the relationships they form through SD, while also learning new skills and developing new insights along each step of the process.

The first stage of SD—determining who should be in dialogue—involves identifying and recruiting dialogue participants based on the topics or relationships that dialogue initiatives aim to address. This initial stage frequently involves tailored outreach to groups contributing to or affected by the community issues that have prompted the dialogue.

The second stage involves developing trust and common purpose within the dialogue group as participants begin to share personal experiences and interrogate issues affecting their community. Moderators ask participants questions about their personal experiences with the community issues at stake to help build understanding and awareness among the group and humanize those who have different experiences and identities from each other.

During the third stage of SD, participants work together to analytically examine the root causes of community issues and the larger social systems and structures that influence how issues play out at the local level. For example, a group dialoguing about an incident of religious intolerance on campus and how each participant experiences religion on campus will shift to thinking about what systems underlie and support religious bias or sentiment on campus. The group shifts to analyzing the root causes of what they experience, "not just discussing the ways it manifests in their lives" (SDCN, 2018, p. 38).

The fourth stage involves developing a plan for action that has been informed by knowledge built within the group, research about community needs, and insights gained from consultation with experts external to the dialogue group. For example, this same group dialoguing about religion on campus may have identified some root causes they wish to address. Now they will begin to make a plan to address that root cause through actions such as awareness-raising campaigns, a speaker series on a particular faith, or trying to hire more professors of a particular faith.

The fifth and final stage is where the dialogue group works to implement the plan that they have developed in collaboration with members of their community. Although the stages in the SD process build on one another, the stages do not have to be experienced in a strictly linear fashion. Groups might revisit various stages throughout their journey together as new insights emerge and as their action plans develop.

The SD model's second core pillar is our relational paradigm that focuses on the dynamic relationships between groups and individuals in conflict. Rather than "focusing first on the problem, we focus on the people within the community affected by or contributing to the problem" (SDCN, 2018, p. 88). In using this paradigm, dialogue participants and facilitators are asked to analyze five key elements of relationships when trying to create change within these relationships. These components are as follows: (a) patterns of interaction; (b) perceptions, misperceptions, and stereotypes; (c) interests; (d) identity; and (e) power. Dialogue facilitators trained in the SD process are prepared to help guide their groups through a dialogue-to-action process and also to lead their group in thoughtfully and analytically examining the relationships involved in the community issue(s) that they are addressing.

Dialogue groups are peer-facilitated with facilitators being identified from within the communities affected by the issues being discussed. The bulk of the work at the SDCN is helping campuses to build community capacity by providing deep training for dialogue facilitators who then run dialogue circles for their own community using the SD model. Although campuses can adapt the model, typically students are trained for 16 hours, which includes learning the SD model, building cultural competency, understanding social justice concepts, and practicing facilitation skills at the beginning of a semester or quarter as peer facilitators and then moderating a weekly, at least 1-hour-long dialogue for the remainder of the semester, or at least 7 times. Each of these dialogue groups should contain 2 trained peer facilitators and approximately 12 to 15 participants.

Primary Audience, Settings, and Examples

SD originally emerged on college campuses as a cocurricular program designed by students, for students. This is still SD's traditional model; it has expanded across a network of more than 40 campuses. Campuses select students differently depending on the content they want to navigate or the specific challenges the campus may want to address. For example, some campuses choose to focus their SD program within residential housing so that students can dialogue with their dormmates. Other campuses focus on other areas of student life, using SD to bring athletes, Greek life, or other specific groups together. Another model is to recruit students college-wide so any student in any year of school can participate. Some campuses recruit topically instead, so recruitment focuses around the issue to be addressed in dialogue, such as race relations or another aspect of social identity, rather than a specific type of student.

Northwestern University provides a powerful example of SD's cocurricular student model. It is led by student leaders who are supported by campus staff in the Social Justice Education Department. One of the assistant directors of Social Justice Education at Northwestern works with a Sustained Dialogue Leadership Team comprising 5 undergraduate students that assists in recruiting students, promoting SD on campus, training moderators, coordinating social get-togethers for moderators, and assisting with moderators' continual training for 60 minutes biweekly throughout the semester. Dialogues run for the quarter (9–10 weeks) and are composed of 2 moderators and up to 18 participants. Meetings last for 90 minutes every week (SDI, n.d.).

In addition to the traditional cocurricular undergraduate student approach, graduate students, faculty, and staff have become involved in dialogues on some campuses. Typically, these are spread across the academic year, so that people are meeting on a biweekly or monthly basis, although some maintain the weekly approach for about 10 weeks. These dialogues are often used to desilo institutions and build a stronger sense of community across the campus. For example, Case Western Reserve University incorporated staff and faculty dialogue groups into their wellness program, which allows employees to access a small financial incentive through their wellness program for participating in dialogues. Participants commit to 10 weeks of dialogue for 1 hour and have attributed a greater sense of belonging on campus to their participation.

Further, SD also helps develop and facilitate retreats to give students an immersive experience with our model. Students are trained as moderators and then as retreat facilitators, totaling 32 hours of training. They then recruit students across all aspects of diversity to attend a 3-and-a-half day, off-campus retreat, typically conducted over a long weekend where students stay overnight. This experience is highly immersive and catapults students through a deeply reflective and transformative experience as they engage in learning around different aspects of social identity followed by intense dialogue. Retreats serve as opportunities to engage students who cannot commit to a weekly dialogue during the academic year to jumpstart dialogue groups who are then able to meet in a sustained way throughout the semester or year. By engaging deeply in the second stage of SD, relationship-building and exploration of issues, during the retreat, the goal is for them to be able to move through the remaining stages of SD more fully and ultimately achieve Stage 5 action more effectively than the cocurricular students often can.

In addition to the cocurricular approaches, some campuses have brought SD formally into the academic curriculum. Courses incorporating SD can be housed in many different disciplines, and the intensity of the SD experience varies from simply integrating pedagogical practices into ongoing courses to a deeper shift of the structure of the class to practice and experience dialogue. Three models have emerged thus far.

The first model is when faculty simply integrate dialogic practices into their current courses. Some focus on incorporating pedagogical practices such as asking questions in a more relational way or creating a more dialogic approach to classroom discussion. Other campuses have designed a seminar that allows a smaller group of students to go deeper using the SD model. In the seminar approach, students learn content of the course during some classes, for example one to two times per week, and engage in sustained dialogues in other sections—for example, once per week. These dialogues are often moderated by peers in the class or students who have been involved in the cocurricular program on campus and have taken the class in the past. These smaller seminars often include a Stage 5 social action project as their capstone project. Examples of this approach include courses at Roger Williams University, Auburn University, and St. John Fisher College.

The second academic model shifts the traditional teaching assistant–led discussion section into a dialogue. Here, the content of the course is taught in the traditional format, but students then meet weekly in a dialogue group, led by other students who have previously taken the course, to engage deeply in how the material they are learning connects with their lives and their experience on campus. At the University of Notre Dame, for instance, an introduction to philosophy class, God and the Good Life, shifted from what was originally a teaching assistant led–discussion section to a deep, peer-led dialogue.

Some campuses infuse a more intensive SD experience into a course so that students are experiencing SD as an integral part, not just a section, of the whole course. This sometimes takes place in a broad, introductory format able to reach more students not typically attracted to dialogue. An example of this third model is found at the University of Alabama, where two dialogue courses are offered concurrently—one a three-credit and the other a one-credit course. In the three-credit course, students learn dialogue moderating skills and deepen their understanding of social identity concepts. Students in this course are hand-selected based on their campus leadership experience as well as their experience in previous semesters as students in the one-credit course. These leaders facilitate dialogue groups composed of students in the one-credit course. Participants in the one-credit course attend once a week and participate in dialogues focused on specific issues of social identity and related student experiences. Students in the three-credit course attend class twice a week, one day receiving materials, feedback on the previous week's dialogue experience, and some skills training, and moderating the dialogues in the one-credit class on their second day. This course context offers the opportunity to be engaged in dialogue to a broad swath of the campus that might not otherwise be attracted to SD in a cocurricular approach.

Key Takeaways, Strengths, and Challenges

The strengths of the SD model are rooted in its long history as a proven peace process replicated across a variety of situations and its focus on relationships. These include its flexibility, its suitability for extreme conflict, its skill-based outcomes, its ability to be replicated through the network of others using the model, and its ability to become institutionalized into a campus culture.

Within higher education, the flexibility of the SD model has allowed it to be adapted to a variety of campus contexts. It has been taught in academic courses as the core content that students learn in order to engage more effectively in democracy, utilized as a pedagogical tool to decrease lecture time and increase thoughtful engagement with course content by integrating the small-group dialogue process into the structure of the class, and structured in a retreat format to learn key concepts around social justice and difference. It has even been implemented by campuses, with the support of the SDCN, as a large-scale, formal process by which the campus seeks to make decisions and, ultimately, create a culture of dialogue where student meetings, administrative task forces, committees, courses, and departments begin to integrate the skills and expectations of dialogue.

SD has a long history of producing strong community leadership skills, especially among those who participate in SD on their campuses and subsequently dedicate themselves to learning the five-stage process, which includes facilitation and intercultural fluency skills and how to lead a group toward action. For staff who participate, the outcomes are linked to desiloed workplace relationships. Faculty and instructors note transformations in their teaching, including increased confidence in opening the classroom to robust discussions and skill in restructuring course content. Student participant outcomes include finding one's voice and learning to listen to the needs of others (Pettit, 2018).

Yet the fact that SD bridges community leadership, social justice, and peacekeeping also brings challenges to this approach. Organizational rigor, long-term commitment, and adherence to its intent can present certain challenges for participants and campuses.

First, SD facilitators go through serious training, which in this model takes at least 16 hours and is provided by the SDCN, focusing on learning the SD model, building cultural fluency, honing emotional intelligence, understanding social justice concepts, and building skills in active listening and asking questions. This training, the sustained commitment to regular meetings with the same participants over time, and the high-touch nature of the process can result in attendance issues in busy environments and demotivated participants, stunting the impact and progression of the five stages.

Second, the SD process is flexible to the extent that it is often misunderstood and implemented in limited ways. It can be misused by novices as a one-time intervention, confused with other processes, or repackaged without key aspects. For example, even though certain broad-reaching cocurricular models introduce SD to lots of students, Stage 5 action is often left out of the curriculum.

Third, SD requires full dedication. In campus environments where committing to a high-touch program is not common or where nonadministrators are not involved in high levels of making campus change, SD can be misused for insignificant challenges, diluting the gravity of its goals.

Although there are many challenges to implementing SD effectively and fully on campuses, impact data suggest that, when done well, it can have a transformative effect on campus culture and climate. Its flexibility enables SD to be used in a variety of settings—cocurriculum, academic courses, resident housing, orientation, first-year seminars, and with faculty and staff—creating the possibility for all areas of a college campus to be touched by its power to reframe how we interact with each other, build relationships, and engage with those with whom we disagree. In this time of deep polarization when it is increasingly difficult to talk across lines of difference and when, simultaneously, students, faculty, and staff face an increasingly globalized world, SD offers a method for building the important skills required for engaging constructively with one another, for understanding each other, and for effectively working together to improve campus climate. One cannot imagine a more important skill set to develop to engage effectively in a democracy.

References

Pettit, E. (2018). *SDCN annual survey results* [Unpublished full report 2017–2018]. Available by request from the Sustained Dialogue Campus Network.

"Prince" board honors Sustained Dialogue. (2001, May 13). *The Daily Princetonian.* Retrieved from http://www.dailyprincetonian.com/article/2001/05/prince-board-honors-sustained-dialogue

Saunders, H. H. (1999). *A public peace process: Sustained dialogue to transform racial and ethnic conflicts.* New York, NY: St. Martin's Press.

Saunders, H. H. (2008, March 16). *Sustained Dialogue: Synergizing practice and theory.* Presentation at Women in Security, Conflict Management, and Peace, New Delhi, India.

Saunders, H. H. (2011). *Sustained dialogue in conflicts: Transformation and change.* New York, NY: Palgrave Macmillan.

Saunders, H. H., & Slim, R. (2001). The inter-Tajik dialogue: From civil war to civil society. *Accord, 10.* Retrieved from http://www.c-r.org/accord-article/inter-tajik-dialogue-civil-war-towards-civil-society

Sustained Dialogue Campus Network. (2018). *Moderator manual 2018–2019.* Washington DC: Sustained Dialogue Institute.

Sustained Dialogue Institute. (n.d.). Dialogue resources for higher education. Retrieved from https://compact.org/resource-posts/dialogue-resources-for-higher-education/

8

EDUCATIONAL JUSTICE USING INTERGROUP DIALOGUE

Stephanie Hicks and Hamida Bhagirathy

Intergroup Dialogue in Higher Education: General Model, Principles, and Practices

Intergroup dialogue for higher education was developed at the University of Michigan and is currently being implemented on more than 100 campuses around the country (Gurin, Nagda, & Zúñiga, 2013). Intergroup dialogue is rooted in the assumption that intergroup and interpersonal relationships are affected by the histories and current realities of intergroup contact in the United States and that this conflict can be explored through dialogue (Zúñiga, Nagda, Chesler, & Cytron-Walker, 2007). Ximena Zúñiga and colleagues (2007) note that "its pedagogical practices incorporate philosophical and cultural traditions that have valued dialogue as a method of communication and inquiry" (p. 5). The University of Michigan's Program on Intergroup Relations describes intergroup dialogue as a pedagogy in which

> courses are carefully structured to explore social group identity, conflict, community, and social justice. Each intergroup dialogue involves identity groups defined by race, ethnicity, religion, socioeconomic class, gender, sexual orientation, or national origin. Each identity group is represented in the dialogue by a balanced number of student participants, usually 5–7 participants from each group. Trained student facilitators—one from each represented identity group—encourage dialogue rather than debate. Students examine and discuss reading materials that address issues and experiences relevant to the groups in the dialogue, in relation to both the University setting and general society. Facilitators and participants explore similarities

and differences among and across groups, and strive toward building a multicultural and democratic community. Past dialogues have included gender, race & ethnicity, socio economic class, white racial identity, religion, Arab/Jewish relations, international/US relations, sexual orientation, and ableism. (Program on Intergroup Relations, 2011)

Intergroup dialogue follows a rich tradition of practices that scholars concerned with democratic education have hailed as useful. John Dewey, while at Teachers College in the 1930s and 1940s, proposed that having students work on real-world problems in a democratic way (through dialogue) would result in a better society (Zúñiga et al., 2007). He thought that the democratic process in the greater society would be nourished by democracy in the classroom. More critical theorists later argued that the classroom practices should push harder, so to speak, that democracy in society requires creating speech situations that allow people to speak across cultural and status differences. Dialogue-based learning, it seems, would be just that kind of praxis.

Unlike many academic courses, intergroup dialogue uses a critical dialogic approach, as opposed to the banking model found in courses across disciplines. In the banking model, students are thought to be like empty vessels that teachers fill with knowledge. It is assumed that the only bearer of knowledge is the teacher and students know nothing until they are given information by said teacher. In the critical dialogic model, however, students are thought to enter the classroom with a vast amount of knowledge that they have gained from their experiences inside and outside of the classroom (Friere, 1970). They have something to teach, and teachers also have something to learn from them.

As a way to offer an alternative to the banking model of education, the Michigan model of intergroup dialogue is based on its use of peer facilitators in dialogue, with an intent to support the notion that students as learners already embody knowledge within themselves. As Zúñiga and colleagues (2007) put it,

> Peer facilitation suggests that students can learn outside the traditional patterns of faculty control and direction of the instructional process. Thus, it can make specific contributions to intergroup encounters and more broadly to the empowerment of learners, both in intergroup dialogue and in other areas of higher education. (p. 52)

In the Michigan model, which will be explained in depth in later sections, peer facilitators undergo an extensive two-semester experience that includes an interview process and two courses. First, training occurs prior to their facilitation, and second, peer facilitators participate in a practicum that occurs in tandem with their facilitation. Both academic credit-bearing courses work to lay and strengthen a common foundation for peer facilitators by establishing competence in "intergroup issues, including knowledge and awareness of their own and others' social identities and histories and structures of privilege and oppression" and "small group leadership, including the concepts and skills involved in providing instructional leadership to a group of their peers" (Beale, Thompson, & Chesler, 2001, p. 227). Peer facilitators help students process content knowledge about the historical and social factors that shape their social identities. What is more, the students use that knowledge, along with knowledge of their own personal experiences, to engage in dialogue as a means of challenging themselves and others to create more just environments.

The critical dialogic approach is used in intergroup dialogue to achieve three educational goals: consciousness-raising, building relationships across difference and conflicts, and strengthening individual and collective capacities to promote social justice (Zúñiga et al., 2007).

Consciousness-raising endeavors enhance participants' understanding by introducing the concepts of privilege and marginalization and its multiple levels of manifestation. Consciousness-raising is couched in sociological concepts and aims to introduce the notion of structural inequities in a manner that galvanizes its gravitas across identities (Zúñiga et al., 2007). This double-sided intellectual and affective approach makes the case for its credibility with participants who hold mostly privileged identities (and as a result may not readily connect their lived experiences with these concepts), and validates and contextualizes the lived experiences of participants who hold mostly marginalized identities. This consciousness then enables participants to understand how privilege and marginalization have informed their own and others' life experiences, making the connection that "the 'we' that's in trouble is all of us" (Johnson, 2006, p. 7).

Building relationships across differences seeks to foster relationships among participants with an awareness of social identities, privilege and marginalization, and the conflicts and tensions that may exist among groups due to histories and contemporary realities. Relationship-building across differences asks participants to discover their hidden commonalities and challenges them to expand their understandings of what it means to navigate the world by sharing and attending to their peers' anecdotes of their own varied navigational experiences (Zúñiga et al., 2007). This blending of shared and varied experiences serves to expand participants' understandings of each other and disrupt reductionist views and stereotypes of what it means to hold particular social identities.

Strengthening individual and collective capacities to promote social justice aims to create an actionable component of prior educational goals (Zúñiga et al., 2007). The combination of intellectual and experiential knowledge around privilege and marginalization, along with the skills to navigate conflicts rooted in social identity, are intended to spur participants to action. Capacity-building may occur in a number of ways, including building skills to serve as an effective ally/accomplice, creating and maintaining coalitions, and engaging in activism work. This third goal relies upon participants' prior learning of structural and experiential inequities, and relationships across difference, as catalysts to compel both the brain and the heart to understand that there is work to be done and to cultivate a desire to gain and utilize skills that will lead to systemic change.

These goals are achieved through a four-stage model. The first stage of intergroup dialogue entails creating a shared understanding of values, learning what it means to be in dialogue as opposed to other means of communication, and building the relational foundation for authentic dialogic engagement. The second stage of intergroup dialogue explores the ways difference manifests in society through examples of participants' lived experiences of prejudice and discrimination, and the ways those experiences compound to create structural systems of oppression. In this stage participants are encouraged to engage in active listening and perspective-taking to gain an understanding of the ways privilege and marginalization unfold for peers who hold social identities different from their own. The third stage of intergroup dialogue explores contemporary hot-button issues and how participants' experiences of interpersonal, cultural, structural, and historical contexts of privilege and marginalization inform their perspectives on controversial issues. In this stage, participants are encouraged to engage in honest, informed, and meaningful dialogue in the spirit of appreciative inquiry. The fourth stage of intergroup dialogue calls participants to action, which ranges from furthering their social justice education to actively engaging in work for social change. In this final stage participants are asked to critically examine their passion, awareness, skills, and knowledge around social justice and chart their next steps for impacting social change (Zúñiga et al., 2007).

Intergroup Dialogue Peer Cofacilitation Training: Concepts and Skills

In the Michigan model, undergraduate students take a credit-bearing course, Training Processes in Intergroup Dialogue Facilitation, before going on to cofacilitate. The training course addresses concepts and skills such as active listening and inquiry. Students learn to use these skills and to model them for the participants in their dialogue.

Active Listening

Students are taught to use the listen/affirm/respond/add information (or inquire) (LARA/I) method. In small groups, students practice *listening* to each other with their full presence (not giving verbal or nonverbal responses or interrupting), *affirming* what has been shared by other participants, *responding* with their considered, informed perspectives, and *adding* information to what has been shared by others and/or *inquiring*—asking open-ended questions that probe for deeper understanding and meaning.

Inquiry

Affirming inquiry, which builds on the practice of appreciative inquiry, is one of the most complex concepts/skills for students to grasp, providing continuous opportunities for learning. Affirming inquiry is composed of the following four pillars:

1. Shared/mutual risk-taking and vulnerability among intergroup dialogue participants
2. Shared/mutual responsibilities for contributions of participants
3. Shared/mutual benefit
4. A participant's need and/or desire to know, learn, and/or experience must be subjugated to the agency of others to answer their inquiries

In the topical dialogues, a different kind of inquiry is used to animate the semester-long process: critical appreciative inquiry (CAI), which

> is an expansion of Appreciative Inquiry that melds social justice, critical theory and appreciative inquiry. Appreciative Inquiry is a paradigm shift in approaches to human systems change that moves away from problem solving and a focus on the deficits in the system . . . by examining strengths and successes. (Gold, Sargeant, Cockell, & McArthur-Blair, 2014, p. 44)

Because all potential dialogue students are trained together and the vast majority of them will cofacilitate a traditional dialogue, traditional inquiry is the kind of inquiry focused on in the training course. This means that students who facilitate a topical dialogue have training in affirming inquiry, but not specifically CAI. Their inquiry skills may be strong enough to engage participants in the traditional intergroup dialogue but are somewhat insufficient in the topical dialogue setting.

Topical Intergroup Dialogues: Strengths, Challenges, and Opportunities

The Program on Intergroup Relations has trained undergraduates for decades to cofacilitate intergroup dialogues with their peers on race, socioeconomic status, gender, sexual orientation, religion, ability status, and citizenship, among other identities. In recent years, students have expressed a deep interest in using their dialogue skills to engage not only social identities but also specific kinds of institutional and structural oppression. Although Stage 3 of intergroup dialogue focuses on topics related to identity, students asked for—and faculty and staff in the program wanted to create—an opportunity to spend an entire semester delving into a specific manifestation of oppression with an eye toward solutions.

As a result, as part of the bicentennial celebration of the University of Michigan in 2017, the Program on Intergroup Relations received an internal grant to expand the Intergroup Dialogue course, ALA 122, to include topical dialogues focused on educational inequality and justice. This responded to the student's desire for learning about how their various social identities impacted their education trajectories and how they might work together to create more just educational futures for students coming after them.

Semester-long topical dialogues, like traditional intergroup dialogues, are cofacilitated by two trained undergraduates. Unlike traditional intergroup dialogues, however, the cofacilitators leading the dialogues do not necessarily hold privileged or marginalized identities within a particular social identity category. Furthermore, these topical dialogues are not populated by equal numbers of participants with marginalized and privileged identities. Rather, the students who choose to participate in these dialogues express interest in the given topic, as do the cofacilitators. Some of them have taken classes on the topic or already engage in activism or volunteerism around it, but that is not a prerequisite for participation.

The topical dialogues follow a modified four-stage model and teach and encourage participants to use CAI as the primary mode of engagement with the topic and with each other. In the stages of the topical dialogue semester, students focus on forming and building relationships; (re)conceptualizing intergroup dialogue as an applied methodology; analyzing issues of inequality and injustice; and finally, achieving sustainable and just solution-making and organizing for change.

In traditional dialogues the only people in the classroom are the participants and the cofacilitators (save for observation visits by the lead instructor); however, in the topical dialogues, stakeholders of different kinds are invited into the dialogue classroom to share information and experience that will broaden participants' perspectives and contextualize and challenge how they think about solutions.

For decades, Michigan undergraduates have been challenged and transformed by the experience of participating in traditional intergroup dialogues. These new topical dialogues now provide a different opportunity for students to engage dialogic practice: Students can use the skills and knowledge they gain to imagine new futures for themselves and their peers. The topical dialogues also create an opportunity for faculty and staff to consistently reflect on—and modify—our pedagogy to confront pressing social issues. It enables us to open intergroup dialogue opportunities to more students on campus, most especially those who want to think concretely about policy change and activism around relevant issues of our time. It also, interestingly, has decreased the amount of time it often takes reluctant students to "buy in" to intergroup dialogue. In other words, students sometimes resist intergroup dialogue pedagogy when they experience the cognitive dissonance that can arise when they are confronted with new information about social identities, systems of oppression, and the ways in which we participate in them. The topical dialogue has given students a different point of entry in that they come to the dialogue willing to engage in conversations about educational inequity, difficult as that may be. Students are given the tools and support to engage in dialogue about privilege, power, and marginalization.

In our pilot of the educational inequity dialogue, a challenge for our peer cofacilitators—and thus for our program—has been that students who came to the topical dialogue *without* having taken a traditional dialogue had less experience with understanding their membership in social identity groups (race, ethnicity, social class, gender, etc.). Because of this, students found it more difficult to think about educational inequality in terms of racial, ethnic, class, and gender disparities. For example, students were less able to connect social systems that grant privilege to dominant racial and class groups to the prevalence of standardized testing and metal detectors in schools. Further, they were less able to understand how their own racial, ethnic, class, and gender identities may have impacted the experiences they had in their own educational trajectories.

Because of ways students' memberships in privileged social identity groups have impacted their life experiences—and their misunderstanding of the interconnectedness of oppression—some students have exhibited "savior" tendencies when coming up with solutions for problems of educational inequity. This has led some dialogue participants to focus more on "helping" people they deem disadvantaged gain access to the privileged experiences dialogue participants have had, as opposed to wrestling with the complicated ways in which we all participate in oppressive systems that reproduce privilege and marginalization.

Conclusion

The Program on Intergroup Relations pilot of the topical dialogue on educational inequality has provided much insight into the possibilities of intergroup dialogue as a form of democratic education. For instance, we learned that it is important to be attuned to the selection process for the dialogue section. We realized the importance of introducing CAI to intergroup dialogue facilitators earlier in their training process and consistently revisiting it throughout. And we realized the need to modify activities, such as the identity time line activity and privilege walk, along with the process of using caucus groups, to make them more appropriate for traditional or topical dialogues.

The pilot has shown its developers that there is an opportunity to use the Michigan model of intergroup dialogue in higher education to create new ways of engaging students in learning about systems of oppression, social identity, and social change. It has also demonstrated that the pedagogy must adapt to provide students with skills and knowledge that equip them to participate in dialogues about specific topics authentically, with humility and genuine inquiry. The pedagogical foundation provided by the Michigan model, strengthened by honest and critical feedback from student participants, faculty, and staff in the Program on Intergroup Relations, provides a strong base from which to create educational experiences that will continue to contribute to the tradition of democratic education.

The mission of the University of Michigan Program on Intergroup Relations is to "pursue social justice through education" (Program on Intergroup Relations, 2019). This mission aligns with the purpose of intergroup dialogue in higher education, which is to bring students together to dialogue across difference in hopes of creating more just, equitable campuses. It is our hope that the educational justice pilot contributes to not only the mission of our program but also the field of dialogue and deliberation by developing pedagogy that allows students to consider identity through the lenses of structural inequality and eradication of institutional and structural barriers to justice.

References

Beale, R., Thompson, M., & Chesler, M. (2001). Training peer facilitators for intergroup dialogue leadership. In D. L. Schoem & S. Hurtado (Eds.), *Intergroup dialogue: Deliberative democracy in school, college, community, and workplace* (pp. 227–246). Ann Arbor: University of Michigan Press.

Cockell, J., & McArthur-Blair, J. (2012). *Appreciative inquiry in higher education: A transformative force.* San Francisco, CA: Jossey-Bass.

Freire, P. (1970). *Pedagogy of the oppressed* (M. B. Ramos, Trans.). New York, NY: Continuum.

Gurin, P., Nagda, B. A., & Zúñiga, X. (2013). *Dialogue across difference: Practice, theory, and research on intergroup dialogue.* New York, NY: Russell Sage Foundation.

Johnson, A. G. (2006). *Privilege, power, and difference.* Boston, MA: McGraw Hill.

Program on Intergroup Relations. (2011, November 28). Program on Intergroup Relations. Retrieved from irg.umich.edu

Program on Intergroup Relations. (2019). *Intergroup dialogue.* Retrieved from https://igr.umich.edu/article/about-program-intergroup-relations

Zúñiga, X., Nagda, B. A., Chesler, M., & Cytron-Walker, A. (2007). Intergroup dialogue in higher education: Meaningful learning about social justice [Monograph]. *ASHE Higher Education Report, 32*(4), 1–128.

9

THE FREE SOUTHERN THEATER'S STORY CIRCLE PROCESS

Lizzy Cooper Davis

> *I am a storyteller. I say storyteller instead of liar cuz there's a heap o' difference between a storyteller and a liar. A liar's somebody that covers things over mainly for his own private benefit. A storyteller, now that's somebody that uncovers things so everybody can get some good out of it. A heap o' good meaning can be found in a story . . . if you got the mind to hear it.*
>
> —John O'Neal, *Don't Start Me To Talking . . . : Plays of Struggle and Liberation: The Selected Plays of John O'Neal*, 2016

The story circle process is simple. Small groups of people sit in circles and share stories. That's it. There are guidelines for its structure and some key principles of practice—which I will outline later—but, in essence, it is simply about sharing and listening.

This is more radical than it may sound. The core frameworks for the process counter those frequently found in our educational, political, and even artistic spaces. Story circles encourage us to embrace dialogue over debate and to value the nuances of experience over even the best-structured arguments. They ask us to abandon the adversarial stances so often seen as the hallmark of serious engagement and take up postures more conducive to offering and receiving. Ultimately, they teach us that it is through listening to our stories, rather than arguing our points, that we discover who we are.

The story circle process is also about the power of sitting together to listen deeply. I would feel foolish writing about it without echoing the concerns shared by John O'Neal, the process's chief architect and steward, when

---

For John O'Neal (1940–2019), who uncovered so much for so many of us.

embarking on a similar task. His is the seed story of any discussion of this process—the one to which the rest of us are responding—so I'll quote him at length and point you to his "Story Circles Discussion Paper." He writes:

> I hesitate to present these suggestions for the operation of the Story Circle process in writing because the process, like the stories that people use it to share, is essentially oral in nature. When things are written down we have a tendency to treat them as more final than they need to be. On the other hand, when people sit down to actually talk together we have the chance to look at the body language, listen to the tone of voice, to question if you're not clear about something or to challenge if you think that's in order. We even use different words when we write, maybe even a whole different kind of language. I even think differently when I'm writing than when I'm talking. If you, dear reader, were sitting here I wouldn't be bent into the computer keyboard staring at the screen typing or editing what I've already written. I would be engaged with you, concerned about how you react to what I say, changing my direction or my emphasis according to your responses. . . . On the other hand, when I'm writing I can re-write and edit and you'll never know it . . . well, maybe you'll never know it. If you were really here I wouldn't have to imagine as much about who you are and could pay more attention to what you want or maybe need from me in order to understand what I'm trying to communicate and how I feel about it. So, in this case at least, writing is a poor substitute for being there. (O'Neal, n.d.)

In addition to alerting us to the irony of writing about a process defined by its liveness, O'Neal is also highlighting the extent to which the story circle process pushes us toward the relational.[2] It is not a way to hear a series of monologues; it is an intentional process for structuring equitable dialogue.

With that said, I will try—while "bent into the computer keyboard staring at the screen"—to tell my story circles story.

"A New Area of Protest": The Free Southern Theater and Junebug Productions

I learned the story circle process from four remarkable teachers: Jawole Willa Jo Zollar, founding artistic director of the Brooklyn-based dance

---

2. For discussions of cultural and psychological barriers to relational behavior, see *Enacting Pleasure* (Davis & Davis, 2001), in which artists and scholars respond to a call "to conquer a culturally embedded fear of love and give play to the pursuit of relational pleasure" (p. 5).

company Urban Bush Women; Stephanie McKee, artistic director of Junebug Productions; Wendi O'Neal, New Orleans–based cultural organizer; and her father and cofounder of the Free Southern Theater (FST), John O'Neal. Each of these artists works deliberately to activate black traditions of culture and protest within their broader efforts toward community wellness, justice, and joy. They also each have deep connections to New Orleans, Louisiana—a city whose unique slave history has fostered practices of black cultural resistance like no other in the country and in which the story circle process developed and thrived.[3] My use of story circles and study of their history is indebted to each of these teachers and so my story begins by naming and offering gratitude to them.

Story circles were developed by the FST, which, although not born in New Orleans, had its coming of age there. In 1963 John O'Neal and Doris Derby, two field directors from the Student Nonviolent Coordinating Committee (SNCC), along with Gilbert Moses, a journalist from the *Mississippi Free Press*, decided theater could be a powerful way to engage rural black communities frequently excluded from the planning tables of the civil rights movement. With an initial donation from Langston Hughes and support from other artists and activists, they launched the FST as the theatrical arm of SNCC. Founded in Mississippi but soon relocating to New Orleans, the integrated FST brought free presentations and postshow discussions of works by writers as diverse as Ossie Davis, Samuel Beckett, and Bertolt Brecht to public and community spaces across the U.S. South. Their founding treatise identified the following goals: "to establish a legitimate theatre in the deep South"; "to stimulate creative and reflective thought among Negroes in Mississippi and other Southern states"; and to cultivate a theatrical form "as unique to the Negro people as the origin of blues and jazz" (Derby, Moses, & O'Neal, 1969, p. 4). Summarizing their charge, they wrote, "Through theatre, we think to open a new area of protest" (p. 4).

The story circle process emerged to push past the limits of the traditional postshow discussion and facilitate more inclusive dialogues. Rather than ask audiences to talk back to those on stage, audiences and actors sat together in circles to share personal stories evoked by the show. The FST was, after all, less interested in showcasing the talents of their artists or pushing movement propaganda than in using theater to open community conversations—conversations facilitated by SNCC field secretaries and other

---

3. For more on the New Orleans history of black cultural resistance see Arend (2009); Flaherty (2010); Johnson, R. (2016); Johnson, W. (1999); Rasmussen (2011); Sublette (2009); and Turner (2009).

movement organizers such as Fannie Lou Hamer (Dent & Schechner, 1969). As FST members Thomas C. Dent, Richard Schechner, John O'Neal, and Gilbert Moses wrote,

> It is not simply that the artists and poets and actors and directors who have made the FST wish to say something. More importantly, there is an audience which cries to express itself. In this sense, the FST has always been, and continues to be, a popular theatre. The audience is articulate and active—no one who has seen an FST performance can fail to recognize that the audience is the most important and expressive element in it. (Dent & Schechner, 1969, p. xii)

The FST's goal was not to awe or impress but to engage and activate. The theatrical performance was merely the prompt. The real action was the personal storytelling and subsequent discussion about issues of concern and the growing movement to address them. Story circles helped facilitate this work.

This upending of traditional theatrical structures by centering audiences rather than artists emerged from the movement's commitment to radical democracy and bottom-up leadership as articulated and enacted by SNCC—particularly its matriarch, Ella Jo Baker. Baker was a life-long organizer for racial and economic justice whom Stokely Carmichael described as "the most powerful person in the struggle of the sixties" (quoted in Olson, 2001, p. 150). With a leadership style more facilitative than didactic, Baker called a national meeting of student organizers to support those making headlines at lunch counters in Greensboro, North Carolina. Her goal was not to dictate what should be done but to create a space where students could strategize for themselves. As SNCC member Clayborne Carson (1995) recalls, "The letter [inviting young leaders to the gathering] assured students that, although 'Adult Freedom Fighters would be present for counsel and guidance,' the conference would be 'youth centered'" (p. 20). This now-historic meeting of April 1960 resulted in the birth of SNCC.

Baker's critique of hierarchical leadership models permeated her work with SNCC. Despite being the elder organizer, for example, she facilitated democratic planning meetings in circles rather than deliver lectures or directives from the front of the room (Michna, 2009, p. 539). She also pushed SNCC's student organizers to embrace the core value that those most affected by a problem should lead the strategizing around its solutions. This was a challenge for many of the largely northern and comparatively privileged students flooding the South to support the movement. As scholar and activist Barbara Ransby (2003) writes of Baker's approach,

Talented and educated young black people were persuaded to forfeit their privileged claim to leadership of the race, a status that would naturally have been afforded them according to pre-World War II uplift ideology, and instead to defer to the collective wisdom of sharecroppers, maids, and manual laborers, many of whom lacked even a high school education. White activists were encouraged to reject existing race and class hierarchies and do the same. This was a fundamental break with black politics as usual. Poor southern black people were not merely SNCC's constituency; they were revered for their knowledge, commitment, and sacrifice. (p. 365)

Summarizing Baker's leadership, SNCC member Joanne Grant (2012) recalls, "She taught SNCC students the importance of nurturing local leaders, the value of organizing local groups who would make their own decisions, and the vital concept of a group-centered leadership as opposed to a leadership-centered group" (p. 309). The FST sought to put these same values into practice, not only by using theatrical tools to engage those most affected but also by refashioning theatrical structures to put new voices at the center. As John O'Neal—himself an English and philosophy major from Southern Illinois University—said to an audience sitting in folding chairs and on the ground behind a house in Ruleville, Mississippi, "You are the actors" (quoted in Sutherland, 1969, p. 24).[4]

As civil rights struggles shifted into the 1960s and 1970s, O'Neal felt the FST's mission and work needed revising. The company's final production was the 1980 tour of his solo show, *Don't Start Me to Talking or I'll Tell Everything I Know* (O'Neal, 2016), which showcased the wit and wisdom of ordinary people through the SNCC-created character Junebug Jabbo Jones. After this production, O'Neal laid the FST to rest and announced the company's rebirth as Junebug Productions—a new theater for a new time. In 1986, he gave the FST a traditional New Orleans funeral—complete with coffin, brass band, second line parade, and eulogy—and hosted a conference on the role of arts in society called "The Funeral for the Free Southern Theater: A Valediction Without Mourning" (Cohen-Cruz, 2006; Considine, 2016; O'Quinn, 1986).

Junebug quickly embarked on a series of collaborations that solidified the story circle process and its centrality to their work at the intersection of community arts, dialogue, and action. Two such projects, both multiyear endeavors, were "Junebug/Jack"—a collaboration with Dudley Cocke of Appalachia's Roadside Theater that brought black and white communities

---

4. For more on Baker, see Grant (1981, 2012).

together to talk about racism—and "The Color Line Project"—a national tour of what had become the trilogy of Junebug Jabbo Jones plays (O'Neal, 2016) accompanied by community dialogues about local civil rights histories. Carlton Turner, a Mississippi-based artist, organizer, and mentee of O'Neal's, who describes story circles as his "most important tool," points to this period in the 1990s and early 2000s as the process's most formative. According to Turner, it was through these and other cross-cultural partnerships—with Roadside as well as New York's Pregones/Puerto Rican Traveling Theater, San Francisco's Traveling Jewish Theater, and others—that O'Neal and his collaborators honed in on the story circle's power to bridge divides and speak across difference. As he says, "The circle represents our common humanity—that everyone is created equal and everyone has a voice. This tool allows us to live in that practice" (C. Turner, personal communication, August 30, 2018).

Junebug continues to work from its base in New Orleans and remains rooted in FST's original mission of creating theater with and for communities in the Black Belt South. The company is now helmed by Stephanie McKee as artistic director and the story circle process remains a core practice.

Continued Spread and Contemporary Use

Story circles are used widely by theater artists to support ensemble-building and generate material for playmaking, by organizers to surface core concerns and guide planning and action, by educators to keep student voices at the center of learning, and by those at the intersection of these various roles for myriad purposes. Junebug Productions—particularly O'Neal, McKee, theater artist Kiyoko McCrae, and singer and cultural worker Wendi O'Neal—has been central to this growing use, through not only practice but also deliberate documentation, teaching, and exchange (McCrae, McKee, O'Neal, & O'Neal, 2009–2012).

Many New Orleanian organizers adopted the practice in the wake of the civil rights era, making it a hallmark of the city's approach to grassroots mobilization. "Color Line Project" partner Curtis Muhammad and another former SNCC member, Kalamu ya Salaam, for example, have both centered story circles in their work—Muhammad in his organizing for racial and economic justice and Salaam through Students at the Center, the high school–based writing program he cofounded with educator Jim Randals to support youth organizing for educational justice (Buras, 2011; Flaherty, 2010; Michna, 2009). The practice has spread among organizers through a number of means, including the meeting grounds offered by Alternate ROOTS, a Georgia-based organization for southern cultural organizers that Turner led from 2001 to 2017, and the Highlander Research and Education Center, a national organizing hub based in Tennessee. Among community-engaged theater artists, Linda Parris Bailey of Carpetbag Theater in Knoxville, Tennessee, and "Junebug/Jack" collaborator Dudley Cocke of Roadside in Norton, Virginia, are two who have made story circles a core company practice for both art-making and community dialogue. Independent artists who regularly use story circles due to their mentorship from civil rights–era organizers include Eboni Noelle Golden, Shani Jamila (O'Neal's niece), Paloma McGregor, and Harold Steward.

Although many have long brought story circles to their teaching in university settings, the practice is increasingly finding its place among those interested in humanistic pedagogies and university-community collaborations. This broadened dissemination within higher education has largely been facilitated by Imagining America (IA), a national consortium of scholars, artists, and activists committed to campus-based organizing and community engagement, as well as its offshoot, the U.S. Department of Arts and Culture. Jan Cohen-Cruz, a scholar and practitioner of community-based theater, was IA's director from 2007 to 2012 and invited Carlton Turner and Dudley Cocke to consortium events and projects along with Carole Bebelle, a longtime Junebug partner and cofounder and executive director of the Ashé Cultural Arts Center in New Orleans. Through them and others, story circles became, as current director Erica Kohl-Arenas describes it, "part of IA's DNA" (E. Kohl-Arenas, personal communication, January 9, 2019). They are used during staff meetings (ross & Peters, 2018) as well as in national convenings and have been adopted by many of its members to foster equitable dialogue in and beyond the classroom. Describing their particular power in higher education, Cohen-Cruz says:

> Experiencing story circles has opened many of my students to the varied ways people come to know things worth knowing, much of which has not come from formal educational settings. . . . [It] teaches them in a powerful way that is often missing in "higher education." Higher than what, I often ask. Indeed, the term higher ed is a dead giveaway of yet another great lesson that story circles impart to university students—the humility of what people know simply from their lives, and not because they "got in" to this

or that school, or that they are part of some elite group; a story circle is a great leveler. (Personal communication, January 7, 2019)

Story Circle Guidelines

The story circle process is not a unique practice. It resonates in important ways, for example, with circle practices of many Indigenous populations and restorative justice work, liberatory pedagogies of educators like bell hooks (1994, 1999) and Paulo Freire (2000), and methods for community dialogue forged by artists like Augusto Boal (1993) and Liz Lerman (2003). It is, however, a *particular* practice. It emerged from black-led organizing of the civil rights era in the United States. When facilitating the process, it is important to honor its history and name your teachers.

The process, as I learned it, uses the following structure. The process begins with the offering of a theme or seed story to which others will respond. A theme could be something as broad as finding lessons in surprising places and a seed story could be a story told by the facilitator, an experience the group has just shared (i.e., a play or current event), or a text the group has read. The process then goes as follows:

1. Sit in groups of no more than about eight people, depending on numbers and your sense of how long the group will be able to sit and listen.
2. Honor the circle. It is a radically democratic arrangement that puts us in equitable relationship to one another. Sitting in that arrangement is an important practice. To test the circle, I often ask that participants make sure no one has to move to see anyone else.
3. Ensure that time is shared equitably. Everyone will have three minutes for their story. Storytellers do not have to use the full time but cannot go over.
4. Ensure the task of timekeeping is shared equitably. Stories are told sequentially around the circle and the person who has just shared serves as timekeeper for their neighbor. Timekeepers should signal when there is about a minute remaining and gently alert storytellers when their time is up.
5. If you do not have a story when it is your turn, you can pass and the circle will return to you at the end.
6. There is no note-taking or recording. Remembering the lessons of oral tradition, the process honors what Wendi O'Neal calls our "original

recording devices"—our ears, hearts, minds, and bodies. If, however, the process is being used explicitly to gather information—for playmaking or assessment, for example—and everyone consents, stories can be recorded. It is important, however, to not underestimate the ways both telling and listening are affected when notes are being taken or audio or video is being captured.

7. There are no interruptions or clarifying questions while stories are being offered. There will be time for conversation later.
8. Be sure what you're telling is a story—not an opinion or argument—and be sure it is yours to tell. A story is a personal experience with a beginning, middle, and end and it must be a story that happened to you.
9. John O'Neal (n.d.) says, and I've heard my teachers repeat it, "You don't have to like the story being told but you have to respect the storyteller's right to tell it."
10. O'Neal also stresses "the law of listening" (para.10). He writes, "In storytelling, listening is always more important than talking. If you're thinking about your story while someone else is telling theirs, you won't hear what they say. If you trust the circle, when it comes your turn to tell, a story will be there" (para.10).
11. After everyone has told their story, allow time for crosstalk within the circles. I often start this by asking people to first offer images they are left with from the stories. Once this comes to a natural close, open dialogue can begin.
12. When crosstalk is complete, provide some sort of synthesizing or closing activity. This can be as simple as a full group conversation or as complex as asking each group to devise a three-minute performance piece or poem about their group story.

I use story circles in a number of contexts—in processes of community-based conversation and art-making, in classrooms to illustrate and activate student-centered and humanistic teaching and learning, and as "a leveling tool"—as both Carlton Turner (personal communication, August 30, 2018) and Jan Cohen-Cruz describe them—among people with varying degrees of status or privilege.

The story circle process has brought me to some of my dearest teachers, collaborators, and friends and led me to listen to an array of stories about history, pedagogy, and politics. I have been working with Jawole Zollar and Stephanie McKee for over a decade and have been exploring the histories discussed previously for just as long. These people and ideas ground my own teaching and work and have led me, among other things, to center Ella Jo

Baker in histories of liberatory pedagogy and feature the FST in histories of North American Theater.[5] Their frequent omission highlights the extent to which certain stories—particularly those of people of color—are spoken over in our historical narratives. It is time to tell new stories.

John O'Neal says, "When we tell stories we are sharing with each other how we put things together" (O'Neal, n.d., para. 7). Indeed, everyone who uses this process has their own story—their own way of putting its history and practice together. The story I have told is not *the* story circles story but only *my* story circles story. In keeping with the spirit of the circle, I am indebted to those I've heard before and look forward to those coming next.

References

Arend, O. (2009). *Showdown in Desire: The Black Panthers take a stand in New Orleans*. Fayetteville: The University of Arkansas Press.

Boal, A. (1993). *Theatre of the oppressed* (TCG ed.). New York, NY: Theater Communications Group.

Buras, K. L. (with Randals, J., ya Salaam, K., & the students at the center). (2011). *Pedagogy, policy, and the privatized city: Stories of dispossession and defiance from New Orleans*. New York, NY: Teachers College Press.

Carson, C. (1995). *In struggle: SNCC and the black awakening of the 1960s*. Cambridge, MA: Harvard University Press.

Charron, K. M. (2009). *Freedom's teacher: The life of Septima Clark*. Chapel Hill: University of North Carolina Press.

Clark, S. P. (1962). *Echo in my soul* (1st ed.). New York, NY: Dutton.

Clark, S. P. (1986). *Ready from within: Septima Clark and the Civil Rights Movement*. Navarro, CA: Wild Trees Press.

Cohen-Cruz, J. (2006). Comforting the afflicted and afflicting the comfortable: The legacy of the Free Southern Theater. In J. M. Harding & C. Rosenthal (Eds.), *Restaging the sixties: Radical theaters and their legacies*. Ann Arbor: University of Michigan Press.

Considine, A. (2016, August 2). Know a theatre: Junebug Productions of New Orleans. *American Theatre*. Retrieved from https://www.americantheatre.org/2016/08/02/know-a-theatre-junebug-productions-of-new-orleans/

Davis, P. C., & Davis, L. C. (Eds.). (2001). *Enacting pleasure: Artists and scholars respond to Carol Gilligan's New Map of Love*. Chicago, IL: Seagull Books.

Dent, T. C., & Schechner, R. (Eds.). (1969). *The Free Southern Theater by the Free Southern Theater*. New York, NY: Bobbs-Merrill.

---

5. Septima Clark is another civil rights–era organizer who, through her Citizenship Schools, forged a pedagogy much aligned with Baker's. For more, see Clark (1962, 1986) and Charron (2009).

Derby, D., Moses, G., & O'Neal, J. (1969). A general prospectus for the establishment of a Free Southern Theater. In T. C. Dent & R. Schechner (Eds.), *The Free Southern Theater by the Free Southern Theater* (pp. 3–4). New York, NY: Bobbs-Merrill.

Flaherty, J. (2010). *Floodlines: Community and resistance from Katrina to the Jena Six.* Chicago, IL: Haymarket Books.

Freire, P. (2000). *Pedagogy of the oppressed* (30th Anniv. ed.). New York, NY: Continuum.

Grant, J. (Producer and Director). (1981). *Fundi: The story of Ella Baker* [Documentary film]. United States: Icarus Films.

Grant, J. (2012). My friend Ella Baker. In F. S. Holsaert, M. Prescod, N. Noonan, J. Richardson, B. G. Robinson, J. S. Young, & D. M. Zellner (Eds.), *Hands on the freedom plow: Personal accounts by women in SNCC.* Urbana: University of Illinois Press.

hooks, b. (1994). *Teaching to transgress: Education as the practice of freedom.* New York, NY: Routledge.

hooks, b. (1999). *Happy to be nappy.* New York, NY: Jump at the Sun.

Johnson, R. (2016). *Slavery's metropolis: Unfree labor in New Orleans during the Age of Revolutions.* Cambridge, UK: Cambridge University Press.

Johnson, W. (1999). *Soul by soul: Life inside the antebellum slave market.* Cambridge, MA: Harvard University Press.

Lerman, L. (2003). *Liz Lerman's critical response process: A method for getting useful feedback on anything you make, from dance to dessert.* Takoma Park, MD: Dance Exchange.

McCrae, K., McKee, S., O'Neal, J., & O'Neal, W. (2009–2012). *Free Southern Theater Institute syllabi.* Authors' collection.

Michna, C. (2009). Stories at the center: Story circles, educational organizing, and fate of neighborhood public schools in New Orleans. *American Quarterly, 61*(3), 529–555.

O'Neal, J. (2016). *Don't start me to talking . . . : Plays of struggle and liberation: The selected plays of John O'Neal.* New York, NY: Theater Communications Group.

O'Neal, J. (n.d.). *Story circle process discussion paper.* Retrieved from http://www.racematters.org/storycircleprocess.htm

Olson, L. (2001). *Freedom's daughters: The unsung heroines of the civil rights movement from 1830 to 1970.* New York, NY: Scribner.

O'Quinn, J. (1986, March). Free at last. *American Theatre,* 27–28.

Ransby, B. (2003). *Ella Baker and the black freedom movement: A radical democratic vision.* Chapel Hill: University of North Carolina Press.

Rasmussen, D. (2011). *American uprising: The untold story of America's largest slave revolt.* New York, NY: Harper Collins.

ross, j. m., & Peters, S. (2018, October 1). IA story share [Podcast]. *Imagining America.* Retrieved from https://www.stitcher.com/podcast/imagining-america-iastoryshare/iastoryshare/e/56505366

Sublette, N. (2009). *The world that made New Orleans: From Spanish silver to Congo Square.* Chicago, IL: Chicago Review Press.

Sutherland, E. (1969). Theater of the Meaningful. In T. Dent, & R. Schechner, R. (Eds.). *The Free Southern Theater by the Free Southern Theater* (pp. 24–29). New York, NY: Bobbs-Merrill,(Reprinted from *The Nation*, October 19, 1964).

Turner, R. B. (2009). *Jazz religion, the second line, and black New Orleans*. Bloomington: Indiana University Press.

10

THE NATIONAL ISSUES FORUMS

"Choicework" as an Indispensable Civic Skill

Jean Johnson and Keith Melville

Several years ago, in his book *College: What It Was and Should Be*, Andrew Delbanco (2012) commented: "The American college has long been devoted to the principle that the college classroom is a rehearsal space for democracy, a place where students learn to speak and listen with civility to peers whose perspective differs from their own" (p. xiii).

At a time when constructive political dialogue is lacking, when toxic messages drown out thoughtful exchange, and when the partisan divide grows deeper, it is more important than ever for college educators to use this "rehearsal space for democracy" to help students learn how to engage in civil conversations. But how can educators tackle this demanding task? What does a "rehearsal space for democracy" look like? What specific skills do we want students to develop and practice?

Today, when uncivil and unproductive exchanges are all too common, the National Issues Forums (NIF) provide places for citizens of all ages to engage in productive deliberation on some of the toughest issues facing the United States—immigration, health care, foreign policy, safety and justice, and others.

NIF is a national network of nonpartisan community-based organizations. Forums are locally organized and sponsored. Local conveners—including community colleges, four-year colleges and universities, libraries, K–12 schools, senior and youth centers, and religious and other community organizations—share a common interest in finding more productive ways for citizens to address shared concerns. The network grew out of a long-term collaboration between the Charles F. Kettering Foundation, an operating foundation focused on strengthening democracy worldwide, and Public Agenda, a research organization aimed at narrowing the divide between America's leaders and the public.

Since it started in 1981, NIF has regularly found partners in American higher education. NIF deliberations are now included in college-level courses, in on-campus conversations, and in forums sponsored by higher education institutions but open to the broader community.

Over the years, the network has hosted citizen deliberations on dozens of issues. Every NIF forum, no matter what the subject, revolves around the concept of *choicework*. Using materials and methods developed in concert with Kettering, participants in NIF forums weigh alternative approaches to urgent problems. They look at the advantages and tradeoffs of different courses of action. They listen to the ideas and experiences of others. They deliberate on the choices they face as individuals, neighbors, voters, and citizens in a democracy.

As David Mathews (2005), Kettering's president and an astute advocate of deliberation, explains: "To deliberate is not just to talk about problems.... It means weighing carefully both the consequences of various options for actions and the views of others" (p. 72).

In today's fractured society, a key NIF goal is to bring people together from across the political spectrum to talk about public problems. In 2018, for example, the NIF convened deliberations about U.S. immigration policy in 33 states and more than 80 different venues. More than half of these forums took place on college campuses. In 2017, community members met with police officials and rank-and-file police officers to talk about how to provide safety and justice in their own neighborhoods. NIF's mission—whether the topic is immigration, the economy, or the nation's foreign policy—is to offer what is often missing, a place where citizens who do not necessarily share the same views can engage in candid, civil exchanges.

The basic idea is to arm citizens with the understanding, perspective, and confidence to act as more powerful players in the democratic process. In contemporary American politics, people often become active only after decisions have been made. Citizens most often show up as critics or angry citizen-spectators to speak out in protest when something threatens them in their own backyard, when something has gone wrong, or when they think government is headed in the wrong direction.

At the center of widely shared discontent with the democratic process today is the sense that crucial decisions that decisively shape American public life are made without much public consultation or understanding of the tradeoffs citizens are willing to make. Yet there are few occasions where citizens engage in dialogue with each other about common concerns and decisions that affect their communities or the nation as a whole.

Many commentators have identified this as a missing element in the American political process. Public opinion analyst Daniel Yankelovich (1991), cofounder of Public Agenda, studied public thinking over the course of several decades. He wrote persuasively about the need to offer citizens better opportunities to develop what he terms *public judgment*. For Yankelovich, public judgment is a more stable, thoughtful, and realistic kind of public thinking, which contrasts with the often uninformed, top-of-the-head responses captured in polls.

As Jared Duval (2010) writes in *Next Generation Democracy*, "Before we can make innovative progress on nearly any large-scale challenge before us, there must first be bold reform of the process by which we make decisions as a society" (p. 200). NIF forums are intended to address this deficiency. They offer both a place for effective public problem-solving and a space in which citizens learn a key civic skill—the skill of choicework.

NIF Forums: Political Learning Through Deliberation

If you attend any of the NIF forums held around the country that focus on specific issues, it may not be apparent what is different about these gatherings. NIF forums focus on issues that are frequently debated by political leaders and covered in the media, such as immigration, the federal debt, health-care costs, safety and justice, the opioid crisis, and the challenge of making ends meet. But as participants in hundreds of forums held each year will tell you, these exchanges are occasions for a different kind of public conversation. In postforum questionnaires collected by the NIF, nearly 4 in 10 participants say they heard ideas in the forum that they hadn't considered before. About 1 in 5 report having second thoughts about a proposal they thought they supported before the forum. Most of all, these forums are different in their tone, which is a striking contrast to the uncivil and often toxic tone of many exchanges about public issues.

One way to describe NIF forums is to say what they are not. These exchanges are not free-for-alls. They are not occasions for a simple exchange of opinions. They are not debates in which one side or the other is declared a winner. And they are not like public hearings in which experts stand at the front of the room and lay out their proposed actions, field questions, and then listen to what people have to say, one after another, as they are handed the microphone. Perhaps most importantly, at a time when many public exchanges are acrimonious, these forums are not occasions for partisan slugfests. They focus on issues, not personalities or partisan divisions.

NIF forums are carefully structured discussions designed to prompt deliberation, listening, reconsideration, and second thoughts. The guides and videos that launch NIF deliberations offer a baseline of facts and background information and lay out three or four distinct options, each reflecting different values and priorities, each representing a different way of thinking about how a problem could be solved.

In forums, participants ask themselves how these different approaches would affect different people and sectors in our society and how each would play out in the near term and the long term. Deliberations often revolve around weighing costs, identifying unintended consequences, and exchanging views with others about what is fair or unfair. Working through these questions and considerations is the essence of choicework.

As practiced in NIF forums, choicework rests on several key assertions about political decision-making:

- Few major issues, once they reach the national stage, offer risk-free, cost-free, universally supported solutions. The choices these issues present to us are difficult.
- Understanding key facts and proposals is important but insufficient. To make sound decisions, people need to weigh the goals, risks, and tradeoffs of the different approaches presented. Juxtaposing different courses of action is crucial to sound judgment.
- Exchanging views with others is an essential element. Participants benefit from hearing and absorbing the perspectives of others. Listening is a prerequisite to public learning.

NIF choicework does not consist of people reviewing and vetting a long list of policy proposals devised by experts or advocacy groups. Instead, participants think through several broad strategies that reflect different aspirations and require different courses of action. These actions often include legislation or public investments, but they may also include steps taken by individuals and/or at the neighborhood or local level.

Although NIF discussion guides are prepared for nonexperts and extensively reviewed for balance and readability, their basic purpose is not so different from the briefing books prepared for the president or corporate executives. These high-level background materials lay out an array of options, generally in response to a specific threat or challenge. Their role is to ensure that decision-makers understand the costs, consequences, and tradeoffs associated with each possible action before moving ahead.

For NIF, citizens are the decision-makers. They have the right—and the responsibility—to understand the implications of the choices they and their elected officials face.

In David Mathews's (2005) words:

> People who would rule themselves have to make countless collective decisions: which policies will result in the greatest good, which candidates for office will best represent us, which projects will most improve our community.... Citizens have to make judgments, not only about what to do, but also about what is most important. The fate of a democratic society is determined by the soundness of these decisions. (pp. 74–75)

Why Does Choicework Matter?

Public decisions are proposed and made every day at various levels of public decision-making—in local communities; state capitols; and in Washington, DC. For better or for worse, decisions about the nation's energy options, health-care reform, immigration policy, and fixing the economy will shape society for decades to come. Some decisions redefine the rules of the game, modify the social contract, and affect the nation's prospects for security and prosperity. Should health care be considered a right of all citizens, paid for as a shared expense? Should public programs be expanded or contracted, and who should bear more of the burden of paying for them? Should immigration be restricted to protect jobs and wages, particularly those of less educated Americans?

When major initiatives are proposed, major cutbacks undertaken, or the rules of the game are changed, such decisions should not be made mainly by political insiders or a small band of experts. They should be topics for public deliberation and debate. Yet public participation for most Americans is limited to voting, paying taxes, and other routine acts of citizenship. There are few places where citizens can gather to weigh proposals and move toward well-considered judgments about which measures are in the public interest.

The premise of the NIF process and the deliberative democracy movement as a whole is that citizens are capable of addressing and discussing major public issues in democratically meaningful ways. However, citizens need to learn how to do choicework, and they need occasions that invite and facilitate this key act of democratic citizenship. For educators who share DelBanco's (2012) view that higher education should offer a "rehearsal space for democracy," the challenge is to help students learn the civic skills needed to participate in deliberative conversations. The best way to learn these skills is by doing them in forums where students practice these skills in the course of deliberating about real-world public concerns.

This is no small task. People often approach complex issues like health care, immigration, and the federal debt with a mixture of confusion, skepticism, and defensiveness. But helping citizens move beyond cynicism or blame is often the first step toward public judgment, a step that has an even greater urgency in today's political climate, where public confidence in government and other institutions is so low.

Public Agenda's Alison Kadlec and Will Friedman (2010) describe how public cynicism can block deliberation and problem-solving and how it can short-circuit public choicework. They summarize a public meeting they observed:

> When the conversation got bogged down in venting about corrupt and greedy leaders it seemed to circumvent people's curiosity about the nature of the problem. Venting about malfeasance furnished a kind of explanatory framework that makes people less interested in exploring the causes and nature of the problem. Or perhaps it simply gives people an excuse not to work very hard by letting them fall back on pat explanations. (p. 102)

Wrestling with choices helps people move beyond unproductive blaming. In many instances wrestling with choices also helps people move beyond partisan responses to a fresh understanding of what they had not considered before.

Based on our experience and those of colleagues who have observed forums and analyzed postforum surveys, choicework often results in important learning for individuals and communities:

- *Choicework helps forum participants to feel less manipulated.* In today's hyperpartisan era, citizens are often suspicious of new information and resistant to alternative ways of thinking. Wrestling with choices helps reduce skepticism and defensiveness.
- *Choicework enables people to be more realistic.* The process of struggling with choices helps people to become more realistic as they assess several options for public action. People who engage in deliberative conversations are better informed and less likely to engage in wishful thinking.
- *Choicework expedites public learning.* Most people need a framework for understanding issues that are unfamiliar and multifaceted. Wrestling with choices helps people clarify and think through complex problems.

- *Choicework empowers citizens.* Issue frameworks prompt citizens to think more clearly about what is in the public interest and what they can reasonably expect from elected leaders and public officials.

Over the past 40 years, this nationwide network of community-based conveners has served as a testing ground for claims about what citizens who engage in deliberative forums can accomplish. These forums are, in effect, a school for citizenship. This nationwide network is no longer an experiment or a visionary enterprise. Deliberative forums have become an integral part of the civic routines in hundreds of communities, a familiar way for communities to respond when they are confronted with public problems.

For college educators, holding deliberative forums is not just a way to make classroom learning more engaging or campus activities more inclusive. Deliberative forums that revolve around choicework are occasions for students to learn a fundamental civic skill. The question today is whether colleges committed to civic education choose to incorporate this key dimension of democratic citizenship into the educational experience of undergraduates.

References

DelBanco, A. (2012, May 22). College: The best rehearsal spaces we have for democracy [Broadcast interview]. *PBS NewsHour*. Arlington, VA: WETA/PBS.

Duval, J. (2010). *Next generation democracy: What the open-source revolution means for power, politics, and change.* London, UK: Bloomsbury.

Kadlec, A., & Friedman, W. (2010). Thirty-five years of working on public judgment at Public Agenda. In D. Yankelovich & W. Friedman (Eds.), *Toward wiser public judgment* (pp. 73–109). Nashville, TN: Vanderbilt University Press.

Mathews, D. (2005). Listening to the public: A new agenda for higher education. In A. Kezar, T. Chambers, & J. Burkhardt (Eds.), *Higher education for the public good* (pp. 71–86). San Francisco, CA: Jossey-Bass.

Yankelovich, D. (1991). *Coming to public judgment: Making democracy work in a complex world.* Syracuse, NY: Syracuse University Press.

11

WHAT IF?

The Interactivity Foundation and Student-Facilitated Discussion Teams

Jeff Prudhomme and Shannon Wheatley Hartman

The Interactivity Foundation is a small nonprofit and nonadvocacy foundation that uses small-group discussions to expand the possibilities for dealing with complex topics. The organization is commonly abbreviated as "IF," in part to convey the core motif of exploring possibilities, to ask, "What if . . . ?" This chapter introduces the organization, its discussion process, and how this process can be adapted for higher education contexts, offering a specific focus on the case of Wesleyan College.

History

Jay Stern, a West Virginia businessman and public philosopher, created the nonprofit that would become the Interactivity Foundation in 1965. Under the name of the Upper Ohio Valley Self-Help Organization, its initial focus was on policies for economic development in West Virginia. Over time, Stern realized that his interests went beyond economic development and in 1987, after his retirement, he renamed the organization the Interactivity Foundation (IF).

IF grew from Stern's concern that a healthy democratic society should anticipate issues rather than lurch reactively from crisis to crisis. In his words:

> Wouldn't it be better if there were mechanisms that allowed leaders to examine alternative approaches before decisions absolutely had to be made? Wouldn't it be better if leaders had the advantage of deliberation on possibilities from both experts and those of practical bent? Wouldn't there be

some benefit in combining the reflections of wise advisers with ideas that tapped citizen understandings of what choices should be made? (quoted in Hopkinson, 2010, p. 4)

After experimenting with these questions, Stern relaunched IF in 2002 as an operating foundation that would conduct its own projects. He brought on a small, full-time staff of fellows who helped codevelop IF's discussion process and who would go on to conduct citizen discussion projects to generate contrasting policy possibilities for complex areas of public concern. IF's motivation is to engage more citizens in thinking imaginatively and expansively about policy possibilities for a healthy democratic society. After years of experimentation, IF has developed a process that it employs today in community and classroom discussions.

The IF Process

IF discussion projects are sustained, exploratory discussions with expert and generalist panels. Participants in these panels come together as thinking groups to explore a particular area of concern (a *thinking group* explores what could be, whereas a *study group* investigates what is or has been the case). Projects have included topics such as climate change, food, higher education, human migration, freshwater, cities and towns, childhood, art, and agriculture. An IF fellow manages the project, which includes recruiting participants, facilitating discussions to help the participants explore different ways to frame the core concerns and questions surrounding the topic, and writing up the results of these discussions. The end product is an array of policy possibilities that represents different ways to frame possible societal choices. These possibilities are captured in the form of citizen discussion guides—guides generated by citizens and offered to other citizens as a way to expand their thinking about the possibilities for an area of public concern. The guides are always anticipatory, not reactive. They encourage discussion groups to coimagine the "future of . . ." an area of concern rather than problem-solve current aspects of the topic. The guides, which are made available free of charge in print or in electronic format via IF's website, do not make specific recommendations. Their aim is to encourage people to develop their own thinking by considering more possibilities than they might otherwise. Core principles within this discussion process include the concepts and practices of (a) sanctuary, (b) sustained engagement, (c) collaboration by difference, and (d) facilitation.

Internally, the small-group discussions are sometimes described as *sanctuary discussions*. *Sanctuary* means a space protected from the rush toward evaluation and decision-making, protected from the need for achieving social approval (e.g., judgments about what might be politically or economically feasible), and protected from the constraints of the status quo or past conventions. Accordingly, participants in discussion projects tend to remain anonymous and are never connected with a particular idea that is published in the discussion guide. It does take time for participants to feel comfortable with sharing ideas that may push the boundaries of conventional thinking. This requires an unhurried approach that is developed through the practice of sustained engagement.

Sustained dialogue over a series of discussion events, generally once a month over the course of a year, creates a space for unearthing and interrogating presuppositions, for exploring divergent perspectives, and for generating alternative possibilities that might flow from these divergent presuppositions and perspectives. Sustained discussions with the same thinking group also build trust, which is essential for genuine collaboration. Of course, participating in such a sustained discussion project may be a luxury that many everyday citizens cannot afford. To encourage participation by people who might otherwise be excluded, IF supports transportation, provides childcare, and offers a modest honorarium to the participants of sustained discussion projects. IF has also experimented with videoconferencing and other online discussions to address geographic limitations and transportation barriers.

The IF discussion process is animated by the notion of *collaboration by difference*—collaboration not for the sake of reaching consensus or narrowing to a preferred solution but collaboration intended to expand the range of diverse perspectives and possibilities under consideration (Davidson, 2011). IF discussions aim to be additive and generative rather than reductive. They also are intended to flow in an organic, nonlinear manner. To ensure interactivity and robust participation of all the participants, the discussion groups typically include roughly 6 to 10 people. Ideally, the IF process focuses on helping a group develop and expand its thinking over time. It is usually intended for more than stand-alone or one-off discussions, but it can be adapted to shorter uses. Typically, IF discussions flow progressively through stages of exploring alternative ways to frame core questions and concerns, developing contrasting possible responses to those questions, and then testing and revising those possible responses through imaginative exploration. IF discussion guides are designed to walk participants through this process without a professional facilitator; however, facilitation (formal or informal) is still an important aspect of a successful IF discussion.

Facilitation plays a key role in service of an IF discussion group, a role that takes practice and intentional focus. Facilitators in the IF process should be active, but neutral, embodying what Martín Carcasson refers to as "passionate impartiality" (Sprain & Carcasson, 2013). Facilitators bring everyone into the discussion, manage the discussion flow, and challenge the group to develop overlooked or alternative perspectives, but they do not steer the discussion to a predetermined destination. They take notes, typically while standing at a flipchart easel, to capture the thinking of the group, enabling the participants to see and review the statements. For extended series of discussions, facilitators write up these notes as thematic summaries to help the group to organize its thinking and to move forward over time. The shared notes become an important form of legacy documentation for the group, helping the group to retain insights and develop ideas cumulatively. This practice can be adapted to classroom settings by having students rotate as facilitators.

IF discussions tend to follow a few basic guidelines that are often personalized by IF facilitators to best communicate with their participants. Some of these overlapping guidelines include the following:

- *Practice creative agreement* ("Yes—and . . ."). Build on ideas rather than critiquing them as they emerge. Practice generosity of spirit, keeping in mind that these are not zero-sum debates. Engage with the content of ideas, not the persons who introduce them.
- *Foster divergence* ("Be yourself—and an other"). Participants should share their own perspectives *and* also use their imaginations to introduce other perspectives (Ask, "Who's missing from this discussion?").
- *Be bold and go deep.* Bring up ideas regardless of whether they might meet approval or whether they are fully formed. Try to uncover root issues and underlying assumptions. Participants should help each other flesh out fragmentary ideas and explore interconnections among different ideas.
- *Establish a sense of "sanctuary" as a protected space for exploratory discussion.* Protect the discussions from the rush to decision-making, from the need for immediate social approval, and from the constraints of current or past approaches. Because innovative possibilities often break with convention, it's important not to rule out ideas prematurely.

IF in Higher Education

The IF process is designed to encourage brave exploration of a complex topic, what is often called a wicked problem. The IF process is most useful for those interested in exploring a wide range of possibilities—even possibilities that may seem unlikely or disagreeable to one or more participants. This may frustrate anyone who expects the discussions to lead directly to action. Still, the consideration of unusual or disagreeable possibilities can be helpful for clarifying values surrounding a topic, regardless of whether the participants would ever promote a given possibility or set of possibilities. The overall purpose is to exercise imaginative collaboration to promote a more robust democratic society of engaged citizens. The IF process and discussion guides have been most commonly used in two settings: community discussions (Gundersen & Lea, 2013) and education activities. This chapter focuses on IF's work in higher education.

Since 2006, IF has worked with more than 50 faculty members around the United States (and some international faculty members) through a series of summer institutes and workshops. These training events have focused on introducing faculty members to the discussion process and supporting their efforts to design courses that integrate this process. IF has also worked with dozens of individual faculty members and departmental programs on a case-by-case basis and in a variety of institutions ranging from large research institutions, such as Arizona State University, Kansas State University, and the University of Alabama at Birmingham, to smaller, liberal arts colleges such as Dartmouth and Haverford. As the focus is more about process than specific content, IF has been able to collaborate with faculty partners in a wide range of academic disciplines, curricular and cocurricular circumstances, and with online or in-person delivery. IF's interest in the curricular use of the discussion process is twofold—as a way to enhance student learning of course content and as a way for students to learn essential twenty-first-century communication, interpersonal, and civic skills.

WISe 101: A First-Year Experience at Wesleyan College

One specific institution where the IF process has taken root is Wesleyan College, a small liberal arts college for women in Macon, Georgia. IF worked with a team of faculty partners and convened an on-campus summer institute in 2012 to help with Wesleyan's redesign of their mandatory first-year seminar. This course, WISe 101, is team-taught from a common syllabus by faculty from each academic division. The original Wesleyan summer institute included all 12 faculty who would teach the course over a 2-year rotation. This began a project of collaboration between IF and Wesleyan College that continues today. The fall 2019 semester will mark the eighth iteration of the seminar, with approximately 125 students enrolled per year.

There are several motivations for integrating IF discussions into a first-year seminar. The first-year seminar at Wesleyan, as elsewhere, targets the development of students' communication and critical thinking skills. By learning how to facilitate and participate in generative discussions surrounding the course content, students engage practical oral communication skills like active listening, exploring dissent or disagreement in a positive manner, resolving conflict within a group, and communicating across cultures. Critical thinking is engaged by the discussion process's emphasis on creative or divergent thinking, exploring multiple ways to frame issues, and summarizing major points from each discussion. Having students work in discussion teams, and having faculty coach them through the process, encourages students to see education as a collaborative process of constructing meaning rather than a process of rote learning. To have students start their college experience facilitating discussion teams conveys a sense of students' ownership of their learning. Ultimately, embedding the practice of these skills in a first-year experience creates an important building block for students' growth beyond the first year—and across other aspects of campus life.

The standing format for the seminar is a mix of common sessions (the entire first-year class) and individual class sessions (course sections of roughly 18 students). Faculty modified this structure to integrate the IF process into one-third of the class time. In a Monday-Wednesday-Friday schedule, Fridays are devoted to student-facilitated discussions ("IF Fridays"). The organizing thematic question for the course is "What does it mean to be part of an academic community?" Students use their weekly small-group discussions to explore different aspects of this theme through the lens of the week's texts and common sessions.

At the beginning of the semester, instructors divide their course sections into three groups and set up a rotating schedule of student facilitators. Faculty members aim to create balanced and diverse groups in terms of students' academic records, comfort with speaking or leading in class, race, ethnicity, and country of origin (Wesleyan has a relatively high percentage of international students). Instructors introduce and demonstrate the basic guidelines for IF discussions, including having a strong but neutral facilitator, having everyone participate, practicing creative agreement, seeking divergent perspectives, thinking boldly and deeply, and embodying a spirit of sanctuary. Student discussion teams start by generating a group contract that lists agreements to govern their team's behavior. These agreements address things such as timely attendance, coming prepared to facilitate and/or participate, being respectful and supportive of divergent points of view, helping each other explore the class topics, and so on.

Faculty use the initial common session to introduce students to the IF discussion process and explain how they will be using it. Additionally, the faculty use their individual class sessions to model facilitation practices. In each 50-minute "IF Friday," there are roughly 5 minutes of introductory whole-group discussion and setup, followed by roughly 30 minutes for the student discussion teams. This allows time for a whole-group closing debriefing discussion. In the small-group sessions, students are responsible for facilitating their own discussions. The role of facilitator rotates so that each student facilitates at least twice over the course of the semester. Discussion topics vary depending on the week's texts and common sessions. At the end of the semester each IF discussion team shares a group project presenting different ways to answer the question of what it means to be part of a thriving academic community.

Faculty use a combination of pre- and postfacilitation meetings with students to coach the facilitation process. In weekly prefacilitation meetings, instructors meet with their class's facilitators as a group. Facilitators are responsible for developing a facilitation plan to sustain a collaborative exploration of divergent perspectives on the week's topics. Meeting as a group enables the facilitators to learn from each other's ideas (over time the students accumulated a shared toolkit of discussion activities). Faculty use these prefacilitation meetings to offer advance guidance. During the actual small-group discussions, the facilitators introduce activities and pose questions to promote an in-depth discussion. The discussion teams typically meet at different corners of large classrooms. Faculty observe the teams from a central location and, at times, offer coaching advice if a group seems at an impasse. Faculty take notes on the facilitator's, and group's, performance in order to provide targeted feedback. The facilitators record the comments of group members on flipchart paper, posting notes on the wall as they proceed. After the discussion, the facilitator sends summary notes to group members and the instructor. Students schedule one-on-one postfacilitation debriefings with the instructor. These debriefing sessions provide an opportunity for instructors to give targeted feedback to help students with their facilitation skills. Students complete a self-evaluation sheet of their facilitation. During the postfacilitation meeting they discuss what worked well in the facilitation and what areas to target for future improvement. Each discussion team also completes an evaluation of how well members performed as a group.

The faculty member's role in the IF process is more as a coach than as a dispenser of knowledge. Faculty see their roles as helping students to be successful in their facilitation of, and participation in, collaborative discussions that are geared toward expanding students' thinking about the course topics. As one faculty member commented:

As someone who feels a constant need to be lecturing and in control of class discussions, I went in very dubious that the IF sessions would be effective. I can't stress enough how impressed I was by my students' response to the IF process on a variety of fronts. . . . IF Fridays may feel odd to new faculty, as one stands in the center of the room and quietly observes and records what's happening in each of the three small discussion groups—it's definitely the antithesis of lecture-mode. The observation process requires focused attention and a careful balance of positive reinforcement that doesn't distract or discourage the student facilitating the discussion. What surprised me the most was how little I needed to intercede and keep students on task. In fact, the students loved the IF process. (Prudhomme, 2012, p. 2)

Wesleyan faculty took a number of different approaches toward assessing the impact of this pedagogical intervention. Assessment has most recently focused on faculty and student ratings of skill development. Student and faculty ratings concurred that students were improving on skills specific to the IF process, including thinking of multiple ways to frame issues, summarize major points, and communicate effectively across cultures. Students reported that small groups allowed them to discuss topics that would be less comfortable if done in front of the whole class. They indicated that they appreciate diversity and that learning about their classmates' diverse perspectives is useful for their learning experience. Faculty ratings also showed improvements of students' thinking divergently, facilitating team contributions, interacting cross-culturally, and encouraging a collaborative environment, among other IF-related skills. Faculty also report that students stay on task and explore disagreements more productively than in other class discussions they have experienced. Students similarly reported that they now looked forward to hearing divergent points of view, whereas previously they would have simply tried to refute opposing points of view. They also report that the discussion process has spread throughout the culture of the school. Overall the WISe-IF collaboration has been welcomed as having a positive impact on the Wesleyan student experience.

From that first-year course the use of the discussion process has expanded across campus. Instructors report using variations on the process in their other courses, which is made easier by the fact that they can build on the students' background from the first-year experience. Faculty and students use the IF dialogue methods outside of classroom educational contexts, including in faculty meetings and within student organizations. The discussion process has become part of the civic infrastructure of the college.

One specific outgrowth is Wesleyan's program of Diversity and Inclusion Discussions (DID). In response to incidents of hate speech in 2016, a group of students proposed using their facilitation skills to convene peer-to-peer discussions around the themes of diversity and inclusion. With IF's support, the faculty diversity liaison and the assistant dean of students for diversity and inclusion launched DID. In this program, which will be in its fourth year in the fall of 2019, students work in pairs to recruit student participants for a short series of small-group exploratory dialogues around the theme of making the campus more welcoming of diversity. The student facilitators also facilitate discussions with faculty and staff where they present the possibilities for campus inclusion that emerged from the student dialogues.

Key Observations, Strengths, and Challenges

IF has worked with faculty members at more than 40 institutions to develop the pedagogical use of the IF discussion process. IF continues to work with a number of colleges and universities to support curricular (in-person and online) and cocurricular exploratory discussion spaces. The approach is adaptable to all disciplines as long as the course and discussion opportunity lend themselves to the exploration of diverse perspectives and the development of multiple alternative frameworks for approaching the topic.

Partnerships with colleges and universities are not without their own challenges. For example, faculty need to have buy-in and support to do this work well. It does not work well with reluctant instructors or those resistant to pedagogical experimentation. It works best where educators are rewarded for pedagogical development and innovation. Incentives for teaching performance have often been neglected in higher education and this well-known institutional problem can dampen the willingness or ability of faculty to teach with student-facilitated discussions. One factor that helped expand the impact of the IF discussion process at Wesleyan was the high level of support by the administration.

Using this pedagogical intervention is labor intensive, especially early in the process. Many instructors report that the upfront labor of incorporating student facilitation into the classroom, whether for in-person or online courses, is an investment that pays off. Faculty members consistently report expanding their use of the process to other courses, which indicates their perception of its value. Like other flipped-class formats, instructors are eventually able to take a step back and observe the students' discussions and meta-discussions unfold. At this point, faculty are no longer the drivers of daily discursive interactions. Faculty report that this is one of the strengths of using student-facilitated dialogues in the classroom. As described by a faculty member using the IF process in an online course:

> I have been teaching online courses for several years, and I have long felt the weight of having to drive discussion and sometimes to "chase" students to get them to participate, but I didn't feel that way at all this summer. I wouldn't say that I had less work to do, but my work was different; rather than me feeling responsible for all aspects of the discussion, I could observe my students, evaluate them, and then reflect on their work and their progress. (Hartman, 2014, p. 2)

Assessment is always a key challenge for pedagogical interventions. A plausible case can be made that the use of student-facilitated discussions could positively impact beliefs and attitudes associated with enhanced student learning. It is difficult, however, to trace any such positive effects from one specific intervention in a one-semester course. Instructor and student ratings of specific skills related to the IF discussion process do show evidence of positive skill development, yet there will always be questions about interrater reliability. Finding ways to better demonstrate the positive impacts of the IF discussion process in educational settings remains a key challenge to communicating the value of this particular pedagogical intervention to likely adopters. This focus on measuring skill development could prove to be an important pathway for demonstrating growing levels of students' competency in facilitation and civil discourse skills. Providing a means for students to attest their discursive competencies, such as through certificate programs or badging, could encourage their repeat engagement with facilitation and discussion experiences and could help them to communicate their growing levels of mastery for outside audiences, such as future employers.

The use of the IF discussion process in the classroom can call into question epistemological assumptions in a way that could make some educators and students uncomfortable. For the process to work well, faculty and students have to be open to discovery learning. Students cocreate content through their discussions rather than receiving the content through faculty lectures. To some, this sort of learning-by-doing and learning-by-discussing may not seem like the serious business of higher education. It could be perceived by students as being a "light" course. These perceptions, however, are a challenge for all pedagogical approaches that attempt to decenter traditional notions of knowledge and understanding. Faculty who have used the process report favorably about the seriousness of purpose in their students' discussions. They also report that initial concerns about content coverage were not warranted, because students find their way to the core of the course content through discovery learning.

Finally, for both faculty and students, it takes time and direct experience to learn how to do this well. People tend to say they "get it" before they really do—often because they think facilitation is synonymous with leading a discussion or they think an exploratory discussion is an "anything goes" type of experience. This is clearly untrue. Beyond training services, IF also provides facilitation guidelines, prediscussion worksheets, facilitation evaluation rubrics, student-evaluation surveys, and postdiscussion debriefing exercises to help counter these assumptions. These are all available via request or for free download on the IF website.

Conclusion

IF is an evolving organization dedicated to improving the health of democracy through exploratory discussion. Although these discussions can take many forms, they tend to be facilitated, small-group, sustained, and characterized by expanding rather than foreclosing possibilities. Through collaboration by difference, participants seek out divergent ideas and surround any particular area of concern with bold, anticipatory, and imaginative thinking. IF began with a small group of fellows developing this process and has since expanded to a growing community of practitioners. IF is also expanding into classroom experiences for the purpose of employing students as facilitators and generators of content. The hope is that this helps to educate students in twenty-first-century civic skills.

As described in this chapter, the core element to the success of the Wesleyan College experience with the IF process is the fostering of a community of practice that could provide mutual support for the use of facilitated small-group discussions in instructional and other campus settings. By training a group of interested instructors at one campus, the IF summer institute enabled those instructors to continue to confer and consult with each other after the initial training. To create this opportunity, it was beneficial to have the support of respected advocates among the faculty, people who had experienced the IF process and experimented with it in their individual courses. Developing a critical mass of support among a group of faculty members was essential. This in turn helped generate support from the administration, who recognized the value of this particular pedagogical innovation. Similarly, students at Wesleyan were able to build on their shared experience of the discussion process through the common first-year experience. The development of a community of practice at Wesleyan has meant that faculty and students feel empowered to continue to innovate with their discursive skills, both inside and outside of the classroom. Faculty and students report how the spirit of exploratory dialogues, of the IF discussion process, now permeates the culture of the college. A key consideration we are left with is how this model, with a specific orientation toward fostering a community of practice, could extend to other colleges and universities.

References

Davidson, C. N. (2011). *Now you see it: How technology and brain science will transform schools and business for the 21st century.* New York, NY: Penguin Books.

Gundersen, A. G., & Lea, S. G. (2013). *Let's talk politics: Restoring civility through exploratory discussion.* Parkersburg, WV: Interactivity Foundation.

Hartman, S. W. (2014). *Online discussion guidebook summer project.* Unpublished internal report, Interactivity Foundation, Parkersburg, WV (not publicly available for download).

Hopkinson, N. (2010). *Julius "Jay" Stern: A biography.* Parkersburg, WV: Interactivity Foundation.

Prudhomme, J. (2012). *WISe-IT faculty advice to future teachers.* Unpublished internal report, Interactivity Foundation, Parkersburg, WV (not publicly available for download).

Sprain, L., & Carcasson, M. (2013). Democratic engagement through the ethic of passionate impartiality. *Tamara: Journal for Critical Organization Inquiry, 11*(4), 13–26.

PART THREE

DIALOGUE AND DELIBERATION IN THE CURRICULUM

12

THE STUDENT AS LOCAL DELIBERATIVE CATALYST

The CSU Center for Public Deliberation

Martín Carcasson

The Colorado State University Center for Public Deliberation (CPD) was founded in 2006 and serves as an impartial resource for the Northern Colorado community. It is based on the idea that democratic living requires high-quality communication to function well. Unfortunately, our communities rarely experience such communication. Indeed, the opposite—polarized and hyperpartisan communication patterns that reward poor arguments; punish stronger ones; and foster outrage, cynicism, and distrust in each other and our institutions—is much more likely to occur naturally. The CPD is thus an ongoing experiment focused on the idea of what happens when a local institution focuses all its time, energy, and expertise on elevating the conversation rather than trying to win arguments.

This chapter presents the CPD as a model for a campus-based deliberative center. From the beginning, the goal was for the CPD to be replicated, and over the last 12 years—with a considerable assist from the Kettering Foundation's Centers for Public Life program—that has become a reality several times (i.e., similar centers have been developed at the University of Houston-Downtown, James Madison University, University of Iowa, Washington State University Vancouver, St. Edward's University, University of Utah, and Baylor University). I continue to believe that every college and university in the country should host and support an organization similar to the CPD and argue that as more of these centers are established, they will continue to have a profound impact on the quality of our local communities, and ultimately our national political culture.

This chapter proceeds in three parts. First, I review the founding of the CPD and its overall principles and practices. Second, I discuss our key successes and challenges. Third, I conclude this chapter with a focus on recommendations and resources for other campuses.

General Model, Principles, and Practices

I developed the CPD based on my experiences as a researcher and teacher of rhetorical studies and argumentation (Carcasson, 2017). My research has always focused on how we talk about difficult issues in the United States and the nexus of expertise and democracy, but as I finished graduate school I had already grown weary of analyzing national politics, precisely because the system seemed almost unredeemable. As I was completing a research project on President Clinton's 1997 National Conversation on Race (Carcasson & Rice, 1999), I was exposed to materials that the administration had developed and that were designed to help people have difficult conversations on race. They introduced me to dialogue and deliberation as key interactive communication technologies, quite distinct from the debate my work had focused on up until that point. I immediately saw the value of these new tools in helping us address difficult issues and began to study them more closely by connecting with organizations such as the National Issues Forums, the National Coalition for Dialogue and Deliberation (NCDD), and the Deliberative Democracy Consortium. When I was hired by CSU in 2003, my work shifted more directly from a national scope to a local one and from being a critic to being a *pracademic* (i.e., a practitioner and academic hybrid). I first transformed my classes to focus on equipping students with the skills related to dialogue and deliberation, alongside argumentation and debate. After seeing the positive impact of those skill sets, the CPD became the next critical step—working to provide genuine dialogue and deliberation opportunities in our local community.

From the beginning, the CPD has been exceedingly student-centric yet community-focused. Each semester, the CPD student associate program brings in around 15 undergraduate students for a yearlong curricular experience. They take a 3-credit-hour class their first semester—a course entitled Applied Deliberative Techniques—that trains them as small-group deliberative facilitators and note-takers. They then all return for a second semester and complete at least a one-hour practicum. The second semester can be repeated for credit, which many students take advantage of, and ensures that we can begin each semester with a core group of experienced students. The student facilitators assist with numerous events in the community, partnering with the city, county, school district, and a wide variety of community organizations. Processes are designed by connected faculty and graduate students, often with assistance from more experienced students. We use the National Issues Forums model as our base training process, but then rely on a broad range of deliberative and dialogic practices and techniques, depending on the issue and environment. Process tools such as NCDD's streams of engagement (Heierbacher, 2010), the *Deliberative Democracy Handbook* (Gastil & Levine, 2005), and *The Change Handbook* (Holman, Devane, & Cady, 2007) have been critical staples in our work.

With the students, we can essentially take a crowd of 100 participants who arrive to discuss a difficult issue, and rather than have them sit and listen to a panel of experts or walk up to a microphone one at a time and talk past each other, we can transform them into 15 small groups of 6 to 8. The student facilitators—combined with various other key deliberative components such as naming and framing the issue well, establishing ground rules, relying on small groups, utilizing quality background material and processes designed to support deliberation, and so on—create genuine opportunities for the kind of deliberative conversations our communities must have to thrive. Student note-takers capture the insights from these discussions to share with our partners and fuel our research programs.

The CPD student associate program was the first of its kind in the nation in terms of having dedicated coursework focused on providing students facilitation training in deliberative techniques to support local projects. The decision to rely on students was essentially a necessity given my teaching responsibilities at CSU (half my appointment); any other model would have stretched me too thin, allowing too little dedicated time to the CPD. With time, we have come to realize relying on students worked better than ever anticipated. Facilitation is clearly a self-reflective practice, and having a year of time in class for training, preparing for events, and reflecting on their experiences has led to particularly high-quality facilitation. Overwhelmingly, the students have connected to the work passionately, finding it particularly hopeful and pragmatic in a political culture that is often neither.

In many ways, the CPD represents the epitome of a modern land-grant university engagement program. It naturally cuts across the university's teaching, research, and service responsibilities, with each positively complementing the others. Indeed, the CPD allows the connected faculty and graduate students to constantly bounce back and forth between theory and practice in ways that are critical for the growth of the young interdisciplinary field of deliberative engagement. The particular form of engagement is also a strong fit for current community needs, considering the increasing polarization, partisanship, and erosion of trust in expertise and institutions

(Carcasson, in press; Kavanaugh & Rich, 2018). Deliberative engagement goes beyond the traditional university engagement strategy of providing expert answers to a community and focuses more on providing capacity for the community to come together to work productively through tough issues and ultimately cocreate potential collaborative actions, a process we have termed *deliberative inquiry* (Carcasson & Sprain, 2016). When done well, deliberative inquiry also works to negotiate the ongoing tensions between democracy/inclusion and expertise/hierarchy. Many of our deliberative events explicitly work to combine expert and public voices in productive ways, which is a role universities should play much more often and explicitly than they do.

Key Successes and Challenges

The clearest success derived from the CPD experience in its first 12 years involves its positive reception in the community. It has been obvious that the community in many ways was yearning for authentic engagement, and the CPD served a role in helping fill that void. We learned that it is possible for people to not only have better conversations on tough issues but also enjoy them. The CPD grew faster than designed or expected, because with each event we hosted, the community responded by asking us to assist with others. Despite our expectations for people to challenge their assumptions and work through difficult discussions, it became apparent that participants saw the value of engaging in this way and wanted more. We grew quickly as key local institutions—the school district, city government, United Way, the local newspaper, and so on—also saw the value of deeper engagement and provided us steady, meaningful projects.

Our projects and partners have varied greatly over the years. At times, we are approached by partners with a broad issue and a goal of engaging the public, but little else. They have come to trust us to design the project, develop the materials, run the event, and then share the results. Other times, our partners are more in control of various aspects, but rely on us as process consultants reacting to their plans and then assisting them the day of the event with our facilitators. For most of the history of the CPD, we have been able, due to some funding support from the university and a local philanthropic organization, to complete the projects as a public service. As we have grown and honed the quality and professional nature of the work, however, we are moving now to more of a fee-for-service model for some of our work that will allow us to cover the costs of dedicated staff to support the work.

Because of the growing demand, we have also shifted from being an organization that primarily runs individual events to an organization that serves as a key catalyst and capacity builder in an evolving local deliberative system (Parkinson & Mansbridge, 2012). Although the events are still the most visible and tangible aspect of our work, our efforts before and after events working to build capacity in numerous local institutions have become essential. We began to offer workshops on deliberative engagement for community leaders and now serve on various steering committees and advisory boards. Our mission more clearly has become building capacity for a robust community that relies on quality engagement (Carcasson, 2009). Our internal capacity grew as well. In our 12 years, we have added additional faculty with time dedicated to the CPD; developed a deliberative track to our MA program; and in the summer of 2017, hired a full-time program director.

The biggest challenges remain the amount of time necessary to do the work well and the funds necessary to support that time. Elevating the quality of a community conversation is a never-ending task. Working to balance the various calls and challenges to our work—to engage representative and inclusive audiences, to provide quality data and address misinformation, to inform while primarily providing opportunities for voice—all while building and maintaining a reputation for impartiality and fairness, is an ongoing challenge. Yet it is a challenge that is interesting, motivating, and rewarding.

Recommendations for Other Campuses

The CPD was formed based on the recognition that democracy requires high-quality communication. Our experiences have clearly supported the value and potential of campus-based centers to build capacity for the kinds of conversations our communities need to thrive, and to provide a viable alternative to the worst impulses of our hyperpartisan political culture. We believe such centers provide a reciprocal win-win-win-win for the students, faculty, institution, and local community (Carcasson, 2014). Most importantly, we see the power of providing students deep and meaningful opportunities to engage in democratic practices while at the same time providing the community with critical capacity.

In considering recommendations for institutions considering following the model, we stress the importance of connecting the work to all three of the pillars of higher education: teaching, research, and service. This insight was originally derived from an analysis of institutional histories of centers connected to the National Issues Forums (Carcasson, 2008), and the CPD experience lends further support to that insight. Attempting to do this work simply through a service lens provides too little time and support, while also missing the significant pedagogical and research benefits. Having a dedicated curriculum provides many more hours (from both faculty and students); likely leads to sustainability (programs may continue after founders leave); and, most importantly, provides an exceedingly valuable pedagogical experience to students (Shaffer, Longo, Manosevitch, & Thomas, 2017). Producing published research works to satisfy expectations and typical incentive structures for faculty, while also improving the practice and expanding its stature academically.

The most significant challenge for universities developing deliberative programs is tied to the likelihood that demand for the work will be overwhelming. The good news is there is a growing network of support and examples to follow. Since 2011, the Kettering Foundation's Centers for Public Life program has provided training for institutions to develop centers like the CPD (I have been on the faculty/mentor team since its inception). Institutions in a wide variety of situations have participated in the program, from established campus institutions with extensive budgets to individuals with only an initial idea to build something new. In these efforts, it has been my experience that in the dialogue and deliberative field, people are most often more than willing to share resources and their time to help others.[1] As more and more colleges and universities develop these programs and share experiences, the easier it will be for new programs to be established and learn and contribute to the growing community of practice.

References

Carcasson, M. (2008). *Democracy's hubs: College and university centers as platforms for deliberative practice* (Research report). Dayton, OH: Kettering Foundation.

Carcasson, M. (2009). *Beginning with the end in mind: A call for purpose-driven deliberative practice* (Occasional Paper No. 2, Center for Advances in Public Engagement, Public Agenda). Retrieved from https://www.publicagenda.org/files/PA_CAPE_Paper2_Beginning_SinglePgs_Rev.pdf

Carcasson, M. (2014). The critical role of local centers and institutes in advancing deliberative democracy. *Journal of Public Deliberation, 10*(1), 1–4. Retrieved from http://www.publicdeliberation.net/jpd/vol10/iss1/art11

---

1. NCDD's website (www.ncdd.org) is a particularly useful resource that includes introductions to the field and a broad selection of tools, training guides, and videos related to a wide variety of deliberation and dialogue practices.

Carcasson, M. (2017). Engaging students in our democracy: Lessons from the CSU Center for Public Deliberation and its student associate program. In I. Marin & R. Minor (Eds.), *Beyond politics as usual: Paths for engaging college students in politics* (pp. 171–187). Dayton, OH: Kettering Foundation.

Carcasson, M. (in press). From crisis to opportunity: Rethinking the civic role of universities in the face of wicked problems, hyper-partisanship, and truth decay. In W. V. Flores & K. S. Rogers (Eds.), *Democracy, civic engagement and citizenship in higher education*. Lanham, MD: Lexington Books.

Carcasson, M., & Rice, M. F. (1999). The promise and failure of President Clinton's Race Initiative of 1997–1998: A rhetorical perspective. *Rhetoric & Public Affairs, 2*, 243–274.

Carcasson, M., & Sprain, L. (2016). Beyond problem solving: Re-conceptualizing the work of public deliberation as deliberative inquiry. *Communication Theory, 26*, 41–63.

Gastil, J., & Levine, P. (Eds.). (2005). *The deliberative democracy handbook: Strategies for effective civic engagement in the 21st century*. San Francisco, CA: Jossey-Bass.

Heierbacher, S. (2010). *Resource guide on public engagement: National Coalition for Dialogue and Deliberation*. Retrieved from http://www.ncdd.org/files/NCDD2010_Resource_Guide.pdf

Holman, P., Devane, T., & Cady, S. (2007). *The change handbook: The definitive resource on today's best methods for engaging whole systems* (2nd ed.). San Francisco, CA: Berrett-Koehler.

Kavanaugh, J., & Rich, M. D. (2018). *Truth decay: An initial exploration of the diminishing role of facts and analysis in American public life*. Santa Monica, CA: Rand Corporation.

Parkinson, J., & Mansbridge, J. (Eds.). (2012). *Deliberative systems: Deliberative democracy at the large scale*. New York, NY: Cambridge University Press.

Shaffer, T., Longo, N., Manosevitch, I., & Thomas, M. S. (Eds.). (2017). *Deliberative pedagogy: Teaching and learning for democratic engagement*. Lansing, MI: Michigan State University Press.

13

DIALOGUE AS A TEACHING TOOL FOR DEMOCRATIZING HIGHER EDUCATION

The Simon Fraser University Semester in Dialogue

Janet Moore and Mark L. Winston

Dialogue changed my life. Simple as that.
—SFU Semester in Dialogue student

The Simon Fraser University (SFU) Semester in Dialogue is a one-semester, full-time program designed to inspire students with a sense of civic responsibility and encourage their passion for improving society. The semester is the only undergraduate program at SFU outside of our traditional department and faculty administrative structure, an unusual position for any university teaching program. This chapter is a description of the program, its history, context, and a brief outline of the experience and practice of teaching dialogue in an immersive, semester-long format.

The Morris J. Wosk Centre for Dialogue was conceived at Simon Fraser University in 2000 to encourage public assembly through dialogue-based programs and conferences that address social issues. Mark L. Winston, a professor in biological sciences renowned for studies of bee biology (Winston, 2014), proposed that the new Centre for Dialogue find a way to put undergraduate students at the center of the initiative. Winston founded the Semester in Dialogue in 2002 to expand the boundaries of traditional education by creating deeper, experiential learning opportunities that provide students with the inspiration and tools necessary to become active citizens. He aimed to provide mentorship opportunities and expand the university's connections to the community. The semester began as a pilot project in the fall of 2002 and is thriving 17 years later, having completed 44 unique semester offerings.

Janet Moore joined the Semester in Dialogue team in 2006 to increase the size of the teaching team to offer three Semesters in Dialogue per year. Each term a team of between two and four faculty coteach on a timely and relevant topic that is connected directly to community issues. Course themes have included Semester in Energy Futures, Governance for the Twenty-First Century, Leading Social Change, Health Issues and Ethics, Sustainable Food Systems, and Decolonizing: Dialogues, Solidarities and Activism, among many others.

Each Semester in Dialogue program offers an original, interdisciplinary experience that bridges the university and the community, and also creates space for students to reflect on what they are doing and why it matters. Our approach to learning helps students to better define their personal and professional goals while gaining effective skills in communication and group work. We aim to inspire students with a sense of civic responsibility by encouraging their passion and commitment to discover who they want to be in the world.

Why Dialogue?

In our experience higher education is traditionally based on the premise that the person at the front of the room has the knowledge and expertise and the students are there to learn from the experts. The Semester in Dialogue aims to have students recognize their own expertise and transform how we share power in the classroom.

The program aims to inspire students to take responsibility for and contribute to the world around them; it also provides them ways to communicate and be effective change agents using tools such as dialogue. Dialogue involves collaborative listening and learning to discover meaning among diverse participants and is best conducted in the context of citizenship and civic engagement. Dialogue offers helpful ways to relate to one another and can lead to better quality outcomes than the adversarial, position-based discussions that typically characterize debate about complex issues. *Dialogue* in our classroom is defined as a form of respectful conversation, where deep listening, mutual understanding, collaborative process, and empathy act as alternatives to more adversarial approaches. Faculty members challenge students to let go of judgment and remain curious while exploring issues from a variety of perspectives.

The dialogue circle is a powerful way of being in a classroom. Spending time in a circle with the same group of people, without an agenda, goal, or preconceived outcome is a different way of being in a university classroom. The key to dialogue is telling stories about your experience in the world and remaining curious about other persons telling their stories. The typical dialogue with a thought leader lasts two and a half hours. We encourage students to suspend judgment, to listen deeply before preparing their response, and to remain curious. We ask big questions in dialogue: What matters most? How did you experience the conversation? What do you need? What does the group need? These kinds of questions elicit responses about personal identity, our connections and disconnections to community, and the nature of power and relationship in society.

The classroom culture is cocreated with the students, who are encouraged to "make" the course instead of "take" the course. Dialogue is a tool that inverts power in a room and takes away the typical "front of the room" expertise mentality that is baked into our systems. The classroom becomes a place to try new ways of being with students and each other and take risks. One factor that allows for more risk-taking in the program is that it exists outside the usually constricting department and faculty structure, allowing for ease of coteaching, interdisciplinary engagement of faculty, and easier departures from the rigid information-rich curricula that characterize most university degree requirements.

The following is a typical student description of dialogue from the 2010 cohort of Semester in Dialogue:

> Dialogue might include, as we've learned . . . some awkward pauses. These breaks in conversation provide room for more soft-spoken participants to take a moment to gather their thoughts and contribute, and also give the whole group time to reflect on what was said. Dialogue ultimately provides a space to bring together diverse viewpoints, explore these differences, and work towards understanding them better.

We focus on the pause in dialogue as a key learning outcome. In most groups there are those who are comfortable speaking and are always ready with a response. There are others who take a backseat and wait. There is an obvious moment in each term when those who are speaking too much learn to step back and the quieter students learn to step forward, motivated by individual feedback and debriefs with faculty as well as fellow students. As the group dynamic shifts through the semester, the students learn to "read the room" and pay more attention to the conversation (the content) as well as who has been speaking or is eager to contribute (the process). Students learn to see the conversation as it is happening and learn to reflect on both process and content.

We believe that dialogue-based learning can forge strong links between coursework and community practice as students connect theory from their discipline to the stories and experiences of the thought leaders, faculty, and students. By developing a blend of attitudes, expertise, and intellectual dexterity, students will be better suited to face the myriad and complex problems facing society today.

How Does Semester in Dialogue Work?

The Semester in Dialogue is a rigorous, intensive program, and students have a workload similar to that of a typical full-time semester. The semester is open to students from all departments and disciplines who have completed 45 credit hours. Twenty students from diverse areas of study are selected for each program. Our recruitment process seeks disciplinary and experiential breadth, with admission criteria that emphasises motivation, community engagement, and accomplishments in addition to academic achievement. A typical semester will have students who represent 10 to 15 departments. A recent program, for instance, included students from archaeology, anthropology, biology, communications, economics, English, history, kinesiology, molecular biology, psychology, sociology, and women's studies.

The semester is a full course load (15 credits at SFU) and is presented as a seamless unit, but for grading purposes credits are divided into three simultaneous courses: DIAL 390 (Art and Practice of Dialogue), 391 (Written Assignments), and 392 (Final Project). Students participate in the program Monday through Friday during normal working hours, either for formal class time or to work collaboratively with their peers. Students spend time after class hours on reading, research, and writing.

Faculty members curate unique learning experiences each semester, with themes emerging through consultations with colleagues, cofaculty, and community leaders. Thought leaders are not typically paid for their attendance in class unless they are underemployed. Both traditional university faculty and community experts participate together as teachers and dialogue facilitators. A typical week is spent engaging in dialogue with thought leaders, meeting with faculty, conducting research, going on field trips, and working on individual or group projects.

Three Tenets: Experiential Learning, Community Engagement, and Dialogue

Our educational framework is based on three tenets: experiential learning, community engagement, and dialogue-based communication. Experiential education emphasizes learning through doing. Students apply skills in the real world, reflect on the results, and use this learning to provide context for normally abstract theories. The Semester in Dialogue engages the community in a variety of ways, including partnering with community organizations on projects. Each semester convenes community dialogues to address pressing issues and hosts relevant community thought leaders in the classroom. Each semester students are invited to collectively choose a topic of broad public interest related to the course theme and organize a public dialogue. Students are responsible for planning and executing every aspect of this event, including hosting, facilitating, managing, and reporting.

Assignments

These tenets of experiential education, community engagement, and dialogue-based communication are designed to teach students a variety of communication, leadership, and group-work skills and are embodied in many unique assignments, which might include the following:

> *Growing the Story.* This assignment involves initially building a process for class work, then learning how to engage and facilitate dialogue. We begin the first day of class with a hypothetical scenario concerning a controversial issue, revisiting it a few weeks later. Students develop a skit over the next 24 hours and present it to the class and guests, demonstrating how the scenario might progress using the principles of dialogue covered in earlier sessions. This exercise encourages careful consideration of how diverse groups might interact through adversarial compared to dialogue-based processes.
>
> *Reflections.* Students may be asked to hand in written reflections throughout the semester (one page in length), approximately one reflection every two weeks. The key questions to consider are "What is going on here?" and "What stood out for you?"
>
> *750-Word Op-Ed Piece for a Newspaper.* The goal is to engage with a controversial issue in a manner that is probing, thought-provoking, and nondidactic, while inviting discussion. Students produce a 750-word article to submit as an opinion/commentary piece to a major Canadian newspaper. Typically 3 to 6 are published each semester in publications such as the *Globe and Mail* and *Vancouver Sun.*
>
> *Power in (the City, Health, etc.).* Students identify and interview the five people they would contact to assess how decisions for an ongoing community project are being made. For example, students in an urban-focused course might consider a new rapid transit line under consideration and interview the key stakeholders, including those supporting and opposed to the project. The objective is to determine "how the world works" (i.e., who wields real power on an issue and the dynamics of reaching consensus or conclusion).

"*I Disagree.*" Students frequently become so engrossed and successful at developing respect for the opinions of others that they can become uncomfortable disagreeing with each other. There is a fine line between the spirit of dialogue and a reluctance to engage with controversial material that might disrupt dialogic interactions. This exercise is designed to foster the ability to disagree without becoming adversarial or nasty. We pair students up and one expresses a controversial opinion. The second response beings with "I disagree," and continues on to express an opposing position but using language and an approach that encourage continued conversation rather than polarization.

Community-Based Project. Each semester's students conduct focused projects in small groups and/or as an entire class in collaboration with our designated community partner. Projects have included working to redesign a high-speed rail transit station that had been plagued by crime, a submission used by the city's planning department in presentations to the city council; rewriting the Canada Health Act while also producing a new provincial health budget that reflected values and priorities in the rewritten act; redesigning the alleyways of Vancouver for novel functions, such as playgrounds, gardens, and basketball courts (a project that won a city-wide competition); and developing and adjudicating a public art competition that led to a $60,000 installation.

Community-based projects can often have a major impact. For instance, students in the 2018 Semester in Dialogue at Vancouver City Hall as part of the CityStudio program spent the semester considering the question "What is needed for young people to stay and thrive in Vancouver?" (CityStudio, n.d.). The city is currently experiencing increasing costs of housing and living while wages are stagnant. Magnifying this challenge is the fact that student tuition is rising and student housing has long wait lists. As a response, the students wrote a manifesto for how young people need to be considered in all planning projects. They projected digital images of the manifesto onto the outside walls of Vancouver City Hall and presented it to the newly elected mayor and city councilors to promote student and youth engagement in the new CityPlan.

Individual Final Project. This final assignment asks each student to produce a 3,000-word manuscript or equivalent in another media, suitable for submission to a major public outlet on a topic relevant to the course. Students submit a proposal and pitch their ideas to the class. Examples include a video documentary, shown in a local film festival, that used billboards to explore the history and current issues in a Vancouver neighborhood; a quirky but fascinating piece on urban cemeteries that was published in a local newspaper; and a large oil painting titled *Dying Balance* about lost equilibrium and the increasingly destructive impact of human beings on our planet.

Our Impact

In total, 44 Semesters in Dialogue have graduated 819 students with more than 45 different faculty coteaching and 836 thought leaders engaged in the program (up to and including fall 2018). These semesters have had transformative impacts on students while at the same time creating rich partnerships with the wider community. Extensive student feedback indicates that alumni leave the program with new understandings of leadership, better communication skills, and a renewed sense of who they want to be in the world. Through hosting public dialogues and engaging with experts and community leaders, students develop networks of contacts and discover new interests and opportunities.

We conduct evaluations at the end of each semester, and student satisfaction has always been exceptionally high. In 2018, we conducted an in-depth survey after 15 years of the program to understand the long-term impacts. We were able to contact 550 of our alumni, and 131 responded (17% of all alumni and 24% of those we were able to contact). Overall, the survey confirmed that our alumni move quickly and successfully into their professional lives, with varied careers that hold in common a commitment to community engagement. It was also clear that the Semester in Dialogue's learning objectives have been successful, as our graduates overwhelmingly emphasized how they have incorporated what they learned into their personal and professional lives.

Students have found employment researching urban sprawl; coordinating communications for a nonpartisan youth voting project; managing projects in public consultation for clients such as the Greater Vancouver Regional District and the Ministry of Transportation; developing programs for Vancouver's Office of Cultural Affairs; writing for *Western Living* magazine, the *Vancouver Courier*, *Tyee*, and *Adbusters*; coordinating projects and liaising with members of the Citizens' Assembly for Electoral Reform; and soliciting community input for transit planning at the Vancouver region's transit provider TransLink, among many others. These outcomes were both indirect and direct, first through establishing a broader search image for jobs as the range of students' ambitions increased and second through the tangible network of contacts developed during each semester. Many others have gone on to professional schools in law, medicine, architecture, and urban planning, as well as entering diverse graduate programs.

Extensive student feedback indicates that students leave the Semester in Dialogue with new understandings of the role of dialogue in leadership and other aspects of their lives. As one student reflected:

I have sought to carry the spirit of dialogue into all my endeavours. The quote by William Isaacs, "Dialogue is a conversation with a center not sides," has stuck with me. It reminds me to listen with an open mind, and also speak in a way that moves conversation and understanding forward instead of trying to "win" or "persuade." I take this into my work mentoring students, and even into my personal life with family, partners, and friends.

Concluding Thoughts

The Semester in Dialogue is a unique program with a strong commitment to small class size, intensive mentorship, and the power of dialogue in a group setting. As instructors we don't believe that every course at the university needs to be run this way—yet it would be ideal to have an early semester and a final capstone semester that expose students to a more open and dialogic focus on community issues. We are also experimenting with new models, such as a seven-week summer Semester in Dialogue and supporting departments in creating their own versions of the program, beginning with the faculty of Communication, Art, and Technology.

Spending 13 weeks deeply immersed in dialogue with young people and a range of community thought leaders has incredible benefits for faculty and students alike. After teaching in the semester for well over a decade, we find ourselves still curious about and engaged with the experience and interests of our students. We have come to recognize, and celebrate, the truly innovate ideas that young people are capable of when we provide intensive opportunities for experiential learning, community engagement, and dialogue such as the Semester in Dialogue. It is our hope that colleges and universities offer more opportunities for intensive experiences with dialogue that connect undergraduate students who are full of creativity, hope, and optimism with the communities into which they will graduate.

References

CityStudio. (n.d.). Home page. Retrieved from https://www.citystudiovancouver.com/

Winston, M. L. (2014). *Bee time: Lessons from the hive*. Cambridge, MA: Harvard University Press.

14

CONVERSATIONS THAT MATTER

Spoma Jovanovic

Democracy depends on the active engagement of ordinary people to express themselves and share their stories of hopes and dreams as well as challenges and burdens to fashion a life with others that is fair and just for all. According to Danielle Allen (2014), "Our only chance to achieve collective happiness comes through extensive conversation punctuated here and there with votes, which will themselves, over time, in their imperfection, simply demand of us more talk" (p. 82).

Toward that end, colleges and universities play a pivotal role in providing instruction on democratic expression through conversation that promotes equality and freedom. With such preparation in the classroom, students become more confident and practiced to interact with new ideas and views gleaned from readings, peers' experiences, and faculty research (Hess & McAvoy, 2015). For some students, talking and arguing about political concerns of the day may even lead to plans for action and organizing others as their political identities are activated.

At the same time, students are poised to flex their civic muscles, though, a national report on incoming freshmen indicates students are also consumed with personal concerns of how to finance the increasing costs of college, as well as how to manage their higher incidences of depression, disabilities, and mental health concerns (Eaton et al., 2017). The stress, students say, is palpable.

Our contemporary world poses yet more obstacles for students to learn the skills and habits of face-to-face conversation, especially across differing ideologies and values. The rise of time spent on smartphones coupled with social media analytics often pushes users toward like-minded people. When students report spending nearly half their waking hours texting or posting messages via their smartphones, the opportunity may seem to exist for vigorous conversation, yet nearly half report they have never shared their opinions with others publicly (Eaton et al., 2017). This phenomenon parallels Robert Putnam's (2000) thesis in *Bowling Alone* that there is a decline in social capital, in which friends, families, and associations keep us connected to public life. Putnam's research documented the plummeting levels of political action and even bowling leagues in the second half of the twentieth century, in favor of solo acts of charity, service, and leisure events. College student life often mirrors this trend, despite technological advances, and thus students are left absent the skills to participate successfully with others in public concerns.

Putnam's insights, and those of others who have written about record levels of social, political, and economic inequalities, note that the fate of our democracy is tied to engagement, expressions of dissent, and collective action (Allen, 2014; Baldwin, 1963; Giroux, 2013). They offer a clarion call to college instructors and administrators everywhere. As we educate students in the twenty-first century, we need to be mindful of students' complex situations while making the case for the value of dialogue and deliberation as key pathways to lifelong learning and engagement in our democracy. From that foundation, the course Conversations That Matter was developed to ignite students' desire to participate in public conversations.

Dialogue and Deliberation—Central to Academic Studies and Activism

Contrary to the popular trope of apathy, students are, generally speaking, concerned about community and global concerns (Russell & Jovanovic, 2018). However, they may be unprepared to talk about and take action on issues that older and more experienced leaders have not been able to solve. Students who have not been invited into political conversations or instructed in how to welcome others into dialogue about critical issues that can generate positive results see plenty of examples of divisive speech from their elected leaders but few, if any, constructive deliberations. They have witnessed what Deborah Tannen (1998) describes, in her book of the same name, "the argument culture," where talk in the public sphere is dominated by words that are adversarial, aggressive, and warlike. Communication scholars Josina Makau and Debian Marty (2013) responded to Tannen's thesis with an antidote, namely that we need to exhibit compassion in dialogue to encourage communication "on our minds and in our hearts . . . to find out what matters to those who see things differently" (p. 64).

The task of college teaching is formidable when the goal is to teach students how to be active members of the community in ways that advance their intellectual capacities, collective compassion, and moral outrage for injustice. To move toward that goal, students need to explore local, regional, national, and international disputes. Students need to listen intently, ask thought-provoking questions, read plenty, participate in community programs, and explore just solutions to difficult matters.

Within this context, the course Conversations That Matter, offered through the Communication Studies Department at the University of North Carolina at Greensboro, was designed to offer students the knowledge and tools to engage with crucial public conversations that invite openness, inclusion, critical inquiry, and even forgiveness. In doing so, students practice how to express ethical values including responsibility, compassion, justice, and respect. A student who completed the course explained it this way in her final reflection paper: "This class forces you to look at the world with new eyes, wonder why a community is the way it is, and wonder if it could be better."

A Course That Models Democratic Action and Commitments

Throughout the semester, students read and discuss issues in the news to help make them interesting conversation partners and unafraid to ask questions about what matters in the world. They turn to the local newspaper and national publications like the *New York Times* to enter the public sphere, and they investigate other topics of interest, aided by university librarians on how to vet resources for credibility. The students also study and synthesize texts on dialogue and deliberation to consider—for instance, how various facilitation instruments including sticks, bells, questions, and dramatic impressions can be useful tools in conversation (Landreman, 2013; Makau & Marty, 2013). The students attend public meetings on campus and in the community to see firsthand and then analyze what meeting models are used to tap into the pulse and passion of the community. Research skills are another component of the course. Students explore the various standpoints on a contemporary topic that does not suggest easy solutions. Finally, students facilitate conversations, based on their research, that keep people on all sides of the issue talking together for the purpose of organizing for action.

Conversations That Matter follows James Baldwin's (1963) challenge that education is a moral endeavor to teach students how to change the world. Speaking up is central to that proposition, as self-confidence, to enter into or start a conversation that can prompt changes for a more just world

(Jovanovic, 2013). During the course, students reflect in weekly writing assignments, as well as verbally, on what difficult conversations are necessary, why, and for what purpose. Critically considering these questions encourages students to think deeply about their speaking choices, such as framing information in ways that invite people into conversation or purposely being either vague or crystal clear in articulating a position in order to encourage different responses (Palmerton, 1992).

By the end of the semester, students will have participated in a dozen or more critical conversations in class and in the community. They consider the benefits and the drawbacks of their initial and (sometimes different) final positions on such topics as gender and racial equality, human trafficking, education funding, and media impacts. As they consider the different views on transparency in government or criminal justice matters, they also consider options in inevitable decision-making about funding and programming, as well as the priority those issues should hold in balance with other concerns. By the end of the semester, students see more than problems in their community, of which there are many. The goal is for students to see hope in the dialogues and deliberations they have experienced to consider potential ways forward in addressing the real, day-to-day problems we encounter in public life. One student, reluctant to speak in class at first, finished the course standing up and sharing with classmates, "Why wouldn't we engage in community conversations? I mean the worst-case scenario is that we become more knowledgeable."

The course leaves room, as all courses committed to democracy must, for students to shape and refine its trajectory. For instance, in one iteration of the course, students learned about pop-up civic spaces (Cioffi, 2015) that included taking dining room chairs onto public streets for spontaneous, informal political discussion. Enamored with that idea, the students surveyed 300 campus members about conversations important to them. Next, they researched the top issues that emerged from the survey, in order to host an afternoon of "pop-up dialogues" on campus. That spring afternoon, the students engaged in both short conversations—5 to 10 minutes long—along with longer conversations—up to 2 hours—with those who walked by a main thoroughfare of campus. Passers-by included the new dean of the university library, who enthusiastically joined in with others and then invited the students to propose conversations in partnership with the library in the future.

In a subsequent semester, the Conversations That Matter class hosted a final dialogue on police accountability. Students wrote press releases and public service announcements to invite the community as well as campus members to the event. They also invited police officers and grassroots activists involved in local police review processes. Of note is that the students specifically asked these stakeholders to attend as audience members, not experts. The result was a two-hour session where stories were shared, tears shed, and actions proposed for reducing racial profiling and arrests in the community.

Ample Success and Some Challenges

In assessing the impact of the course, students have been consistent. They find the student-directed nature of the class meetings and the peer and professor feedback provided akin to coaching. These critical features allow students to (a) explore provocative topics without fear of reprisals, (b) practice facilitating and contributing to public conversations, (c) reconsider their own views on public issues, and (d) reflect on the challenges that talking about controversial matters engender.

Students self-organize into small groups so that by the third week of class they can identify a public issue worthy of dialogue and deliberation and facilitate 45- to 60-minute in-class discussions attentive to the following major areas: the content of the public issue; specific dialogue and deliberation features from our texts such as constructive confrontation, discernment, or procedural norms for decision-making; and inclusive and just facilitation methods. Students develop a group plan for facilitation that explains what discussion model they will use, why, and the intended or hoped-for dialogue and deliberation results. The discussion models students first read about and then modify for their use include those from Essential Partners, the National Issues Forums Institute, Everyday Democracy, and Liberating Structures. Underlying all of those models is the framework of social justice facilitation that can shed light on matters of equality, voice, and community-building. While participants do not necessarily emerge with common views, even within the same group, the processes used enable and encourage all to speak freely and listen deeply.

Following each small group's facilitation, group members reflect on the experience with the professor verbally and then write more extended comments to submit within 48 hours. Those written reflections consider the facilitation team process as well as the conversation that ensued, along with thoughts on how to improve in the future. Other students in the class offer concrete feedback to the small group in writing given directly to the professor. Within a week, the facilitation team receives a detailed report from the professor that collates the positive comments, suggestions, and critiques from various sources—the facilitation team members themselves, the student audience members, and the professor.

At the conclusion of the course, each student reflects on what skills or competencies are most necessary for participating in public conversations to ensure a robust democracy. Among the most frequently cited of those skills and capacities are the following:

1. *Active listening.* Students regard listening to understand others who hold different perspectives and views as the most important feature of strong dialogue. Having empathy, they say, is critical to active listening as is being open-minded even to the point of being uncomfortable. Through this process of listening, students saw conflict differently. A student explained, in her written summary of the class, "Constructive conflict is okay! Societal and community issues need the involvement of many, in order to be resolved, and listening and conflict are inevitable features."

2. *Education.* Students agree that doing research, being willing to ask stimulating questions designed to elicit insights and information, and following the news are vital to the democratic process where people are vested with the responsibility for self-governance. In doing so, students report a greater desire to initiate conversations that are often skirted in their circles.

3. *A welcoming environment.* Students recognize that having participants with diverse views in a conversation of relative importance is necessary to consider all the relevant facts and needs of a public issue. Being inclusive and respectful demonstrates positive regard for others. Relatedly, acknowledging the contributions of others and seeing our interdependence—embodied in the Bantu term *Ubuntu*—are seen as foundational features for strong deliberation.

4. *Truth and honesty.* Students find that generalizations inhibit the possibility of deep conversation. Instead, they point to the value of truth—in personal stories, history, and facts—as essential to constructing good reasons necessary for robust conversation and outcomes. Students see being inquisitive, discerning, and maybe even a little suspicious as positive ways to unpack complex matters rather than defaulting to polemic discourse. As one student wrote in her final paper, "Sometimes we are afraid of arguments or are uncomfortable having them, however they are necessary to discover truth and for justice to prevail."

5. *Courage and humility.* Students point to the need to challenge the status quo, stand with others who are speaking out, and acknowledge the corrosive impacts of economic disparities on notions of equality necessary for a democracy. With that, they learn the value of dissent and the need to have their knowledge and convictions challenged. The students point out

that using their passion for the good of the community is an important foundation for their civic duty and that to act for social change where injustices persist is in fact their responsibility.

The challenges in teaching Conversations That Matter revolve around ensuring participation and quality experiences. For students who are less comfortable speaking out loud, one-on-one encouragement is suggested for them to take small risks at first. One way to do so is by suggesting students speak on less controversial topics that are still issues of public concern.

Another challenge is the lack of good models for public dialogue, which specifically manifests itself in the difficulty with finding meaningful public meetings for students to attend. We have all seen how some meetings can devolve quickly (as some college classes do) into a recitation of facts by particular advocates, to the consternation of others in attendance. Although those meetings may provide important lessons of worst practices for dialogue and deliberation, students report finding greater learning from seeing dialogue practiced well. To find those places and people having productive conversations where students are welcome requires that the instructor have previous and ongoing relationships with community partners. There is no easy way to cultivate this knowledge; it takes time and personal commitment. The goal, however, is that courses like Conversations That Matter will make engaging and thought-provoking public dialogues more common.

Recommendations for Creating More Conversations That Matter

Encouraging more dialogue and deliberation about issues that matter to students offers an opportunity, as one student explained in the final written reflection, to "create purpose and serve as a space where the imagination gets sparked in order to find solutions in the most appropriate and constructive forms." These courses make meaningful a discipline's content and in so doing help students develop as public intellectuals who can actively advance democratic action in the world.

Conversations That Matter, as discussed in this chapter, is a stand-alone course that devotes considerable time and attention to conversation features in a college setting. However, the concepts and themes can be adapted for a course module or rewritten as one or more assignments to complement other activities. Engaging conversations that matter in the world can find resonance in diverse disciplines. To further the potential of courses like Conversations That Matter, instructors may consider encouraging students to involve their friends, peers, and community guests in their conversations to bridge the learning with insights from other courses and experiences. Doing so ensures that more people witness the power of discussing democracy that features respect, creativity, critical questions, collaborative inquiry, and a call to action.

References

Allen, D. (2014). *Our declaration: A reading of the Declaration of Independence in defense of equality.* New York, NY: Liveright.

Baldwin, J. (1963, December 21). A talk to teachers. *Saturday Review.* Retrieved from http://zinnedprojectt.org/materails/baldwin-james/

Cioffi, L. (2015, March 26). *The American townhall on anything.* Retrieved from https://americantownhalls.wordpress.com/2015/03/26/the-american-townhall-on-anything/

Eaton, K., Stolzenberg, E. B., Zimmerman, H. B., Aragon, M. C., Sayson, H. W., & Rios-Aguilar, C. (2017). *The American freshman: National norms fall 2016.* Los Angeles, CA: Higher Education Research Institute, UCLA.

Giroux, H. (2013). *America's education deficit and the war on youth.* New York, NY: Monthly Review Press.

Hess, D. E., & McAvoy, A. (2015). *The political classroom: Evidence and ethics in democratic education.* New York, NY: Routledge.

Jovanovic, S. (2013, April 16). *Conversation is the starting point* (Greensboro TEDx talk) [Video file]. Retrieved from https://www.youtube.com/watch?v=MOoUe7-nzLk

Landreman, L. M. (Ed.). (2013). *The art of effective facilitation: Reflections from social justice educators.* Sterling, VA: Stylus.

Makau, J., & Marty, D. (2013). *Dialogue and deliberation.* Long Grove, IL: Waveland Press.

Palmerton, P. R. (1992). Teaching skills or teaching thinking? *Journal of Applied Communication Research, 20*(3), 335–341.

Putnam, R. D. (2000). *Bowling alone: The collapse and revival of American community.* New York, NY: Simon & Schuster.

Russell, V., & Jovanovic, S. (2018). Academic allies and millennial voices for democratic practice. In A. Atay and M. Z. Ashlock (Eds.), *Millennial culture and communication pedagogies: Narratives from the classroom and higher education* (pp. 43–58). Lanham, MD: Lexington Books.

Tannen, D. (1998). *The argument culture: Stopping America's war of words.* New York, NY: Ballantine Books.

15

TALKING DEMOCRACY

David Hoffman and Romy Hübler

The two of us teach a seminar in the Honors College at the University of Maryland, Baltimore County (UMBC) called Talking Democracy. The course is designed to help students become critically aware of the interplay among communication styles and techniques, democratic values, and the civic health of communities. Its premise is that democracy is a way of life, not merely a form of government, and can be enacted "in the living relations of person to person in all social forms and institutions" (Dewey, 1937, p. 474). By the end of the semester, we want students to have a good sense of how to create spaces and conversations in which people can express themselves honestly, work through disagreements, identify collective goals and priorities, and take action together. The course is part of a broader UMBC approach to fostering a thriving democratic culture by helping people develop the knowledge, skills, and dispositions to communicate effectively and build strong communities together.

To set the stage for experimentation in our course, we assign readings highlighting a variety of challenges to democratic communication. In the United States in the twenty-first century, those challenges are daunting. They include social media algorithms that isolate people in perspective-reinforcing bubbles (El-Bermawy, 2016; Snyder, 2018); media conventions that turn news stories into divisive spectacles (Kellner, 2003); trolling and predatory behavior in online forums (Domise, 2018; Hess, 2017); and systemic biases reflected in a wide variety of cultural and linguistic practices (see, e.g., Frye, 2008). Collectively, these influences can turn human beings into mere objects and abstractions in each other's eyes.

More subtle barriers to democratic communication include conventions in social and institutional life that can reduce people to their roles and keep them at a distance from each other. Such conventions undoubtedly guide interactions in many college classrooms: chairs facing the front symbolizing the instructor's role as primary actor and the students' as more passive recipients of information; forms of address affirming students' deference to the instructor's authority and expertise, such as "doctor" or "professor"; and rituals of performative participation in class discussions through which students offer answers for the sake of appearing to engage in class without necessarily experiencing a connection between their contributions and their lives. If you have been immersed in such environments for long enough, it may be difficult to conceptualize the other people going through the same motions as fully human beings, as opposed to simply the roles they have been playing.

We grapple with all of these challenges alongside the students in our course, in part by testing conversation formats that can help bridge divides. All of us experience and reflect together on story circles (Roadside Theater, 2012; see also Davis, chapter 9 of this volume); restorative practices (Pranis, Stewart, & Wedge, 2003); "brave space"–style facilitated dialogues (Arao & Clemens, 2013); and deliberative dialogues facilitated using a National Issues Forums guide (2017; see also Johnson & Melville, chapter 10 of this volume). In addition, we conceptualize the class itself as a civic space and encourage critical thinking about our shared experiences.

We do this in part by intentionally departing from taken-for-granted conventions. Rather than simply calling on students to speak or taking the lead in facilitating discussions, we work with the group to establish guidelines for turn-taking in class, helping students envision protocols that serve everyone's interests. When the class breaks into small groups for analytical or reflective conversations, the two of us join groups rather than hovering above them. When we engage in personal sharing activities such as a story circle, the two of us participate. The first written assignment in the course is a personal reflection on how all of us came to hold our perspectives on what it means to be a responsible participant in civic life. The two of us complete this assignment along with the students. For the next class session, we ask students to read all of the papers, including our written reflections. Throughout the semester, all of us reflect together on the process by which our experiences of the various conversation formats, and of our departures from common classroom scripts, humanize us among one another.

Fostering a Humane Civic Culture

What we have found, not surprisingly, is that locating a structured deliberative dialogue in the context of these cultural supports for authentic conversations and humane connections impacts both the way people experience the deliberative dialogue and their thoughts about the issues being discussed. A student who participated in an in-class deliberation using the National Issues Forums' Safety and Justice issue guide, for instance, shared during the post-activity group reflection that she had never considered the idea of community policing as a viable approach to keeping communities safe, in part because she had known police officers only as distant outsiders and could not envision them being integrated into the fabric of community life. However, she had found herself newly receptive to the idea during the deliberation because her imagination had been sparked by her interactions in class. Here, she said, we've created an environment in which the instructors had become integral to a vibrant *talking democracy* community in which students and instructors were all stakeholders, and all human beings, not just our assigned roles. And what is possible for instructors in a classroom is also, in principle, possible for police officers in a community beyond the campus.

That kind of breakthrough moment has become a staple of UMBC's culture, thanks in part to an intentional, loosely coordinated, campus-wide approach to helping students develop civic skills and dispositions. These civic skills include being able to initiate and participate in deliberative dialogues and other meaningful conversations across difference. The dispositions include people seeing each other as fully human and seeing themselves as having the power to make contributions that matter to their communities. The coordination has occurred through a grassroots organizing process involving students, faculty, and staff. Our provost, Philip Rous, has supported the process through a grant program, BreakingGround, that awards startup funds for courses and programs promoting democratic communication, social justice, and individual and collective agency.

The array of courses affording students opportunities to develop the skills and dispositions for effective democratic communication is impressive: more than three dozen launched with BreakingGround grants over six years, spanning disciplines from visual arts to geography and environmental systems to mechanical engineering. These courses afford students opportunities to share their stories, develop meaningful relationships with people in Baltimore neighborhoods and agencies, and leverage their learning to produce positive social impacts. In addition, students and staff have developed new civic programs and organizations. The BreakingGround-funded projects alone number more than two dozen. Many connect UMBC people with partners in external communities, in ways designed to avoid the objectification and abstraction of people experiencing social challenges that can occur in poorly designed service programs. Others strengthen UMBC as a civic community—destigmatizing mental illness, combating sexual assault and relationship violence, establishing a community garden, and more.

These initiatives, and others funded from different campus sources, fall into four broad categories, all aligned in their cultural objective of making democratic communication ubiquitous at UMBC. The opportunities listed in each of the following categories are just some from the many available to students:

1. *Skill development programs.* Students can learn basic techniques for engaging successfully in everyday conversations with peers through the Division of Student Affairs' Interact Program; reflect on the connections between their own stories and their civic aspirations, and learn about effective participation in groups, at the Center for Democracy and Civic Life's immersive STRiVE retreat; and work with peers to sample and share democratic conversation formats with RealTalk, an organization launched and run by students who had experienced the Talking Democracy course and STRiVE retreat.
2. *Facilitated conversations.* Students can join conversations about controversial issues organized by UMBC's Women's Center and Mosaic Center for Culture and Diversity; hear from speakers from across the political spectrum and engage in small-group conversations at events in the Student Government Association's Between Elections: Coffee and Conversation series; and join peers, faculty, and staff for informal dialogues about issues affecting specific regions in Maryland at Dinner with Friends, hosted by the Student Government Association and Center for Democracy and Civic Life.
3. *Campus leadership and governance positions.* Students can serve on campus shared governance committees, administer justice in student conduct cases as members of the Student Hearing Board, and engage peers in dialogue about healthy behaviors as peer health educators.
4. *External community engagement.* Students can engage in semester-long service-learning at a variety of sites coordinated through our Shriver Center or immerse themselves for a week during Alternative Spring Break in student-led learning experiences coordinated through the Center for Democracy and Civic Life, focused on issues affecting people in Baltimore.

New Platforms and Resources

Most recently, UMBC established the Center for Democracy and Civic Life to coordinate the BreakingGround grant program and support and help connect all of these efforts. The center's explicit aim is to foster cultures of deep engagement, full participation (Sturm, Eatman, Saltmarsh, & Bush, 2011), and effective democratic communication at UMBC and in communities touched by the center's work.

This approach to teaching effective, democratic communication by attending to both skill development and the cultural dimensions of people's interactions aligns with the civic learning and democratic engagement theory of change developed with partners in the American Association of State Colleges and Universities' American Democracy Project, NASPA: Student Affairs Administrators in Higher Education, and the Democracy Commitment (Hoffman, Domagal-Goldman, King, & Robinson, 2018). The theory of change highlights the importance of developing civic capacities to foster a thriving democracy. These capacities include "recognition of the intrinsic worth and equality of all human beings, capacity to envision and identify with each other's struggles, and disposition to work for the full participation of all Americans in our democratic life" and the ability to "engage in civil, unscripted, honest communication . . . about issues [even when] individuals disagree" (Hoffman et al., 2018, p. 11). With other leaders in the networks working on the theory of change, including Melissa Baker-Boosamra,[1] Craig Berger,[2] Jennifer Domagal-Goldman,[3] and Stephanie King,[4] we are developing tools to assist in pursuing these cultural objectives within our institutions.[5]

We are fortunate to be part of an institution where an initiative focused on cultivating people's abilities to communicate their differences and build power through collaboration has deep resonance. Our president, Freeman A. Hrabowski, participated in the Birmingham Children's March for civil rights when he was 12 years old. In his quarter century at UMBC's helm, he has helped build a robust culture of inclusive excellence. As a result, our challenges in building a campus movement around democracy as a way of life, including the recognition of each other's humanity in all the ways we communicate, have been relatively modest and manageable. We still must contend with the difficulty of reaching across campus roles, authority silos, and disciplines to build commitments to new practices and pedagogies. However,

---

1. Associate director of student life, civic engagement and assessment, Grand Valley State University.
2. Assistant director, Community Engaged Learning, Kent State University.
3. Executive director, ALL IN Campus Democracy Challenge.
4. Director of civic engagement and knowledge community initiatives, NASPA.
5. NASPA has collected resources relating to the theory of change on its Lead Initiative website (www.naspa.org/constituent-groups/groups/lead-initiative/initiatives).

we have found support in many corners of the institution from people who have appreciated the chance to bring their whole selves, not just their expertise, to the work of educating for a thriving democracy.

As the final project in our Talking Democracy course, students work in groups to develop and demonstrate new conversation formats that can encourage productive relationship-building and problem-solving. Having been steeped in the culture of the class and of UMBC, the students typically propose formats that not only have deliberative elements but also attend to the need to humanize the participants to each other. These humanizing components might include pairing off to sit knee-to-knee and maintaining eye contact while taking turns answering questions about their personal histories. Or they might involve gathering personal reflections from the participants and then sharing them anonymously to reveal common hopes and fears and make real communication less intimidating. Not all of these ideas work well in practice, but some are remarkably effective. All reflect the aspiration to produce wise, inclusive, collective judgments while fostering the human connections that can support healthy conversations and communities. We believe those human connections are necessary for deliberative democracy to thrive and that building cultures that support them should be central to the work of higher education.

References

Arao, B., & Clemens, K. (2013). From safe spaces to brave space. In L. Landreman (Ed.), *The art of effective facilitation: Reflections of social justice educators* (pp. 135–150). Sterling, VA: Stylus.

Dewey, J. (1937). Education and social change. *Bulletin of the American Association of University Professors, 23*(6), 472–474.

Domise, A. (2018). It's too late for civility in American politics. *Maclean's.* Retrieved from https://www.macleans.ca/opinion/its-too-late-for-civility-in-american-politics/

El-Bermawy, M. M. (2016). Your filter bubble is destroying democracy. *Wired.* Retrieved from https://www.wired.com/2016/11/filter-bubble-destroying-democracy/

Frye, M. (2008). Oppression. In K. E. Rosenblum & T. C. Travis (Eds.), *The meaning of difference: American constructions of race, sex and gender, social class, sexual orientation, and disability* (pp. 363–368). New York, NY: McGraw-Hill.

Hess, A. (2017, February 28). How the trolls stole Washington. *New York Times Magazine.* Retrieved from https://www.nytimes.com/2017/02/28/magazine/how-the-trolls-stole-washington.html

Hoffman, D., Domagal-Goldman, J., King, S., & Robinson, V. (2018). *Higher education's role in enacting a thriving democracy: Civic learning and democratic engagement theory of change*. Washington DC: American Association of State Colleges and Universities' American Democracy Project, NASPA, and the Democracy Commitment. Retrieved from http://apps.naspa.org/files/CLDE-Theory-of-Change.pdf

Kellner, D. (2003). *Media spectacle*. New York, NY: Routledge.

National Issues Forums. (2017). *Safety and justice: How should communities reduce violence?* Dayton, OH: National Issues Forums Institute.

Roadside Theater (2012). *Story circles*. Retrieved from https://roadside.org/sites/default/files/storycircle.description.web_.2012.pdf

Pranis, K., Stewart, B., & Wedge, M. (2003). *Peacemaking circles: From crime to community*. St. Paul, MN: Living Justice Press.

Snyder, T. (2018, May 21). Fascism is back. Blame the Internet. *Washington Post*. Retrieved from https://www.washingtonpost.com/news/posteverything/wp/2018/05/21/fascism-is-back-blame-the-internet/

Sturm, S., Eatman, T., Saltmarsh, J., & Bush, A. (2011). Full participation: Building the architecture for diversity and public engagement in higher education. *Imagining America*, 17. Retrieved from http://surface.syr.edu/ia/17

PART FOUR

DIALOGUE AND DELIBERATION USING CAMPUS SPACES

16

DEMOCRACY PLAZA AT IUPUI

Amanda L. Bonilla and Lorrie A. Brown

Democracy Plaza's Origins

Like many campus innovations, Indiana University–Purdue University Indianapolis's (IUPUI) Democracy Plaza (DP) sprang to life through the energy of student leaders and the serendipity of occurring at the right place at the right time. As the nation's attention focused on the upcoming 2004 presidential election, the NBC television network designated a space outside of Rockefeller Center, called Democracy Plaza, where they would broadcast about political issues. Although the original Democracy Plaza did not last beyond that election, DP at IUPUI remains an active force on campus and serves as an inspiration for democracy walls on many other campuses.

Inspired by NBC's concept of an open space designated for democracy, several ambitious leaders in the undergraduate student government (USG), in partnership with a political science professor, the Student Life Office, and the Campus Facilities Department, conceptualized, designed, and oversaw the construction of IUPUI's DP initiative. Financial support was obtained primarily through student activity fees, which were accessible by the USG. The outdoor structure was created to be an avenue for freedom of expression and public discourse, by way of a physical space for civic and political issue-focused programming (Goldfinger, 2009).

The original DP structure consisted of four 4×8-foot wooden chalkboards, constructed by IUPUI Campus Facilities and located underneath a building breezeway. Eventually this was expanded with the addition of two shorter boards, forming a U-shaped structure. DP was purposely built in a prominent location—just off the campus quad—where hundreds of students and other campus inhabitants pass by the boards every week. A consistent process has been for student leaders to craft questions, which they write weekly on the boards, and leave chalk for others to respond through written comments.

DP's founders deliberately chose chalkboards as a writing surface rather than white dry-erase boards. Knowing that there would be dissenting opinions, the original creators felt that whiteboards were too easy to erase—with a swipe of a hand, a comment can disappear, be censored, or be otherwise altered. Chalk, however, was harder to erase without erasers (which were not provided) and so instead allowed for an ongoing written dialogue to occur. Even if a comment is scratched out, it is often still visible, creating a conversation as new comments are written to respond to older ones. Timely cleaning of the chalkboards is essential because participation wanes as the boards fill up and space to write becomes limited. Scheduled cleaning also allows the boards to be cleared of the personal and off-topic comments that are inevitably written.

The visibility of the space encourages both active and passive participation. Students (and others on campus) can actively engage in the discussion by answering a question or commenting on others' posts. But just as important in influencing IUPUI's campus culture is the opportunity for passive participation—reading comments on the boards and seeing what others think about current issues. This practice of openness to different opinions is an essential dimension of public discourse at IUPUI. This was of particular value to IUPUI's campus a decade ago, when most students were commuters and the campus culture did not support student cocurricular involvement as much as it does today.

Student Leadership

Student leaders have always been an integral part of the DP space and programming. Since 2005, student leaders, called DP Scholars, have been awarded financial aid through a civic engagement–based scholarship program, starting with 1 scholar in 2004 and growing to 6 by the mid-2010s. This financial support for IUPUI students has proven to be a key aspect in supporting student leadership in cocurricular activities. IUPUI students work off campus more than students at peer urban institutions, averaging 20 to 30 hours per week, leaving little time to get involved outside of the classroom. Scholarship funding could therefore ease some of the financial pressure on students and allow them free time to get involved in activities on campus. The commitment that IUPUI has made to providing scholarships to deepen students' civic involvement is what has allowed activities such as DP to thrive over time (Hatcher, Bringle, Brown, & Fleischhacker, 2006).

Since the beginning, DP has included a programming component alongside the physical structure. Some of the first events served to convene the campus around national events, including a tribute to Virginia Tech after the campus shooting and Hurricane Katrina relief projects. One of the initial events was "Pass the Mic," led by a communication studies professor who had his class research and lead discussions weekly at the chalkboards. Pass the Mic still endures, where student leaders provide education on a provocative topic, pose questions, and moderate a dialogue among participants by passing a microphone to those who want to speak.

Student leaders of the original DP organization took a strong nonpartisan stance, eventually creating guidelines for questions that reflected this philosophy. They also crafted a vision statement and posted it prominently at the chalkboards. After some discussions with the university's legal counsel, the decision was also made to not censor any speech, but instead to contact the IUPUI Police Department if any hate speech was expressed toward individuals. This proved to be difficult because it placed student leaders as monitors of the boards and in charge of determining what constitutes hate speech. As a result, this policy has evolved over time, as is discussed in this chapter.

DP Today

Expansion and Transition

As engagement with DP grew, so did the desire to expand the physical space. In 2012 DP expanded from the outdoor location to include a new three-board wall located inside of the IUPUI Campus Center. This space was funded by the Campus Center leadership and was designated to be placed on the highly trafficked first floor of the building. Staying true to the original goal of the outdoor DP space, three boards with space for questions and responses were created. However these boards were created out of dry-erase materials, instead of chalkboards, to match with the building aesthetics and architecture.

In 2014, DP and the DP Scholars transitioned to the portfolio of IUPUI's Social Justice Education Department. This shift was reflective of the demands by the student body to expand DP's focus on political issues to include diverse social issues as well. The updated mission of DP is "to support the development of well-informed and engaged students through critical thinking and civil discourse on political, cultural, and societal issues through a social justice lens" (Indiana University–Purdue University Indianapolis,

2019). This mission expanded the types of questions the scholars posed to the campus every week and invited even more engagement with the boards as students continue to use both spaces to discuss local, national, and international issues.

DP Scholars also evolved into a more expansive scholarship known as Social Justice Scholars. Social Justice Scholars consists of several student-led programs through a variety of platforms with the goal of providing educational opportunities that raise awareness and promote inclusivity and an understanding of oneself and others. As a result DP and Pass the Mic became two separate individual programs that Social Justice Scholars supports along with a storytelling café, shop talks on identity, history tours, and a student-led podcast. Under this new structure two scholars were selected to work with DP, which allows DP Scholars to focus solely on creating questions for both the indoor and outdoor boards as well as taking the questions to an online platform through social media. DP Online uses Facebook and Twitter to post articles and stories relevant to the mission of DP and posted the questions placed on the boards online. The DP Scholars also provide the opportunity for other campus partners to utilize the space with thought-provoking questions through a DP question submission form, which is widely utilized among a variety of student organizations and departments.

Campus Impact

DP has evolved to become a significant physical space not only for programming on critical social issues but also for gathering. Over the years several candlelight vigils and healing circles have been held in DP's outdoor location, as well as silent protests, sit-ins, and rallies. DP has also become a popular stop on campus tours for prospective students to highlight the campus's commitment to civil discourse and being a welcoming campus.

In an effort to understand the level of engagement with DP from the campus, the DP Scholars collect data on the boards and categorize the responses weekly. Each response is sorted into 1 of 3 categories: written responses, characters or symbols, and pictures. At the end of any given week there is an average breakdown of about 70% written responses, 20% characters or symbols, and 10% pictures. The majority of the written responses are sentences, phrases, or paragraphs directly linked to the questions posed by the DP Scholars. This includes statements that are in opposition to or in agreement with responses by other contributors to the board and often includes subconversations that begin in response to another's written comment. The characters and pictures on the boards fall into the following categories: (a) those that connect written responses to one another, often in the form of arrows or lines linking responses together; cartoons, stars, hearts, smile or frown faces; or exclamation marks and (b) irrelevant drawings and responses that range from advertisements to social media handles and inappropriate drawings (indicating one of the challenges of monitoring responses, among other challenges discussed in the following section).

Challenges

Inclement Weather

One of the most challenging aspects of DP is the deterioration of the outside boards. Weather and other elements have taken their toll on this space and securing funding to update the structure has proved difficult. Because of the freezing temperatures in the winter in Indiana, the DP boards located outside must be closed for the season once temperatures reach 45 degrees Fahrenheit as the scholars are unable to clean the boards or use chalk to write the questions. This causes all of the 6 outside boards to be offline for several months each year, limiting the dialogue space to the 3 indoor boards in the Campus Center.

Free Speech

Another challenging issue with DP is the inability to regulate the type of speech that is written on the boards. Although DP is committed to free speech and creative expression of ideas, there is no mechanism in place for harmful or hateful speech. With the anonymity of individuals engaging on the boards, this lack of identifying information limits the ability to know who writes what comments (or even if they are affiliated with the university), because the boards are located in public spaces on a public campus. The DP boards located inside of the Campus Center, however, do tend to have much less hateful speech written on them because there is an information desk staffed with student workers located adjacent to the boards and the center itself closes at 11:00 p.m.

DP scholars will only erase a written response when it directly targets an individual, as advised by our campus police. Currently, if individuals have concerns about the views expressed on the boards, they are encouraged to contact campus police, which often leaves our DP Scholars feeling helpless in creating a welcoming space for all students. But students are also then encouraged to use other dialogue-based programs put on by the Social Justice Scholars that are not anonymous to express their concerns and opinions.

Recommendations

Creating space for critical social and political engagement has never been more relevant, and there are lessons to be learned from the past 15 years of DP at IUPUI—most notably, location, location, location. The placement of DP plays an important role in its success. Although the first DP was created in a highly trafficked public outdoor space, decades later the ability to maintain, monitor, and improve said space has been challenging. In contrast, the DP boards located inside of the Campus Center have been more successful. As a result, it is recommended that institutions look for high-traffic indoor spaces frequently used by the student population for democracy plaza dialogue spaces.

Securing financial support for the students who work with DP has also proven to be important. Because we create opportunities for students who are passionate about social change to have financial compensation in the form of scholarship funding, our students are better able to commit to becoming Social Justice Scholars. Funding considerations should include not only scholarship funds but also staff time and a budget for maintenance of the physical spaces. Securing annual funds for maintaining the physical boards was not considered in the early planning and has proven to be one of the greatest challenges for DP nearly two decades later.

Overall, DP at IUPUI continues to provide the campus community a critical space for public discourse as well as political and social issue–focused programming space central to democracy on campus. The creation of a democracy plaza is a model that can be widely adapted across other institutions to foster community and understanding for all who engage.

References

Goldfinger, J. (2009). Democracy Plaza: A campus space for civic engagement. *Innovative Higher Education, 34*(2), 69–77.

Hatcher, J. A., Bringle, R. G., Brown, L. A., & Fleischhacker, D. A. (2006). Supporting student involvement through service-based scholarships. In E. Zlotkowski, N. Longo, & J. Williams (Eds.), *Students as colleagues: Expanding the circle of service-learning leadership* (pp. 35–48). Providence, RI: Campus Compact.

Indiana University Purdue University Indianapolis. (2019). *Democracy Plaza mission statement.* Division of Diversity, Equity, and Inclusion. Retrieved from https://diversity.iupui.edu/offices/mc/socialjustice/scholars.html

17

ACADEMIC LIBRARIES AS CIVIC AGENTS

Nancy Kranich

Practicing the arts of democracy can be infused across disciplines, and it can be built into nearly all structures on campus, such as student clubs and activities, athletic programs, cultural and intellectual events, residential life, and volunteer opportunities. Every venue on campus can be a practice ground for democracy. (Thomas, 2010, p. 9)

One practice ground for democracy often overlooked is the academic library. In fact, until recently, academic libraries were "conspicuous by their absence in the engaged university" (Westley, 2006, p. 200). Although academic libraries are well recognized for their role informing scholarship; promoting access to a diversity of ideas; and serving as depositories for government, community, and other useful information, many are just now beginning to move up the International Association for Public Participation (IAP2) Public Participation Spectrum (2014)—a widely recognized descriptor of levels and resources of public participation processes—from informing toward involving, collaborating with, and empowering future citizens on the issues of the day. Academic librarians are natural allies in the quest to create a more engaged citizenry, given their liaison responsibilities across the curriculum with such campus hubs of democracy (Carcasson, 2008) as political science, education, journalism, social work, communication, and Cooperative Extension.

Like public libraries, academic libraries began transforming their civic engagement identities over the past decade, hosting deliberative dialogues, offering safe (and brave) spaces for public discourse, appointing civic engagement librarians, partnering with campus and community organizations, participating in service-learning, and collaborating across the curriculum to enhance civic literacy. In 2007, George Mehaffy, vice president for academic leadership and change at the American Association of State Colleges and Universities (AASCU), told academic librarians about his work on campuses through the American Democracy Project, emphasizing that he saw academic libraries as "citizenship centers . . . more relevant now than ever in history" (Mehaffy, 2007). In 2009, Elizabeth Hollander, the late director of Campus Compact, encouraged academic librarians attending the American Library Association (ALA) annual conference to get involved with civic engagement. Up until that time, though, most of the dialogue about academic library participation in civic activities on their campuses was simply that—dialogue about possible roles, not actual experiences (Kranich, 2010, 2012; Kranich, Reid, & Willingham, 2004; Leong, 2013).

Thomas Jefferson espoused the value of an informed citizenry to a healthy democracy. Two hundred years later, the Knight Commission on the Information Needs of Communities in a Democracy (2009) urged that Americans need an informed *and* engaged populace if democracy is to thrive in the digital age. This means that libraries and universities must shift from an environment of "*informing*" to "*involving*," because an involved—not just informed—citizenry is more likely to participate in democratic political processes (Lievrouw, 1994, p. 350). Jaeger and Burnett (2005) suggest redefining the role of information in a society that relies on "libraries, as established guardians of diverse perspectives of information, . . . to protect and preserve information access *and exchange* . . . facilitating and fueling deliberative democracy" (p. 464, emphasis added). Following a series of highly polarizing elections, escalating amounts of fake news, and widening economic divides in the United States, librarians are rising to the occasion, identifying a new role that promotes not just informing but also fostering civic literacy and building safe/brave civic spaces that connect academe with community and global issues.

Traditional library services such as reference assistance, collection development, organization of information, preservation, and archiving are vital to civic engagement. Students and faculty are often unaware of local information and data resources and need help navigating through documents and other primary source materials essential to mapping the civic sphere. A simple research guide to the terrain—often produced in collaboration with campus partners—such as the Rutgers University Libraries-Camden's *Civic Engagement LibGuide* (Wilkinson, 2018) or the University of Texas at El Paso Library's *Center for Civic Engagement LibGuide* (2018) offers a perfect starting point for anyone naming, framing, and deliberating about public issues. These LibGuides are easy-to-use tools deployed by thousands of libraries to curate knowledge, share information, and identify subject-specific resources that get students started in finding information about their local community.

With tools like these, librarians teach how to find, evaluate, and use information (from the bewildering amount available) essential to analyzing community issues and fostering civic literacy.

Academic libraries also provide comfortable, inviting, neutral, safe spaces conducive to democratic discourse—spaces where citizens can work together to solve public problems. As Ray Oldenburg (1989) describes in *The Great Good Place*, libraries are places essential to the political processes of democracy—places that reinforce the American notion of association.

The challenge for academic librarians is to go beyond the delivery of expert opinion through texts and presentations to a more interactive platform where students and faculty can work together to solve public problems. It is not that academic librarians do not want to participate in civic engagement initiatives; they are just unsure how. After all, few have learned the skills necessary to foster public deliberation in master's programs in library and information science (MLIS), although at least five MLIS programs including Rutgers now offer community engagement courses. Recent efforts to deepen involvement by academic librarians—promoted by an ALA (2018) training program—represent a turning point and provide tools specifically geared toward academic librarians, demonstrating how they can contribute to and learn about the civic work underway across their institutions.

At the nexus of multiple academic disciplines, academic libraries are well positioned to prepare future generations as leaders of an increasingly complex and divided world. Beyond safe space, academic librarians can contribute by naming, framing, convening, and moderating deliberative forums that teach students how to make public choices together and demonstrate the value of the deliberative process as a curricular tool. Librarians can also teach the theory and scholarship behind public politics along with the methods of convening and moderating deliberative discussions. To amplify such efforts, they should work in concert with other civic initiatives already underway on campus. A number of examples including those undertaken at Rutgers University illuminate possibilities for academic library partnerships across campus and beyond.

Access to Civic Engagement Scholarship

Librarians have traditionally made information, including local resources, available through campus libraries. With increased involvement in the civic sphere, they are finding new ways to leverage their resources to prepare students, faculty, and staff for service-learning experiences and to provide physical and online spaces for planning and sharing projects as well as programs (Gruber, 2017a, 2017b). A University of Kansas community engagement librarian who curates a Campus Compact Knowledge Hub titled "The Role of Libraries in Engagement Work" (Thiel, n.d.) has recorded a webinar (Gruber & Thiel, 2017) that showcases creative ways to increase access to the research of engaged campus and community scholars and to expand the tent and build bridges across different civic engagement constituencies on campus. These approaches help students, faculty, and staff gain a more realistic understanding of a local community and develop cultural competence; assist service-learning programs with capturing, collecting, sharing, archiving, and preserving a record of their activities through campus institutional repositories; and create relevant community-focused materials including video documentaries using the library's computer labs and maker spaces.

At Rutgers University Libraries, we worked with public libraries near our campuses in Camden, Newark, and New Brunswick on an ALA/National Endowment for the Humanities grant using the PBS series *Latino Americans: 500 Years of History*. Through that project, we connected the academy with the community by creating a LibGuide (Kranich, 2016); identified scholars to interpret the six PBS videos shown at participating libraries; and collected reports, archival materials, and newsletters available through the Rutgers New Jersey collection and institutional repository—RUCore. Previous to that collaboration, the library had limited success collecting materials about the century-old experience of Latinos in the state. This effort allowed us to build relationships between and among the Latino and research communities, while documenting the rich history and scholarship in this arena. The initiative opened the door to deeper community engagement efforts and linked scholars to both the public and academic libraries in new and meaningful ways.

Strengthening Civic Literacy

Academic librarians have long led their campuses in teaching information literacy skills based on standards and frameworks developed by the Association of College and Research Libraries (2016). To date, these efforts have focused primarily on college and career, but as librarians increase their role in civic engagement, they can benefit students by emphasizing a third c—citizenship. As learners confront fake news, clicktivism, and slacktivism, librarians are well positioned to seize this teachable moment to enhance civic literacy— "the knowledge and ability of citizens to make sense of their world and to act as competent citizens" (Milner, 2002, p. 3). According to the recently adopted core curriculum C3 Framework for Social Studies,

> Active and responsible citizens are able to identify and analyze public problems, deliberate with other people about how to define and address issues, take constructive action together, reflect on their actions, create and sustain groups, and influence institutions both large and small. (National Council for Social Studies, n.d., p. 19).

To help students become civic actors instilled with a sense of civic agency (Boyte, 2007), academic librarians can incorporate such civic literacy skills into their training strategies. At the David & Lorraine Cheng Library on the campus of William Paterson University in New Jersey, librarians are doing just that through their Civic Literacy Initiative in partnership with the Office of Campus Activities and Student Leadership. The library offers students an academic learning component to complement service-learning opportunities on campus, piloting programs with the student Model UN and Political Science Club. Participants in the program earn credit toward their Civic Engagement Badges (Marks, 2018).

Naming, Framing, and Moderating Deliberative Forums

Academic librarians can provide valuable support for naming, framing, and moderating deliberative forums on campus and beyond. A number of them have participated in deliberative dialogue for years. For example, librarians at Ripon College in Wisconsin, McDaniel College in Maryland, and Franklin Pierce College in New Hampshire joined faculty, clubs, and the student radio stations to promote campus deliberative forums. Kansas State University Libraries' association with the school's Institute for Civic Discourse and Democracy resulted in the naming, framing, and convening of deliberative forums around broadband deployment in a number of statewide settings, including public libraries. The Lyndon Baines Johnson Presidential Library worked with the University of Texas, the Texas State Humanities Council, and the Texas Library Association to help Texans deliberate about the achievement gap. In Georgia, the Jimmy Carter Presidential Library teamed up with the Richard B. Russell Library for Political Research and Studies at the University of Georgia to train students to conduct forums at public libraries and other locations around the state. At Oklahoma State University, the Edmon Low Library worked with the Stillwater Public Library, public schools, and Oklahoma State University

Extension to offer National Issues Forums (NIF) through a local organization called Stillwater Speaks. And at the Illinois State University Library, librarians joined the AASCU campus American Democracy Project, participating in voter registration; service-learning; candidate debates; conducting research; and naming, framing, and moderating forums at the public library on the Illinois budget.

For nearly a decade, the ALA Center for Civic Life—established in partnership with the Kettering Foundation—has trained librarians in dialogue and deliberation techniques and has named and framed issues of common concern to librarians; "Who Should I Trust to Protect My Privacy?" (ALA, n.d.), was convened at the Rutgers University Libraries in New Brunswick as part of the observance of Banned Books Week. In 2017 and 2018, the ALA (2018) *Libraries Transform Communities: Models for Change* initiative included a webinar and in-person training program on moderating NIF deliberative forums specifically targeted at academic librarians. Following the training, librarians from Rutgers University sponsored a series entitled "Newark Talks the Talk: Introduction to Deliberative Forums" for the Rutgers University-Newark and city of Newark communities. They convened three sessions using NIF materials, one of which incorporated a training module for participants. The series was cosponsored by the Rutgers-Newark Collaboratory for Pedagogy, Professional Development and Publicly-Engaged Scholarship, graduate students across disciplines, and Newark community leaders.

Lessons Learned, Challenges, and Opportunities

It will take a collective effort within the library and across the campus to cultivate deep and meaningful democratic practices for a new generation of citizens. Anyone engaged in the civic sphere likely agrees that the hardest part is not learning to use new tools but convincing others to subscribe to deliberative-type practices. Over the last decade, academic librarians have sponsored several deliberative forums. More recently, a larger cohort participated in dialogue and deliberation training programs. When this group returned to their own campuses, they also learned the need for intensive relationship-building first—a lesson enunciated to Rutgers-Newark librarians following the 2018 training after they scheduled a series of three NIF forums, only to find themselves lacking much of an audience for the sessions. And similar to the experiences of other academic librarians, their involvement with this work remains episodic, dependent on individual champions rather than an organization-wide effort. For Rutgers and other academic librarians around the country, sustaining and expanding these efforts is difficult at best. Although many are eager to work more closely *with* rather than *for* campus colleagues involved with community-building, they rarely feel a vital part of the endeavor. To illustrate, Rutgers-New Brunswick librarians discovered that service-learning and civic engagement activists on their campuses were actively working closely with the local public library, but they never involved campus librarians with this opportunity to deepen relationships. Somehow, such gaps must narrow if academic librarians are to contribute as civic agents in meaningful and relevant ways.

The larger challenge calls for academic libraries to transform to an engaged model of civic engagement. Moving up the IAP2 spectrum (2014) of public engagement beyond informing toward involving, collaborating with, and empowering future citizens—although an appealing trajectory for many academic librarians—may not sync with the priorities of administrators during a period of budgetary retrenchment. Although notable efforts to deepen the civic work of academic librarians abound, conversion of the nation's 5,000 academic libraries into civic agents remains in its infancy. A survey of the civic-mindedness of academic librarians by Laura Barry, Maureen Lowe, and Sarah Twill (2017) found that only those already demonstrating an interest in or experience with community-related service were significantly more civic-minded. And as Albert Dzur (2008) points out, democratic civic-minded professionals—or *positive deviants*—may succeed in influencing their colleagues but cannot single-handedly turn their professions outward toward their communities. In short, academic librarians face hurdles convincing their own as well as faculty colleagues that they should become essential contributors to deliberative dialogue endeavors on campus and beyond.

Recommendations

College and university librarians have begun to stimulate civic engagement by working with their professional associations as well as higher education and civic organizations including the Association of American Colleges & Universities' Civic Learning and Democratic Engagement initiative, AASCU's American Democracy Project (ADP), the American Association of University Professors, Campus Compact, the National Issues Forums Institute, and the National Coalition on Dialogue and Deliberation (NCDD). Librarians attend and present at ADP and NCDD national conferences and now have a library group that meets at Campus Compact network meetings. College and university librarians also link up with civic actors at state and campus-level meetings of these organizations, opening up closer collaboration opportunities.

On campus, librarians, faculty, and community organizations can join forces through service-learning courses, learning communities, political and civic institutes, and numerous other campus hubs (Carcasson, 2008). These partnerships can start simply by offering space for activities. For example, after students told library staff that they did not know how voter registration worked, the libraries at Rutgers hosted a voter registration table in the library. Students expressed how glad they were that we were there to help. Librarians benefit from building partnerships with campus and community groups already working together and looking for the added value that librarians offer. They can also enlist academic departments, administrators, development officers, library friends groups, alumni, and trustees. Within the community, they can begin with a common starting point by connecting with their colleagues in public and school libraries, serving as a welcome bridge between town and gown as they work together to promote and deepen their role in civic engagement.

With colleges initiating exciting new programs to enhance participation, librarians have an unprecedented opportunity to collaborate with their campus colleagues to strengthen the ability of tomorrow's leaders to practice civic engagement and participation. By sponsoring and promoting deliberative forums and participating in service-learning initiatives, librarians can foster student learning and faculty research while expanding linkages between campus and community.

Now is the time for academic libraries to assume their rightful role in creating a new generation of informed citizens capable of acting to address complex, urgent social problems. By committing themselves to joining the civic mission of higher education, academic librarians will become leaders and catalysts for preparing students to participate actively in a flourishing twenty-first-century democracy. As John Dewey (1916) framed the issue, "democracy needs to be reborn in each generation and education is its midwife" (p. 22).

References

American Library Association. (2018). *Libraries transform communities: Models for change—Academic libraries.* Chicago, IL: American Library Association. Retrieved from http://www.ala.org/tools/librariestransform/libraries-transforming-communities/academic

American Library Association. (n.d.). *Who do I trust to protect my privacy?* (Deliberative dialogue issue map and guide). Chicago, IL: American Library Association. Retrieved from https://chooseprivacyeveryday.org/programs/civic-engagement/

Association of College and Research Libraries. (2016). *Framework for information literacy for higher education*. Chicago, IL: American Library Association. Retrieved from http://www.ala.org/acrl/standards/ilframework

Barry, M., Lowe, L. A., & Twill, S. (2017). Academic librarians' attitudes about civic-mindedness and service learning. *Library Quarterly: Information, Community, Policy, 87*(1), 1–16.

Boyte, H. (2007, November 21). Building civic agency: The public-work approach. *Open Democracy*. Retrieved from https://www.opendemocracy.net/en/building_civic_agency_the_public_work_approach

Carcasson, M. (2008). *Democracy's hubs: College and university centers as platforms for deliberative practice* (Report to the Kettering Foundation). Dayton, OH: Kettering Foundation. Retrieved from https://my.lwv.org/sites/default/files/carcasson.democracys_hubs_report.pdf

Dewey, J. (1916). *Democracy and education: An introduction to the philosophy of education*. New York, NY: Macmillan.

Dzur, A. W. (2008). *Democratic professionalism: Citizen participation and the reconstruction of professional ethics, identity, and practice*. University Park: Pennsylvania State University.

Gruber, A. M. (2017a, November 4). Academic libraries tell the story: Archiving community engagement projects. *Service Learning Librarian*. Retrieved from https://sllibrarian.uni.edu/articles/201711/academic-libraries-tell-story-archiving-community-engagement-projects

Gruber, A. M. (2017b). Community engagement in higher education: Online information sources. *College and Research Libraries News, 78*(10), 563. Retrieved from http://crln.acrl.org/index.php/crlnews/article/view/16809/18387

Gruber, A. M., & Thiel, S. G. (2017). *Libraries and civic engagement* [Webinar]. Retrieved from http://illinoiscampuscompact.org/resource-posts/webinar-libraries-civic-engagement/

IAP2 International Association for Public Participation. (2014). *IAP2's public participation spectrum*. Louisville, CO: IAP2 International Federation. Retrieved from https://www.iap2.org.au/Tenant/C0000004/00000001/files/IAP2_Public_Participation_Spectrum.pdf

Jaeger, P. & Burnett. G. (2005). Information access and exchange among small worlds in a democratic society: The role of policy in shaping information behavior in the post-9/11 United States. *Library Quarterly, 75*(4), 464-495.

Knight Commission on the Information Needs of Communities in a Democracy. (2009). *Informing communities: Sustaining democracy in the digital age*. Washington DC: Aspen Institute. Retrieved from https://production.aspeninstitute.org/publications/informing-communities-sustaining-democracy-digital-age/

Kranich, N. (2010). Academic libraries as hubs for deliberative democracy. *Journal of Public Deliberation* (special issue on Higher Education and Deliberative Democracy), 6(1), article 4. Retrieved from http://services.bepress.com/jpd/vol6/iss1/art4

Kranich, N. (2012). Libraries and civic engagement. *The Library and Book Trade Annual, 2012*, 75–97. Retrieved from https://doi.org/doi:10.7282/T3VX0DWS

Kranich, N. (2016). *Latino Americans: 500 years of history—100 years in New Jersey*. New Brunswick, NJ: Rutgers University Libraries. Retrieved from https://libguides.rutgers.edu/latinoamericans500

Kranich, N., Reid, M., & Willingham, T. (2004). Civic engagement and academic libraries. *College and Research Libraries News, 65*(4), 380–383, 388, 393. Retrieved from http://crln.acrl.org/content/65/7/380.full.pdf+html

Leong, J. H. T. (2013). Community engagement—Building bridges between university and community by academic libraries in the 21st century. *Libri, 63*(3), 220–231.

Lievrouw, L. (1994). Information resources and democracy: Understanding the paradox. *Journal of the American Society for Information Science, 45*(6), 350–357.

Marks, G. (2018, April 27). *Civic literacy initiative: Campus partnerships to develop civic leaders*. Civic Engagement and Academic Libraries Roundtable Workshop, Raritan Valley Community College, Branchburg, NJ.

Mehaffy, G. (2007, May 1). The American Democracy Project. Presented at the Association of College and Research Libraries Library Legislative Day Luncheon. [From notes taken at the speech by the author.]

Milner, H. (2002). *Civic literacy: How informed citizens make democracy work*. Hanover, NH: University Press of New England.

National Council for Social Studies. (n.d.). *College, career, and civic life: C3 framework for social studies state standards*. Retrieved from http://www.socialstudies.org/sites/default/files/c3/C3-Framework-for-Social-Studies.pdf

Nutefall, J. (2016). *Service learning, information literacy, and libraries*. Westport, CT: Libraries Unlimited.

Oldenburg, R. (1989). *The great good place*. New York, NY: Paragon.

Thiel, S. G. (n.d.). *The role of libraries in engagement work*. Boston, MA: Campus Compact. Retrieved from https://compact.org/resource-posts/role-libraries-engagement-work/

Thomas, N. (2010). Why it is imperative to strengthen American democracy through study, dialogue and change in higher education. *Journal of Public Deliberation, 6*(1), article 10. Retrieved from http://www.publicdeliberation.net/jpd/vol6/iss1/art10

University of Texas at El Paso (UTEP) Library. (2018). *Center for Civic Engagement LibGuide*. El Paso, TX: Author. Retrieved from http://libguides.utep.edu/c.php?g=430029&p=2932147

Westley, L. (2006, Spring). Conspicuous by their absence: Academic librarians in the engaged university. *Reference & User Services Quarterly, 45*, 200–202.

Wilkinson, Z. (2018). *Civic engagement LibGuide*. Camden, NJ: Rutgers University Libraries-Camden. Retrieved from https://libguides.rutgers.edu/c.php?g=337477&p=2271056

18

RESIDENCE HALLS AS SITES OF DEMOCRATIC PRACTICE

Laurel B. Kennedy

Denison University's mission is to "inspire and educate autonomous thinkers, discerning moral agents, and active citizens of a democratic society" (Vision and Values, n.d.). Many college mission statements are obscure and inaccessible to students, but Denison students know, understand, and regularly invoke our mission. We thus feel obliged to bring not only the words and spirit but also the direct charge of our mission into the reach of our students. Active citizenship, we believe, relies on not only knowledge of democratic theory but also what Alexis de Tocqueville (1835/2012) called "habits of the heart" (p. 466)—ways of living day-to-day that foster the common good. This day-to-day approach is important because it is the situations that confront us in our own neighborhoods that actually test our capacity for and commitment to democratic principles. On the Denison campus, those neighborhoods are our residence halls. This chapter documents our efforts to transform these spaces into sites for learning the practices of democratic engagement.[1]

Adam Weinberg (2017a), Denison's president since 2013, writes that residential spaces offer an opportunity to deepen such learning about how to respond to difference and conflict:

---

1. Tremendous leadership was provided for this work by Denison students, especially those who staff residential communities, and Ben Daleiden and Cari Meng, who were associate directors in Res Comm during the period described here. Dean of Student Leadership and Community Engagement Erik Farley, Dean of First-Year Students Mark Moller, and Director of Residential Communities and Community Values Léna Crain continue to mastermind the work and contributed to this chapter.

Residential halls function as design studios for acquiring the skills for democratic living. Our student population is diverse in many different ways (e.g., race, ethnicity, religious practices, political views, geographic origins, class, sexual identity). This means that students bring into our residential halls an array of needs, likes and dislikes, passions, habits and goals. These differences create opportunities for students to learn to communicate more effectively, resolve conflict, and solve problems creatively to build and sustain community. (para. 7)

These skills and habits are not widely cultivated and, broadly speaking, colleges and universities have rarely been intentional in fostering them. Brian Rosenberg (2016) writes of the folly of bringing together students from vastly different life experiences and expecting them, "as if by spontaneous chemical reaction" (p. 36) to form a robust community.

Our efforts to redress these concerns about student living and engaging one another across difference have included significant program development in recent years regarding dialogue and listening. Examples of these efforts include long-standing sustained dialogue and campus interfaith dialogue groups, several ad hoc campus programs using dialogue to solve emergent issues, and the restorative justice orientation in our conduct work. In addition to these programs, we focus on skill-building with listening as a core component of human-centered design in our innovation space, the Red Frame Lab. In these diverse ways, the use of dialogue and deliberation has become part of a naturally resonating approach to building strong, democratic campus communities.

General Model, Principles, and Practices

Over the course of the 2016–2017 academic year, we began to have conversations about challenges we were facing in the residential environment, which pointed to a lack of community-mindedness among student residents. Professional staff in the residence halls observed, for example, that students often relied on staff or Campus Safety to solve problems when, in fact, they might better solve these issues themselves. These included vandalism in the residence halls, such as water fountains or exit signs pulled from first-year hall walls on weekend nights, low-level roommate conflicts, and the management of noise and trash from parties. We also believed that students could take greater responsibility for responding to incidents of homophobia, racial bias, and other behaviors that undermine feelings of belonging and inclusion among peers. As a university community, we wanted students to feel a sense of ownership and investment in their own communities. Achieving this required a reconceptualization of residential life.

Asking students to take greater responsibility for the cocreation of their communities required giving students greater authority over their own communities, which we were determined to do. A significant challenge we faced was figuring out how to support them in the development of the skills of neighborliness and civic responsibility. In particular, we needed to clarify our goals and the tools we would use to achieve them.

We began by articulating the essential elements of our residential communities model. The short document we created for internal use provided a shared touchstone for staff working on the design of the new program:

> It is geared to cultivating the skills of democratic living . . . on which democracy depends: to be engaged and responsible for cocreating communities that are respectful, enjoyable, safe, and interesting, and in which students find a sense of home.
>
> It fosters life skills that enable students to be at their best and to achieve the goals that brought them to college.
>
> It establishes that exploring diversity (race/ethnicity, class, political views, sexual orientation and gender identity, religion) and diverse perspectives is essential to learning and growth.
>
> It encourages exploration of self, the time and space for reflection, and the expectation that college should, at least once in a while, cause us to question our own ideas (and sometimes to change our mind).
>
> It asks for patience as our ideas and views evolve, and generosity in the face of mistakes and mis-steps. (Kennedy, 2017)

We set to work on the practical questions of how the residential communities would operate. Our thinking was shaped by Harry Boyte's (2011) conception of *public work*, the sustained effort by a mix of ordinary people to create something of lasting civic value, while developing civic capacity along the way. We saw that our students could identify and even diagnose problems in their own communities (in this case, their residence halls) but did not see themselves as agents of change. This condition corresponded with the loss of "civic muscle" that Boyte (2018, p. 17) associates with the delegation of civic responsibility to others. We were inspired by Boyte's ideas about how we might prepare our students to be citizens through their everyday work. "Citizen politics and public work greatly expand the concepts of democracy, citizenship, power and politics itself. They convey a generative experience of politics. And they point to a much deeper story about democracy" (p. 77).

Boyte describes Denison's project as one of empowering our students to be "artisans of possibility" (pp. 143).

Residential life programs virtually everywhere identify community-building as a goal, but most rely on tools (like educational bulletin board displays) that bear little relationship to how communities form and grow strong. Denison's own resident assistant (RA) training was heavily focused on policy, administrative documentation, and facilities management rather than community-building. Student residents, faculty members, and parents frequently complained that RAs were inaccessible. Students who struggled to make friends or find community sometimes reported to the dean of first-year students or to faculty members that RAs were unavailable or lacked the skills needed to help them. An immediate need, therefore, was to reimagine the role and training of our student staff as facilitators of relationships.

To signal a changed role, student staff were renamed as community advisers, and training was refocused to emphasize relationship-building. We turned to the public achievement model (see Siracusa & Elpers, chapter 22 of this volume) developed by Harry Boyte and Dennis Donovan (Hildreth, 2014). The model employs strategies associated with political organizing and deliberative public work to inform relationship-building. During a series of visits, Donovan trained our student staff to use one-to-one relational meetings as a way both to get to know their residents and to model ways of forming new relationships.

One-to-one meetings use a structured format to invite conversation, storytelling, and the practice of deep listening. Community advisers schedule these meetings formally and with the express purpose of learning more about the resident. Most talking during a one-to-one is by the resident; community advisers pose questions and listen to learn: *Why are you in college? Why did you choose Denison? What do you hope to accomplish here? What values and goals shape your life?* Through these conversations, community advisers discover what excites or worries their residents so that they can point them to opportunities and resources. They also discern points of interest shared by different students, so that they can help form connections between them.

Another essential practice of Denison's Residential Communities model is community problem-solving through "civic deliberations." Civic deliberations can unfold in different ways, but usually involve soliciting all perspectives on the issue's nature and impact, and as many solutions as participants can formulate. Student staff learn how to facilitate group conversations involving students with different life experiences and points of view, creating a forum for speaking and listening across difference. Like one-to-one relational meetings, these are structured engagements, but the group conversations are centered on issues or conflicts, often internal to the group.

Participants consider the consequences of different solutions and ways of testing them. Civic deliberations typically address issues that could divide communities, pitting individuals against one another. Coming together in a structured format to name and describe a problem and then generate solutions transforms the conflict from "us versus them" to "community versus problem." In our residence halls, these experiences serve both to resolve problems and to practice foundational competencies of democratic engagement.

In a first-year hall where familiarity with the practice is just beginning, civic deliberations address differences in how residents maintain common rooms or confront incidents that negatively impact residents, such as vandalism. As students become more experienced, civic deliberations might center on larger campus issues, or national or international topics.[2] The goal of civic deliberations is better understanding among people with different perspectives and the identification of solutions or actions that serve shared interests.

One-to-ones invite stories and the sharing of personal narratives and cultivate compassionate listening and self-reflection. The meetings offer the gift of being recognized and known by another student and encourage students to share their stories with their peers as well. Civic deliberations, in in contrast, rely on skills of effective critique: focusing on issues rather than people, framing questions in positive and nonconfrontational ways, listening with compassion, and adopting an orientation toward the common good. We are finding that these tools incorporate a number of interpersonal skills that equip students to be better citizens, and potentially also better coworkers, family members, and neighbors in the future.

Key Successes and Challenges

Our staff in Residential Communities believe that creating a culture of storytelling and designing formal opportunities to share experiences and goals among their residents has fostered a renewed sense of neighborliness and shared civic life. As community advisers more consistently get to know their residents (over 90% of students are now reached through one-to-one meetings), they are creating communities where anonymity is all but impossible. As we continue to experiment with and develop our new model, we observe a number of changes that signal the stronger, more caring, and more accountable communities that civically conscious students can create:

---

2. A civic deliberation following Brett Kavanaugh's confirmation hearing in fall 2018 centered on whether sexual assault was a partisan issue. The lively deliberation engaged about 80 students from across the political spectrum.

- Across all our residence halls, but especially in the largest of these (where student behavior can be most anonymous), we have seen a sharp reduction in callous or mean-spirited actions, like writing slurs on door-mounted whiteboards. Reports of bias-related behaviors declined 70% in the first year of the new approach.[3]
- There has also been a noticeable decline in the type of minor vandalism we typically see in residence halls. Certain behaviors are highly predictable, like prank fire alarms, which previously averaged six per year. These dropped to zero in the first year of the new model, and both student and professional staff observed a greater sense of ownership for and personal connection to the living environment. Costs associated with vandalism dropped 35% in the program's first year.
- Our dean of first-year students reports that fewer parents now seek his intercession in roommate conflicts and residential issues. He concludes that as issues are preempted or resolved early, fewer students complain to parents who then escalate matters to his attention. He observes that students are trying harder to resolve issues by themselves, are more respectful of each other, and trust their community advisers to partner with them in managing situations that arise.
- Community advisers say they are treated with a greater degree of respect by fellow students and feel increased comfort addressing conflict. Community advisers speak about their conduct-related functions as "documenting the situation" rather than "writing someone up," a marked departure from past approaches. This shift allows community advisers to fulfill their responsibility to community while maintaining relationships with individuals, including those involved in difficult interactions.
- We have observed a changing composition of the applicant pool for the community adviser position with each successive year. Although in the past the RA role was particularly prized for its financial benefits, applicants now increasingly express interest in social change, community organizing, conflict resolution, and matters of student well-being. In our second year, a record number of new applicants pursued the role, and a record number of community advisers were returning staff members.

---

3. The measures reported here are indirect assessments of the program's effectiveness and could be associated with other, unrelated causal factors. Their cumulative impact on the atmosphere of the campus, however, was palpable.

Although we have also experienced challenges, these have been comparatively modest:

- We selected student staff before we had a thorough understanding of the qualities we would need in community advisers. Our applicant pool included many students who had served—effectively—under the old model and were renewed. Training the staff thus required overcoming uncertainty and resistance to change. Further, some of the staff had limited capacity for the new model, especially its more relational aspects. For that reason, we had to find ways to manage those shortfalls by strategically leveraging staff talents.
- Similarly, we had to rebuild significant components of student staff training. Policy-related and incident response components are still job duties, but these needed to be reframed, as described. Our training in conflict resolution skills (expectation setting, empathy, deep listening, dialogue, and compromise) now corresponds with the practices and principles of one-to-one relational meetings and civic deliberation.
- We struggled to find a director for the Residential Communities department who understood both the practical requirements of undergraduate housing and the nuances of our civic education goals. We were fortunate that our dean of first-year students was willing to lead the department in its inaugural year, when so much of the program's invention occurred. During that year, we discovered that our conflict resolution (conduct) director, who was new to the college, had an intuitive understanding of our goals. These aligned with her approach to conflict resolution and community development, and she now serves in a dual role and is leading the development of the model.

None of these challenges caused us to question our approach. Further, anticipated concerns, such as pressures we expected from students and parents for staff to intervene as problem-solvers, didn't materialize. Instead, we have grown increasingly confident with the language and practices of the model and our capacity to elaborate its concepts. We have begun to discern interesting points of intersection between the residential communities model and work in other areas of the cocurriculum. From conflict resolution and student wellness to leadership development and diversity and inclusion initiatives, we are seeing changes in our campus community. We find ourselves increasingly promoting the skills of dialogue and deliberation in these other areas of student life. These nudges to more consciously integrate dialogue and deliberative practices underscore for us the coherence in the model and affirm its utility for our community.

Conclusion

de Tocqueville (2012) wrote in *Democracy in America* that democracy is an ongoing process of people coming together to create and recreate the communities in which they want to live. Our vision is consistent with this longstanding tradition of democracy. But as Boyte (2018) reflects, "Co-creative citizenship and its skills, values, habits and identities have to be learned. . . . People are not born knowing how to be 'citizen co-creators'" (p. 107).

Colleges must do this educational work and residential halls can operate as sites for doing it effectively. Denison's residence halls present opportune spaces for students to learn to work together, often across difference, and to create things of lasting public value. As Denison University President Adam Weinberg (2017b) wrote in a recent Kettering Foundation piece, "This conception of democracy moves beyond the laudable actions of voting and community service to the nuanced and difficult process of people acting together to solve problems. It is a citizen-centered view of democratic living" (p. 37). Working together to solve day-to-day problems in their residential communities, students develop understanding, build human relationships, and cultivate the civic agency to be cocreators of their communities, a conception of citizenship that goes far beyond mere legal status and that is increasingly essential to democracy today.

References

Boyte, H. C. (2011). Constructive politics as public work: Organizing the literature. *Political Theory, 39*, 630–660.

Boyte, H. C. (2018). *Awakening democracy through public work: Pedagogies of empowerment*. Nashville, TN: Vanderbilt University Press.

de Tocqueville, A. (1835/2012). *Democracy in America* (Vol. 1). Retrieved from https://oll.libertyfund.org/titles/2735

Hildreth, R. (2014). *A coach's guide to public achievement*. Minneapolis, MN: Center for Democracy and Citizenship.

Kennedy, L. (2017). *ResComm 1.1*. Unpublished internal document.

Rosenberg, B. (2016). Creating diverse communities. *Trusteeship, 24*(1), 36.

Vision & Values. (n.d.). Retrieved from https://denison.edu/campus/about/vision-values

Weinberg, A. (2017a). The civic responsibilities of colleges. *Huffington Post*. Retrieved from https://www.huffpost.com/entry/the-civic-responsibilitie_b_9194106

Weinberg, A. (2017b). Being a civically engaged college that contributes to democratic ways of living: Reflections of a college president. *Connections* (Annual Journal of the Kettering Foundation). Retrieved from https://www.kettering.org/sites/default/files/product-downloads/connections_2017.pdf

PART FIVE

DIALOGUE AND DELIBERATION IN THE COMMUNITY

19

PROVIDENCE COLLEGE/ SMITH HILL ANNEX

Keith Morton and Leslie Hernandez

In April 2012, following a year of informal conversations, experimentation, and use, Providence College began formally leasing 1,000 square feet of space in the Smith Hill Community Development Corporation's (SHCDC) Capitol Square development. The development—6 storefronts at ground level and 13 condominiums above—was part of a major effort by a longtime community partner to provide affordable housing and revitalize a major artery running through the Smith Hill neighborhood of Providence, Rhode Island. The development had opened in 2008, literally on the day the national financial and real estate meltdown began; prospective tenants walked away and by 2012 the storefronts and most of the condos had been empty for more than 3 years. An immediate goal of the new Providence College/Smith Hill Annex was to serve as an anchor tenant; the SHCDC hoped to leverage the project to fill the other spaces. We also hoped to serve as a catalyzing space for dialogue with a primary mission of "fostering conversation in a wide range of configurations between members of the campus and community, with longer-term goals of greater mutual understanding and opportunities for collaboration" (Feinstein Institute for Public Service, 2012). In this chapter, we provide an overview of the Providence College/Smith Hill Annex as a model for mutual relationships and dialogue between campus and community.

Why Dialogue: Founding the Annex

The organizing work that resulted in the Annex was inspired by a local, street-involved teenage hip-hop artist whom one of us had known for several years.

Stevie talked often of his wish for a place in the neighborhood where he and his crew could be welcome and safe and could meet, practice, and perform. We soon realized that his crew did not need a space for their sole use, but rather a space they could access on a consistent basis as full members of the community. It would be fine if that space were shared with other community members. As we understood it, being a "full member" meant that our partners controlled their access to the space and shared power and decision-making in determining its overall organization. This realization led us to connect Stevie's hope to other conversations taking place among Providence College's Feinstein Institute for Public Service staff and others from the local community. We began to collectively imagine a space that had the potential to enlarge and connect our social networks, support opportunities for personal and collective growth, and bring campus and community members into closer proximity. Looking back, we recognize that a larger experiment, in which all of this was embedded, was learning how a large institution of higher education could authentically share resources and power with grassroots community members.

The "us" involved in the planning was initially an informal group of conversation partners, including staff and students of the Feinstein Institute, staff and board members of the Smith Hill CDC, neighborhood residents, and students and faculty of several of the college's departments. As the core concept of the Annex began to take shape, we expanded the conversation to include members of the college's executive staff, including the provost, the chief financial officer, the associate vice president for external affairs, and several local political leaders. One of the contributors to this chapter was then coleading a weekly youth program at a neighborhood rec center (where they met Stevie and his friends), and we used people gathering at the rec center as a sounding board for the ideas that emerged.

Although we did initially consider other spaces, a storefront in the Capitol Square development project fit the criteria that had emerged from our conversations: It was located in a highly visible spot on a major thoroughfare in the neighborhood; it was geographically and politically positioned to leverage additional development activity in the neighborhood; it allowed the college to provide support to the SHCDC, a valued and financially vulnerable community organization that was working to stabilize the neighborhood; it was a space we could rent, rather than buy; and it was an unfinished space we could build out and make hospitable to a wide range of uses.

Historical and Philosophical Foundations

As we began to formalize the idea of using a storefront as a space shared by campus and community, we reframed our goals into a more deliberate experiment: We began searching for a structure and methods for bringing campus and community members together in an authentic and equitable way. More specifically, we began to lean explicitly on the work of Margaret Wheatley (2002), and especially her book *Turning to One Another: Simple Conversations to Restore Hope to the Future*. Building on the dialogical insights of Paulo Freire, and filtering these through a lifetime of organizing, advocacy, and systems thinking, Wheatley argues that the fundamental starting point for individual and communal thriving is conversation across perceived barriers of difference and separation. She writes, "There is no more powerful way to initiate significant change than to convene a conversation. . . . When a community of people discovers that they share a concern, change begins. There is no power equal to a community discovering what it cares about" (p. 26).

Wheatley's perspective was (and is) relevant to the Annex for multiple reasons: It emphasizes the importance of convening a conversation; it also deemphasizes managing toward predetermined ends, or having one perspective take ownership. Wheatley points to a particular strategy of positive social change: building community, where community is a dense system of relationships strengthened and sometimes created by hearing, telling, and making room for stories that convey meaning, values, and identity. She argues that the power necessary to make change emerges from a community of people who have named and shared what they care about. We asked ourselves, What could we do with this space to facilitate such conversations within and among members of the campus and community?

We were helped in our deliberations by locating the Annex in a historic tradition, attempting to represent something of the dialogical spirit that informed the founding of Jane Addams's (1910) Hull House in 1890; the folk education spirit of Myles Horton's (1997) Highlander Education Center, a place so pivotal in the civil rights movement of the 1950s through the 1970s; and the hospitality and inclusiveness of Dorothy Day and Peter Maurin's Catholic Worker movement (Troester, 1993). We were also inspired by more contemporary experiments with the power of conversation and stories, such as work of the Conversation Café (Robin & Pogue, 2018).

Because we were focused on relationships, boundary crossing, and values such as authenticity, we anchored our conversations about putting Wheatley's perspective into practice in three intertwined analytical frameworks: critical service-learning (Mitchell, 2008); asset-based community development (Battistoni, Longo, & Morton, 2014; Kretzmann & McKnight, 1993); and systems theory (Meadows, 2008). We wanted to meet in a manner that promoted equity, where people were free to put into and get out of the process what they chose. We wanted to be able to have campus and community members meet across the cultural boundaries separating them on the basis of their respective interests, strengths, assets, and potentials, rather than their weaknesses, deficits, or needs. And we assumed that individuals and the larger community had the potential insights, resources, and abilities needed to be successful on their own terms. We wanted a space that invited listening, more than telling, and we wanted to have people practice and learn to listen with respect. And we wanted all of this to happen in an environment that encouraged participants to use their conversations, relationships, and learning to work toward positive action. Conversation, storytelling, and listening across perceived boundaries has the potential to reveal the systems in place, create shared knowledge, and identify the leverage points for change. Our foundational assumption was the insight that everyone wants to live a meaningful life.

As complex as our conceptual model was, we recognized the value of making it as simple as possible in practice: We defined what we thought were the minimum requirements for structuring a space that was available for free to any configuration of campus and community partners and the potential to increase conversation among them. This presented a classic problem of community-building: balancing structure and antistructure (Turner, 1974). At its extreme, antistructure is the experiential moment of beginning in time and space when everything and anything is possible—an opportunity of pure potential. Structure, at the other end of the spectrum, means that institutional power has been organized to determine, or overdetermine, what is possible or allowed and how people will behave in a given time and space, removing their autonomy and creativity and reducing their potential to make meaning. We wanted a space that provided enough structure and kept open the opportunity of beginning again, a balance that Turner calls *communitas*: a space that "does not merge identities; [but] liberates them from conformity to general norms, though this is necessarily a transient condition if society is to continue to operate in an orderly fashion" (p. 274). Authentic community, we believed, would be best supported by creating a consistent, minimalist structure; establishing a small and clear set of shared expectations; and encouraging continuous fluidity and creativity.

Our goal was a space that had enough structure for a wide variety of participants to easily use it, while retaining an energy that was perpetually liminal, a space that resisted becoming institutionalized or filled with prior experiences, expectations, and histories. We did not want it to become a place symbolically owned by some groups while unintentionally excluding others. We wanted a space that allowed people using it to self-organize and name for themselves the things they cared about and their ways of doing them.

General Model, Principles, and Practices

For each of its 7 years of operation, the Annex has averaged 17 to 20 campus and community groups using the space on a regular (generally weekly) basis, and an additional 20 to 30 groups using it on an occasional basis (monthly or a couple of times per year). The uses represent the wide array we were hoping for: The space has been used by a group teaching English to recent immigrants as they prepare for citizenship tests, learn about their rights, and exercise their political imaginations. The Guatemalan and Honduran Associations meet weekly at the Annex, opening their meetings to campus members as they are asked. Project 401, a hip-hop collaborative (of which Stevie is a member), uses the space to practice, teach, and occasionally perform, grounding their work in values of community and nonviolence. A local small business owner and activist, connected to the Honduran Association, periodically offers a 12-week entrepreneurship class to current and aspiring small business owners. Common Grounds Gamers, a loose collective of 30 or so members, meets weekly to share and play current and vintage video games. The Smith Hill Jam hosts a weekly get-together for people who want to play folk music.

The Annex also houses college courses that fit with the mission of the space. For instance, Providence College's Department of Public and Community Service Studies has, for six years, collaborated with College Unbound (a college for working adults) to offer a for-credit course titled "The City and . . . ." In this course, Providence College's students—mostly White, mostly middle- and upper-middle-class, mostly suburban—partner with College Unbound's working adults—mostly from Providence and very diverse—around a theme that requires exploring the city together: the city and its youth, its storytellers, its neighborhoods, its artifacts. Other courses at the Annex are from global studies and education and take up topics such as urban education, dialogue, and community-engaged research. As another example, a campus staff member pursuing certification as a doula organized a series of trainings for other students seeking certification. All of these courses invite campus and community participation in one way or another.

Periodic learning circles, led mostly by community practitioners, are open to all and explore a wide range of topics—most recently on educating black boys and immigration and advocacy in the Latino community. The space is also used by nonprofit organizations ranging from the regional United Way to local service organizations such as Sojourner House (a local domestic violence organization) for gatherings, workshops, toy drives, and other events. A few times a year we hold potlucks and invite everyone to join in.

Physically, the Annex is a rectangular, 1,000-square-foot space with a bathroom in one corner and a walled-off storage area in another corner. There is a full-size refrigerator. The space has tall glass windows on 3 sides, doors opening onto the street, and a small parking lot at the rear. The Annex has 8 folding tables, 40 stackable chairs, and 4 easy chairs. It offers flipchart stands, WiFi, and a projector that can be linked to a laptop computer. Its concrete floor is covered with carpet designed to resist staining, and it is lit by fluorescent ceiling lights. Art is limited to a large plywood mural of the neighborhood done by a youth program that says "Smith Hill" and a graffiti-art sign in the front window that says "Annex," a gift from Project 401. Each group is given a key and an orientation, and left to set up and break down on their own. We provide basic amenities such as toilet paper, garbage bags, and paper towels. We have turned down offers of furniture, art, and other objects that would define the space; keeping it this simple allows everyone who comes in to own it equally and set it up according to their own needs.

Holding the Annex together is a small commitment of staff time and a flexible management structure. As a faculty member with a one-course release to work with Providence College's Feinstein Institute for Public Service, one of us has been able to make establishing and managing the Annex a small part of their work. A portion of time from three-plus years of AmeriCorps/VISTA volunteers did much of the heavy lifting getting the project established. Now one of us works with the Annex as a graduate assistant to coordinate its day-to-day operation—a position that has been in place for nearly three years.

The Annex has a web page on the college's website that displays its calendar; it maintains a presence on Facebook and sends out a weekly e-mail update to a sizeable list. The update is built around the weekly calendar, sharing basic information but also reinforcing the mission of the Annex and linking everyone on the contact list to its shared work. At the request of Annex groups, we use these resources and occasional e-mail blasts across campus to help publicize opportunities.

Organizationally, the Annex inhabits an unusual place in the institutional life of the college. Although it was initiated through the college's Feinstein Institute and is managed day-to-day by a graduate assistant and a faculty member associated with the institute, it formally "belongs" to the Office of the Provost and Vice President for Academic Affairs (VPAA), which is where its operating budget of approximately $17,000 per year is located (the graduate assistantship, valued at approximately $20,000 for stipend and tuition remission, comes from another budget line, and is supervised through the Feinstein Institute for Public Service). The office of the VPAA and the Feinstein Institute are coconveners of the Annex's campus-based management committee. This committee exercises no direct influence on Annex programming, but helps navigate the college's bureaucracy, publicize events, and oversee the business side of the project. It addresses practical issues such as leases, utilities, insurance, access, and security, as well as policy questions such as requests to use the space by overtly partisan groups during elections. The committee includes administrators and staff from the college, and the executive director of the SHCDC, who has played a significant role in the life of the Annex, regularly attends the meetings.

The Annex acts as one conduit between campus and community and builds a reservoir of goodwill—a "third" space that allows people to discuss potentially divisive or tense concerns informally and provisionally. The Annex figures, in a modest way, in the college's ongoing discussions with the city of Providence about "payment in lieu of taxes." Our Annex network regularly provides introductions to community members when college committees or advisory groups that want to include community members are being formed. We help the college practice its expressed goal, spoken at the Annex's ribbon-cutting by the college president, to "be a good neighbor," rather than a gated community that ventures out to do episodic service. And finally, the Annex contributes in small ways to improving campus and community members' perceptions of one another.

Key Successes and Challenges

The biggest successes of the Annex are the congruence of its mission and structure, and its consistency of purpose over time. It was created and is maintained now by the exercise of its primary purpose: conversation among a diverse group of community and campus members. Its mission has led to deeper college support of the SHCDC, including a 3-year grant totaling $750,000; inspired a startup (if short-lived) café; and led to the creation of the Smith Hill Partners Initiative, a group of 30 or so nonprofit leaders, community residents, and local political leaders that meets monthly to share and collaborate. The Smith Hill Block Party—led by the Partners Initiative—now draws over 1,000 people every August; Annex members help run, participate in, and perform at the party. The Annex also served as one important source of inspiration for the college's new on-campus, multicultural, creative space, the Center at Moore Hall.

The ongoing challenge of the Annex is maintaining its original simplicity and its liminality even as its sedimentary history of use accumulates: balancing structure and antistructure in a manner that encourages the experience of authentic community. It is this balance, we believe, that creates space for deep, difficult dialogue, a space in which, to quote one participant, "the things not spoken can be spoken." Although we are excited and supportive of the successes of groups using the space, we are careful to understand the Annex as an open, free space waiting to be filled in a unique way by each group that appears. We are not trying to position the Annex as a laboratory in which the Feinstein Institute or other units of the college can practice their expertise on behalf of the community. We argue that the college, as a permanent institutional presence in the neighborhood, has the resources and a learning-focused mission that allow it to hold this space as a good neighbor. What we value in the space is the diversity of groups and people using it, and the multiplicity of their worldviews and lived experiences.

Our goal is to maintain a space hospitable to that diversity. We invite users of the Annex, who might not know one another, to meet and talk. We do not offer the Annex as a space for finding organizers, consultants, or leaders—though it is often visited by all three. As coordinators of the Annex we are hosts, sometimes conversation partners, and occasionally conveners, but that is it. The groups using the Annex organize it conceptually and physically, bringing their knowledge, wisdom, analysis, and leadership. This is the subtle but important insight learned through the Annex: If colleges and universities want to include their community partners as full and authentic members in the shared work of strengthening communities, democracy, and public life, we begin by making space where stories built on the lived experiences of campus and community members are shared, helping us to learn about and improve the system in which we live, together.

References

Addams, J. (1910). *Twenty years at Hull House.* New York, NY: Macmillan.

Battistoni, R., Longo, N., & Morton, K. (2014). Co-creating mutual spaces for campuses and communities. In J. Plaut, J. Hammerlink, & L. Worell (Eds.), *Asset-based campus-community partnerships* (pp. 59-66). Minneapolis: Minnesota Campus Compact.

Feinstein Institute for Public Service. (2012). *Mission statement.* Smith Hill Annex. Providence College, Providence, RI.

Horton, M. (1997). *The long haul: An autobiography* (J. Kohl & H. Kohl, Eds.). New York, NY: Teachers College Press.

Kretzman, J., & McKnight, J. (1993). *Building communities from the inside out: A path toward finding and mobilizing a community's assets.* Evanston, IL: Institute for Policy Research.

Meadows, D. H. (2008). *Thinking in systems: A primer*. White River Junction, VT: Chelsea Green Publishing.
Mitchell, T. (2008). Traditional versus critical service learning. *Michigan Journal of Community Service Learning, 14*(2), 50–65.
Robin, V., & Pogue, J. (2018). *History* (Conversation Café). Retrieved from http://www.conversationcafe.org/history/
Troester, R. R. (1993). *Voices from the Catholic Worker*. Philadelphia, PA: Temple University Press.
Turner, V. (1974). *Dramas, fields and metaphors: Symbolic action in human society*. Ithaca, NY: Cornell University Press.
Wheatley, M. (2002). *Turning to one another: Simple conversations to restore hope to the future*. San Francisco, CA: Berrett-Koehler.

20

LESSONS FROM THE FRONT PORCH

Fostering Strengthened Community Partnerships Through Dialogue

Suchitra V. Gururaj and Virginia A. Cumberbatch

The Role of Dialogue for Community Engagement at the University of Texas at Austin

Engagement efforts by institutions of higher education are most credible and sustainable when they are both strategic and responsive. A university may effectively create partnerships between its scholarly resources and communities to meet community priorities or stated needs. However, maintaining and stewarding these partnerships involves continuously addressing and reassessing the uneven power structures between the university and the community (Holland, 2005; Maurasse, 2001). Since 2015, the Division of Diversity and Community Engagement (DDCE) at the University of Texas at Austin (UT Austin) has developed and reenvisioned a series of dialogues to help us undertake the difficult work of effective and reciprocal community engagement.

Both the state's flagship institution and its most elite public institution, UT Austin holds *responsibility* as a core value of its public service mission, with expectations that its students will "serve as a catalyst for positive change in Texas and beyond" and that the university itself will "transform lives for the benefit of society" (University of Texas at Austin, n.d.). In 2007, President Williams Powers Jr. created the DDCE as a demonstration of his commitment to public service. A collection of programs from around the university, including student affairs, academic affairs, external affairs, and community relations, the DDCE is a place where dialogue has the potential to create positive impact and connect diverse stakeholders including students, engaged faculty, and community.

This potential is especially important in light of the university's long history with the city of Austin. Segregated by policy decisions delineated in the city's 1928 Master Plan, Austin was redefined with a white population west of (now) Interstate 35 and a "negro district" to its east (Koch & Fowler, 1928). During the university's growth in the 1980s, swaths of East Austin were purchased—or obtained through practices not rooted in equity—by the university and land-use developers working with the university. These decisions opened the floodgates to alarming rates of residential and commercial development on the eastside and helped encourage the gentrification and displacement seen today that is slowly dismantling the structures of the vibrant black and Latinx communities that were relegated to the eastside through inequitable policy.

Aligned with UT Austin's relationship with Austin is its mirrored microcosmic political and social history of integration on campus. Integrated at the graduate level in 1950 with the *Sweatt v. Painter* lawsuit, UT Austin's tumultuous and arguably ongoing process of integration has modeled an approach to build external community trust and reconciliation. The historical narratives higher education institutions choose to recognize, document, and curate often shape institutional memory and set a precedent for an institution's values and priorities. Such is certainly the case for UT Austin. As such, UT Austin and DDCE have committed (particularly through coauthor Virginia A. Cumberbatch's 2018 book *As We Saw It: The Story of Integration at the University of Texas at Austin*) to documenting the stories of individuals, black alums, and other alumni of color who pioneered the way for today's continued conversations on race, diversity, and inclusion. This commitment has informed UT Austin's interactive, reactive, and intentional dialogue with the community surrounding the campus and furthers the potential for the DDCE to catalyze for positive impact.

Meanwhile, considered a "creative class" (Florida, 2002) city and a politically progressive dot in a solidly conservative state, Austin's popularity has grown at unprecedented rates, with Asian and Latino populations growing the fastest. From 2000 to 2014, Austin's population increased by 20.4%, thus making it the third fastest-growing city during that period; yet, according to Eric Tang and Chunhui Ren (2014), Austin was also the only major metropolitan area that experienced a loss in its population of African Americans, many of whom were being displaced from previously black East Austin.

It was in this context that the DDCE began reaching out to a community that was experiencing rapid growth and seemingly inevitable change, engendered, in part, by the university itself. For this reason, the community engagement goal of the DDCE's strategic plan explicitly states our purpose of "cultivating mutually beneficial community-university partnerships that further the mission of UT Austin to serve Texas and beyond, with an emphasis on historically and currently underserved communities" (Division of Diversity and Community Engagement Strategic Plan, 2016) and to address past inequity by fostering substantive connections between the university and our communities. The DDCE's Community Engagement Center (CEC) unit, located in the heart of East Austin, has served as a meeting point between the university and the community and, thus, as a natural site of dialogue.

The Development of a Model for Dialogue

The CEC undertook a strategic shift in 2014, from serving as the unit charged with community relations to one involved in actual engagement. At this time, Suchitra V. Gururaj and DDCE's vice president's team internally redefined the CEC as the division's *front porch*—the place where folks might gather before feeling that they could be invited in to a university that was intimidating, both in its size and in its power.

That year, the CEC hosted a talk given by a DDCE faculty fellow, Eric Tang (Tang & Ren, 2014), whose work on gentrification in Austin and the unusual decrease in the number of black families in East Austin had recently spurred local consternation and activism. At this first talk—not yet defined as a *dialogue*—Tang presented his data, then opened the conversation to the 60 people in the room. The roomful of listeners represented several generations of East Austin—from the civil rights leaders of the 1960s and 1970s to young non-black students renting in the area to students of color from Huston-Tillotson, Austin's historically black university. The gathering became increasingly conversational and the "audience" spoke and responded directly to Tang, who, as a former organizer, especially valued the role of listener. Elder listeners offered their own conjectures—based on their personal experiences—for the loss of black families and the crumbling of community and asserted that the hard data only told part of the story. Younger listeners wondered aloud what they might do to stanch the rapid cultural changes in their new neighborhoods and work more closely with the older generation to preserve them. Tang responded as a community-based researcher: He asked the older residents if they might be willing to be interviewed about why they stayed in the neighborhood, despite the rapid changes taking place. The list of names and e-mails collected that night served as one foundation for a later study, *Those Who Stayed* (Tang & Falola, 2016). The collaboration that emerged from a simple invitation to have a conversation with an engaged faculty member was the inspiration for the development of the

Community Engagement (CE) Dialogues, which was launched in academic year 2015–2016.

Drawing on the model of asset-based community development (Kretzmann & McKnight, 1993), the dialogues were intended to convene Austin-area participants as "full contributors to the community-building process" (Kretzmann & McKnight, 1993, p. 6), acknowledging that the people of UT Austin were also Austin-area participants with an interest in the cocreation of knowledge and solutions for complex problems. In addition, we recognized that *listening* was at the core of community change and development and the success of these convenings would depend on creating a "process of genuine interaction through which human beings listen to each other deeply enough to be changed by what they learn" (Sustained Dialogue Institute, 2017, p. 3).

That pilot year, we offered dialogues on topics such as "Gentrification in East Austin," "Economic Segregation," and "Health Inequity" with context-setting experts from the university and the community in various locations on campus and at locations of partner organizations in East Austin that were well known to us, including community centers and local black churches. Advertising was done through e-mails, social media, newspaper ads, and word of mouth. At the event, attendees and speakers ate the dinner provided, usually sandwiches, drinks, and dessert from a restaurant with an existing UT Austin contract. Three or four experts in the area—whether faculty, nonprofit leaders, community leaders, or councilpeople—were called on to speak for three to five minutes each to provide context, and the conversation was then opened up for dialogue with an assembly of students, community members, faculty, and nonprofit leaders.

Participants were asked to complete an evaluation after the dialogue that asked about their affiliations and interests, especially as related to a desire or need to connect to the university's resources. The last session was conducted with grant funding from Bridging Theory to Practice and enabled us to ask the summative question "How can UT Austin be a better collaborator as it relates to our students, our faculty, and our staff?" The intent of this last session was to seek information that would inform the student-, faculty-, and community-focused programming created in our center.

Key Successes and Lessons Learned: CE Dialogues

Attendance for the CE Dialogues ranged between 18 and 75 participants. Of the 40 evaluations completed during the first series of dialogues, a majority replied affirmatively to questions such as "Are you interested in connecting with UT Austin?" and "Would you attend another CE Dialogue?" The final convening of the year identified 3 areas of improvement for UT Austin: increasing communication with community partners, designating one point of contact at UT Austin, and establishing individual projects in the neighborhood. Overall, comments from the assessment, including "I can't wait for more," "Look forward to the next," and "Would like to see more," indicated an interest in this format, which was still novel for the university.

Yet postdialogue informal discussions revealed that participants wanted to spend less time *talking* about problems and more time *mobilizing* around solutions. As in their evaluations, both students and community members alike asked, "What do we do?" and stated, "I look forward to helping with solutions and possible volunteer opportunities." Participants asked for more opportunities for partnership-building. Moreover, community feedback indicated the need to "feature fewer participants" and cull their "talking points" in the spirit of brevity and providing space for conversation.

In that way, we discovered that, despite our intention to create collaborative spaces, the CE Dialogues evolved to undermine community members' authority as full contributors (Kretzmann & McKnight, 1996). The three to five minutes allotted each speaker for context-setting often became protracted and dialogues frequently reverted into the traditional "sage-on-the-stage" model, where "experts"—faculty, community leaders, or politicians—speak in one direction and the "audience" responds.

We learned two important lessons from this CE Dialogues pilot. First, although convened in the spirit of an asset-based community development meeting where each individual is seen to have gifts (McKnight & Kretzmann, 1993), the CE Dialogues perpetuated prevailing power dynamics. Second, community members no longer wished to dialogue bidirectionally but to mobilize collaboratively to address the issue. In this manner, we had yet to deliver on the promise of asset-based community development.

Revision of the Model

When Virginia A. Cumberbatch joined the team and accepted the challenge to revision the CE Dialogues, the name Front Porch Gatherings (FPG) stood out as both a nod to our center's evolving story and a symbol of what we hoped the series would become—a gathering of people, all of whom had lived experiences, collaborating toward sustained community-building. The term *dialogue* no longer described our intention. In addition, we had to strive to keep individuals at the core by truly elevating community members as "full contributors to the community-building process" (Kretzman & McKnight,

1993, p. 6) and by fostering "genuine interaction" (Sustained Dialogue Institute, 2017, p. 3). This process could be effected through storytelling.

And so we repositioned community members—not necessarily leaders and not necessarily faculty—as the experts in the room, both philosophically and physically. Rather than faculty statistics (used in some cases), the context-setting mechanisms were community testimonials, switching the emphasis from statistics and data to that of human-centered story and experience. Participants were invited intentionally, and we made an effort to include a critical mass of participants from each stakeholder group. After context-setting, participants were placed by group number in breakout sessions facilitated by a trained student, faculty, or community member facilitator, who was charged with keeping conversation moving along predetermined questions and preventing one voice from dominating. Undergraduate and graduate student scribes recorded the conversation on flipchart paper for full transparency. A final sharing session helped to determine action items for the collaborators in the room, whether they sought to work with UT Austin or not. The purpose of the debrief at the end of the session was not only to present each group's ideas and discuss some of their overlaps and contradictions but also to then present the expectation that the individuals and groups in the room continue their collaborative interactions toward creating "informed community change" (Sustained Dialogue Institute, 2017, p. 3).

Location was also critical, as it helped set the tone for community trust. As such, accessible locations were scouted. In forging a partnership with Austin's historically black university, we set the standard for collaboration. Dinner was provided at each event with an effort to contract with local businesses, primarily operated by owners of color, bringing restaurant proprietors in, too, as experts to the conversations in their neighborhoods. Finally, scribe notes were shared within days on the CEC blog (e.g., see Community Engagement Center, 2016). In sharing a recap of the FPGs, we not only kept our community contract to be transparent and to continue communication beyond the evening's conversation but also engaged stakeholders and community members who were unable to attend so that they too could join in on all of our efforts to hold all of ourselves accountable for change. As with the CE Dialogues, we attempted to hold FPGs on the same night of every month; the need to curate FPGs more deliberately necessitated increased and improved communications so that people could plan to attend.

In the first year of FPGs, we addressed several topics that emerged during the CE Dialogues, which served as a type of informal assessment to understand topics of interest in the community. Given the interactive nature of gatherings, these topics, along with facilitator questions, were developed in conversation with key community partners. The first two years of FPGs addressed issues such as "The Role of the Black Church in East Austin," "Affordability and Re-Entry," "The Impact of Immigration Policy at the Local Level," and "Stopping the School to Prison Pipeline"—and were hosted at local black churches, Austin's historically black university, the local community college system, and community centers. For these convenings, most context-setters were community members, nonprofit leaders, and faith leaders in the community; only a couple were university faculty.

Keys to Success and Lessons Learned: Front Porch Gatherings

The success of the FPGs is evident in the collected statistics. Over 2 years, the FPGs have convened more than 50 community partners, 65 student volunteers, 30 university faculty, and more than 645 individuals overall. Collaborations with media partners, in addition, ensured that anyone with an Internet connection could be part of the gathering by viewing the livestream.

This new format resulted in collaborations among community partners as well as connections with UT Austin. We learned that participants' productivity, regardless of their affiliations, was enhanced by the new structure of the gatherings. One facilitator said, "The focus on formative outcomes really shone through and I heard from many in the small group that they appreciated the opportunity for an authentic dialogue." With the new format, instead of a dialogue between two entities, this process fostered a dialogue among all participants—all of whom were treated as experts in the room. Students may have found themselves inadvertently on the sideline of the initial CE Dialogues; at the FPGs, however, they were cocreators of knowledge and played a significant role in developing action plans. In their evaluation testimonial, one student commented, "Thank you for intentionally creating space to expose some, engage others and most importantly drive action. I am very hopeful especially after yesterday's discussion that we are not far from reallocating resources in an appropriate way. I love it!"

The revised format of the FPGs taught several lessons. First, we needed to acknowledge the power dynamic between the university and its communities and seek to actively dismantle it by intentionally creating a format that engages every participant in active ways. Second, engagement cannot be limited to listening, but rather is the basis for scaffolding to action. To that end, the purpose of the post-FPG debrief was to not only present each group's ideas and discuss some of their overlaps and contradictions but also set the expectation that the individuals and groups in the room continue their collaborative interactions toward creating "informed community change" (Sustained Dialogue Institute, 2017, p. 3).

Recommendations for Other Campuses

Our models for community-university dialogues may be replicable for many universities and colleges in a variety of contexts. Based on our experience with developing this model, we offer the following recommendations for tailoring a model like this to a particular institution:

1. *Know your context.* Our models were created in the historical and cultural context of our community. In the last decade, the DDCE has cultivated relationships with more than 400 community partners and incubated dozens of local nonprofits with time and funding, and our staff keeps abreast of topics in the community through these groups. Nonetheless, we find value in continuously assessing our programs. We use assessments to reenvision the FPGs and our center programming, and we recently completed a community assessment survey of more than 120 community members and leaders to redetermine the priority issues in Austin.
2. *Acknowledge self-interest.* The defendant in the *Fisher v. The University of Texas* case and the locus for some of the first conversations about Confederate statuary on campuses, UT Austin owns its historical role in encouraging equities and its current role in helping to repair and restore them. We also acknowledge that the community-based programs we help create are tied to our role as a state institution that is often part of national policy conversations. Constructing spaces in which citizens can engage in deliberate decision-making is without a doubt tied to the health of our democracy, which, as a state public institution, we are bound to serve.
3. *Expand the circle of beneficiaries.* Developed immediately after we completed the application process for the Carnegie Classification for Community Engagement, the CE Dialogues chose to focus on the types of traditional engagement assessed in that application—namely, the relationship between a higher education institution's students or faculty with its community. In focusing only on this dynamic, we missed the opportunity to provide time and space to facilitate collaborations among community partners—which could still result in opportunities for UT Austin students and faculty.
4. *Embrace the role of event planner.* Revisioning the CE Dialogues included critical considerations of event planning. In the end, we reassessed not only the ways in which content was shared but also the arrangement of chairs, catering menus and contracts, external communications, event signage, and accessibility. No detail is too small.

5. *Trust, but assess, the process.* Most importantly, the model we developed at UT Austin was an iterative process that required thoughtful consideration—and trial and error—over time. It also benefited from the perspectives of two different programmatic leads at unique moments in the program's history who initially considered and later reconsidered the communities to be served, the redefinition of goals, and the center's changing mission.

These lessons are useful in the larger landscape of higher education, and especially of public higher education, the mission of which includes serving communities. Being of service cannot be characterized by a one-way interaction in which the institution bestows resources to the public in the name of capacity-building but rather by mutually beneficial relationships between the university and its communities. Though intended as participatory events, the CE Dialogues naturally reverted to the sage-on-the-stage model that often typifies the role of the privileged institution that casts itself as both creator and owner of expertise. But our addressing this problem in a timely, inclusive, and deliberate manner enabled us to create programming through which expertise was acknowledged to be one of the many gifts of each and every participant.

Representing in the community an institution as prominent and with as storied a past as UT Austin can be challenging. However, through these dialogues, we attempted to, as much as possible, set aside the UT Austin brand to create an "organic" process (London, 2010, p. iv) that stood apart from the institution and that would create a culture characterized by civic partnerships and citizen-led action that could indeed "transform lives for the benefit of society" (University of Texas at Austin, n.d.). In this manner, this iterative process enabled UT Austin to deliver on the promise of public higher education to acknowledge individuals as the deep assets of a place—and as both the beneficiaries of and the reason for higher education.

References

Community Engagement Center. (2016, September 30). *September 2016 recap: The role of the black church in East Austin.* Retrieved from http://diversity.utexas.edu/communitycenter/2016/09/september-recap-the-role-of-the-black-church-in-east-austin/

Division of Diversity and Community Engagement Strategic Plan. (2016). Community engagement strategic goal. Retrieved from http://diversity.utexas.edu/strategic-plan-2016/the-plan/#Community

Florida, R. (2002). *The rise of the creative class: And how it's transforming work, leisure, community, and everyday life*. New York, NY: Basic Books.

Holland, B. (2005). Reflections on community-campus partnerships: What has been learned? What are the next challenges? In P. A. Pasque, B. L. Mallory, R. E. Smerek, B. Dwyer, and N. Bowman (Eds.), Higher education collaboratives for community engagement and improvement. *Education Scholarship*, 4, pp. 10–17. https://scholars.unh.edu/educ_facpub/4

Koch & Fowler, Consulting Engineers. (1928). *A city plan for Austin, Texas*. Retrieved from ftp://ftp.austintexas.gov/GIS-Data/planning/compplan/1927_Plan.pdf

Kretzmann, J. P., & McKnight, J. L. (1993). *Building communities from the inside out: A path toward finding and mobilizing a community's assets*. Evanston, IL: Institute for Policy Research.

London, S. (2010). *Doing democracy*. Washington DC: The Kettering Foundation.

Maurasse, D. J. (2001). *Beyond the campus*. New York, NY: Routledge.

Sustained Dialogue Institute. (2017). *What is Sustained Dialogue? It's not just using issue sheets*. Washington DC: Author.

Tang, E., & Falola, B. (2016). *Those who stayed: The impact of gentrification on long-standing residents of East Austin*. Retrieved from https://liberalarts.utexas.edu/iupra/_files/Those-Who-Stayed.pdf

Tang, E., & Ren, C. (2014). *Outlier: The case of Austin's declining African-American population*. Retrieved from https://liberalarts.utexas.edu/iupra/_files/pdf/Austin%20AA%20pop%20policy%20brief_FINAL.pdf

University of Texas at Austin. (n.d.). *Mission and values*. Retrieved from https://www.utexas.edu/about/mission-and-values

21

LOCAL PARTICIPATION AND LIVED EXPERIENCE

Dialogue and Deliberation Through Participatory Processes in Landscape Architecture

Katie Kingery-Page

Many landscape architects tacitly accept dialogue and deliberation as an assumed part of practice, but seldom is the explicit language of deliberation used. Thus, some translation is required to understand the profession's history of building critical theory about community participation as a deliberative process. Though arising from the history of palatial and estate garden design in Europe and early America, the profession quickly became significant in the shaping of North American cities through parks, squares, and streets (Rogers, 2001). A focus on the intersection of ecological and human systems made it fertile ground for the rise of what Randolph Hester (2006) called "ecological democracy" (p. 77), a vision for a holistic built and natural environment, designed through inclusive processes.

The work of landscape architecture often occurs in the context of community decision-making with tangible outcomes such as the design of public places, parks, and schoolyards. Given this focus, methods for democratic deliberation about design of public places has blossomed in landscape architecture, framed as *participatory design* and *codesign* processes (Beardsley, Ross, & Gragg, 2009; Hester, 2012; Juarez & Brown, 2008). This chapter presents key principles of dialogue and deliberation in landscape architecture, explores models for dialogue and deliberation in a community-based project conducted by Kansas State University (K-State) faculty and graduate students, and concludes with lessons learned from the landscape architecture models of dialogue and deliberation.

Key Principles for a Profession: Local Community Participation in Design and Valuing Lived Experiences of Place

Rapid urbanization during the landscape architecture profession's first full century of growth in the United States brought the competing pressures of new development and community continuity to the forefront. The profession's focus on outdoor, urban green space made it a natural testing ground for concerns about local knowledge, community involvement, and/or exclusion from design processes (Halprin, 1969; Hester, 1975; Merriman, 2010). To understand the development of key principles for dialogue and deliberation in landscape architecture, it is essential to become acquainted with the work of Lawrence Halprin and Randolph T. Hester.

Halprin's landscape architecture included community site planning, design of public plazas and fountains, and typological exploration of movement spaces such as streets and freeways (Halprin, 1966). Halprin developed a design framework he dubbed *RSVP Cycles* and later adapted as a participatory approach he called *Take Part* (Halprin, 1969; Merriman, 2010). The model emphasizes the feedback loop of participation and includes special attention to the patterns, movements, and realities of people. Halprin's work was shaped by his collaboration with Anna Halprin, his life partner and a pioneer of postmodern dance (Merriman, 2010; Wasserman, 2012). Together, they held experiential movement workshops in the context of community projects. They encouraged people to explore embodied experience of place and bring their lived experiences as input to design dialogue (Merriman, 2010). Halprin's involvement with freeway planning as an adviser to the Federal Highway Administration in the 1960s developed his awareness of tensions in community planning and design (Halprin, 2005). By his own admission, Halprin's ethos of participation arose from the anger he encountered when he did not include communities in the design of their places (Halprin, 2005).

Hester (1984) laid out a 12-step process in his seminal work on participatory design process, *Planning Neighborhood Space With People*, beginning with listening and goal-setting to capitalize on local knowledge. In the 1970s and 1980s, Hester challenged conventional wisdom in landscape architecture that the designer determined goals and that local residents had limited ability to determine the future of their places. Hester (1975) defined *meaningful participation* as "based on the premise that no single public good exists. Since wealthy special interests often determine the public good, this process simply allows less powerful minority interests to be represented in the decision-making discussions" (p. 180). Hester (2006) recommended that participatory design be "informed by local wisdom, attachment to place, and networks of interconnectedness and ecological thinking" (p. 10).

Both Halprin and Hester helped inform participatory design as a form of dialogue and then codesign as a fully deliberative process. Hester often uses "transactive" (Hester, 1975, p. 180) or "design *with* people" (Hester, 2002, p. 53). *Codesign* is another way of saying design *with* people: community members' full participation throughout dialogue and deliberation and their active presence when decisions are made (Howard & Somerville, 2014).

Models for Participatory Design and Codesign in Faculty- and Student-Led Projects

Hester and Halprin's principles inform my work with graduate students through the use of adapted ethnography to learn about people's lived, embodied experiences (Kingery-Page, Glastetter, DeOrsey, & Falcone, 2016). We begin by gathering broad input in mixed groups of stakeholders, seek to understand who is missing from the dialogue, and then develop a plan to invite those people into the process. We use methods including focus groups, one-on-one interviews, passive observation, participatory observation, and arts-based collective creativity events.

"Enclave" deliberation can be a vital part of a democratic process if it empowers otherwise suppressed people to engage in dialogue (Himmelroos, Rapeli, & Grönlund, 2016, p. 150). In landscape architecture, enclave deliberation is known as "smaller" public group or "field-based" participation and is also understood to empower marginalized groups (Juarez & Brown, 2008, p. 201). Literature on enclave deliberation emphasizes the need for inclusion in larger processes—in other words, using enclave-level dialogue to develop interests and agency, then bringing these agendas to the larger democratic process (Abdullah, Karpowitz, & Raphael, 2016). The concept of enclave or small-group deliberation is essential to the adapted ethnography model.

Chester I. Lewis Reflection Square Park: Memorial to a Civil Rights–Era Icon

At the request of the Downtown Wichita Development Corporation, Wichita Parks and Recreation, and a downtown arts collective known as FischHaus, my students and I began to craft an inclusive process to discuss the future of an underused public park. Our goal was a redesign of the park to strengthen its historic significance and provide inclusive green space in the downtown area. Wichita is a metropolitan area of approximately 400,000 population, but as of the 2010 census, less than 1% of Wichitans lived downtown. Downtown Wichita has been working to create a more pedestrian-friendly, livable environment, in part by assisting new residential infill development and by investing in public open spaces (Downtown Wichita, 2017).

Chester I. Lewis Reflection Square Park (Lewis Park) commemorates the life of a prominent lawyer of the Young Turks era of the NAACP. The Young Turks, as they were called, pushed for the NAACP to lead and promote direct action as a means of achieving civil rights (Eick, 2001). Part of Lewis's legacy, the Dockum Drugstore sit-in of 1958, was the first sit-in of the civil rights movement, although not sanctioned by the NAACP (Eick, 2001). Lewis, then a young lawyer, backed high school and college-aged youth in their sit-in to integrate the Dockum Drugstore lunch counter even as the NAACP did not support this direct action. As a result, Lewis split from the NAACP, though he continued to achieve many milestones of desegregation, including integrating Wichita's swimming pools and fighting against police brutality and public employment discrimination (Eick, 2001; Lewis, n.d.).

The downtown park that would become Lewis Park opened in 2000 but was not designated to commemorate Chester Lewis until 2007. At that time, the city installed a sculpture representing a lunch counter as the park was located within blocks of the actual Dockum Drugstore sit-in site. The park is a low-activity area with mature shade trees over a concrete hardscape and a backdrop of a custom-built wall fountain that is frequently in disrepair. In its current condition, Lewis Park is underutilized but does provide a shady respite for homeless individuals.

Participatory design of the project began by empowering community members to give input, enabling knowledgeable locals to guide the process. An initial convenience sample of local residents, NAACP members, city agency leaders, and public officials made up a first stakeholder meeting (see Figure 21.1). Following that meeting, students identified enclaves based upon interests, lived experiences of downtown, and demographics. The design team used focus groups, one-on-one interviews, participant observation, passive observation, and collective creativity methods to learn about community needs and dreams for the downtown park. Content analysis of the dialogue data ensured that pragmatic needs were prioritized, but also identified what Hester (2012) refers to as the emotional aspect of community input—people's feelings about the place.

One graduate student, Wei Sun, recruited participants by going door to door in apartment buildings and businesses near Lewis Park. She was interested in learning how residents and workers in the immediate vicinity

Figure 21.1. Lewis Park initial stakeholder meeting facilitated by chapter contributor and MLA students Skylar Brown, Andrea Lemken, and Wei Sun.

Note. Reprinted by permission of photographer, La Barbara James Wigfall.

of Lewis Park currently use or conceive of the park and what (if anything) would cause them to use Lewis Park more. Based on the interviews, Sun assembled a list of potential affordances the park could provide visitors if redesigned (Sun, 2018).

Andrea Lemken, another graduate student, recruited interview participants from minority communities in Wichita through a small snowball sample beginning with initial stakeholders and local community organizations. Lemken hoped to contribute an understanding of whether Wichitans had needs for green space that were unique to their culture of origin (Lemken, 2018). Graduate student Skylar Brown focused his recruitment of interview participants in two enclaves: advocates for Wichita's homeless and living participants and descendants of the Dockum Drugstore sit-in. Homeless advocates who participated in interviews with Brown emphasized the need for including services for homeless persons in downtown spaces. Brown also participated as a volunteer worker in a meal center downtown, observing and making field notes about stories shared by homeless individuals. Both Brown and Lemken found that persons strongly connected to the Dockum Drugstore sit-in emphasized the need for informal learning at the park—opportunities to reflect on the past, present, and future civil rights struggle (Brown, 2018; Lemken, 2018).

The result of this participatory process was a public art exhibit created by the students and curated by faculty at the downtown FischHaus community arts collective. During the exhibit, more than 600 members of the public considered the park's future by leaving their feedback on walls and banners within the exhibit. These posed specific questions such as "What would you like to see in Lewis Park?" and "What does the civil rights movement mean to you? . . . yesterday, today, and tomorrow?" (Figure 21.2). Also, as a result of the public exhibit, students met one of Chester I. Lewis's few living descendants, who agreed to be interviewed for the project. Students then digested this new input and refined a series of proposals for the park.

Figure 21.2. Community Dialogue on Chester I. Lewis Park, an exhibit hosted by the FischHaus, chapter contributor, and MLA students Skylar Brown, Andrea Lemken, and Wei Sun.

Note. Reprinted by permission of photographer, La Barbara James Wigfall.

These new designs sought to propose a park that exemplified Lewis's passion for equity and inclusion, commemorated his life, and also included resources for homeless persons (Brown, 2018; see Figure 21.3).

The graduate student design proposals were not ends in themselves, but rather were intended to promote further community dialogue and fundraising for the park. Each student provided a master's report to project partners, stakeholders, and participants. The students' community-based work has been (or will be) used in a variety of contexts to promote more dialogue, including the recent 60th anniversary celebration of the Dockum Drugstore sit-in and in the context of future Wichita Downtown development corporation roundtables on open space.

Successes and Challenges Using an Adapted Ethnography Model of Participation

The adapted ethnography model aimed to bring unheard voices into the Lewis Park conversation, following Hester's (1975) guidance: "Since wealthy special interests often determine the public good, [participatory design] simply allows less powerful minority interests to be represented in the decision-making discussions" (p. 180). In this spirit, the model engaged

Figure 21.3. Visualization of a future Lewis Park, created to express the possibilities of a commemorative park inclusive of the needs of Wichita's downtown homeless persons.

Note. Reprinted by permission of Skylar Brown.

a broad array of diverse interests in visioning the park's future. The graduate students' work used enclave deliberations, a mixed-group stakeholder meeting, and a large public event to engage publics. More than a single park, the site is a powerful symbol of Wichita's ability to acknowledge civil rights struggles and groundbreaking history. Skylar Brown's facilitation of process shows us that the park's future may also be symbolic of Wichita's willingness (or lack of willingness) to include unhoused people in public open space. Though the future of Lewis Park remains undetermined, the student reports record important dialogue and lay groundwork for future deliberation.

To date, the city of Wichita has no significant designated funding to redesign or refurbish Lewis Park, but the community-based project did create a groundswell of interest during a strategic year, the 60th anniversary of the Dockum Drugstore sit-in. The ideals of codesign, however, were not fully realized. Students' location at K-State while community members live two hours away in Wichita resulted in many design decisions being made in the academic studio, rather than in active sessions with community members. Ultimately, more time would be needed to bring the students' design proposals back to a mixed, diverse community group for decision-making on a final proposal.

In the context of graduate student master's projects, aligning inclusive community input and public-facing events with local community schedules challenged academic calendar constraints. I am not the first to note that sufficient time is the lifeblood of and insufficient time is a barrier to deliberative processes in landscape architecture. "Empowering local people may be critical for landscape architects working with marginalized communities," Jeffrey Juarez and Kyle Brown (2008) write. However, "logistical concerns such as time and access present substantial barriers to further strengthening the presence of landscape architecture within this arena" (p. 194). Hester (2012) adds, "Time affords deep empathy, detailed knowledge, and trusting partnerships that accommodate creative conflict and nurture a working majority politic" (p. 138).

Recommendations for Other Campuses

Why bother engaging deliberative processes in the context of open space design if it is so time-intensive? It is worth it because the benefits to community partners and professional program students are great, chiefly fostering an appreciation for design as a democratic process and underscoring the role of public open space in democracy. A prime challenge of dialogue and deliberation in landscape architecture is the time needed to engage the complexity of public space dilemmas and audiences. Some design colleges sustain outreach centers that may employ students or other staff outside of the typical academic term. This model can be a practical way to connect landscape architecture programs with unmet community needs for public space dialogue and deliberation. For institutions without an outreach center specifically devoted to community design, it is critical that faculty are upfront about any time limitations for student engagement with dialogue and deliberation.

An alternative to a dedicated community design center operating year-round is the possibility of curricula with built-in flexibility to allow students and faculty to engage thorough dialogue and deliberation processes across several academic terms. The landscape architecture program at K-State recently made curricular changes that expand the time frame a student may use for a master's project or report. This may open the possibility for thorough enclave-based deliberation that then contributes to a longer timetable for mixed group decision-making. Ultimately, time is needed to engage the messy process of consulting local knowledge and learning about people's lived experiences.

Acknowledgments

I owe thanks to graduate students Skylar Brown, Andrea Lemken, and Wei Sun for the chance to share aspects of their contributions to deliberative dialogue on Lewis Park. I thank my colleague, La Barbara James Wigfall, for her role as a critic and photographer to the graduate students' work. Colleagues Lorn Clement, Jessica Falcone, and Katrina Lewis, as well as FischHaus director Elizabeth Stevenson, also provided critique to student work in progress. The Downtown Wichita Development Corporation provided seed funds for the public exhibit. Donna Schenck-Hamlin and David Procter (of K-State's Center for Engagement and Community Development) inspired this chapter through their devotion to democratic discourse. Editors Nicholas V. Longo and Timothy J. Shaffer provided insightful and targeted criticism to improve this chapter as a work in progress.

References

Abdullah, C., Karpowitz, C. F., & Raphael, C. (2016). Affinity groups, enclave deliberation, and equity. *Journal of Public Deliberation*, *12*(2), article 6. Retrieved from https://www.publicdeliberation.net/jpd/vol12/iss2/art6/

Beardsley, J., Ross, J., & Gragg, R. (2009). *Where the revolution began: Lawrence Halprin and Anna Halprin and the reinvention of public space*. Washington DC: Spacemaker Press.

Brown, S. (2018). *Narrative and design: Commemorating the Civil Rights Movement through an inclusive design for Chester I. Lewis Park in Wichita, Kansas* (Master's thesis). Retrieved from K-State Research Exchange. (http://hdl.handle.net/2097/38924)

Downtown Wichita. (2017). *2017 State of downtown report*. Retrieved from https://downtownwichita.org/user/file/2017-state-of-downtown-report-download.pdf

Eick, G. C. (2001). *Dissent in Wichita: The Civil Rights Movement in the Midwest, 1954–72*. Urbana: University of Illinois Press.

Halprin, L. (1966). *Freeways*. New York, NY: Reinhold.

Halprin, L. (1969). *The RSVP cycles: Creative processes in the human environment*. New York, NY: George Braziller.

Halprin, L. (2005). *Lawrence Halprin on design: RSVP cycles* [Oral history interviews by Charles Birnbaum]. Retrieved from https://tclf.org/pioneer/oral-history/lawrence-halprin

Hester, R. T. (1975). *Neighborhood space*. Stroudsburg, PA: Dowden, Hutchinson and Ross.

Hester, R. T. (1984). *Planning neighborhood space with people*. New York, NY: Van Nostrand Reinhold.

Hester, R. T. (2002). Community design (1974). In S. Swaffield (Ed.), *Theory in landscape architecture* (pp. 49–56). Philadelphia: University of Pennsylvania Press.

Hester, R. T. (2006). *Design for ecological democracy*. Cambridge, MA: MIT Press.

Hester, R. T. (2012). Scoring collective creativity and legitimizing participatory design. *Landscape Journal*, *31*(1–2), 135–143.

Himmelroos, S., Rapeli, L., & Grönlund, K. (2016). Talking with like-minded people—Equality and efficacy in enclave deliberation. *Social Science Journal*, *54*(2), 148–158.

Howard, Z., & Somerville, M. M. (2014). A comparative study of two design charrettes: Implications for codesign and participatory action research. *CoDesign*, *10*(1), 46–62. Retrieved from https://doi-org.er.lib.k-state.edu/10.1080/15710882.2014.881883

Juarez, J. A., & Brown, K. D. (2008). Extracting or empowering? A critique of participatory methods for marginalized populations. *Landscape Journal*, *27*(2), 190–204.

Kingery-Page, K., Glastetter, A., DeOrsey, D., & Falcone, F. (2016). Examples of adapted ethnographic approaches for participatory design. *Landscape Research Record*, no. 5, 261–275. Retrieved from http://hdl.handle.net/2097/35288

Lemken, A. (2018). *Cultural inclusion in outdoor spaces: A cultural inquiry of Chester I. Lewis Reflection Square Park in Wichita, Kansas* (Master's thesis). Retrieved from K-State Research Exchange. (http://hdl.handle.net/2097/38943How)

Lewis, C. I. (n.d.). Chester I. Lewis Papers, Kansas Collection, RH MS 558. Lawrence: University of Kansas, Kenneth Spencer Research Library, 1948–1961.

Merriman, P. (2010). Architecture/dance: Choreographing and inhabiting spaces with Anna and Lawrence Halprin. *Cultural Geographies, 17*(4), 427–449. doi.org/10.1177/1474474010376011

Rogers, E. B. (2001). *Landscape design: A cultural and architectural history.* New York, NY: Harry N. Abrams.

Sun, W. (2018). *Urban restorative landscape: A cultural inquiry of redesigning Chester I. Lewis Reflection Square Park* (Master's thesis). Retrieved from K-State Research Exchange. (http://hdl.handle.net/2097/38929)

Wasserman, J. (2012). A world in motion: The creative synergy of Lawrence and Anna Halprin. *Landscape Journal, 31*(1–2), 33–52. doi:10.3368/lj.31.1-2.33

22

"GIVE LIGHT AND THE PEOPLE WILL FIND A WAY"

Democratic Deliberation and Public Achievement at Colorado College

Anthony C. Siracusa and Nan Elpers

> *My basic sense of it has always been to get people to understand that in the long run they themselves are the only protection they have against violence or injustice.... People have to be made to understand that they cannot look for salvation anywhere but to themselves.*
>
> —Ella Jo Baker, 1970

A Developmental Style of Politics

Public Achievement (PA) is an international program wherein college students mentor primary and secondary school students through a community organizing process. The program was inspired by the citizenship schools founded by the African American educator Septima Clark and relies heavily on practices of group-based deliberation endemic to the twentieth-century black freedom struggle. In this chapter, we suggest that the core deliberative practices of PA belong to what the historian and sociologist Charles Payne (1995) has called "a distinct philosophical heritage" (p. 93) developed by black Americans discerning how best to fight Jim Crow in the early to mid-1960s. PA uses these practices of democratic deliberation because they were deeply effective in helping activists in the midcentury black freedom movement build collective power, and they remain a powerful mode of developing collective power today. Learning the steps from this deliberative tradition equips PA students with the skills and language needed to act when they find themselves facing social or civic crises in our own time.

PA's foremothers, an influential cohort of black women, showed to the world that political work was not simply giving speeches; they revealed that every person has a critical role to play in public life. PA carries forward this community-driven approach, relying on collective processes of deliberation, decision-making, and action—and the case study later in this chapter illustrates how these deliberative practices were used in the PA program at North Middle School in Colorado Springs in 2018. These middle school students used deliberative processes to do impactful political work, demonstrating that politics are not simply the business of elected and appointed officials but are instead the cocreative work of people working together to leverage their own power and resources to fix the problems they face. These students in Colorado Springs collectively organized toward the goal of closing the Martin Drake coal burning power plant just miles from their school, adding their collective voice to a community chorus calling for the plant's closure. It is this form of deliberative public work—carried forward from the midcentury black freedom movement—that continues to contribute to the civic health of communities today.

PA and Democratic Deliberation

PA was founded by Harry C. Boyte in 1990, the outgrowth of focus groups with young people in Minneapolis-St. Paul. Boyte believed in the work of Septima Clark and the Citizenship Schools, citing them as part of a long and vibrant tradition in the United States of people claiming their own power to collectively decide and collectively organize around the problems they face.[1] In the Citizenship Schools, Clark taught black adults to read and write. She encouraged her students to develop these abilities by sharing stories from their own lives, facilitating personal and collective deliberation as her adult students worked out how to articulate their own experiences to one another. This deliberation provided a foundation for helping students think about how they might transform the basic conditions of their lives.

In 1956, Clark joined the Highlander Folk School as director of workshops. Highlander was founded in 1932 by the white labor organizer Myles Horton as a preparatory school for activists interested in nonviolent approaches to ending labor conflicts, Jim Crow segregation, and racial violence. Clark and Horton believed that communities could achieve

---

1. For a detailed history of how Boyte connects the origins of PA with longer movements in American civic life, see Boyte (2018).

liberation through a collective process of deliberation, and they taught students to first name and explain the conditions of their oppression, and then to prioritize what action to take. This group-based, deliberative approach to community organizing is centered in the notion that communities already possess the knowledge and resources needed to transform structures of cruelty and injustice. The key to accessing this power is discovering power through group-based processes of deliberation. This group-based dialogue and collective deliberation helped people grow together in understanding both the conditions of their oppression and the assets they possess to transform these conditions. This pedagogy remains central to PA and is reflected in the idea of cocreative politics: a group-based process of dialogue and deliberation directed toward a public project that is intended to cultivate the same kind of civic agency in youth that Clark nurtured in adults.

Boyte has held up the citizenship schools as an exemplar of people organizing themselves collectively to create meaningful and durable change and has described this work as citizen-centered, cocreative politics. In seeking to transmit these historical practices of group-based deliberation and dialogue to a new generation of youth, Boyte teamed up in the early 1990s with Dennis Donovan—then a principal at St. Bernard's Elementary in St. Paul, Minnesota. Boyte and Donovan began a program that prepares college-age "coaches" to lead primary and secondary school students through a group-based, deliberative process of discerning individual and collective identity for the purpose of cultivating *civic agency*, defined here as the ability to meaningfully impact the forces and contexts that shape their lives. Boyte (2014) has described the collective public deliberation endemic to the PA process as "one important strand of civic practice" within this "larger movement focused on 'the ability to act together'" in challenging situations (p. 1). Since 2008, students at Colorado College (CC) have partnered with North Middle School in a PA program focused on equipping students with the deliberative public skills needed to exercise their civic agency.

During the 2017–2018 academic year, a team of five CC coaches walked to North Middle School each week to meet with students in grades six through eight, all of whom voluntarily chose week after week to participate in the Public Achievement Club. The CC coaches worked for months to familiarize and equip groups of students with the core concepts of PA: self-interest, relationships, and power. PA defines *self-interest* as the passions that stem from a person's multiple identities and that drive a person to act on an issue or problem. Coaches used one-to-one relational meetings with the students at North to learn about their self-interests, digging deeper into their individual stories by asking respectful questions about a student's family, background, worries, and passions. These one-to-one meetings help coaches discover the components of identity and experience that shape their students' personal and public interests. Perhaps most critically, one-to-one meetings were a precursor to the group process of public deliberation. The meetings allowed coaches to identify the overlap between individual self-interest and the collective interest of the group. As students began to articulate those things about which they cared the most (e.g., many of Alaina's family members suffer from depression, and she cares about bringing early mental health intervention to middle schoolers), they shaped these stories into a "story of us," a public narrative that joined individual self-interest to a collective self-interest of the class. As with students at Highlander and in the Citizenship Schools, this process helps students think critically about their own individual experiences in preparation for a group-based process of deliberation around shared challenges.

PA students at North developed a list of public issues of collective concern that they could begin to research—issues where a collective interest emerged such as gun violence, animal rights, and mental health. This work of joining individual self-interest to collective interest was an essential first step in preparing for the Issue Convention, a group-based process of public deliberation where students run back and forth between colorful supersized sticky notes with the issue name scrawled in big letters. The Issue Convention allowed students to deliberate together, thinking through how their individual concerns might be understood—and worked on—as a collective concern. The pivot from individual interest to collective interest is derived directly from Horton's conviction that it is through group-based processes that people can discover their "collective self-determination" (Payne, 1995, p. 70) and secure the power needed to transform the basic conditions of their lives.

This is how the Issue Convention unfolded at North in 2018: CC coaches scrawled the public issues generated by the North students onto large sticky notes and hung them around the North Middle School library. Students lined up beside the issue they cared about most and were given five minutes as a group to prepare a short speech articulating why this was the most pressing issue facing their community. Once speeches were delivered and questions asked, students were given the option of either remaining at their station or moving to another issue if persuaded by their peers. The students repeated this cycle until issues were narrowed down and only two groups remained.

Although students championed their own causes at the Issue Convention, they ultimately caucused for the purpose of blending their perspectives into a cause of collective concern. The process exemplifies why group-based processes of deliberation are central to cocreative politics: In stark contrast to the often-polarizing fights between individual advocates vying for a focus on their own specific interest, the group-based process of deliberation at the Issue Convention settled on an issue of greatest concern to the group—but individuals were still encouraged to find a way to align this issue with their self-interest. For example, Joseph, a student ringleader in the group focused on racism and discrimination before the convention, realized he could happily join the environmental pollution team after a coach suggested that pollution disproportionately affects poorer neighborhoods and non-white Americans. For Joseph, this process of civic deliberation allowed him to stay focused on his own self-interest—racial injustice—but also enabled him to see how his individual interest intersected with the collective concern of the class.

With an issue selected, CC coaches Max and Liam pivoted to deeper issue research. They helped the students learn about environmental degradation specifically in Colorado Springs, and after exploring several potential local problems to tackle, the students settled on the controversy surrounding the Martin Drake coal burning power plant just miles from their school. CC coaches facilitated a process of group deliberation that assisted students in moving from a broad issue—environmental pollution—to narrowing their focus to a clear problem that they could address through a project.

Max introduced the students to a citywide campaign to close the Martin Drake power plant by 2025—10 years earlier than determined by the Colorado Springs City Council—and the students evaluated possible outcomes and consequences for adding their voice to this chorus. With assistance from their coaches, the "Close Martin Drake" team contacted a Colorado Sierra Club employee to help them learn more about efforts to close the plant before 2035. North students built on the information they gathered in the initial research phase and blended in additional details from this community expert. The CC coaches then taught the students how to make a "power map"—a practice that explores stakeholders and networks of power drawn from the organizing efforts of activists in the Mississippi Freedom Summer of 1964 (Allen, n.d.). Again wielding a giant sticky note and a rainbow of markers, the North students created a spiderweb of potential supporters and dissenters in an effort to understand who had the power to influence the closing of Martin Drake. This power map of stakeholders helped the students determine the best path of action for supporting the early closure of the plant, a visualization of both the extent and limitations of their own political efficacy. Ultimately, the students decided to follow in the footsteps of others supporting the closure of the plant by making a public statement in front of the Colorado Springs City Council—the body they rightly identified in their power mapping phase as having the direct power to close the plant.

On the day of their presentation, the North students and their coaches marched up the marble steps of City Hall and within minutes were greeted by at-large council representative Bill Murray—who supports closing the plant in 2030 or 2035 rather than the earlier date of 2025. Councilman Murray whisked the North students through the halls for a tour of the municipal building. During the public comments period of the City Council meeting, the six middle school PA students offered the following testimony:

> Hello, we are students from North Middle School. As you know, the city is going to shut down the Martin Drake Power Plant by 2035. We are here to ask you to vote to shut it down in 2025. We are asking this of you because the power plant is polluting much more than it is supposed to, and it does not look good to have it in the middle of the city.
>
> Even though we have not been able to see the report the city did on the plant's pollution, other reports have found that Sulfur Dioxide emissions are 2.5 times higher than the standard. Sulfur Dioxide causes asthma, bronchitis, smog, and acid rain. The plant also produces Nitrogen Dioxide and soot, which are also bad for your lungs. These health problems affect children and the elderly more than anyone else. As children, this is why the plant is so concerning to us. Since a lot of you fall into the other category, you should be concerned too.[2]

In this presentation, the students demonstrated how a deliberative group process can lead to collective civic action and public work. They exercised their civic agency by making a request of their elected representatives to close a facility that pollutes their neighborhood, and their speech revealed the careful research, collective investment, and citizen-centered approach to politics that PA cultivates in youth.

Modeling Deliberative Democratic Practice, Then and Now

Although the students at North focused on a very different set of issues than activists in the midcentury black freedom movement, in each case democratic deliberation was the requisite first step in a process of developing

---

2. Statement from North Middle School Students in authors' possession.

collective action. Septima Clark, Ella Baker, and Fannie Lou Hamer all taught group-based processes during their lifetimes—primarily because each believed that people have "the right and the capacity to have some say-so in their own lives" (Payne, 1995, p. 68). Students in PA continue to learn this model today because they come to see—through collective deliberation—that as the people most affected by a community challenge they have unique power in working collectively toward its resolution.

PA prepares students for group-based decision-making by teaching students to find the overlap between individual self-interest and collective interest. As students think through this individual and collective identity, they follow a process that is similar to the one utilized by the Student Nonviolent Coordinating Committee (SNCC). SNCC was famous for making decisions in the early 1960s through consensus—and often in mass meeting spaces. SNCC activist Charles McDew noted that in these collective decision-making spaces, "somebody may have spoken for eight hours . . . and seven hours and fifty-three minutes was utter bullshit, but seven minutes was good" (quoted in Hogan, 2007, p. 104). Joyce Ladner said that SNCC staff meetings in which she participated sometimes lasted days:

> You'd think you're going to arrive at a decision after all this dialectical stuff goes on, and then someone jumps up and says, "Well who gave you the right to decide?" and then you start all over again. . . . It took real effort to find the line of thinking, and make it clear without distorting anything. If I could do that, I could assist in the development of consensus. (quoted in Hogan, 2007, p. 104)

Ella Baker, who mentored the SNCC founders, noticed that young people would often veer off course as they sought consensus in discussion, so she asked questions instead of making statements. She later explained that she used this deliberative approach, rather than an authoritative approach, because she admitted, "I was not too sure that I had the answer" (quoted in Hogan, 2007, p. 104).

PA follows in Baker's footsteps. Coaches seek to ask the right questions of their students to assist them in first understanding their individual self-interest, but most importantly by then helping them to link this individual interest to a collective interest. Coaches then facilitate a process of collective deliberation in an Issue Convention that leads to collective action through a public project. Just as Clark taught people who could barely read to become teachers, PA coaches help K–12 students understand that they can do essential public work—carrying forward the idea that no person is too young, too inexperienced, or too disempowered to participate. PA affirms that every voice matters through group-based deliberation, creating a foundation for effective collective action. This is the power of PA—the ethic of cocreative politics, the notion that people together have the power to remake our communities in just and humane ways. In carrying forward this approach to collective organizing, an approach central to the mid-1960s black freedom movement, students in PA model for adults a historically effective form of deliberative democratic practice.

References

Allen, P. (n.d.). *Freedom Summer power map.* Pamela P. Allen Papers, Freedom School mimeo materials 1963–64, Folder 1, p. 1, Pamela P. Allen papers, 1967–1974, Wisconsin Historical Society, Madison, WI.

Baker, E. (1973). Developing community leadership. In G. Lerner (Ed.), *Black women in white America* (pp. 345–351). New York, NY: Vintage.

Boyte, H. (2014). Deliberative democracy, public work, and civic agency. *Journal of Public Deliberation, 10*(1), article 15. Retrieved from https://www.publicdeliberation.net/jpd/vol10/iss1/art15/

Boyte, H. (2018). *Awakening democracy through public work: Pedagogies of empowerment.* Nashville, TN: Vanderbilt University Press.

Hogan, W. (2007). *Many minds, one heart: SNCC's dream for a new America.* Chapel Hill: University of North Carolina Press.

Payne, C. (1995). *I've got the light of freedom: The organizing tradition and the Mississippi Freedom Struggle.* Berkeley: University of California Press.

PART SIX

DIALOGUE AND DELIBERATION NETWORKS

23

NEW HAMPSHIRE LISTENS

Fulfilling the Land-Grant Mission While Strengthening Democratic Practice

Bruce L. Mallory, Michele Holt-Shannon, and Quixada Moore-Vissing

Many of us employed in land-grant institutions find intellectual and personal satisfaction in work that allows us, indeed rewards us, to have "one foot on campus and one foot in the community." Fostering civic engagement using the tools and aims of deliberation and dialogue is one approach to fulfilling the mission of land-grant universities, requiring that we both advance formal knowledge *and* serve our states through practical applications (cf. Peters, Alter, & Shaffer, 2018). The Carsey School of Public Policy at the University of New Hampshire (UNH) is home to New Hampshire (NH) Listens, launched in 2010. At NH Listens, we have worked both on campus and in communities to build civic infrastructure, design and facilitate inclusive deliberative processes, and engage in research to improve deliberative practices and assess the impact of our work on community decision-making and overall civic health. This chapter describes the efforts of NH Listens both on campus and in communities to achieve the dual aims of knowledge transfer and creating more equitable and participatory civic life.

Our work reflects the evolving understanding of what it means to be a land-grant university with an outward-facing mission. Scott Peters (2006) describes that evolution when he notes, "Instead of public service, extension, and outreach, there is talk of engagement, community-university partnerships, and service-learning. Instead of applied research, we talk of community-based participatory research, action research, the scholarship of engagement, and public scholarship" (p. 4). NH Listens, through the campus- and community-based approaches illustrated in the following paragraphs, seeks to create a more democratic institution of higher learning—one that respects and amplifies student voice—while also working across the state bringing people together to create communities that work for everyone.

Areas of Focus

The four areas of focus that guide our work in 2019 are illustrated in Figure 23.1. When we began nearly a decade ago, our primary purpose was to introduce deliberative practices[1] to municipalities, public sector organizations, and community leaders as a tool for engaging more, and more diverse, residents in the processes of civic and public decision-making. As indicated in the Projects and Partnerships quadrant of Figure 23.1, we focused on building capacity for mutually respectful, action-oriented dialogue (initially relying heavily on study circle formats such as those used widely by Everyday Democracy, which is described in chapter 6 of this book). This reflected our concern for the increasingly contentious, polarized nature of public discourse we were observing in 2009–2010 and the fact that many New Hampshire communities were stuck or unable to resolve significant differences around money-dependent topics such as whether to build a new school, make a traffic intersection safer, or invest in long-term infrastructure to protect against climate change. In the process of responding to community requests for assistance, we also addressed the need to (a) build local capacity for increasing participation and engagement; (b) increase equity with respect to both who participates and how public decisions affect all segments of a community; and (c) facilitate the building of coalitions of stakeholders across sectors, identities, and organizations.

In our early years, we saw the need to act both locally and at the state level. In fact, NH Listens was essentially an effort to scale up the highly successful work of Portsmouth (NH) Listens, which had been founded in the late 1990s and was later recognized for its work in building democratic practice as a finalist for the 2011 Reinhard Mohn Prize for "innovative approaches and effective solutions to sociopolitical problems" (Bertelsmann Stiftung, 2019). Portsmouth Listens is a community-led group focused on integrating equitable, inclusive, deliberative problem-solving into the city's

---

1. This essay will use the terms *dialogue* and *deliberation* in reference to the range of public conversations we have designed and helped communities to employ. Some of those conversations have been more dialogic in the sense of interactive expression of diverse views to explore a topic; others are more deliberative in the sense of weighing alternative options and making recommendations for preferred solutions to local, regional, or statewide challenges. Unless specified, the terms are used interchangeably here, even as we recognize that practitioners and researchers often make distinctions such as those found in Escobar (2011).

Figure 23.1. NH Listens focus areas.

decision-making. We were among the early organizers of Portsmouth Listens and began to envision how that effort could be applied in communities across the state as a way to increase civic participation and build capacity for informed and equitable public problem-solving. This led us to conceptualize a university-based resource that could partner with community leaders in the establishment of Local Listens organizations and at the same time respond to statewide challenges affecting multiple communities.

Our vision was to be both local and global through capacity development in the form of affiliated (but independent) community-based organizations and the design and facilitation of statewide deliberations relevant to state-level policy. An important role of these local partners is to participate in regional or statewide engagement projects that span communities. When a statewide deliberation is scheduled that occurs simultaneously in multiple sites, Local Listens organizations provide logistical, recruitment, and facilitation resources in the communities they know best. The other primary role of Local Listens organizations has been to create local civic infrastructure to support engagement of community residents in deliberation on local matters. Using a range of formats to support *community conversations*, Local Listens groups have addressed concrete problems such as how to design a new Main Street in the state capital to broader, more systemic challenges such as youth empowerment or responding to the opioid crisis. In any case, the purpose of these deliberations is always "talk to action" such that the outcomes of the conversations point to specific activities in the form of community organizing, advocacy, or policy changes that are responsive to the issues under consideration.

At the same time we were committed to building capacity statewide, we wanted to build on ad hoc campus-based dialogues we had led in the early 2000s in our roles as leaders in academic and student affairs at UNH, where we are housed. From the beginning, we wanted to practice (and teach) democratic deliberation with students and staff around such topics as postathletic event student celebrations (some of which were characterized as riots), the implications of the 2003 Michigan affirmative action decisions by the Supreme Court, the tensions between academic freedom and creating safe learning environments, and more recently the impact of the Occupy and fossil fuel divestment movements on UNH. Much of the campus work has attended to the social, cultural, and political identities of students and staff, often explicitly and sometimes implicitly in how issues are framed, what group agreements we use, and how power relations are addressed in the practice of facilitated dialogue.

As NH Listens evolved, we came to understand the need to support leaders who want to strengthen participatory decision-making in their respective communities and organizations. Thus, we developed a range of civic leadership development initiatives, from the highly practical Facilitating for Public Engagement, a daylong training event that we offer three or four times a year, to more advanced versions of facilitator training that address difficult moments around racial or class identity and to intensive, multisession explorations of race, racism, and equity as critical factors in democratic practice and governance. In addition, we have learned that training focused on community conversations alone is not enough. In the absence of a strong civic infrastructure, there will be no opportunity to practice new skills or to sustain the benefits of dialogue and deliberation. For this reason, we are increasingly designing workshops focused on creating, leading, and sustaining community collaborations that can become part of the infrastructure needed to enhance participatory governance as well as a sense of community belonging.

It is in the context of our civic leadership initiatives that we have increased attention to racial equity as a fundamental component and requisite for democratic engagement. Several factors have catalyzed this emphasis. New Hampshire's demographic profile is changing in significant ways, partly as a result of a decline since the Great Recession of in-migration on the part of young professionals, who have historically been white and middle class; increasing numbers of immigrants from South Asia and Africa;

and the growth of Hispanic communities in the southern tier—all of which means a net increase in our cultural, linguistic, and socioeconomic mix. These changes have directly impacted public schools as well as nonprofit agencies, local police departments, employers, and demand for affordable housing. Our civic work now reflects these changes as we use multilingual facilitators, seek out emerging leaders from historically underrepresented populations, and design training events and community conversations that examine implicit bias, historic advantages and disadvantages, and opportunity inequities.

This focus on racial and social equity has been part of our response to challenges to democratic participation that have surfaced in recent years. For example, local and regional conversations on community-police relations (NH Blue and You) have explicitly sought input from marginalized and threatened communities, including Muslims and young people of color. We have explicitly addressed racial equity as both means and end to gaining legitimacy as a trusted, impartial convener of difficult conversations across all forms of difference. We have been supported and encouraged on this journey through our relationship with Everyday Democracy. In 2015, NH Listens became Everyday Democracy's first national anchor partner, signifying our role as an intermediary in supporting their mission and vision. This relationship helped advance our emerging attention to racial equity and gave us access to tools and training to deepen our own resources.

Finally, as a university-based civic engagement program (as visualized in Figure 23.1), we are committed to research on the relationship between equity and civic health. Our research interests focus on disparities in civic health in and across local communities, the impact of socioeconomic stratification on civic health, and the role of civic infrastructure, public institutions, and community-driven problem-solving initiatives as means to foster higher levels of civic health. As part of the Carsey School of Public Policy, we published the statewide *Civic Health Index* (Mallory & Moore-Vissing, 2013), in collaboration with the National Conference on Citizenship. As a next iteration of the *Civic Health Index* (CHI), we are designing a community-based version of the CHI that measures engagement and participation at a more granular level than allowed by census and American Community Survey data. This will enable us to collaborate with colleagues in public administration and communication at UNH to specifically measure the impact of deliberation, overt equity aspirations, and social contact across differences for individuals and communities. This more localized focus on civic health follows the recent research on *civic deserts*, which finds that 60% of rural youth see their communities as lacking ways to engage meaningfully with neighbors as well as decision-makers (Atwell, Bridgeland, & Levine, 2017). To better understand what community-based civic health looks like, we will conduct direct surveys, focus groups, and interviews with everyday residents as well as community leaders to gather their perceptions of opportunities to volunteer, affect local decision-making, learn about municipal governance, and amplify the voices of the historically disenfranchised.

Facing Heroin: A Case Study on Strengthening Our Community

The Facing Heroin community conversation that took place in Berlin, New Hampshire, in the fall of 2015 is an example of how building civic infrastructure at the local level can prepare communities to address significant social challenges as they arise. In the past five years, New Hampshire has experienced the effects of the opioid epidemic at higher rates than almost any other state in the country. We have the second highest death rate from opioid overdoses in the nation; the rate of overdose deaths tripled from 2013 to 2016. In towns and cities experiencing severe economic challenges related to the decline of manufacturing and extraction industries (logging in this case), exacerbated by the Great Recession, the incidence of addiction and opioid-related deaths is especially high. As addiction-related crime was perceived to increase in the Berlin area during this time and as families experienced the consequences of addiction, residents began expressing concerns that police and city leaders were not taking action. This led to a call for community dialogue, supported by North Country Listens in partnership with the city of Berlin police department and the regional public health consortium.

North Country Listens is 1 of 10 local or regional Local Listens organizations we have helped to establish over the past 9 years. Created in 2014 with the support of the Neil and Louise Tillotson Fund of the New Hampshire Charitable Foundation, North Country Listens works across greater Coos County to support engagement and dialogue. The region includes about one-third of the land in the state of New Hampshire, but is sparsely populated with a shrinking population of about 33,000 in 2019. Operating with a part-time program coordinator, North Country Listens has responded to a range of requests for support in engaging residents around local challenges, from early childhood education to support for young adults to resolving competing uses of woodland trails.

The Facing Heroin conversation in Berlin drew more than 250 people, double the number expected. The result of the small-group facilitated dialogues was a set of priority actions in each of three areas: prevention, treatment, and recovery. For example, with respect to prevention, there was widespread agreement that prevention education for children and new parents should begin as early as possible and be reinforced throughout the school years. The city schools have since begun to put that curriculum in place with the aid of federal grants, with a focus on children's overall behavioral health. In the area of treatment, there was a call for a community coalition to oversee and initiate action to address the heroin epidemic, including treatment options for adolescents that were closer to home and increasing the visibility of the recovery community. This led to the creation of Stand Up for Androscoggin Valley, a regional coalition of stakeholders who remain active in support and advocacy work. Recovery-related actions included a goal to create transition housing as well as the need to educate providers and the public about the harm of stigma for those in recovery.

These examples of campus and community work are representative of the range of dialogue-based engagement activities and topics that NH Listens supports. We have had "one foot on campus and one foot in the community" since our inception, although the balance of our work to date has been off campus. One goal for the future will be to bring lessons learned in community deliberation work back to our research colleagues at the university. Community-based deliberation and other forms of engagement create opportunities to experience and learn about the complexity of social institutions and systems through multiple disciplinary lenses. In this sense, the link between engagement and scholarship is enhanced through grounded, applied research that both advances knowledge production and helps community members to address the complex problems they face.

Knowledge Production and Transfer

This case, and our broader experiences with NH Listens, are directly connected to a core part of the land-grant, research university mission—knowledge production and transfer. NH Listens has participated in efforts that reflect our role as partners with research colleagues in the framing and sharing of research findings to inform local and regional decision-making.

From 2014 to 2017, for instance, NH Listens worked with UNH climate scientists and state and federal agency representatives to design and implement public engagement processes focused on the effects of extreme weather events and rising sea level on coastal communities. Our role was to frame public engagement practices that could connect scientists with decision-makers and everyday citizens, so that both groups could be informed and weigh a range of policy options in light of available data. Climate scientists provided information about current and projected patterns of weather and sea level rise and in turn heard from elected officials and residents about the traditions, values, and economic conditions of the communities. Decisions about long-term infrastructure investments in storm water, sewage treatment, erosion barriers, and ecosystem management were the topic of participatory processes supported by NH Listens. Both community values and empirical data were part of the deliberations that occurred. Preservation of historic coastal sites, first responder access to elderly residents during floods, property rights, tourist economies, local tax rates, and conservation versus development goals were all addressed in the engagement processes.

Our efforts to support knowledge transfer using public engagement processes have also focused on youth opportunity in rural communities. Social science researchers at the Carsey School have been tracking longitudinal cohorts of high school students in the northern tier of the state since 2008 (Staunton & Jaffee, 2014). A significant amount of information has been collected about virtually every student in the region, beginning in the eighth grade. Variables include student aspirations and perceptions of regional opportunities, community attachment, the role of mentors, substance use and mental health, in- and out-of-school engagement, and decisions about leaving the region after graduation. In a region with a shrinking population, especially among young adults, the data are highly useful for understanding what keeps students in the region and what drives them away. NH Listens has convened a series of public conversations with youth, educators, service providers, and decision-makers in the region to review the research findings and identify ways to improve student outcomes and encourage young people to stay (or return). This partnership has helped university researchers to translate findings into deliberation topics for policy and practice changes at the community level.

In both cases, NH Listens was instrumental in making research data available and accessible to decision-makers and everyday citizens, who could then weigh that data against local knowledge about the history, customs, and values of their communities. Both audiences—decision-makers (elected and appointed municipal officials) and everyday citizens—benefit from inclusive and facilitated deliberative processes. Decision-makers have access to a broader swath of public input and opinion than is typically generated in the public comment portions of public meetings.

The give-and-take, listening-and-speaking aspects of deliberation create opportunities for decision-makers to both listen to constituents in a more intimate and interactive manner and to ask questions for clarification or deeper understanding before they arrive at formal decisions. Community residents, whose interests are connected to their personal well-being and that of their neighbors, have opportunities to ask questions of decision-makers (generally not part of public comment portions of meeting agendas), hear each other's perspectives, and gain an understanding of the tradeoffs behind official actions. When highly value-laden topics are under consideration, such as community-police relations or funding of public schools, sustained, equitable dialogue helps surface the complexities that affect the issue. Recognizing that public decisions depend on consideration of both objective information as well as personal values is critical to participatory governance practices.

Concluding Reflections

NH Listens is one example of how a land-grant university is addressing its mission to improve the lives of the residents of the state (and beyond). Situated in a school for public policy, led by faculty and professional staff with expertise in community psychology and development, higher education, student development, and civic engagement, we have provided a range of tools for both campus and community leaders to strengthen participatory democratic practices. We have committed to a set of core principles that include bringing people together from all walks of life; providing time for in-depth, informed conversations; respecting differences as well as seeking common ground; and achieving outcomes that lead to informed community solutions.

We seek to help communities increase civic engagement, create more equitable approaches to including all voices (especially those that have been historically disenfranchised), and become more resilient as economic and social challenges arise. We strengthen civic health through greater participation and more open, transparent decision-making processes. And we provide concrete, adaptable tools for improved community problem-solving through deliberative and other public processes. The work is complex, multidisciplinary, and long term. Much of it is hard to fit into the traditional reward system for faculty and curriculum structures for students. Yet it is what is needed in a time of threats to democracy and growing skepticism about the public value of higher education.

References

Atwell, M. N., Bridgeland, J., & Levine, P. (2017). *Civic deserts: America's civic health challenge.* Washington DC: National Conference on Citizenship.

Bertelsmann Stiftung. (2019). *Richard Mohn Prize.* Retrieved from https://www.bertelsmann-stiftung.de/en/our-projects/reinhard-mohn-prize/

Escobar, O. (2011). *Public dialogue and deliberation. A communication perspective for public engagement practitioners.* Edinburgh, UK: Beacons for Public Engagement.

Mallory, B., & Moore-Vissing, Q. (2013). *2012 New Hampshire Civic Health Index.* Durham, NH: Carsey Institute/University of New Hampshire and National Conference on Citizenship.

Peters, S. (2006). Changing the story about higher education's public purposes and work: Land-grants, liberty, and the little country theatre. *Imagining America, 3.* Retrieved from https://surface.syr.edu/ia/3

Peters, S. J., Alter, T. R., & Shaffer, T. (2018). *Jumping into civic life: Stories of work from extension professionals.* Dayton, OH: Kettering Foundation Press.

Staunton, M., & Jaffee, E. M. (2014). *Key findings and recommendations from the Coos Youth Study: Research from the first half of the study.* Durham, NH: Carsey School of Public Policy, University of New Hampshire. Retrieved from https://scholars.unh.edu/cgi/viewcontent.cgi?referer=&httpsredir=1&article=1219&context=carsey

24

START TALKING, STOP TALKING, AND TOXIC TALKING

Resources for Engaging Difficult Dialogues in Higher Education

Libby Roderick

I gave an assignment to bring a symbol of cultural pride into my course on cultural identity. A student brought in a T-shirt with a Confederate flag as her symbol of cultural pride. What should I do?

I teach students about racial disparities in access to health care. Whenever I raise these issues, some students become defensive; others clam up. What should I do?

I know I need to teach my students about climate change, but the issue is so polarized, I'm afraid to even go there. What should I do?

Posters have surfaced all over campus with the statement "It's OK to be White." Because of free speech laws, we aren't allowed to take them down. Our students of color are extremely distressed. What should we do?

A colleague in my department is making my life miserable, writing critical e-mails, yelling at me, withholding vital information. Who do I turn to?

Questions like these—and thousands more—surface on U.S. campuses every day. The Southern Poverty Law Center (www.splcenter.org/20161129/ten-days-after-harassment-and-intimidation-aftermath-election) and the Anti-Defamation League's Center on Extremism (https://www.npr.org/2019/02/20/696217158/u-s-hate-groups-rose-sharply-in-recent-years-watchdog-group-reports) have reported spikes in bias incidents and hate crimes on campuses since the 2016 national election. Where can people turn for answers?

Fortunately, as this book conveys, a number of efforts exist to help faculty, students, student affairs professionals, and administrators respond in ways that promote learning and a sense of connectedness rather than further divisiveness, disruption, and academic and emotional derailment. In this chapter, we offer the Difficult Dialogue Initiative as a method that strives to expand innovative approaches to civil discourse on controversial topics and complex issues at the college level.

Model History

Over the past decade and a half at the University of Alaska Anchorage (UAA), we have developed a wide range of resources (books, film, website, workshops) designed to help university communities respond more effectively to complex, divisive issues on campuses and in the nation. Our project addresses the following key areas: (a) increasing faculty skills at successfully introducing controversial topics into the classroom; (b) engaging difficult dialogues between Indigenous and academic communities, primarily through introducing non-Indigenous faculty to Indigenous ways of teaching and learning; and (c) supporting productive discussions on responding to and preventing faculty bullying and toxic behavior in academic departments. In 2006, UAA, a public university with 5 campuses serving roughly 20,000 students, joined with Alaska Pacific University (APU), a nearby small private university, to successfully apply for a Ford Foundation Difficult Dialogues grant. That grant (and a subsequent grant in 2008) permitted us to launch faculty development work on both campuses to

- build the skills, networks, and confidence to cultivate learning environments in which all viewpoints are respected and civil discourse is taught and modeled;
- develop learning climates more inclusive of minority voices/ways of knowing and safer places for the free exchange of ideas; and
- cultivate deeper understandings between Indigenous and academic communities.

Since that time, we've offered a multitude of workshops and launched a host of faculty learning communities on these topics for faculty throughout the United States and in South Africa.

Our project started with the 2005 Ford Foundation call to all accredited universities in the United States to apply for grants under its national Difficult

Dialogues Initiative. In response to a rise in religious and racial tensions and threats to academic freedom on U.S. campuses following 9/11, the program aimed to promote and protect academic freedom and religious, cultural, and political pluralism on college and university campuses across the nation. More than 700 universities applied for 2-year grants addressing the unique dialogue challenges on their campuses; 26 were awarded $100,000, and an additional handful received $10,000 awards. Large grantees included Yale University, Barnard College, Emory University, the University of Missouri, the University of Texas at Austin, Portland Community College, the University of California Irvine, the University of Michigan, Clark University, UAA/APU, and 16 others. Project issues varied, including the Middle East conflict, fundamentalism and secularism, racial and ethnic relations, religion and the university, and sexual orientation and academic freedom. In addressing these issues, initiatives took the form of student programs, interactive theater, and public forums, as well as curriculum, pedagogical, and faculty development. The UAA Difficult Dialogues work has been primarily aimed at supporting faculty in the classroom and department. However, all the work is transferable to other constituencies (staff, students, administrators, etc.) and learning environments.

After the 2008 fiscal crisis, the Ford Foundation shifted its priorities and closed out the Difficult Dialogues Initiative; a consortium of institutions and individuals committed to advancing meaningful difficult-dialogue practices in higher education created a nonprofit to continue the work. Representatives from UAA, the University of Texas at Austin, the University of Missouri, the University of Michigan, and Emory, as well as various interested individuals, joined together to create the Difficult Dialogues National Resource Center (DDNRC) to continue the work on a national basis. The DDNRC offers a national conference on difficult dialogues in higher education every two years. The first was held in 2014 at the University of Texas at Austin, the second at the University of Michigan, and the third at the University of Maryland.

General Model, Principles, and Practices: UAA's Difficult Dialogues Initiative

The UAA Difficult Dialogues Initiative includes three tracks: Start Talking, Stop Talking, and Toxic Friday. All three projects—as well as other projects and resources from across the United States and the world—are showcased on the UAA Difficult Dialogues website (www.difficultdialoguesuaa.org).

Start Talking introduces faculty and other university constituencies to a wide range of strategies for proactively and successfully introducing and managing difficult dialogues in the classroom and other learning environments. The Start Talking track includes the following:

- *Faculty development workshops and learning communities.* Groups are organized with the aim of increasing skill levels among faculty for introducing difficult dialogues into the classroom.
- *A Books of the Year program.* Texts addressing controversial issues are discussed in classrooms and the community, using two-year themes as a basis.
- *Start Talking: A Handbook for Engaging Difficult Dialogues in Higher Education.* A nationally acclaimed field manual describes the UAA/APU model, shares the experiences of program participants, and explains strategies for classroom use. (Landis, K., ed. (2008) *Start talking: A handbook for engaging difficult dialogues in higher education.* Anchorage: University of Alaska Anchorage.)

Stop Talking introduces faculty to 10,000-year-old Indigenous ways of teaching, learning, and addressing conflict, and to key difficult dialogues between academic and Indigenous communities. The Stop Talking track includes:

- *Faculty development workshops and learning communities.* Non-Indigenous faculty are introduced to traditional Indigenous best practices for teaching and learning as well as key difficult dialogues between Indigenous and academic communities.
- *ePortfolios.* Electronic documents show faculty efforts to apply these new ways of teaching in their classrooms.
- *Stop Talking: Indigenous Ways of Teaching and Learning and Difficult Dialogues in Higher Education.* This book includes descriptions of Indigenous-designed and -run intensive faculty development efforts, along with strategies for applying Indigenous pedagogies in Western learning environments, reflections on education by Alaska Native Elders, and reports from participants on what they have learned and tried in their classrooms. (Merculieff, L., & Roderick, L. (2013). *Stop talking: Indigenous ways of teaching and learning and difficult dialogues in higher education.* Anchorage: University of Alaska Anchorage.)

Toxic Friday offers a range of resources for engaging faculty and other university constituencies in important discussions about how best to prevent and respond to toxic behavior in academic departments. The Toxic Friday track includes the following:

- The book and online video *Toxic Friday: Resources for Addressing Faculty Bullying in Higher Education,* which jointly aim to promote

constructive discussions about how to respond to bullying and toxic behavior in academic departments.
- *Faculty workshops and learning communities* organized around the book and video.

Ongoing UAA Difficult Dialogues Activities

In addition to the activities described previously, the UAA Difficult Dialogues Initiative includes several other ongoing activities, including public policy debates and faculty forums; for-credit courses (e.g., Race, Ethnicity and Identity in the Social Sciences) in which students learn not only the course content but also the processes for engaging in respectful dialogue with those holding differing viewpoints; and interactive theater performances and discussions on eliminating bias in faculty hiring processes.

The UAA Difficult Dialogues program has been a model for campuses across the United States and in South Africa. We have been invited to present and/or train faculty, staff, and administrators at multiple universities and conferences, including Yale University, Tufts University, Virginia Tech, the University of Virginia, the University of Wisconsin, Villanova University, Clemson University, Valparaiso University, the University of Maryland, Michigan State University, and many more. UAA also partnered with the Institute for Reconciliation and Social Justice and the Centre for Teaching and Learning at the University of the Free State in Blomfontein, South Africa, to help design and deliver weeklong faculty development intensives based on the model described in the *Start Talking* book. And UAA has partnered with various community groups in its home city of Anchorage to assist in the design and facilitation of difficult dialogues on a range of community topics, including homelessness, racial equity, the climate crisis, art and politics, and more. Partnering organizations have included museums, nonprofits, senior learning programs, arts organizations, and churches.

Key Takeaways/Strengths and Challenges

The key strength of the UAA Difficult Dialogues offerings might be summed up in a single word: *practicality*. All the work offered—whether aimed at strengthening faculty capacity to intentionally and successfully introduce discussions on controversial topics in the classroom, begin to understand and apply traditional Indigenous pedagogies and/or engage in difficult dialogues between Indigenous and academic communities, or host conversations around toxic behavior in departments—is designed for on-the-ground, real-world applications for busy members of the academic community (as well as nonacademics). The strategies and information offered have been ground-tested and shown to have demonstrated effectiveness. Another key strength of the Stop Talking work is how Indigenous approaches are quickly able to decouple learners from their usual cultural constructs and allow them to see the world and their work freshly, permitting more innovative, inspiring and relevant teaching to occur, particularly in this era of climate threat.

Challenges vary for the three different tracks of UAA's Difficult Dialogues work. For the Start Talking work, a key challenge is that the strategies are designed to be used by professors with varying levels of awareness around their own identities and biases. Because the vast majority of difficult dialogues center around issues of power, privilege, and identity, the work is even more effective when paired with additional offerings that focus on helping professors from privileged groups wrestle more deeply over time with the impact of their own identities and biases on their students and learning environments.

For the Stop Talking work, a key challenge involves the time allotted to presenting the material to non-Indigenous populations. Most workshops in academic cultures are a few hours; occasionally, a few days are made available. Although deep and lasting shifts in awareness and understanding can and do occur on a regular basis in these shorter sessions, more lasting applications and transformation in the classroom are best supported over longer periods of time (which can often be accomplished through ongoing learning communities, including those based on the free *Stop Talking* book). Connecting or reconnecting with living natural systems is at the heart of Indigenous education; few academic timetables allow for this process to take deep root.

For the Toxic Friday work, a key challenge is translating ideas for how to prevent and respond to toxic behavior in academic departments into protocols and policies that have traction within institutions.

As with every model, a challenge for the Difficult Dialogues work is the fact that, in most cases, attendance is voluntary and institutions provide few, if any, incentives to participate. Hence, the repeated refrain across the nation that those who most need to be exposed to the work rarely attend. However, the feedback we regularly receive from the many faculty (and others) who do attend—including those who are required to participate—is that the tools and resources are extremely useful in grappling with challenging issues both inside and outside the classroom. As racial, religious, gender, and political tensions continue to mount on campuses throughout the United States, the Difficult Dialogues Initiative at UAA will continue to support academic communities in developing the skills and knowledge necessary to successfully grapple with a wide range of difficult dialogues.

25

ENACTING DEMOCRACY IN "DEMOCRACY'S COLLEGES"

Carrie B. Kisker, John J. Theis, and Alberto Olivas

The phrase "Democracy's Colleges" was first applied to land-grant universities as early as 1862 in recognition of their work on important public (often agricultural) problems and their enrollment of ordinary citizens who, in years prior, would have been excluded from the more selective system of liberal arts colleges and elite research universities operating in the United States (Cohen & Kisker, 2010; Ross, 1942). Since at least the 1960s, however, the moniker "Democracy's Colleges" has been more often applied to the nation's community colleges, both because of the close relationships they maintain with their local communities and because they perform a critical democratizing function in American higher education by accepting all comers, regardless of age, race, religion, socioeconomic status, educational preparedness, or professional/vocational goals.

Yet, although democratizing opportunity and facilitating social mobility is unquestionably important, we believe that America's community colleges—Democracy's Colleges—have a responsibility to go even further: They must, as Bernie Ronan (2012) has argued, also "*do* the work of democracy" (p. 34, italics added). Community colleges must engage students in transformative experiences that not only help them learn about civic or political ideas but also ask them to be "active, critical, reflective, and empathetic member[s] of a community of equals, capable of exchanging ideas on the basis of respect and understanding with people from many different backgrounds" (p. 4). Community colleges have a responsibility to help students grapple with complex or *wicked* problems for which there are no clear-cut solutions (Carcasson, 2013; Rittle & Weber, 1973), engage in those issues with others, discover shared identities despite profound differences, and ultimately take action on issues important to them or their communities (Ronan, 2011). In other words, Democracy's Colleges must guide students in performing, or enacting, democracy.

Community colleges are uniquely suited to this kind of work (Kisker & Ronan, 2012). Community colleges educate two-thirds of all young people who enroll in higher education, and the vast majority of their students hail from nearby communities and return to them to work and raise families. Community colleges engage with K–12 school systems and community organizations. They offer education and training programs for adults and traditional-age learners alike. They send hundreds of thousands of transfer students to universities each year and collaborate with regional economic development agencies to design occupational programs in emerging and high-demand fields. In short, they are true stewards of place (Mathews, 2014), and as such their efforts to enact democracy can create ripple effects that extend far beyond campus or community borders.

Community colleges engage in multiple activities that help students learn about or participate in public life. These include service-learning, voter registration and get-out-the-vote drives, classroom discussion of policy issues, civic agency programs, candidate and election-issue forums, and community organizing and advocacy (Kisker, 2016; Ronan & Kisker, 2016). As we explore in this chapter, community colleges also participate in a robust set of deliberative dialogue projects. There is value in all of these approaches to civic engagement, but as we have argued elsewhere (Kisker, Theis, & Olivas, 2016), with the exception of deliberative dialogues and some civic agency programs, "most collegiate civic efforts focus on the problems that occur *in* democracy (i.e., specific policy issues), as opposed to the problems *of* democracy, or how citizens can help make democracy work better" (p. 3). This chapter describes a three-year project to build community colleges' capacity to deal with these *problems of democracy* through the art of deliberation.

Deliberation, which is frequently taught and practiced on college campuses through structured deliberative dialogues, provides a way for students to address wicked or endemic (as opposed to solvable) problems of democracy and become deeply involved in public decision-making (Shaffer, Longo, Manosevitch, & Thomas, 2017). Deliberation helps students understand issues from multiple perspectives, along the way building a skill set that is both relevant to the marketplace and critical for political participation. It also assists colleges in rediscovering and publicizing their civic mission and provides communities with residents who are well-versed in deliberative practices and able to apply their skills locally (Carcasson, 2013). As such, deliberation is one of the most effective ways in which community colleges can engage students in enacting democracy.

Embedding Deliberation in Community Colleges

It is with this belief that the Center for the Study of Community Colleges, the Democracy Commitment, and the Kettering Foundation embarked on a three-year project to embed deliberation as a civic skill in community colleges. In 2015, we began convening cohorts of faculty and staff from community colleges around the country.[1] All members of the Democracy Commitment—a national organization of geographically diverse institutions supporting the development and expansion of civic learning and democratic engagement within community colleges[2]—have acted as test cases for how we might work to establish deliberation as an essential practice within the community college sector as a whole.

The colleges participating in our project were divided into three cohorts, and each fall one or two cohorts came to the Kettering Foundation's Dayton, Ohio, campus to participate in a research exchange. It was during these exchanges that participants discussed concepts such as wicked problems, how deliberation provides transformative opportunities for students to explore these difficult issues, and ways in which community colleges can act as stewards of place in tackling complex community challenges. Following each research exchange, we worked with institutions in that year's cohort to train faculty, staff, and students in the art of hosting and moderating deliberations, and in subsequent months, each college held least one deliberative forum with students and/or community members. Members from the previous year's cohort returned to Kettering the following fall—together with the incoming cohort—to share their experiences and reflect on the year's work.

In designing the project in this way, our intention was to train the trainers. When faculty and staff are equipped to become the resident experts in deliberative practices on their own campuses, they become ambassadors for the promise and practice of deliberation over time. They can also train successive cohorts of students to act as moderators for deliberative dialogues among their peers and community members, which helps build a critical set of skills that will benefit the students for years to come (Theis, Kisker, & Olivas, 2018). Furthermore, we sought to develop a network of community

---

1. Participating colleges were Tarrant County Community College-Southeast (TX), Guttman Community College (NY), Lane Community College (OR), Delta Community College (MN), Monroe Community College (NY), St. Paul Community and Technical College (MN), Santa Fe College (FL), College of the Canyons (CA), Kirkwood Community College (IA), Piedmont Virginia Community College (VA), and Wright Community College (IL).

2. The Democracy Commitment is now an initiative of Campus Compact. More information can be found at its website (www.compact.org/the-democracy-commitment/).

colleges, experienced in deliberation, that would connect to and augment existing Kettering networks. Our train-the-trainer project design, described in more detail in the following section, has also led to numerous successes and challenges, which we share in hopes that they will help community colleges and other institutions embed deliberation as a civic skill on their campuses.

Our Train-the-Trainer Approach

Following each research exchange, John Theis and Alberto Olivas visited the colleges in that year's cohort to train a group of roughly 20 to 25 faculty, administrators, student leaders, and/or community members in the theory behind deliberation, as well as the practice of holding and moderating deliberative dialogues. Whether the project lead at the campus level ought to be located within college administration (e.g., student life office, president's office, or a center for civic engagement) or within an academic discipline (e.g., communications or political science) is an unresolved question, and there are successful examples of both models. Regardless, we found it especially important to ensure participation of an interdisciplinary group of faculty members in these trainings, as—given their ability to reach a large and diverse set of students—they are frequently the most effective ambassadors for deliberation on campus. However, helping college leaders and other administrators gain an understanding of and appreciation for the power of deliberation is also useful, as they can then act as champions for this type of transformative civic work on campus and in the community (Kisker et al., 2016). In many ways, our deliberation trainings emphasized the ways in which colleges can build the capacity to continue training future moderators and champions, thus creating self-sustaining deliberation programs.

The deliberation training itself consists of engaging trainees in considering the role of the community college as a steward of place and how institutions can facilitate dialogues among students, faculty, staff, and community members that enable them to work through differences and discover common ground, priorities, and values that are widely held in the community. During this part of the training, we describe the differences between deliberative dialogue (where expert knowledge is eschewed and emphasis is placed on the citizen as a problem-solver) and the more familiar adversarial models, such as debate and persuasive speechmaking. This helps clarify the strengths, limitations, and useful applications for each dialogue model, so that deliberation is presented not as superior to debate, but rather as better suited to dealing with many of the most challenging issues in our communities. We use the concept of wicked problems to explain the differences between dialogue and debate, and to highlight the need for deliberative dialogue on campus. In particular, we stress that deliberation is an effective strategy for productively engaging students and community members in understanding and developing strategies to address the persistent and endemic problems in their communities.

Our deliberation trainings also offer opportunities for attendees to experience a deliberative dialogue moderated by one of our trainers, as well as a chance to practice moderating in simulated deliberative settings. Through these experiences, trainees are introduced to key concepts and principles of effective public engagement practices, methods for identifying an issue's stakeholders and convening representative and diverse members of the community to engage in deliberation, and the practices and strategies of effective moderators and recorders (note-takers), including how to troubleshoot and evaluate dialogues. Throughout the trainings, experienced moderators provide feedback to participants and pose practical questions about issues they may face when moderating deliberative events on or off campus (see Kisker et al., 2016, for more detail about our deliberation trainings).[3]

In the weeks or months following each college's deliberation training, faculty or staff representatives organized and hosted at least one deliberative event on campus. Some campuses utilized faculty or staff moderators at these events; most focused on training and using student moderators. Likely as a result, most of these first deliberations were held in classroom settings, which allowed student moderators to gain experience facilitating dialogues among peers. New moderators often perceive classroom dialogues to be "lower stakes" than larger campus or community deliberations, although the latter can be made less intimidating by assigning each moderator to a small-group discussion. Classroom deliberations are also useful to a college's overall work to embed deliberation as a critical skill on campus, as students who find participating in a dialogue to be a transformative experience are frequently eager to become moderators themselves.

The community colleges that participated in our project implemented deliberative practices in a number of other settings, too, including campus-wide conversations or events, campus-community events, faculty professional development seminars, interactive conference presentations, first-year honors seminars, town halls with local representatives, and so forth. Additionally, several colleges are beginning to work with community organizations to host deliberations related to problems of homelessness, drug abuse, peace-building, and so forth.

---

3. Visit www.youtube.com/watch?v=_DdjHCfgPjY for a video about deliberative dialogues at community colleges.

As community colleges introduce and work to establish the practice of deliberation on campus, we encourage them to provide multiple opportunities for students and others to moderate dialogues and as much constructive feedback and support to new moderators as possible. This allows students to strengthen their own moderating skills, and when good practices and suggestions for improvement are discussed in a supportive, small-group environment, moderators can also learn from their peers' experiences. Although formal trainings for new moderators are important—often trainings can be accomplished in two-hour sessions acquainting students with basic moderating skills, followed by opportunities to hone those skills in classroom or campus forums—the act of providing and receiving feedback from peers and more experienced moderators can be an effective way to ensure a consistent supply of moderators, as newly trained students take the places of those who transfer or enter the workforce.

Project Successes

As part of our annual Kettering research exchanges, faculty and staff representatives from the participating colleges reflected on their successes and challenges, and some provided feedback from students. Over the three years of this project, several commonalities emerged. One common success was the sheer number of students, faculty, and staff attending deliberation training events and dialogues, in some cases exceeding expectations, as well as the level of support—both verbal and financial—lent to the initiative by presidents and other senior administrators. Deliberation trainings were also very well received by faculty participants, many of whom reported being able to immediately apply elements of the training session to their classrooms, in particular strategies for promoting discussion among students.

Perhaps more importantly, the introduction of deliberation on campus appears to have an enormous impact on students' views and perspectives on the world. As one student participant wrote, "Everyone is a little ignorant of what everyone else is going through. . . . I learned a lot about individual experiences that I never would have considered." Another student shared similar sentiments: "This was a good opportunity to hear a broad range of ideas from different people of different backgrounds. By the end of the discussion we seemed to have one thing in common: a desire for change." (See Theis, et al., 2018, for a more in-depth discussion of how deliberation affects students' perspectives and views of the world.)

Project participants also reported that students who participated in a deliberative dialogue and/or moderator training made substantial gains in civic learning and critical thinking. As one faculty member wrote:

"Deliberation is an opportunity to build critical thinking and reasoning skills. Students not only have to think about the entirety of an issue but also must do so in a rational and logical manner." Another concurred, noting that by participating in a deliberation, "students learn to make connections between what is taught in the classroom and the problems they face, or eventually will face, within their federal, state, and local government, community, and democracy." Many colleagues believed that these gains in civic learning and critical thinking would have a direct impact on students' persistence rates and success in school.

Finally, project participants also felt that deliberation positively affected students' sense of civic agency, or their view of themselves as individuals who can make an impact on the world and/or promote social or political change. In some cases, student participants in a deliberative dialogue were quite clear about the effects of that experience on their civic agency. As one wrote, "My perspective has dramatically changed towards poverty and towards getting involved in my community." Similarly, another student related that they now have "a deeper understanding of how change can happen." Project colleagues felt strongly that this growth benefits not only the students but also the campus and community as a whole. As one wrote: "Dialogues are helping the college to promote a sense of 'public work' among the campus community, as well as to foster greater civic responsibility amongst our student population." A common refrain among colleagues in our research exchange was that dialogues can help students practice active citizenship, as opposed to passive citizenship. This, one participant wrote, "is the moral obligation of the community college to its students, community, and nation."

Challenges in Using Deliberative Practices on Campus

Despite these successes, project participants also noted several challenges inherent in embedding deliberation on campus. Some of these are logistic in nature and might be experienced at any institution. These include difficulty securing space on campus to hold deliberations or moderator trainings; challenges securing the participation of key campus stakeholders given other events or commitments; and relatively high levels of faculty and staff turnover, which can impede progress toward institutionalizing a culture of deliberation.

Other challenges may be more inherent to community colleges. For example, some colleges have found it difficult to embed deliberative practices into a quarter system or among a highly transient group of students. Similarly, several project participants noted that a major challenge was the fact that "community college students don't do optional." Because many students have work or family conflicts and/or commute to campus, recruiting students to deliberations or moderator trainings outside of regular class hours can be challenging, although offering food or extra credit as incentives can be effective.

Other challenges to embedding deliberative practices in community colleges have to do with faculty or administrative fears about holding such events. These fears can take many forms (see Kauffman, 2016, for a detailed analysis of faculty fears about engaging in civic work on campus). At one participating college, for example, faculty and staff worried that the "usual suspects" (i.e., those who already have established beliefs that are so firmly held that they will impede civil dialogue) would be the only ones who would show up to deliberative events. Although this can happen, project colleagues noted that this does not necessarily negate the impact of the dialogue on the "usual suspects" or other attendees, as participants typically feel heard and understood, even if they do not change their own or anyone else's minds. Another frequent discomfort has to do with moderating dialogues, and specifically the lack of an "expert" as a moderator. Although most participants understood that deliberation is not meant to reduce the value of expert knowledge but rather to elevate the experiences and beliefs of all citizens, several felt that it might be useful to have deliberations—especially those including community members—moderated by someone who has substantial subject-matter expertise.

A final challenge relates to institutionalizing the deliberative process on campus—in other words, securing its practice, funding, and support among college leaders. As one colleague reflected,

> The hardest task likely may be building a culture of deliberation both on campus and in the community . . . and [to] clearly connect the practice to the college mission. More importantly, scheduling and discovering an effective process for public involvement will be key going forward.

Another colleague argued that institutionalizing deliberation on campus would be only the first step. As she wrote,

> Only when civic engagement becomes part of the . . . community college lexicon will it begin to be a statewide movement. In addition, the concept must become part of the larger dialogues taking place within a system, especially those concerned with equity and student success, as well as guided pathways. It is essential that civic engagement become part of these system-wide conversations; otherwise, some campuses will continue to move forward with their own local efforts while others will lag behind.

Training moderators and holding deliberations without external support and buy-in from the campus community will not be enough to ensure that deliberation becomes and remains a critical component of how colleges engage students in political discourse. Faculty must also form internal networks on campus, develop discipline-specific topics and approaches to deliberation that are connected to the curriculum, and periodically revisit the role of deliberation as a part of the teaching and learning dynamic (Kisker et al., 2016). Furthermore, college leaders and other administrators must create opportunities for community members to come to campus to participate in deliberative events and act as champions for the practice, both on campus and off. For colleges located proximally to other institutions of higher education, this may include building a reputation as a regional center of excellence in deliberation and offering trainings and other resources to nearby colleges, universities, and community organizations.

Conclusion

As we have learned in the course of this project, deliberation is far more than simply an opportunity to discuss democracy. It provides students and others with essential skills related to public discourse (Carcasson, 2013), but it also has the power to be transformative in students' lives, enriching their "capacity to act together to solve social problems" (Mair, 2016, p. 113). By participating in and moderating deliberative dialogues, students actually get to experience democracy working as it should. Moreover, they realize that they have the ability—through listening, empathizing, and seeking common ground—to facilitate this enactment of democracy. These opportunities are perhaps the most important and long-lasting gifts that Democracy's Colleges can bestow on their students and other members of the campus and surrounding communities.

References

Carcasson. M. (2013). *Rethinking civic engagement on campus: The overarching potential of deliberative practice.* Dayton, OH: Kettering Foundation.

Cohen, A. M., & Kisker, C. B. (2010). *The shaping of American higher education: Emergence and growth of the contemporary system* (2nd ed.). San Francisco, CA: Jossey-Bass.

Kauffman, C. (2016). Overcoming faculty fears about civic work: Reclaiming higher education's civic purpose. In B. Ronan and C. B. Kisker (Eds.), *Civic learning and democratic engagement* (New Directions for Community Colleges, No. 73, pp. 63–70). San Francisco, CA: Jossey-Bass.

Kisker, C. B. (2016). An inventory of civic programs and practices. In B. Ronan and C. B. Kisker (Eds.), *Civic learning and democratic engagement* (New Directions for Community Colleges, No. 73, pp. 3–23). San Francisco, CA: Jossey-Bass.

Kisker, C. B., & Ronan, B. R. (2012). *Civic engagement in community colleges: Mission, institutionalization, and future prospects.* Dayton, OH: Kettering Foundation.

Kisker, C. B., Theis, J. J., & Olivas, A. (2016). Community colleges and educating for democracy. *eJournal of Public Affairs issue on Educating for Democracy, 5*(2), 2–232. Retrieved from http://ejopa.missouristate.edu/index.php/ejournal/article/view/54

Mair, J. (2016). Empowering and transforming a community of learners via a student-centered approach to campus dialogue and deliberation. In B. Ronan and C. B. Kisker (Eds.), *Civic learning and democratic engagement* (New Directions for Community Colleges, No. 73, pp. 111–119). San Francisco, CA: Jossey-Bass.

Mathews, D. (2014). *The ecology of democracy: Finding ways to have a stronger hand in shaping our future.* Dayton, OH: Kettering Foundation Press.

Nussbaum, M. (2010). *Not for profit: Why democracy needs the humanities.* Princeton, NJ: Princeton University Press.

Rittel, H. W. J., & Webber, M. M. (1973). Dilemmas in a general theory of planning. *Policy Sciences, 4*(2), 55–69.

Ronan, B. R. (2012). Community colleges and the work of democracy. *Connections: Educating for Democracy, 2012,* 31–33.

Ronan, B. R. (2011). *The civic spectrum: How students become engaged citizens.* Dayton, OH: Kettering Foundation Press.

Ronan, B. R., & Kisker, C. B. (Eds.). (2016). *Civic learning and democratic engagement* (New Directions for Community Colleges, No. 73). San Francisco, CA: Jossey-Bass.

Ross, E. D. (1942). *Democracy's college: The land-grant movement in the formative stage.* Ames: Iowa State College Press.

Shaffer, T. J., Longo, N. V., Manosevitch, I., & Thomas, M. S. (2017). *Deliberative pedagogy: Teaching and learning for democratic engagement.* East Lansing: Michigan State University Press.

Theis, J. J., Kisker, C. B., & Olivas, A. (2018). Deepening deliberation in community colleges: Reflections on our research. *Higher Education Exchange, 2018,* 39–50.

CONCLUSION

Sources of Democratic Professionalism in the University

Albert Dzur

That is the uncommon school we want. Instead of noblemen, let us have noble villages of men.

—H.D. Thoreau

Uncommon Schools

This book is being published at a time of pervasive pessimism about American democracy: worries about concentrations of oligarchic and neoliberal power, on the one hand, and alarms about too broad a dispersion of populist and demotic influence, on the other. Historically low levels of trust in politics and politicians pervade every level and branch of government, not to mention citizens' own views of each other, all rendering the prospects of long-term constructive social change dim indeed. This pessimism and distrust is *overdetermined*, as social scientists say, because there are many sources, but the deep wellspring is our nonparticipatory, professionally managed public world. Put simply, the organization of modern life is unfriendly to democracy—from the schools we attend as children and young adults; to the workplaces we enter; to our hospitals, clinics, and asylums; and to the courts we use in times of trouble and conflict.

If we know where to look, however, we will see signs of democratic renewal. Although it usually does not announce itself in bright lights blinking "democracy happening here," collective work in unassuming places is happening all around us. For a number of years, I have been studying innovators I call *democratic professionals* in fields like education, criminal justice, health care, journalism, and city government. They are democratic professionals not because they do democracy professionally but because they do professionalism democratically. They are professional in their commitments to competence in a specific field, to achieving specialized skills, and to obtaining the knowledge necessary for acting well in difficult situations. And like traditional professionals they see their work as having an important normative purpose: as serving society somehow. But, drawing from the lessons of social critics and from their own frustrations with dysfunctional institutions, democratic professionals understand their relationship to society in a particular way; rather than using their expertise for the good of others as they—the professionals—see fit, democratic professionals wish to understand the patient, the offender, the student, the citizen on *their* terms and work collaboratively on issues recognized as common problems.

Democratic professionals rely on the tools of dialogue, deliberation, and public engagement; they are driven to these processes by their substantive commitments to develop *both* the demos and the profession. The knowledge and agency of the layperson is now a significant component of producing what can all too easily be seen as a strictly professional matter: education, news, government, health, justice. I have been interested in particular in the ways democratic professionals open institutions to this kind of load-bearing citizen participation and how they sustain such practices amid the great pressures to streamline, manage, and standardize. I call this process "rational disorganization" because, though including laypeople is rational if you want a more participatory democracy, it will appear more disorganized than conventional professional practices.

Can colleges and universities cultivate democratic professionalism? The answer is yes, but it comes with a caveat: only when they become more aware of the undemocratic professionalism they have routinely cultivated for many decades. The criminologist and democratic professional Nils Christie was once asked to give an inaugurating lecture for a new research institute. Christie (1977) began his talk, which later became an intellectual foundation of the restorative justice movement, by saying, "Maybe we should not have any criminology. Maybe we should rather abolish institutes, not open them. Maybe the social consequences of criminology are more dubious than we like to think. I think they are" (p. 1). Christie was concerned with the ways universities promote a kind of professionalism that "steals" what are really public problems, through the process of what he called "task monopoly": self-perpetuating cultures of expertise and certification that disqualify laypeople from identifying and handling issues best dealt with collectively. Before they can enable, in other words, universities need to come to grips with the often very subtle ways they disable.

The chapters in this book make clear that this is, indeed, possible, if difficult. Colleges and universities are gatekeepers to the professional world, where access requires increasingly specialized degrees and advanced training.

Catalysts of normative orientation, college programs such as those described in the case studies from the diverse set of campuses experimenting with dialogue and deliberation are places where young people can articulate their concerns about the working world they are entering, gain skills, and develop tools for change. Yet, with a few exceptions, the democratic professionals I have interviewed as part of my ongoing research are emerging despite university training, not because of it. Rather than serving as sites of possible leverage to help professions transition to a more democratic model, universities are often marked by the kinds of technocratic and self-serving tendencies that operate in other professional fields as barriers to more participatory norms.

People in Glass Houses

I became aware of the problem even before I started my research on innovative democratic professionals. For years I have included on some of my syllabi the *Port Huron Statement* written by Tom Hayden and others in the Students for a Democratic Society (Students for a Democratic Society, 1984). Hayden advocates cooperative workplaces, open social relations, and citizen-oriented governing institutions. He urges his fellow students to recognize and make use of their universities as sites of transformative change—as models of participatory democracy and channels for transmitting these values into the outside world. Committed to collegiality and truth-seeking, faculty listen to good reasons, and their seminars are places of critical dialogue in which students can challenge repressive, hierarchical, and self-interested practices on campus and in society at large, thus sensitizing and activating their fellows in close proximity in classrooms and campus gathering places. As graduates take their places in corporate and public worlds, they will incrementally democratize the institutions therein.

Hayden's narrative pictures the university as more egalitarian and invested in cultural change than it sometimes appears; underneath the tweeds, the ivy, and the scholasticism is a commitment to unconventional and disruptive ideas that clear new paths in math, science, and the humanities. Yet students reading *Port Huron* in my seminars tend to be unmoved. They care about reforming institutions and are far from apathetic, but the trouble is that students recognize their university is less democratic than it seems on the surface and is therefore an unsteady platform for transformative change. Academic creativity seems insular, self-referential, and mostly beneficial to elites on and off campus. Universities are collegial in their comportment, yet their departments are anchored in closed-off and hierarchical management structures. Relying on private search firms, trustees choose presidents and provosts with scant authentic input from below; once ensconced, these top administrators are typically evaluated with relatively nontransparent and nonparticipatory procedures. Administrative professionalism tends to follow a full-fledged social trustee model—thinking and acting *for* rather than *with*—and consulting faculty, student, and community opinion without any seriousness. The absence of a vibrant democratic professionalism is evident, too, in the classroom and in daily faculty-student noninteraction. Though research and disciplinary specialization are commonly blamed for these academic tendencies, the deeper problem is a proximity deficit: faculty members' inability to see and act with students as fellow citizens, as collaborators—if only neophytes—in a common public project of understanding and improving shared social, political, and economic structures.

To contribute to democratic renewal, universities must convey through their own practices that institutions can change; they are composed of real people with discernment, agency, fallibility, and a willingness to work across disciplinary, managerial, and generational divisions. Core ingredients of a more democratic academic culture include a commitment to power sharing that in turn requires free speech, collegial respect, reciprocity, absence of unnecessary hierarchy, suspicion of lock-step proceduralism, and commitment to collective decision-making. Though many American colleges and universities systemically fail to live up to these norms, which are overpowered by institutional forces of bureaucracy, routinization, legal accountability, risk management, and market definitions of *efficiency* and *productivity*, this book indicates that there is no small number of students, faculty, and administrators seeking openings to a more participatory culture. Without such a culture, experiments in dialogue and deliberation will fade into public relations.

Administrators who take up the challenge to become democratic professionals have a significant role to play in fostering dialogue with faculty and student committees with real responsibilities. For their part, faculty who accept the challenge can do much more to recognize students as cocreators of their education. Beyond receptivity to student voice and influence in seminars and in the shaping of curricula, there is the fundamental issue of how little time there is for research, student interaction, campus obligations, and work with community organizations. There is never enough time. To better cultivate norms of democratic practice, stakeholders need to find the time—fewer students per class, fewer classes per faculty member, fewer credits necessary to graduate—through some kind of calculus that respects research, students, and community.

Dangerous Outposts of a Humane Civilization?

Along with being more self-aware about their internal counterdemocratic tendencies, to be contributors rather than barriers to democratic renewal, colleges and universities need to look more carefully into the ways they think about instruction in professional and skilled work. Are they fostering—through their conceptual models, disciplinary knowledge, and training programs—widespread citizen agency and democratic self-determination, or are they mostly cultivating their own? Without a doubt, campus civic engagement programs and offices are thriving, but they are often freewheels spinning alongside the university's driving imperatives, which remain squarely attached to the social trustee model of managerial, technocratic professionalism.

Some of the very basic professional education choices to be made include, with specific reference to the examples from the campus case studies in this book, the following:

- Faculty can continue to pass along tried and true curricula fitting for largely passive classrooms or they can help students see themselves as learners with voice and agency in coproducing their education.
- Student affairs professionals can train student leaders to preserve hierarchical structures, maintain order, and deliver services to groups of followers or they can be taught to include students in clubs and residence halls as citizens in cocreating democratic living and learning communities.
- Campus organizations can be prompted to provide service or attempt to fix problems for community residents or they can be encouraged to create mutual spaces that involve local citizens as coeducators and partners in the knowledge-creation process.

The social trustee status quo will persist by default as long as higher education professionals complacently fail to recognize the costs of business as usual, which are paid out in the counterdemocratic trends in contemporary institutions and concomitant levels of civic lethargy and public distrust. Students have a powerful role here, too, to question the professional fields many will enter upon leaving university: What skills am I acquiring that can help me succeed, not only in terms of status and financial reward but also in working with future colleagues to do better than our predecessors in humanizing our public institutions?

There are openings for critically minded and constructive students to press these issues on campus, to be sure, and there exist receptive professionals across disciplines in a wide variety of public, private, research, liberal arts, and specialized academic institutions (see, e.g., Boyte, 2014; Peters, Alter, & Shaffer, 2018). Yet it is an uphill struggle for students and faculty alike. Many appear to be aware of the costs of the status quo, realizing the world the previous generations helped shape is one populated by providers and clients, producers and consumers, a world with profoundly undemocratic institutions that every day assert without even having to say it: Lay citizens cannot do justice and cannot do public safety because we, the professionals, do that work for you. Internal problems plague mainstream professionalism, too, for institutions that treat people primarily as clients and consumers rather than active agents and partners do not adequately deliver goods like justice and public safety, and they are unfulfilling to work in because they separate professionals from important social sources of emotional nourishment and practical local knowledge.

The democratic professionals I have met reject institutional hypocrisy: the school that says it is educating citizens while providing no opportunities for self-government or the prison that is so closed off to the public world that it cannot provide an avenue back into society for norm-violators. Undergraduates, graduate students, and faculty working in the natural and social sciences, arts and humanities, law, education, medicine, and engineering struggle with a similar situation. What many of us find desirable about our academic work—the freedom to choose intellectual projects; the collaborative aspect of research; the power-sharing in a laboratory, institute, or department; and the horizontal learning as new cohorts circulate through campus—is just what is being squeezed out of the misaligned and counterdemocratic institutional domains we are unthinkingly supporting through our campuses' professional education and credentialing processes. We who administer, teach, and study in professional education programs need to ask harder questions about what it means to be a professional today, and we need to seek some outside advice. Academics talk about the need for public outreach to spread ideas and best practices from the university out into the community; what I have in mind is the opposite. We need some in-reach.

My suggestion here is humility. Academics are no vanguard, either in modeling democratic norms or offering theoretical models. We need to listen more, to take up the knowledge of people outside our normal disciplinary channels, to learn about the different modes of task-sharing, collaboration, co-ownership, and democratic divisions of labor that nonacademic innovators are manifesting in daily life. We can help them form networks to share information and build platforms for problem-solving. The chapters in this book illustrate many creative approaches to opening up the university to outside perspectives. By listening and learning through the deliberative process, we can also incorporate some of their lessons of new democratic practice into higher education, striving toward the "dangerous outposts of a humane civilization" that Dewey (1922, p. 141) hoped schools could become.

A good example of this sort of recursiveness for higher education is a class on school redesign that democratic professional K–12 educator Helen Beattie recently taught at a Vermont college:

> Four schools are involved in this course. Each school has adults and students, teams of two to four from each school. The adults earn six graduate credits and the students are awarded college credit for a year-long class. We think we can't talk effectively about school redesign without the two primary stakeholders at the table.
>
> We are doing an action research design. This class is also going to be creating tools that will help guide students in fostering transformative dialogues. It will be a common language because the students are not going to let tools be developed that do not feel comfortable for them, and when it is comfortable for them it is comfortable for every stakeholder. There is nobody more masterful than students in getting to the heart of things. They play an essential role in co-creating what will serve their schools well as new strategies and techniques begin to take shape in response to state policy. These strategies are going to be steeped with youth-adult partnership. (Dzur, 2018, p. 145)

Beattie's class shows how academia can be a platform for horizontal collaboration with democratic professionals: not *training*, *instructing*, or *guiding* them but *learning from* them and even, in the best circumstances, *coproducing* with them. University *in-reach* allows reform-minded practitioners to practice dialogue inside seminars and workshops to foster new thinking about professional skills.

Beyond Legislators and Interpreters: Coproducing Theories of Change

Although this book tends to be mostly about practice, offering a diverse set of examples of dialogical and deliberative methods and models, I want to conclude by focusing on the small territory of academia I work in—democratic theory. More specifically, I want to offer some reflections on how we who categorize, compare, and conceptualize might also do the kind of "in-reach" that could better relate to people actively shaping institutions on and off campus. This is harder than it might seem. Writing and thinking are such solitary activities—democracy is not. Worse, time spent writing and thinking is surely time not spent in an elected office making decisions, or in a neighborhood organizing a collective effort, or in a public space articulating grievances. Democratic theory, therefore, is always gnawing away against itself to some extent; in only the barest, most abstract sense does it seek others outside the world of thinking and writing. And this may explain why the others outside are not seeking us much, either.

One of the most sobering insights gained indirectly through my research is how distant democratic theory is from the work of people who are good at doing democracy. They become as smart as they are about democracy by doing it, by reflecting on it with others, but—this is the sobering part—never by dwelling on the texts I cherish in the academic canon. Democratic professionals do their work without help from any theory that resembles what we academics write. Names instantly recognizable to political theorists draw blank looks. This suggests completely different fields of thought and action rather than one shared field that has only to overcome a barrier between theory and practice.

To face this problem squarely in higher education institutions, I think at least some faculty and students need to practice democratic theory as a catalytic rather than traditionally academic discipline—meaning that our research is done with and for the people being studied. *With* means listening carefully to democratic innovators, correcting and adjusting conceptual frameworks as one goes along, and taking suggestions on other lines of inquiry. *For* means contributing somehow to the success of their work by broadcasting it, encouraging discussion, and making links across professional domains to grow and diversify networks. Such an unabashedly open-ended and reform-minded methodological stance is not the only way to do democratic theory, of course, but it seems an appropriate expression of academic democratic professionalism: an admission of intellectual fallibility, sensitivity to the power of naming, humility in constructing theoretical frameworks, a commitment to task-sharing in concept-building, and solidarity with those engaged in the never-ending project of humanizing the institutional world we shape and are shaped by.

Zygmunt Bauman (1987) classified modern intellectuals into two categories: legislators and interpreters. The former is a rational planner who seeks to influence law, policy, and culture to shape productive and fulfilling lives and relationships. The latter—aware, on the one hand, of the failures of rational social planning, yet appreciative, on the other hand, of the wild diversity of productive and fulfilling lives—eschews the planning and shaping role and takes up the task of learning about other ways of life, and then translates these so that people might understand one another better. As Bauman himself realized, neither type of intellectual seems to matter in contemporary life, though they still offer their services in abundance in op-ed essays, think tank reports, and TED talks. The institutions outside of academia are humming along without the goods proffered by intellectuals, and the people purportedly in need of shaping or interpreting are not paying much attention, either.

Legislators and interpreters are both *meta-professionals*, people specializing in reason and careful methods who are somehow above and beyond practitioners as well as those others who are merely living their lives. To blaze a democratic professional rather than meta-professional path, however, I propose a third possibility: *active listeners*. Active listeners do not build systems, yet we also do not just translate fixed meanings from one group to another; we are coequal—or try to be—in meaning-making and system-building. The sites of dialogue and deliberation described in this book illustrate ways this process can start and become sustained. We open our ears, our eyes, our hearts, our minds, and we try to hear and see and feel and think more acutely, and, in our institution-shaping work and dialogue with others, we hold them to those expectations as well. We care about democracy, and we are troubled by the sneaky ways our own habits, norms, practices, and social structures on and off campus block and disable it.

I do not yet know how to make adequate use of active listening, nor what narrative forms are the best vehicles for expressing what is coproduced, but it is evident that some of the most practically useful and theoretically rich texts in democratic theory are fascinating hybrids written by active listeners—from Montesquieu's (1900) *Spirit of the Laws* to de Tocqueville's (1835/2012) *Democracy in America* to Dewey's (1916) *Democracy and Education* and Mansbridge's (1983) *Beyond Adversary Democracy*. And pressures to reconnect the social sciences and humanities to social problems at the ground level have produced significant recent methodological fermentation leading to more horizontal, inclusive, and action-oriented programs for dialogue and deliberation highlighted in this book, examples that are emerging among a number of contemporary disciplines (Schram, 2014).

As we exercise democracy within higher education, we will notice more democratic possibility in the world at large and we will better understand what we might contribute to it. Routine use of dialogue and deliberation reveals the ways knowledge is cocreated. Concepts and theories move forward in conjunction with dialogue, and with ground-level awareness earned through qualitative and participatory action research. As readers, too, we should ask if there is room in a theory for us, for our experiences, abilities, ideas, fears, and hopes. Democratic theory should not legislate for us, nor merely interpret what we already know, but rather, invite us into the common project. Especially in these anxious times, there is much left to be done and much still to learn about each other as we rebuild our public world—together.

References

Bauman, Z. (1987). *Legislators and interpreters: On modernity, post-modernity and intellectuals*. Ithaca, NY: Cornell University Press.
Boyte, H. C. (Ed.). (2014). *Democracy's education: Public work, citizenship, and the future of colleges and universities*. Nashville, TN: Vanderbilt University Press.
Christie, N. (1977). Conflicts as property. *British Journal of Criminology, 17*, 1–15.
de Tocqueville, A. (1835/2012). *Democracy in America (Vol. 1)*. Retrieved from https://oll.libertyfund.org/titles/2735.
Dewey, J. (1916). *Democracy and education: An introduction to the philosophy of education*. New York, NY: Macmillan.
Dewey, J. (1922, October 4). Education as politics. *The New Republic, 32*, 139–141.
Dzur, A. W. (2018). *Democracy inside: Participatory innovation in unlikely places*. New York, NY: Oxford University Press.
Mansbridge, J. J. (1983). *Beyond adversary democracy*. Chicago, IL: University of Chicago Press.
Montesquieu, C. de Secondat., Prichard, J. V., Neugent, T. (1900). *The spirit of the laws*. [Aldine ed.] New York: D. Appleton and company.
Peters, S. J., Alter, T. R., & Shaffer, T. J. (2018). *Jumping into civic life: Stories of public work from extension professionals*. Dayton, OH: Kettering Foundation Press.
Schram, S. (2014). Citizen-centered research for civic studies: Bottom up, problem driven, mixed methods, interdisciplinary. In P. Levine and K. Sołtan (Eds.), *Civic studies: Approaches to the emerging field* (pp. 91–102). Washington DC: Bringing Theory to Practice.
Students for a Democratic Society. (1984). The Port Huron statement. In J. C. Albert and S. Albert (Eds.), *The sixties papers: Documents of a rebellious decade*. New York, NY: Praeger.

RESOURCES

Higher Education Organizations

The following are organizations that promote the civic purposes of higher education and offer resources and support for dialogue and deliberation as part of this mission.

American Democracy Project, American Association of State Colleges and Universities
www.aascu.org/ADP

Association of American Colleges and Universities
www.aacu.org

Bonner Foundation
http://bonner.pbworks.com/w/page/119404902/Dialogue%20Across%20Diversity%20and%20Inclusion%20Trainings

Campus Compact
www.compact.org/resource-posts/dialogue-resources-for-higher-education/

Imagining America
www.imaginingamerica.org

Resource Organizations

The following are national organizations that have dialogue or deliberation as central to their mission. These organizations develop resource guides, conduct trainings and support, and/or host dialogues and deliberations for communities and educational institutions, including colleges and universities.

Better Angels
www.better-angels.org

Essential Partners
https://highered.whatisessential.org

Everyday Democracy
www.everyday-democracy.org

Highlander Research and Education Center
www.highlandercenter.org

Initiative to Revive Civility
www.revivecivility.org

Interactivity Foundation
www.interactivityfoundation.org

Institute for Democracy and Higher Education, Tufts University
https://idhe.tufts.edu

Junebug Productions
www.junebugproductions.org

Kettering Foundation
www.kettering.org

National Issues Forums Institute
www.nifi.org

Program on Intergroup Relations
https://igr.umich.edu

Public Agenda
www.publicagenda.org

Public Dialogue Consortium
www.publicdialogue.org

Sustained Dialogue Campus Network
www.sustaineddialogue.org

Networks

The following are networks of organizations and practitioners that provide resources, share best practices, and create learning communities around dialogue and deliberation.

Deliberative Democracy Consortium
www.deliberative-democracy.net

Deliberative Pedagogy Lab
www.deliberativepedagogy.org

Difficult Dialogues National Resource Center
www.difficultdialogues.org

National Coalition for Dialogue and Deliberation
www.ncdd.org

National Institute for Civil Discourse
https://nicd.arizona.edu

New Hampshire Listens
https://carsey.unh.edu/new-hampshire-listens

Methods

The following are distinctive methods of dialogue and deliberation, many of which are highlighted in this book.

Art of Hosting
www.artofhosting.org

Conversation Café
www.conversationcafe.org

Deliberative Forums
www.nifi.org/en/deliberation

Dialogue to Change
www.everyday-democracy.org/dialogue-to-change/about

Exploratory Discussion
www.interactivityfoundation.org/if-discussions

Intergroup Dialogue
www.intergroupresources.com/intergroup-dialogues

Jefferson Dinner
www.jeffersondinner.org

Open Space Technology
www.openspaceworld.org/wp2/what-is

Reflective Structured Dialogue
www.whatisessential.org/our-method

Story Circles
www.roadside.org/program/story-circles

Sustained Dialogue
www.sustaineddialogue.org/our-approach

World Café
www.theworldcafe.com

Journals

The following are academic journals that publish research on dialogue and deliberation or closely related topics.

Dialogic Pedagogy: An International Online Journal
https://dpj.pitt.edu/ojs/index.php/dpj1/index

The Good Society
www.psupress.org/Journals/jnls_GS.html

Journal of Dialogue Studies
www.dialoguestudies.org

Journal of Public Deliberation
www.publicdeliberation.net

Conferences

The following are conferences that focus on dialogue and deliberation.

Difficult Dialogues National Resource Center/Higher Education Conference
www.difficultdialogues.org/conferences

Frontiers of Democracy Conference
https://tischcollege.tufts.edu/civic-studies/frontiers-democracy-conference

National Conference on Dialogue and Deliberation
http://ncdd.org/events/about-ncdds-events

National Intergroup Dialogue Institute
https://igr.umich.edu/article/institute

Books

The following is a selection of books that focus on dialogue and deliberation.

Abbott, J. Y., McDorman, T. F., Timmerman, D. M., & Lamberton, L. J. (2015). *Public speaking and democratic participation: Speech, deliberation, and analysis in the civic realm.* New York, NY: Oxford University Press.
Allen, D. (2004). *Talking to strangers: Anxieties of citizenship since Brown v. Board of Education.* Chicago, IL: University of Chicago Press.
Bächtiger, A., Dryzek, J. S., Mansbridge, J., & Warren, M. (Eds.). (2018). *The Oxford handbook of deliberative democracy.* New York, NY: Oxford University Press.
Barker, D., McAfee, N., & McIvor, D. (Eds.). (2012). *Democratizing deliberation: A political theory anthology.* Dayton, OH: Kettering Foundation Press.
Boyte, H. C. (Ed.). (2015). *Democracy's education: Public work, citizenship, and the future of colleges and universities.* Nashville, TN: Vanderbilt University Press.
Buber, M. (1958). *I and thou* (2nd ed., R. G. Smith, Trans.). New York, NY: Charles Scribner's Sons.
Dedrick, J. R., Grattan, L., & Dienstfrey, H. (Eds.). (2008). *Deliberation and the work of higher education: Innovations for the classroom, the campus, and the community.* Dayton, OH: Kettering Foundation Press.
De la Pena, D., Allen, D. J., Hester, R. T., Hou, J., Lawson, L. J., & McNally, M. J. (2017). *Design as democracy: Techniques for collective creativity.* Washington DC: Island Press.
Escobar, O. (2011). *Public dialogue and deliberation: A communication perspective for public engagement practitioners.* Edinburgh, UK: Edinburgh Beltane.
Freire, P. (2018). *Pedagogy of the oppressed* (50th Anniversary ed., M. B. Ramos, Trans.). New York, NY: Bloomsbury.
Gastil, J. (2014). *Democracy in small groups: Participation, decision making and communication* (2nd ed.). State College, PA: Efficacy Press.
Gastil, J., & Levine, P. (Eds.). (2005). *The deliberative democracy handbook: Strategies for effective civic engagement in the twenty-first century.* San Francisco, CA: Jossey-Bass.
Gutmann, A., & Thompson, D. F. (2004). *Why deliberative democracy?* Princeton, NJ: Princeton University Press.

hooks, b. (1994). *Teaching to transgress: Education as the practice of freedom*. London, UK: Routledge.

Horton, M., & Freire, P. (1990). *We make the road by walking: Conversations on education and social change*. Philadelphia, PA: Temple University Press.

Jacobs, L. R., Cook, F. L., & Delli Carpini, M. X. (2009). *Talking together: Public deliberation and political participation in America*. Chicago, IL: University of Chicago Press.

Jovanovic, S. (2012). *Democracy, dialogue, and community action: Truth and reconciliation in Greensboro*. Fayetteville: University of Arkansas Press.

Karpowitz, C. F., & Raphael, C. (2014). *Deliberation, democracy, and civic forums: Improving equality and publicity*. New York, NY: Cambridge University Press.

Levine, P. (2013). *We are the ones we have been waiting for: The promise of civic renewal in America*. New York, NY: Oxford University Press.

Magolda, P. M., Magolda, M. B. B., & Carducci, R. (Eds.). (2019). *Contested issues in troubled times: Student affairs dialogues on equity, civility, and safety*. Sterling, VA: Stylus.

Mathews, D. (2014). *The ecology of democracy: Finding ways to have a stronger hand in shaping our future*. Dayton, OH: Kettering Foundation Press.

Molnar-Main, S. (2017). *Deliberation in the classroom: Fostering critical thinking, community, and citizenship in schools*. Dayton, OH: Kettering Foundation.

Nabatchi, T., Gastil, J., Weiksner, G. M., & Leighninger, M. (Eds.). (2012). *Democracy in motion: Evaluating the practice and impact of deliberative civic engagement*. New York, NY: Oxford University Press.

Pearce, K. A. (2010). *Public engagement and civic maturity: A public dialogue consortium perspective*. n.p.: Lulu.

Saunders, H. H. (2005). *Politics is about relationship: A blueprint for the citizens' century* (Revised ed.). New York, NY: Palgrave Macmillan.

Shaffer, T. J., Longo, N. V., Manosevitch, I., & Thomas, M. S. (Eds.). (2017). *Deliberative pedagogy: Teaching and learning for democratic engagement*. East Lansing: Michigan State University Press.

Thomas, N. L. (Ed.). (2010). *Educating for deliberative democracy* (New Directions for Higher Education, No. 152). San Francisco, CA: Jossey-Bass.

Wheatley, M. (2009). *Turning to one another: Simple conversations to restore hope in the future*. San Francisco, CA: Berrett-Koehler.

Yankelovich, D. (1999). *The magic of dialogue: Transforming conflict into cooperation*. New York, NY: Simon & Schuster.

Yankelovich, D., & Friedman, W. (Eds.). (2010). *Toward wiser public judgment*. Nashville, TN: Vanderbilt University Press.

EDITORS AND CONTRIBUTORS

Editors

Nicholas V. Longo is a professor in the Departments of Public and Community Service Studies and Global Studies and a faculty fellow for engaged scholarship with the Center for Teaching Excellence at Providence College. He is also on the faculty and board of College Unbound, a college focused on reinventing higher education for returning adult learners. He served as a program officer at the Charles F. Kettering Foundation in the area of civic education, the inaugural director of the Harry T. Wilks Leadership Institute at Miami University in Ohio, and the director of Campus Compact's national youth civic engagement initiative Raise Your Voice.

Longo is author of a number of books, articles, and reports on issues of youth civic education, engaged scholarship, deliberative pedagogy, global citizenship, and service-learning. His publications include *Why Community Matters: Connecting Education with Civic Life* (SUNY Press, 2007) and several coedited volumes, including *From Command to Community: A New Approach to Leadership Education in Colleges and Universities* (Tufts University Press, 2011), *Publicly Engaged Scholars: Next Generation Engagement and the Future of Higher Education* (Stylus Publishing, 2016), and *Deliberative Pedagogy: Teaching and Learning for Democratic Engagement* (Michigan State University Press, 2017). He was awarded the Early Career Research Award from the International Association for Research on Service-Learning and Community Engagement (IARSLCE) in 2009 and holds an MA in public affairs from the Humphrey Institute and a PhD in education from the University of Minnesota.

Longo lives in Providence, Rhode Island, with his wife, Aleida. Together, they have a great passion for educating the next generation of democratic citizens, starting with their children Maya and Noah.

Timothy J. Shaffer is an assistant professor in the Department of Communication Studies and assistant director of the Institute for Civic Discourse and Democracy at Kansas State University. He is also principal research specialist with the National Institute for Civil Discourse at the University of Arizona. Connected to these efforts, Shaffer serves as an associate editor of the *Journal of Public Deliberation* and as a country expert on deliberative democracy with the Varieties of Democracy project based at the University of Gothenburg. His research centers on the advancement of democratic practices through deliberative politics and civic engagement in higher education and other institutional and community settings using civic studies as a theoretical framework and empirical approach.

His publications include *Deliberative Pedagogy: Teaching and Learning for Democratic Engagement* (Michigan State University Press, 2017), *Jumping in to Civic Life: Stories of Public Work from Extension Professionals* (Kettering Foundation Press, 2018), *Agri-Culture and Future of Farming: An Interactivity Foundation Discussion Guidebook* (Interactivity Foundation, 2018), and *A Crisis of Civility?: Political Discourse and Its Discontents* (Routledge, 2019). He has published dozens of articles and book chapters on civic engagement, civic studies, public deliberation, higher education, and democratic professionalism.

In recognition of his commitment to engaged scholarship, Shaffer received the Early Career Recognition Award from IARSLCE in 2018. He received his BA from St. Bonaventure University, MA and MPA from the University of Dayton, and his PhD from Cornell University.

Shaffer lives in Manhattan, Kansas, with his wife Ellen and their four children—Jane, Margaret, William, and Katherine.

Contributors

Derek W.M. Barker is a program officer at the Kettering Foundation. With a background in political theory, he works primarily on research concerning the democratic role of higher education institutions, philanthropy and nonprofit organizations, journalism, and the professions. Barker is the coeditor (with Alex Lovit) of Kettering's *Higher Education Exchange* and also works closely with the foundation's team of resident researchers. Barker's academic publications include the book *Tragedy and Citizenship: Conflict, Reconciliation, and Democracy from Haemon to Hegel* (SUNY Press, 2009). He recently published an article on the intersection between deliberative democratic theory and virtue ethics in *Political Theory*. He has also published scholarly articles on topics such as oligarchy and modern representative government, Wilson C. McWilliams and the state of contemporary populism, and conceptual frameworks for "engaged" forms of scholarship. Barker's previous experience includes an appointment as visiting assistant professor of political studies at Pitzer College. He holds a PhD in political science from Rutgers University.

Hamida Bhagirathy is a senior program manager at the Program on Intergroup Relations (IGR). She holds an MA in higher education with a concentration in diversity and social justice in higher education from the University of Michigan. Bhagirathy's first encounter with intergroup dialogue was the Psych 405 course (now ALA 421) as a newly minted resident adviser in 2004, and this dialogue experience informed the trajectory of her professional and academic careers. Bhagirathy's undergraduate background is in sociology, political science, and classical archaeology. In her graduate and postgraduate work Bhagirathy explored issues of difference and how they may be bridged, from interrogating sources of inequities in the workplace, classroom, and residential settings to artistic methods of dialoguing. Prior to IGR, Bhagirathy worked at University of Michigan Housing supporting undergraduate students, graduate students, and university affiliates. In her spare time, she enjoys working on writing projects that are in varying states of (in)completion, experimenting with cooking, and exploring the green spaces of Ann Arbor.

Amanda L. Bonilla is the assistant director for social justice education in the Division of Diversity, Equity and Inclusion at Indiana University–Purdue University Indianapolis. She serves as the program director for the Social Justice Scholars program, which prepares students to be agents of positive social change through critical conversations and civil discourse. Since completing her MA in higher education and student affairs at Indiana University in 2011, Bonilla has been involved in a variety of professional leadership roles, including serving as the former associate director of multicultural programs and services at Clemson University. She has also been involved in national organizations including the National Association of Student Personnel Administrators' Latino Knowledge community as the South Carolina state representative, NCORE (National Conference on Race and Ethnicity) as a Latino Caucus representative, and LeaderShape serving as a cluster facilitator. She also cofounded the Inclusion Consultant Network LLC, a minority women–owned business focused on increasing cultural competency through discussion and dialogue for optimal work and learning environments.

Lorrie A. Brown is responsible for the oversight of major cocurricular community service initiatives at Indiana University–Purdue University Indianapolis (IUPUI), including the administration of the Sam H. Jones Community Service Scholarship program. For the past 20 years, Brown has worked to create responsive and well-structured community engagement experiences for students on campus while also actively sharing best practices on a local and national level. She collaborates with numerous IUPUI campus partners in both academic and nonacademic units to support the inclusion of all students in educationally meaningful civic activities. Brown received her undergraduate degree from Baldwin Wallace University and her graduate degree from Bowling Green State University, both located in Ohio.

Martín Carcasson, PhD, is a professor in the Communication Studies Department of Colorado State University (CSU) and the founder and director of the CSU Center for Public Deliberation (CPD). He is also a senior public engagement fellow with Public Agenda, the chair of the National Coalition for Dialogue and Deliberation Board of Directors, and a faculty mentor for the Kettering Foundation Centers for Public Life program. His research focuses on helping local communities address "wicked problems" more productively through improved public communication, community problem-solving, and collaborative decision-making. The CPD is a practical, applied extension of his work and functions as an impartial resource dedicated to enhancing local democracy in Northern Colorado. He and the CPD staff train students to serve as impartial facilitators, who then work with local governments, school boards, and community organizations to design, facilitate, and report on innovative projects and events on key community issues. His research has been published in *Rhetoric & Public Affairs, Communication Theory, National Civic Review, Colorado Municipalities,* the *International Journal of Conflict Resolution,* and the *Quarterly Journal of Speech.*

Virginia A. Cumberbatch, a creative scholar and organizer, works at the intersection of community advocacy and storytelling. Cumberbatch has served as director of community engagement and social equity for the University of Texas at Austin's Division of Diversity and Community Engagement since 2016, helping drive the university's vision to become less of an ivory tower and more of a community anchor addressing issues of access and equity. Cumberbatch is also the cofounder of Rosa Rebellion, a platform for creative activism by and for women of color.

Born and raised in Austin, Texas, Cumberbatch is a founding board member of Six Square, Austin's black cultural district, and is currently a global shaper (part of the World Economic Forum), on the board of KLRU (PBS), and was vital in relaunching the National Urban League's Young Professionals program in Austin. In 2017, she was appointed to and is currently serving on the mayor of Austin's Task Force on Institutional Racism and Systemic Bias. Given her commitment to disrupt systemic racism and build resources for inclusive practices, she's spoken at SXSWEDU, TEDxUWA, Q Commons, and the University of Western Australia's Social Impact Conference.

She is the recipient of the 2016 Anti-Defamation League of Austin Social Justice Award and the 2018 Austin 40 Under 40 Award for Civics,

Government and Public Affairs. She coedited the book *As We Saw It: The Story of Integration at the University of Texas at Austin* (University of Texas Press, 2018).

Lizzy Cooper Davis, PhD, is an artist and scholar interested in how the arts can facilitate community conversation, resistance, and change. Particularly focused on black freedom movements, she has conducted research in Cuba, Brazil, and New Orleans, and her current project examines the cultural workers of the civil rights era. She trained with Augusto and Julian Boal and used their Theater of the Oppressed in schools, community centers, and prisons, and has worked at the intersection of arts and organizing with Anna Deavere Smith, the Urban Bush Women, Angela's Pulse, Jacob's Pillow, The American Repertory Theater, ArtsEmerson, and the Boston Foundation. Davis has also performed nationally as an actor in such theaters as Second Stage, The Public Theater, The Long Wharf, Berkeley Rep, and The American Repertory Theater and with such directors as Liesl Tommy, Anne Bogart, and Mary Zimmerman in addition to work in television, film, and radio. Davis coedited *Enacting Pleasure: Artists and Scholars Respond to Carol Gilligan's Map of Love* (University of Chicago Press, 2010), wrote on the freedom songs of the civil rights movement for the roots music journal *No Depression*, taught with the Posse Foundation and at Harvard's Mellon School of Theater and Performance, and is an assistant professor at Emerson College.

Sara A. Mehltretter Drury is associate professor of rhetoric and director of the Wabash Democracy and Public Discourse Initiative at Wabash College in Crawfordsville, Indiana. Her research analyzes the quality and character of public discourse in the United States, with specific interests in the theories and practices of democratic deliberation, political rhetoric, and religious rhetoric. Drury has offered workshops on facilitation, problem-solving, conflict resolution, and civic engagement. In her work with Wabash Democracy and Public Discourse, Drury has collaborated on projects across Indiana, Illinois, Kentucky, Delaware, and South Dakota, focusing on topics such as community planning, poverty, race and justice, mental health, and public health. Her research has been published in outlets such as the *Journal of Public Deliberation, Communication Quarterly, Translational Behavioral Medicine*, and *Argumentation and Advocacy*. In 2017–2018, she was a visiting research fellow at the Institute for Advanced Studies in the Humanities at the University of Edinburgh in the United Kingdom, focusing on comparative deliberation in the United States and United Kingdom. Drury received her BA in political science and communication at Boston College and her

MA and PhD in communication arts and sciences at the Pennsylvania State University.

Albert Dzur is a democratic theorist interested in citizen participation and power-sharing innovations in education, criminal justice, and public administration. He is the author of *Democracy Inside: Participatory Innovation in Unlikely Places* (Oxford University Press, 2018); *Rebuilding Public Institutions Together: Professionals and Citizens in a Participatory Democracy* (Cornell University Press, 2017); *Punishment, Participatory Democracy, and the Jury* (Oxford University Press, 2012); *Democratic Professionalism: Citizen Participation and the Reconstruction of Professional Ethics, Identity, and Practice* (Penn State University Press, 2008); and a coeditor of *Democratic Theory and Mass Incarceration* (Oxford University Press, 2016). His interviews with democratic innovators appear in *Boston Review, The Good Society, International Journal of Restorative Justice*, and *National Civic Review*. He is a professor in the Political Science and Philosophy Departments at Bowling Green State University.

Nan Elpers is a junior at the Colorado College, studying psychology and feminist and gender studies. She is interested in the gap in dialogue across critical studies and the scientific disciplines and hopes that feminist studies will inform a research career in psychology. Elpers joined Colorado College's Public Achievement program her first year and has continued to learn about cocreative politics both from the black freedom movement in the 1960s South and from her middle and high school Public Achievement students.

Rhonda Fitzgerald is the managing director of the Sustained Dialogue Campus Network (SDCN), a grassroots, student-led movement that aims to transform differences into strong relationships and launch collaborative community change through an intentional dialogue-to-action process. SDCN supports a growing set of leaders around the globe in the United States, Ethiopia, and Sudan. Fitzgerald has taught Sustained Dialogue for the last 10 years after learning the process as a student at Princeton University and works to shift educational and community spaces through teaching equity and social justice practice, organizing across difference, and facilitation skills. She is from Atlantic City, New Jersey, and now lives in Washington DC.

Michaela Grenier is a program director for the Sustained Dialogue Campus Network (SDCN), where she spends much of her time helping campuses build capacity for dialogue and for collaborative problem-solving. Grenier supports campuses in building and sustaining dialogue initiatives by working with campus teams to apply the Sustained Dialogue model to retreat-based, course-based, and extracurricular settings. Before joining SDCN, Grenier worked in other roles within the fields of higher education and conflict resolution, including supporting student retention on a college campus, designing student civic leadership programming, and working with international and domestic conflict resolution programs for teenagers.

Suchitra V. Gururaj, PhD, serves as assistant vice president for community and economic engagement in the Division of Diversity and Community Engagement at the University of Texas at Austin (UT Austin), where she is the visionary and strategic lead for student engagement programs rooted in service, community-based learning course offerings, public engagement programming, and in-kind sponsorships. A lecturer in the College of Liberal Arts at UT Austin, she teaches courses on community organizing and leadership development. Her research focuses on service-learning outcomes, university-community partnerships, and social inclusion policies in higher education. Gururaj earned a BA in English literature from Yale University, an MA in English from the University of Chicago, and a PhD in educational administration from the University of Texas at Austin. She serves as book review editor for the *Michigan Journal of Community Service Learning*, sits on the editorial board of the *Journal of Higher Education Outreach and Engagement*, and holds a seat on the Executive Committee for the Commission on Economic and Community Engagement for the Association of Public and Land-grant Universities.

Shannon Wheatley Hartman, PhD, is a fellow of the Interactivity Foundation (IF), a not-for-profit, nonpartisan organization focused on improving political discourse through exploratory discussion in communities and classrooms. Since 2011, Hartman has worked on all three components of IF's mission: project discussions, community discussions, and higher education pedagogy. Prior to joining IF, Hartman was a lecturer on international relations at Arizona State University, where she was awarded Teacher of the Year for the School of Politics and Global Studies. Her teaching interests and research focus on critical cosmopolitanism, immigration and border politics, nonviolent resistance, critical security, postcolonial studies, and deliberative democracy. Her publications on the privatization of immigrant detention can be found in *International Political Sociology*, the *Routledge Handbook of Private Security Studies*, and *Critical Approaches to Security: Theories and Methods*. She has also published critical essays on ecotourism and travel writing in the *Journal of Politics* and *Margins, Peripheries, and Excluded Bodies:*

International Relations and States of Exception. Hartman is also currently working at Haverford College as a fellow-in-residence for the Center of Peace and Global Citizenship.

Sandy Heierbacher founded the National Coalition for Dialogue and Deliberation (NCDD) with the 60 volunteers and 50 organizations who worked together to plan NCDD's first conference. NCDD continued in that collaborative spirit and grew to a membership of thousands and a broader community of 35,000 subscribers. Under Heierbacher's leadership, members of NCDD collaborated to create the Engagement Streams Framework, the Core Principles for Public Engagement, and a dozen more national and regional conferences involving more than 3,500 participants. The 2002 NCDD national conference was the first of its kind, bringing together 225 facilitators, nonprofit leaders, public administrators, faculty members and others, and fatefully combining the terms *dialogue* and *deliberation* to help ensure all of the trailblazers who were bringing people together across divides could see themselves and their work in the event.

Based in the Boston area, Heierbacher consults with leading organizations in the field, like Everyday Democracy and the Kettering Foundation, in the areas of network- and community-building, public engagement, racial equity, and participatory event planning. Heierbacher currently serves on the boards of the National Issues Forums Institute and the Participatory Budgeting Project, and is an adviser to Participedia.net. Heierbacher has an MA in intercultural and international management from the School for International Training Graduate Institute.

Leslie Hernandez has a BA in public and community service from Providence College, where she is currently completing an MEd in urban teaching. She is of Dominican descent, born and raised in the South Bronx. She uses her intersectional identity to examine how educational theories are presented in the classroom and in community engagement. She has explored this through narrative development work she has done in the classroom and community throughout her undergraduate and graduate studies. She is a comanager of the Providence College/Smith Hill Annex.

Stephanie Hicks, PhD, is a lecturer at the Program on Intergroup Relations at the University of Michigan (UM) and a faculty affiliate of the Institute for Research on Women and Gender at UM. A scholar in educational policy studies, her teaching and research foci include diversity, equity and inclusion policy in higher education, intergroup dialogue, and social justice education.

A Chicago native, Hicks received a dissertation grant from the Institute for Research on Race and Public Policy at the University of Illinois at Chicago and was named a diversifying higher education faculty fellow by the Illinois Board of Higher Education. Her work has been published in the *National Political Science Review* and the *Black History Bulletin*.

David Hoffman is director of the Center for Democracy and Civic Life at the University of Maryland, Baltimore County (UMBC). He is the principal architect of UMBC's BreakingGround civic organizing initiative, which supports a thriving campus culture of engagement in civic life enacted through programs, courses, relationships, and everyday practices. Hoffman develops and teaches courses about civic communication and culture as a faculty fellow in UMBC's Honors College and has created and facilitated dozens of programs in which students develop the knowledge, skills, dispositions, and relationships needed to help their communities thrive. Hoffman serves as a member of the National Advisory Board for Imagining America and the Steering Committee for the American Association of State Colleges and Universities' American Democracy Project. As a member of the inaugural cohort of American Democracy Project Civic Fellows, he developed the framework for the civic learning and democratic engagement theory of change and works with a group of national partners to amplify and implement it. He writes about students' civic agency journeys, and pedagogies and strategies for supporting those journeys. He earned his BA at University of California, Los Angeles; JD and MPP degrees at Harvard University; and PhD in language, literacy, and culture at UMBC.

Michele Holt-Shannon is a cofounder and director for New Hampshire Listens (NH Listens) in the Carsey School of Public Policy at the University of New Hampshire. The mission of NH Listens is to help New Hampshire residents talk and talk and act together to create communities that work for everyone. Her work on and off campus is focused on inclusive civic engagement, community problem-solving, and building coalitions for community-initiated change efforts. She joined Carsey in 2011 to focus on process design to ensure fair, inclusive, and informed outcomes for local and statewide projects. She works to bring people together across perspectives and backgrounds to solve problems and create equitable solutions for their communities. Holt-Shannon is consulted on navigating controversial community issues and fostering organizational and community cultures of sustainable civic engagement. Recent projects include statewide conversations on the American dream and New Hampshire's kids, mental health and substance use, community police relations, race and equity, and water sustainability. Holt-Shannon is a senior associate with Everyday Democracy and a 2018 Better Selves Knoll Farm fellow. She is a graduate of Leadership New Hampshire, class of 2013. She earned her MA in higher education and human development from Bowling Green State University, an MTS in world religions and theological studies from Boston College, and a BS in biology and psychology from the University of Alabama.

Romy Hübler is assistant director of the Center for Democracy and Civic Life at University of Maryland, Baltimore County (UMBC). She works with students, staff, and faculty to advance a thriving civic culture through experiential learning programs, activities, and practices that foster reflection and dialogue to empower individuals and communities. Hübler holds a faculty fellowship in UMBC's Honors College, where she teaches courses that illuminate students' capacity for civic agency and support them in cocreating their communities, including the classroom and the university. For the past seven years, Hübler has also served as a key strategist for UMBC's BreakingGround initiative, which supports students, staff, and faculty in designing or reenvisioning projects and courses to include experiential learning and community engagement components. She is a member of the core team developing and writing about the civic learning and democratic engagement theory of change and has published articles and chapters on experiential learning, institutional change, career preparation for community engagement professionals, and graduate students' civic engagement. Hübler has held fellowships with Campus Compact, the International Center on Nonviolent Conflict, and Imagining America. She earned her BA in modern languages and linguistics; MA in intercultural communication; and PhD in language, literacy, and culture at UMBC.

Katie Hyten is the coexecutive director of Essential Partners, training groups in effective communication across differences, facilitating conversations in communities as they navigate difficult moments, and supporting internal operations and evaluation within the organization. Outside of Essential Partners, she is a visiting fellow at Tufts University, where she coteaches a course titled Dialogue, Identity, and Civic Action. She is also a mediator and an independent consultant in conflict resolution processes. Prior to joining Essential Partners, Hyten completed her MA in international negotiation and conflict resolution at Tufts University's Fletcher School, where her research addressed foreign policy in religious conflicts. In 2013, she was awarded Harvard's Program on Negotiation Summer Fellowship to support her research and work with Search for Common Ground in Lebanon. Hyten also spent over two years at Pepperdine University, where she helped develop and manage the Glazer Institute for Jewish Studies, a university-wide interreligious institute, and a summer internship program for graduate and undergraduate students in Israel-Palestine.

Jean Johnson, a vice president of the National Issues Forums Institute and senior fellow at Public Agenda, has studied public attitudes for more than three decades. She is the principal author of a series of influential Public Agenda reports on K–12 and higher education. She has published articles in *USA Today* and the *Huffington Post* and appeared on *Bill Moyers' Journal*, CNN, and MSNBC. Between 2008 and 2012, she coauthored three books with Scott Bittle: *Where Does the Money Go? Your Guided Tour to the Federal Budget Crisis* (HarperCollins, 2011); *Who Turned Out the Lights? Your Guided Tour to the Energy Crisis* (HarperCollins, 2009); and *Where Did the Jobs Go? –and How Do We Get Them Back?: Your Guided Tour to America's Employment Crisis* (HarperCollins, 2012). She also authored *You Can't Do It Alone: A Communications and Engagement Manual for School Leaders Committed to Reform* (Rowman & Littlefield, 2011). Johnson holds degrees from Mount Holyoke College, Brown University, and Simmons College.

Spoma Jovanovic, PhD, is a professor in the Department of Communication Studies at the University of North Carolina at Greensboro. Since 2001, she has been teaching students there how to collaborate with community members on programs and activist strategies designed to enhance ethical conversations and action related to civic literacy, cultural understanding, democratic participation, and social justice. Her research highlights how positive, meaningful social change begins with a conversation, develops into a story, and culminates with a new narrative to advance democracy.

She is the author of the book *Democracy, Dialogue and Community Action: Truth and Reconciliation in Greensboro* (University of Arkansas Press, 2012) and editor of *Partnerships: A Journal of Service-Learning and Civic Engagement*. Jovanovic's scholarship has been featured in dozens of academic journal articles and book chapters, as well as in national magazines, daily newspapers, and a 2013 TEDx Greensboro talk.

Her recent communication activism has included a 10-year service-learning program with an urban high school to promote political engagement and work alongside a grassroots effort to bring Participatory Budgeting to Greensboro, where thousands of people now participate in proposing ideas, developing budgets, and voting for $500,000 worth of projects and programs of their own design for the city.

Laurel B. Kennedy serves Denison University as vice president for student development. Kennedy began her professional career at National Public

Radio working in satellite distribution and then pursued a PhD to study uses of communication technology for social and economic development. She completed her dissertation as a Fulbright scholar in Malaysia and began teaching in the field of communication with a focus on international and comparative media systems and the history of U.S. media. Drawn to understanding the impacts of systems on people, Kennedy was prompted by local community concerns to explore service-learning and, in her faculty role, designed a series of seminars that took students into the community to provide direct service and community-based research. Kennedy led Denison's service-learning program through curricular expansion and deepened engagement with community leaders. Since becoming Denison's chief student affairs officer in 2010, Kennedy has focused her division's efforts on student well-being, diversity and inclusion, strong career development programs (including support for the cultivation of "citizen-professionals"), and aligning student organizations and residential life around leadership, civic engagement, and creative problem-solving. Kennedy serves on the boards of Newark, Ohio's, local community hospital and a charter school whose mission is to provide wraparound support to its predominantly low-income students and their families.

Katie Kingery-Page is a licensed landscape architect and associate professor in the Department of Landscape Architecture and Regional and Community Planning in the College of Architecture, Planning, and Design at Kansas State University. Her training spans sculpture, art theory, ecology, and landscape architecture. Prior to teaching, she worked in interdisciplinary design practice focused upon urban design. Kingery-Page's work explores the value of humanities knowledge for the practice of landscape architecture. This inquiry is tested through design outreach, often during community-based projects with graduate students. Kingery-Page uses ethnographic methods in a participatory design process to engage the question of whose meaning and values are privileged in public landscapes. Her interest is in participatory design, codesign, and public dialogues for inclusive place-keeping. She wishes to acknowledge the valuable influence of her community process mentors, La Barbara James Wigfall, Connie Pulcipher, and Dorothy K. Billings.

Kingery-Page's work has been published in a variety of journals and anthologies, including in a forthcoming collection of essays edited by Paula Horrigan and Thomas Oles, *Field Work in Landscape Architecture: Methods, Actions, Tools* (Routledge, at press).

Carrie B. Kisker is an education research and policy consultant in Los Angeles, California, and a director of the Center for the Study of Community

Colleges. She engages in applicable research pertaining to community college policy and practice, and regularly consults with college leaders on issues related to civic learning and democratic engagement, student outcomes and accountability, student mobility, and strategic planning. Kisker holds a BA in psychology and education from Dartmouth College, and an MA and PhD in higher education from the University of California, Los Angeles. She cowrote *The American Community College* (Jossey-Bass, 2014) with Arthur M. Cohen and Florence B. Brawer and *The Shaping of American Higher Education: Emergence and Growth of the Contemporary System* (Jossey-Bass, 2010) with Arthur M. Cohen. In 2016, Kisker and Bernie Ronan edited a *New Directions for Community Colleges* (Jossey-Bass) sourcebook on civic learning and democratic engagement.

Nancy Kranich teaches community engagement, information policy, and intellectual freedom at the Rutgers University School of Communication and Information and works on special projects with the Rutgers University Libraries-New Brunswick. A past president of the American Library Association (ALA), Kranich founded ALA's Center for Civic Life and the Libraries Foster Community Engagement Membership Initiative Group. Trained as a public innovator with the Harwood Institute for Public Innovation, she also serves on the board of the Kettering Foundation's National Issues Forums Institute and is a delegate to the U.S.-Russia Dartmouth Conference—a citizen-to-citizen diplomacy dialogue. Kranich holds an MPA from New York University's Wagner School of Public Service and an MA in Library Science and a BA in anthropology from the University of Wisconsin–Madison.

Ottavia Lezzi is earning her MPP with a concentration in women, gender, and sexuality studies from The George Washington University (GW). Her academic work focuses on diversity, equity and inclusion education, and antiviolence activism. She earned her BA in international studies at the University of Washington, during which time she spent a summer in Jordan teaching English in a refugee camp. Lezzi has previously worked at the Women's Funding Alliance and Planned Parenthood Votes Northwest, in the advocacy team. Lezzi also currently works as a graduate assistant at GW, focusing on writing-intensive classes for undergraduates.

Bruce L. Mallory, professor emeritus of education, has been a practitioner and national leader in the deliberative democracy movement for the past 20 years. At the Carsey School of Public Policy at the University of New Hampshire (UNH), he provides technical assistance and leadership related to the use of deliberative processes for citizen engagement. Cofounder and past codirector of New Hampshire Listens, Mallory now serves as senior adviser, focusing on strategic development as well as research and dissemination.

Mallory has served as UNH graduate school dean (1997–2003), provost and executive vice president (2003–2009), and interim director of the Carsey Institute (2011–2014). Prior scholarship focused on the relationship between early childhood disability and poverty, social policy affecting young children with disabilities and their families, the provision of early intervention services in rural communities, and more recently the role of higher education in strengthening democracy through deliberative practices. Mallory is cochair of the Deliberative Democracy Consortium and has served on numerous national committees concerned with higher education and deliberative democracy. He is a member of the board of directors of the Paul J. Aicher Foundation. Mallory earned his PhD from George Peabody College of Vanderbilt University in special education and community psychology in 1979.

Martha L. McCoy is president of the Paul J. Aicher Foundation and executive director of its primary project, Everyday Democracy. The organization and its network are recognized for advancing participatory democracy with a racial equity lens throughout the United States. Their tools, advice, and training support grassroots, public, nonprofit, and business leaders in working across sectors to create inclusive dialogue for sustained, equitable change and democratic governance.

Through their assistance, communities across the country are building their capacity for community engagement that leads to meaningful and measurable change in areas such as policing and the larger criminal justice system, K–12 education, early childhood development, and poverty reduction. Everyday Democracy partners with local, regional, and national organizations that are dedicated to expanding and deepening democratic capacity and infrastructure.

McCoy writes and speaks on grassroots civic engagement, participatory governance, racial and intersectional justice, and on strengthening the emerging U.S. and global movements for participatory, equitable democracy. She serves on several advisory committees, including the Philanthropic Initiative for Racial Equity, the Sillerman Center for the Advancement of Philanthropy at Brandeis, and the Deliberative Democracy Consortium. McCoy is also a member of the American Academy of Arts and Sciences' Commission on the Practice of Democratic Citizenship.

Keith Melville, PhD, is a sociologist who graduated from Columbia University and has been a faculty member at the Fielding Graduate

University since 1983. Throughout his career, his main interests have been in the areas of public policy, higher education, and the uses of social science research.

In the 1970s, he worked in the White House, where he was a writer and staff member for the President's Commission for a National Agenda for the 1980s. Subsequently, he was a senior vice president at Public Agenda in New York, founded by former secretary of state Cyrus Vance and pollster Daniel Yankelovich.

He has worked for more than 30 years with the Kettering Foundation, where he is a senior associate. In recent years, he has written about the progressive tradition in higher education, education for civic literacy and democratic life, and competency development in higher education.

As a writer and general editor, Melville has a long list of publications, including trade books, college-level text books, journal articles, and book chapters. For 14 years, he was executive editor of the National Issues Forums (NIF). He is an adviser to the National Issues Forums Institute and the editorial group that produces the NIF's issue guides. In 2017, he published *A Passion for Adult Learning: How the Fielding Model Is Transforming Doctoral Education* (Fielding University Press, 2017), about the progressive tradition in higher education and the advent of online graduate programs for midcareer adults.

Janet Moore is the cofounder of CityStudio Vancouver and currently the board chair and strategist. She is a professor of professional practice at Simon Fraser University's Morris J. Wosk Centre for Dialogue. She has imagined, designed, and facilitated intensive, interdisciplinary courses that focus on community engagement, resilience, lifestyle activism, food systems, group process, and urban sustainability. As a social innovator she has been involved in breaking ground for sustainability education projects in Vancouver, including early university engagement on sustainability curriculum at the University of British Columbia, where she completed her doctoral dissertation in the fields of community and regional planning and curriculum studies from 1999 to 2004.

Quixada Moore-Vissing, named after Don Quixote, leverages her idealism to support communities in building strong, participatory democratic systems, particularly at the local level. Moore-Vissing leads Public Engagement Partners as a civic researcher and community engagement designer, specializing in creating processes to problem-solve across difference, including race and politics.

Moore-Vissing has collaborated with many national democracy-focused organizations including Public Agenda, Everyday Democracy, the

MacArthur Foundation, the Deliberative Democracy Consortium, and the 92Y's Ben Franklin Circles. She is a fellow at the Carsey School of Public Policy at the University of New Hampshire, the George J. Mitchell Center for Sustainability Solutions at the University of Maine, and the Center for Childhood and Youth Studies at Salem State University. Her scholarship centers on local democracy, rural public engagement, and K–12 and higher education engagement with students and local communities. Moore-Vissing earned her PhD in education from the University of New Hampshire and her MA in communication from the University of Illinois at Urbana Champaign.

Keith Morton is professor and chair of Public and Community Service Studies and director of the Feinstein Institute for Public Service at Providence College. He has worked in the areas of community service and community theory for more than 30 years. His work focuses on how we learn from experience, on service and nonviolence as practices of community-building, and on the historic and present meanings of community and service in people's lives. Much of his work is grounded in the Smith Hill neighborhood of Providence. He is the author of *Getting Out: Youth Gangs, Violence and Positive Change* (University of Massachusetts Press, 2019). He is a comanager of the Providence College/Smith Hill Annex.

Alberto Olivas is the founding executive director of the Congressman Ed Pastor Center for Politics and Public Service at Arizona State University, an initiative to help students learn the skills for effective civic and political engagement. Apart from this role, Olivas provides training and technical assistance on issues related to public dialogue, public engagement, and civic education.

Previously, Olivas served in appointed leadership positions for Arizona governor Jane Dee Hull, as director of the Governor's Office for Equal Opportunity; and as state voter outreach director for Arizona secretary of state Betsey Bayless. Governor Janet Napolitano appointed Olivas to the Arizona Commission of Indian Affairs.

Olivas recently completed a term as board secretary for the National Civic League and serves on the board for Democracy Works, a national civic engagement organization. Locally, he serves on the Court Leadership Institute of Arizona for the Arizona Supreme Court and as vice chair of the Arizona Town Hall Board of Directors. He previously has served as board chair for KidsVoting Arizona and on the boards of directors for Valley Leadership, the Arizona Human Rights Foundation, the Mesa Association of Hispanic Citizens, and the Newtown Community Development Corporation.

Jeff Prudhomme, PhD, is a vice president and fellow of IF. His core activities include participating in the overall guidance of IF's operations, supervising the fellows' project activities, designing and delivering training for educational uses of IF's discussion process, and conducting his own discussion projects.

Now in his eighteenth year with IF, Prudhomme has facilitated citizen discussion projects on such diverse topics as human genetic technology, the future of civic discourse, the design and development of our towns and cities, the future of the family, and the future of sports and society. He maintains a wide range of public policy interests, believing that citizens in a democracy have the capacity and responsibility to think broadly about public matters.

Prudhomme comes to this work from an academic background in philosophy and religious studies. He envisions his work with IF as a way to take philosophical thinking out into the public, beyond the exclusive domain of experts. He sees IF's educational efforts as both a way to expand this civic capacity and a way to enhance student learning. A former Fulbright scholar in Germany, Prudhomme previously taught philosophy and religious studies at the college level. His publications include a book on the philosopher Martin Heidegger, shorter articles and translations, as well as discussion guides and supporting materials for IF.

Libby Roderick is director of the Difficult Dialogues Initiative and associate director of the Center for Advancing Faculty Excellence at the University of Alaska Anchorage and vice chair of the Difficult Dialogues National Resource Center. She is associate editor of *Start Talking: A Handbook for Engaging Difficult Dialogues in Higher Education* (University of Alaska Anchorage and Alaska Pacific University, 2008), coauthor of *Stop Talking: Indigenous Ways of Teaching and Learning* and *Difficult Dialogues in Higher Education* (University of Alaska Anchorage, 2013), and editor of *Alaska Native Cultures and Issues* (University of Chicago Press, 2010) and *Toxic Friday: Resources for Addressing Faculty Bullying in Higher Education* (University of Alaska Anchorage, 2016). She works with faculty across the United States and in South Africa to increase their capacity to effectively conduct difficult dialogues, apply Indigenous ways of teaching and learning in the classroom, and ensure collegiality in academic departments.

Roderick is also an internationally recognized, award-winning singer/songwriter, recording artist, and activist whose music has been featured on CNN and CBS, at the UN Beijing conference, Ms. Foundation, World Wilderness Congress, by the Associated Press, and in many other forums. NASA played one of her songs on Mars to inspire the robot *Spirit*. Her seven recordings have received worldwide airplay and her writing and songs have appeared in many movies and books, including *Home Town* (Random House, 1999) by Pulitzer Prize winner Tracy Kidder, *Moral Ground: Ethical Responses to a Planet in Peril* (Trinity University Press, 2011), and *Prayers for a Thousand Years: Inspiration from Leaders and Visionaries Around the World* (HarperOne, 1999).

John Sarrouf is the coexecutive director of Essential Partners. He studied in the master's program in dispute resolution at the University of Massachusetts. Sarrouf has facilitated dialogues on issues such as guns in America, police-community relations, Israel-Palestine, Muslim-Jewish relations, human sexuality in the Christian church, and race in America.

Sarrouf teaches people how to facilitate dialogues across difference as well as mediate and manage conflict in their own lives and workplaces. He has helped start dialogue programs in universities, organizations, cities, and towns across the country, including the University of San Diego, Tufts University, Wellesley College, Rutgers University, Northeastern University, Bridgewater College, and in his home town of Gloucester, Massachusetts. He served as the assistant director of Difficult Dialogues at Clark University, where he taught dialogue to faculty and students. Sarrouf helped start the peace and conflict studies minor at Gordon College. He teaches reconciliation at the European Center for the Study of War and Peace in Zagreb, Croatia. He is the primary investigator on a team from five universities studying dialogic pedagogy for the development of intellectual humility, conviction, and engagement in the classroom with funding from the Templeton Foundation and the University of Connecticut.

To all of his work he brings a background of 15 years in the theater as an actor and director. He is a member of the stage actors' union, Actors Equity.

Anthony C. Siracusa works at the intersection of race, religion, and politics in modern U.S. history. He has published essays in edited volumes from the University of Kentucky and University of Mississippi Presses, and his work has also appeared in the *Journal of Civil and Human Rights*, the *Journal of African American History*, the *Tennessee Historical Quarterly*, and the *Southwest Tennessee Historical Society Papers*. His book project, *The World as It Should Be: Religion and Nonviolence in the Black Freedom Movement*, explains how and why religious nonviolence became the force that centered black life in U.S. politics in the mid-twentieth century. Siracusa lives with his wife and their dog in Colorado Springs where he serves as the assistant director in the Collaborative for Community Engagement (CCE) at Colorado College.

John J. Theis is the director of the Center for Civic Engagement for Lone Star College–Kingwood and a professor of political science. He also serves as the chair of the steering committee of the Democracy Commitment and a member of the board of directors for the National Issues Forums Institute. He has been involved in civic engagement work for over 20 years, started the Lone Star College–Kingwood Public Achievement program in 2010, and was one of the founders of the Kingwood College Center for Civic Engagement. Theis holds a PhD from the University of Arizona, and among his publications is "The Institutionalization of the American Presidency: 1924–1992," coauthored with Lynn Ragsdale, and "Political Science, Civic Engagement, and the Wicked Problems of Democracy." He has received numerous awards and honors, including being nominated for the E.E. Schattschneider Award for Best Dissertation published in the field of American politics (American Political Science Association), Professor of the Year, Governors Award for Excellence in Teaching, Innovator of the Year, and The John and Suanne Rouche Excellence Award. Theis grew up in South Korea as the son of Methodist missionaries. He has two beautiful daughters, Samantha and Angela, and two granddaughters, Harper and Spencer.

Nancy Thomas directs the Institute for Democracy and Higher Education (IDHE) at Tufts University's Jonathan M. Tisch College of Civic Life. IDHE is an applied research center that studies student political learning, discourse, equity, and participation. Her work and scholarship interests include deliberative democracy, campus climates for student political learning and participation in democracy, political equity and inclusion, and campus free speech and academic freedom. She cofounded The Democracy Imperative, an association of academics and practitioners dedicated to advancing dialogue and deliberation in academia. She wrote several chapters of and edited *Educating for Deliberative Democracy* (Jossey-Bass, 2010), a *New Directions for Higher Education* series monograph. She is also a former editor at the *Journal of Public Deliberation,* a senior associate with Everyday Democracy, and a member of the Scholars Strategy Network. She holds a EdD from the Harvard Graduate School of Education and a JD from Case Western Reserve University's School of Law.

Mark L. Winston is the recipient of the 2015 Governor General's Literary Award for Nonfiction for his book *Bee Time: Lessons From the Hive* (Harvard University Press, 2014). One of the world's leading experts on bees and pollination, Winston is also an internationally recognized researcher, teacher, and writer. He directed Simon Fraser University's Centre for Dialogue for

12 years, where he founded Semester in Dialogue, a program that creates leadership development opportunities that equip and empower students to contribute to social change in communities.

As a consultant and thought leader, Winston partners with universities, corporations, nongovernmental organizations, governments, and communities to advance communication skills, engage public audiences with controversial issues through dialogue, and implement experiential learning and community engagement in educational institutions. As an award-winning writer and editor, he works with students, scientists, other professionals, and writers to develop compelling nonfiction, from proposals and newspaper opinion pieces to manuscripts and books.

He currently is a professor and senior fellow in Simon Fraser University's Centre for Dialogue and a professor of biological sciences.

Elizabeth Wuerz serves as a program consultant, working closely with administrators and staff to organize Sustained Dialogue on their campuses. Prior to her work with the Sustained Dialogue Initiative, she worked in education and conflict resolution supporting the development of student programs to improve campus culture and in the peace-building field facilitating programming and training sessions on conflict management, negotiation and mediation, and researching material for a new citizen security initiative in Central America. Her experience also includes working on economic community development projects in Peru. She received her MA in law and diplomacy from the Fletcher School at Tufts University with a focus in international negotiation and conflict resolution and her BA from Northwestern University. She is based in Boston.

INDEX

8 Ways, 44

Abdullah, C., 240
abortion, 86
academic libraries
  as civic agents, 199–201
  challenges and opportunities for civic engagement, 204–5
  civic engagement scholarship and, 201–2
  deliberative forums and, 203–4
  recommendations for civic engagement, 205–6
  for strengthening civic literacy, 202–3
Acket, S., 92
Act to Restore and Preserve Free Speech, 44
active citizenship, 63
active listening, 123
Adamic, L., 76
Adbusters, 174
Addams, J., 1, 221
Adult Freedom Fighters, 131
Aicher, P., 99
Alaska Pacific University (APU), 270, 271
Alexander, S., 92
ALL IN Campus Democracy Challenge, 188
Allen, D., 78, 176, 177
Allen, P., 253
Allen, R., 106
Alter, T.R., 259, 290
Alternate ROOTS, 134

American Association of State Colleges and Universities, 188, 200, 204, 205
American Association of University Professors, 205
American Community Survey, 263
American Democracy Project, 26, 188, 200, 204, 205
American liberalism, 58
American Library Association, 200, 201, 202, 204
AmeriCorps/VISTA, 224
Andrews, T., 73
Anft, M., 10
Anti-Defamation League, 44, 269
antistructure, 222
Applied Deliberative Techniques, 162
appreciative Inquiry, 123
Arao, B., 185
Arend, O., 130
argument culture, 177
Aristotle, 57
As We Saw It, 229
Ashé Cultural Arts Center, 134
asset-based community development, 221, 231
Association of College and Research Libraries, 202
Atlantic, The, 70
Atwell, M.N., 42, 264
Auburn University, 115
autocratization, 16

Bailey, P., 134
Baker, E.J., 131, 132, 136, 255

Baker, R.A., 44
Baker-Boosamra, M., 188
Bakshy, E., 76
Baldwin, J., 177, 178
banking model of education, 120
Banned Books Week, 204
Barber, B., 61
Barker, D., 26
Barker, D.W.M., 60, 66
Barnard College, 271
Barr, R., 15, 16
Barrett, L.F., 70
Barry, L., 205
Battistoni, R., 221
Bauer-Wolf, J., 70
Bauman, Z., 292, 293
Baylor University, 161
Beale, R., 121
Beattie, H., 291
Beaulieu, B., 105
Bebelle, C., 134
Beckett, S., 130
Beirich, H., 44
Benhabib, S., 58
Ben-Porath, S., 70
Berger, C., 188
Bertelsmann Stiftung, 260
Bessette, J., 57
better speech, 74
Between Facts and Norms, 58
Beyond Adversary Democracy, 293
Bickford, S., 60
Birmingham Children's March, 188
Bjerkaker, S., 99
black freedom movement, 249, 250, 256
Black, L., 22
black nationalists, 44
Blake, H., 16
Boal, A., 135
Bonner Program, 19
Borsenberger, M., 92
Bowling Alone, 177
Boyer, E., 62, 63

Boyer, E.L., 26
Boyte, H., 15, 27, 203, 211, 212, 216
Boyte, H.C., 8, 250, 251, 290
Brammer, L.R., 69
Brandeis, L., 53, 74
brave space, 185
Breadsley, J., 238
BreakingGround, 186, 187
Brecht, B., 130
Bridgeland, J., 42, 264
Bridgewater College, 90, 93
Bridging Theory to Practice, 231
Brigance, W.N., 71
Bringle, R.G., 195
Brookfield, S.D., 26, 27
Brown, A., 15
Brown, J., 24
Brown, K.D., 238, 240, 245
Brown, L.A., 195
Brown, S., 242, 243, 244, 246
Buber, M., 21, 22
Buras, K.L., 133
Burnett, G., 200
Bush, A., 1, 188
Bush, G.H.W., 62
Bushman, D., 90
Busteed, B., 61
Butler, B., 76

Cade, S., 163
Camp David Accords, 110
campus-based deliberative center, 161
Campus Compact, 2, 10, 26, 27, 63, 200, 205, 277
Campus Compact Knowledge Hub, 202
campus interfaith dialogue groups, 210
Canada Health Act, 173
Carcasson, M., 18, 23, 27, 73, 149, 162, 164, 165, 199, 206, 275, 276, 283
Carnegie Classification for Community Engagement, 235
Carsey Institute, 102

Carsey School of Public Policy, 9, 259–60, 263, 266
Carducci, R., 20
Carmichael, S., 131
Carpetbag Theater, 134
Carson, C., 131
Case Western University, 114
Catholic Worker movement, 221
Center for Civic Engagement LibGuide, 200
Center for Civic Life, 204
Center for Democracy and Civic Life, 187
Center for Engagement and Community Development, 246
Center for Public Deliberation (CPD), 7, 161–62
   model of, 162–64
   practices of, 162–64
   principles of, 162–64
   recommendations for other campuses, 165–66
   successes and challenges of, 164–65
Center for the Study of Community Colleges, 9, 277
Center on Extremism, 269
Centers for Public Life, 161, 166
Centre for Teaching and Learning, 273
Chambers, S., 58
Chan, E., 92
Chan, J., 92
Change Handbook, The, 163
Charles F. Kettering Foundation. *See* Kettering Foundation
Charron, K.M., 137
Chasin, R., 87
Checkoway, B., 63
Chesler, M., 20, 119, 121
Chester I. Lewis Reflection Square Park. *See* landscape architecture
"Chicago principles," 71
Christie, Nils, 286
Chufrin, G., 111

Citizens' Assembly for Electoral Reform, 174
Citizenship Schools, 137, 250, 252
CityPlan, 173
CityStudio, 173
civic deserts, 263
Civic Engagement LibGuide, 200
civic engagement movement, 10, 62–64
Civic Health Index, 263
Civic Learning and Democratic Engagement, 205
Civic Literacy Initiative, 203
civic muscle, 211
civic networks, 9
civic studies, 13
civil discourse, 8, 14, 18, 26, 90, 156, 195, 196, 270
civility, 47
Clark, S., 104, 137, 249, 250, 251, 255
Clark University, 271
Clayton, P., 63
Clemens, K., 185
Clement, L., 246
clicktivism, 202
Clinton, B., 62, 162
Cocke, D., 132, 134
codesign, 238, 240, 245
Cogan, N.H., 71
Cohen, A.M., 275
Cohen-Cruz, J., 132, 134, 136
collaboration by difference, 149
College of the Canyons, 277
College Unbound, 223
College: What It Was and Should Be, 140
Color Line Project, 133
Colorado College, 9, 249–50, 251
Colorado Sierra Club, 253
Colorado Springs City Council, 253, 254
Colorado State University, 7, 161
Combs, G., 88
Coming Together for Racial Understanding, 106

Committee on Freedom of Expression, 70
Common Ground Gamers, 223
communication studies, 22
communications theory, 5, 86
communitarianism, 57
communitas, 222
communities, 89
community-based civic health, 264
community-based deliberation, 265
community capitals framework, 105
community colleges, 275–76
    challenges in utilizing deliberative practices, 281–83
    deliberation and, 276, 277–78
    deliberative dialogue project successes, 280–81
    public life and, 276
    responsibility of, 275–76
    train the trainer approach to deliberative dialogue, 278–80
    wicked problems and, 275, 276, 278
community conversations, 261
community engagement, 171
Community Engagement Center, 233
Community Engagement (CE) Dialogues, 231, 232–34
community service, 62
Confederate statues, 85
conflict transformation, 86
Conflict Transformation, 86
Conover, P.J., 19
Considine, A., 132
content analysis, 241
Conversations Café, 221
Conversations That Matter, 7, 176–77
    as a model for democratic action, 178–80
    expansion of, 182–83
    required skills for, 181–82
    successes and challenges, 180–82
Crain, L., 209
Cremin, L.A., 26
criminal justice reform, 43

criminology, 286
critical appreciative inquiry, 123
critical pedagogy, 19
critical service learning, 64, 221
critical synthesis, 4, 79
critical thinking, 69
Crucible Moment, A, 63, 64
culture of dialogue, 116
Cumberbatch, V.A., 229
Cytron-Walker, A., 20, 119

Daleiden, B., 209
Dartmouth Conference, 111
David and Lorraine Cheng Library, 203
Davis, L.C., 129, 185
Davis, O., 130
Davis, P.C., 129
Day, D., 221
De Avila, J., 71
Dedrick, J., 65
Dedrick, J.R., 18, 26
DelBanco, A., 144
deliberation. *See* dialogue and deliberation
deliberative civic engagement, 4, 57, 64–66
deliberative democracy, 3, 4, 6, 7, 26, 28, 42, 57–62, 144, 189, 200
Deliberative Democracy Consortium, 4, 28, 162
Deliberative Democracy Handbook, 163
deliberative democracy movement, 26
deliberative dialogue, 10, 20, 185, 186, 199, 203, 205, 276–83
deliberative inquiry, 164
deliberative pedagogy, 1
Deliberative Pedagogy, 2, 17, 19
deliberative practices, 19
Delivery Organization, 104
Delta Community College, 277
democracy
    current political climate and, 42
    higher education and, 2–3
    in crisis, 16

practicing, 41
readiness approaches to discussing, 45–51
role of colleges and universities, 176–77
Democracy and Education, 293
Democracy and Social Ethics, 1
Democracy Commitment, The, 9, 188, 277
Democracy Imperative, 41
Democracy in America, 216, 293
Democracy Plaza, 8, 193–95
　challenges of, 197
　current program, 195–97
　description of, 193–94
　impact on campus, 196–97
　recommendations for, 198
　student leadership of, 194–95
democracy professionals, 10
democracy walls, 8, 33, 193
Democracy's Colleges. *See* community colleges
"democracy's garden," 73
democratic capacity, 104
democratic deliberation, 250–54
democratic politics, three concepts of, 59
democratic professionals, 285–87, 288–94
democratic recession, 16
Democrats, 43
Denison University, 8, 209, 212, 216
Dent, T.C., 131
DeOrsey, D., 240
Derby, D., 130
Devane, T., 163
Dewey, J., 26, 120, 184, 206, 291, 293
dialogic campus, 90
dialogic open spaces, 27
dialogic pedagogy, 90
dialogue and deliberation, 4–6
　case studies of, 7
　civic networks and, 9
　civil discourse and, 18

　community engagement work and, 8–9
　definition of, 21–22
　deliberative civic engagement and, 64–66
　democratic professionals and, 27
　democracy professionals and, 10
　democratic engagement and, 10
　development of democracy and, 26
　as a form of civic education, 27
　free speech and, 69
　higher education and, 27, 33, 60–62
　learning paradigm and, 15–16
　listening and, 76
　political discussions and 14
　practicing, 71–78
　student affairs offices and, 20
　wicked problems and, 22–25
　Also see Center for Public Deliberation, Conversations that Matter, community colleges, Democracy Plaza, Difficult Dialogues Initiative, Everyday Democracy, Interactivity Foundation, Intergroup Dialogue, landscape architecture, National Issues Forum, New Hampshire Listens, Public Achievement, Semester in Dialogue Program, Sustained Dialogue
dialogue-based communication, 171
dialogue-based learning, 120
dialogue circle, 169–71
dialogue to change, 5, 101
Diamond, L., 16
Dickes, P., 92
Dickinson College, 111
Diebel, A., 107
Dienstfrey, H., 18, 65
Difficult Dialogues Initiative, 9, 28
　indigenous ways of teaching and, 272, 273
　model history, 270–71
　ongoing activities of, 273

principles and practices of, 271–72
Start Talking and, 271, 274
Stop Talking and, 272, 274
strengths and challenges of, 273–74
Toxic Friday, 272, 274
Difficult Dialogues National Resource Center (DDNRC), 271
disciplined perseverance, 111
discursive democracy, 65
discussion leadership and teaching, 53–54
Diversity and Inclusion Discussions (DID), 154
Division of Diversity and Community Engagement (DDCE), 8
Community Engagement Center, 230–31
recommendations for other campuses, 235–36
role of dialogue for community engagement at, 228–30
strategic plan, 230
Dockum Drugstore, 241, 242, 244, 245
Doherty, J., 69
Domagal-Goldman, J., 188
Domise, A., 184
Donovan, D., 212, 251
Don't Start Me to Talking or I'll Tell Everything I Know, 132
Downtown Wichita Development Corporation, 240, 241, 246
DP Scholars, 196
drug addiction, 43
Drury, S.A.M., 69, 73, 74, 77
Dryzek, J., 58, 59, 65
Dryzek, J.S., 26
Duval, J., 142
Dzur, A.W., 14, 205

Eagan, M.K., 14
Eatman, T., 1, 188
Eaton, K., 177, 176
ecological democracy, 238

Edmon Low Library, 203
Egyptian-Israeli Peace Treaty, 110
Eick, G.C., 241
El-Bermawy, M.M., 184
Emory University, 271
emotion, 60
empathetic listening, 69
Enacting Pleasure, 129
enclave deliberation, 240, 245
engaged learning, 19
Engagement Streams Framework, 28, 29, 30 definition of, 21–2232
equity, 19
Escobar, O., 21, *23*, 260
Essential Partners, 4, 5, 24, 28, 85, 180
description of, 86
groups worked with, 88–89, 90, 91
methodology of, 87–88
wicked problems and, 22–25
ethics in government, 43
Evans, S., 15
Evans, S.M., 8
Everyday Democracy, 4, 5, 28, 97–99, 180
about, 99–101
anchor partners of, 102
approach to community change, 101–3
Horizons and, 103–6, 106–7
New Hampshire Listens and, 260, 263
racial equity and, 107
Exec. Order, 2019, 43
experiential learning, 171
Exploratory Discussions, 6

Facebook, 196
facilitation, 149–50
Facing Heroin, 264–65
Facing History, 44
fake news, 202
Falcone, F., 240
Falcone, J., 246
Falola, B., 230
family systems thinking, 5, 86

Farley, E., 209
federal budget deficit, 43
Federal Highway Authority, 239
Federalist Papers, 58
Feinstein Institute for Public Service, 219, 220, 224, 225, 226
Feldman, N., 71
Fingerhut, H., 15, 49
First Amendment, 71
FischHaus, 240, 243, 246
Fisher v. The University of Texas, 235
Fitzgerald, R., 2
Flaherty, C., 69
Flaherty, J., 130, 133
Fleischhacker, D.A., 195
Florida, R., 229
Follett, M.P., 22, 27
Ford Foundation, 21, 270
fossil fuel divestment movement, 262
Fostering Dialogue Across Divides, 88
Frankenberger, T., 92
Franklin Pierce College, 203
free inquiry, 43
Free Southern Theatre, 129–33, 137
free spaces, 8, 15–16
Free Spaces, 15
free speech, 3, 4, 24, 43–45, 69–71, 197
  democracy and, 72–73
  protecting, 72–75
  responsible speech and, 75–77
  silence and, 75–77
  synthesis for public life, 77–78
free speech zones, 43, 70
Freeman, J., 88
Freire, P., 19, 22, 120, 135, 221
Friedman, W., 22, 145
front porch, 230
Front Porch Gatherings, 232, 234, 235
Frontiers of Democracy, 41
Fry, R., 70
Frye, M., 184
Funeral for the Free Southern Theater, 132

Gallup, 44, 49
Garvin, L., 2
Gastil, J., 26, 27, 163
Gibson, C., 21
Gill, S., 44
Giroux, H., 177
Glastetter, A., 240
Globe and Mail, 172
Golden, E.N., 134
Goldfinger, J., 193
Gragg, R., 238
Grand Valley State University, 188
Grant, J., 132
Grattan, L., 18, 65
Great Good Places, The, 15, 201
Grönlund, K., 240
group agreements, 46–48
Gruber, A.M., 202
Guatemalan Association, 223
gun violence, 43
Gundersen, A.G., 151
Gurin, P., 119
Gururaj, S.V., 230
Guttman Community College, 277

Habermas, J., 58, 59, 60
habits of the heart, 209
Haidt, J., 18, 70
Halprin, A., 239
Halprin, L., 239, 240
Hamer, F.L., 131, 255
Hamilton, A., 58
Hanauer, N., 73
Hartley, M., 17, 26, 63
Hartman, S.W., 156
Harvard University, 61
Harwood Group, 18
Hatcher, J.A., 195
hate groups, 44
hate speech, 24, 44
Hayden, T., 287
health care, 43
Heierbacher, S., 163
Held, D., 26
Hess, A., 184

Hess, D.E., 176
Hester, R., 238, 239, 240, 241, 244, 245
Heterodox Academy, 18
Hewitt, G.J., 49
higher education
  civic engagement movement and, 62–64
  cultures of dialogue in, 85–86
  dialogue and deliberation in, 177–78
  influences affecting student learning, 43–45
  Interactivity Foundation and, 150–51
  neutrality challenge, 51–53
  partisan divides and, 14–15
  purpose of, 17–20, 52
  readiness approaches for discussing politics, 45–51
  recursiveness for, 291
  Reflective Structured Dialogue and, 93–95
  viewed as "too liberal," 49
  Also see intergroup dialogue, Semester in Dialogue
high-impact practices, 16
Higher Education Research Institute, 14
Highlander Folk School, 17, 250, 252
Highlander Research and Education Center, 134, 221
Hildreth, R., 212
Hilgendorf, A., 19
Hiltzik, M., 70
Himmelroos, S., 240
Hoelting, J., 104
Hoffman, D., 188
Hogan, W., 255
Holland, B., 228
Hollander, E., 63, 200
Holman, P., 163
Honduran Association, 223
hooks, b., 21, 135
Hopkinson, N., 148

Horizons initiative, 97, 98, 103–6, 106–7
Horton, M., 17, 22, 221, 250, 251, 252
Howard, Z., 240
Hoyt, L., 65
Hrabowski, F.A., 188
Hughes, L., 130
Hull House, 221
Hyten, K., 2

I Too Am Wabash, 76
illegal immigration, 43
Illinois State University Library, 204
Imagining America, 26, 134
Indiana University Purdue University Indianapolis (IUPUI), 193, 195, 198
inquiry, 123
Institute for Civic Discourse and Democracy, 28, 203
Institute for Democracy & Higher Education (IDHE), 41, 48, 49, 50, 51, 54
Institute for Reconciliation and Social Justice, 273
Interactivity Foundation, 4, 6, 147
  benefits to students, 154
  core principles of, 148
  guidelines for facilitators, 150
  in higher education, 150–51
  history of, 147–48
  process of, 148–50
  strengths and challenges of, 155–57
  WISe 101 and, 151–55
Intergroup Dialogue, 5, 20
  consciousness-raising and, 121
  democratic education and, 120
  four-stage model of, 122
  higher education and, 119–22
  peer facilitators and, 120–21, 122–24
  relationship-building and, 121–22

social justice and, 122, 126
strengths and challenges of, 124–26
International Association for Public Participation (IAP2) Public Participation Spectrum, 199, 205
Inter-Tajik Dialogue, 111
Isaccs, D., 24
Issue Convention, 252, 253, 255
IUPUI, 8
Iyengar, S., 43

Jaeger, P., 200
Jaffee, E.M., 266
James Madison University, 161
Jamieson, K.H., 75
Jamila, S., 134
Jay, J., 58
Jefferson, T., 200
Jim Crow laws, 249, 250
Jimmy Carter Presidential Library, 203
Johnson, A.G., 121
Johnson, R., 130
Johnson, W., 130
Jones, C.J., 44
Journal of Democracy, 16
Journal of Public Deliberation, 28
Jovanovic, S., 177, 179
Juarez, J.A., 238, 240, 245
Junebug/Jack, 132, 134
Junebug Productions, 4, 6, 129–33, 133–35

Kadlec, A., 145
Kansas State University, 9, 28, 238–246
Kansas State University Libraries, 203
Karpowitz, C.F., 240
Kauffman, C., 282
Kavanaugh, B., 213
Kavanaugh, J., 164
Keegan, J., 76
Keith, W.M., 27
Kellner, D., 184
Kelly-Woessner, A., 49
Kent State University, 188

Kettering Foundation, 1, 3, 4, 10, 16, 17, 18, 22, 28, 65, 105, 141, 161, 166, 204, 216, 277, 278
Kiesa, A., 18
King, S., 188
Kingery-Page, K., 240
Kirkwood Community College, 277
Kisker, C.B., 275, 276, 278, 283
Kissinger, H., 110
Klinenberg, E., 15
Knight Commission on the Information Needs of Communities in a Democracy, 200
Knight Foundation, 15, 44
Koch & Fowler, 229
Kohl, H., 17
Kohl, J., 17
Kohl-Arenas, E., 134
Kolowich, S., 70
Konitzer, T., 43
Kranich, N., 200, 202
Krause, S., 60
Kretzmann, J., 221, 231, 232
Ku Klux Klan, 44
Kuh, G., 16

Lachapelle, P.R., 106
Ladner, J., 255
land-grant universities, 103, 259–60, 267, 275
Landemore, H., 60
Landreman, L.M., 178
landscape architecture, 9, 238
  adapted ethnography model, 244–45
  Chester I. Lewis Reflection Square Park, 240–44, 246
  community participation and, 238, 239–40
  models for participatory design and codesign, 240
  recommendations for other campuses, 245–46
  twelve-step process for, 239

landscapes of action, 88
landscapes of meaning, 88
Lane Community College, 277
Latino Americans: 500 Years of History, 202
Lea, S.G., 151
Leadership, Equity, Access, and Diversity (LEAD) Fund, 44
learning exchanges, 17
Lederach, J.P., 86
Leighninger, M., 26
Lemken, A., 242, 243, 246
Leong, J.H.T., 200
Lerman, L., 135
Lerner, J., 21
Levine, P., 13, 27, 42, 163, 264
Lewis, C.I., 241
Lewis, K., 246
Liberating Structures, 180
liberalism, 57–58
Libraries Transform Communities: Models for Change, 204
Lievrouw, L., 200
Liu, E., 73
London, S., 18, 236
Longo, N.V., 2, 17, 21, 26, 27, 66, 73, 166, 221, 246, 276
Loss, C.P., 26
Lowe, M., 205
Lührmann, A., 16
Lukianoff, G., 18, 70
Lyndon Baines Johnson Presidential Library, 203

Madison, J., 58, 71
Magolda, M.B.B., 20
Magolda, P.M., 20
Mair, J., 283
Makau, J., 177, 178
Malena, C., 15
Mallory, B., 263
Mangan, K., 70
Manosevitch, I., 2, 17, 66, 73, 166, 276

Mansbridge, J., 58, 165, 293
Margulies, N., 24
Mariani, M.D., 49
Martin Drake Power Plant, 250, 253, 254
Marty, D., 177, 178
Mathews, D., 3, 16, 22, 24, 25, 141, 144, 276
Maurasse, D.J., 228
Maurin, P., 221
Mayhew, M., 49
McAfee, N., 26
McAvoy, A., 176
McCoy, M.L., 101
McCrae, K., 133
McDaniel College, 203
McDew, C., 255
McGregor, P., 134
McIvor, D., 26
McKee, S., 133, 136
McKnight, J., 14, 221, 231, 232
Meadows, D.H., 221
meaningful participation, 239
Mehaffy, G., 199
Meng, C., 209
Merriman, P., 239
Messing, S., 76
Michna, C., 131, 133
Miller, P.R., 19
Mississippi Free Press, 130
Mississippi Freedom Summer of 1964, 253
Mississippi State University, 105
Mitchell, T., 221
Moller, M., 209
Monroe Community College, 277
Montana State University, 105
Montesquieu, 293
Moore, J., 169
Moore-Vessing, Q., 263
Morehouse, D., 103, 105, 106
Morphew, C.C., 17
Morris J. Wosk Centre for Dialogue, 7, 168

Morton, K., 221
Moses, G., 130, 131
Mueller, M., 92
Muhammad, C., 133
Murray, B., 254

NAACP, 241
Nabatchi, T., 26
Nagda, B.A., 20, 119
narrative, 60
narrative therapy, 5, 86
NASPA, 188
National Coalition for Dialogue and Deliberation, 4, 28, 73, 162, 205
National Conference on Citizenship, 263
National Conversation on Race, 162
National Endowment for the Humanities, 202
National Issues Forum, 6, 65, 140–42, 162, 163, 165, 185, 204
  choicework and, 144–46
  goal of, 141
  political learning and, 142–44
  Safety and Justice issues guide, 186
National Issues Forums Institute, 4, 6, 28, 180, 205
National Security Council, 110
National Task Force on Civic Learning and Democratic Engagement, 63, 64
NBC, 193
Negotiation Journal, 111
Neil and Louise Tillotson Fund, 264
neo-Nazis, 44
neutrality challenge, 51–53
New Hampshire Charitable Foundation, 264
New Hampshire Listens, 9, 102, 259–60, 267
  community-based civic health and, 263–64
  Everyday Democracy and, 260, 263
  Facing Heroin and, 264–65

  four areas of focus, 260–64
  knowledge production and transfer, 265–67
  study circle formats used, 260
new knowledge, 104
New Orleans, LA, 130
New York Times, The, 178
Next Generation Democracy, 142
Nguyen, M., 73
North Country Listens, 264
North Middle School (Colorado Springs, CO), 250, 251, 252
Northwest Area Foundation, 97
Northwestern University

Occupy movement, 262
Oklahoma State University, 203
Oklahoma State University Extension, 203
Oldenburg, R., 15, 201
Olivas, A., 276, 278
Olson, L., 131
O'Neal, J., 128–29, 131, 132, 133, 136, 137
O'Neal, W., 130, 133, 135
O'Quinn, J., 132
organic leadership, 26
Organizing Rural and Reservation Communities for Dialogue and Change, 98
original recording devices, 135

Palaces for the People, 15
Palmerton, P.R., 179
Parker, K., 70
Parkinson, J., 165
participatory democracy, 26
participatory design, 238
participatory research methods, 33
partisanship, 43
passionate impartiality, 150
Payne, C., 249, 252, 255
peace process, 110
perspective-reinforcing bubbles, 184

Peters, S., 134
Peters, S.J., 259, 290
Pew Research Center, 14, 42, 43, 49, 70
Phillips, W., 71
Piedmont Virginia Community College, 277
Planning Neighborhood Space With People, 239
Pogue, J., 221
Politifact, 44
pop-up civic spaces, 179
pop-up dialogues, 179
Port Huron Statement, 287
Portland Community College, 271
Portsmouth (NH) Listens, 260, 261
Post, M., 26
poverty, 106
power map, 253
Powers, W. Jr., 228
Pranis, K., 185
Pregones/Puerto Rican Traveling Theater, 133
Preskill, S., 26
Primakov, Y., 111
Princeton University, 111
Proctor, D., 246
Program on Intergroup Dialogue, 5, 119
Program on Intergroup Relations, 4, 28, 124, 126
Project 401, 223
Providence College/Smith Hill Annex, 8, 223
　description of, 224
　dialogue between campus and community, 219–22
　historical and philosophical foundations of, 220–22
　model of, 223–25
　ownership of, 224–25
　practices of, 223–25
　principles of, 223–25
　success and challenges of, 225–26

Public Achievement, 9, 249–50
　democratic deliberation and, 250–54
　group process of public deliberation, 252–54
　Issue Convention, 252, 253, 255
　modeling deliberative democratic practice and, 254 Issue Convention, 25256
Public Achievement Club, 251
Public Agenda, 141, 142, 145
Public Conversations Project, 22–25, 86
public deliberation, 20, 22, 250–54
public dialogue, 18
public judgment, 22
public reasoning, 58
public work, 211
Putnam, R., 177

Quality Enhancement Plan, 90

racial equity, 101
racism, 106
Randals, J., 133
Ransby, B., 131
Rapeli, L., 240
Raphael, C., 240
Rasmussen, D., 130
Rawls, J., 58, 60
Red Frame Lab, 210
reflection, 88
reflective silence, 4, 79
Reflective Structured Dialogue, 5, 86, 87, 92–93, 93–95
Reid, M., 200
Reinhard Mohn Prize, 260
Ren, C., 229, 230
Republicans, 43, 61
resident assistant training, 212
residence halls
　democratic practice sites, 209–10
　democratic principles, 210–13
　model for democratic practices, 210–13

practices of, 210–13
   successes and challenges for, 213
      democratic principles, 210–1315
resilience, 85, 92
responsible speech, 75–77
restorative practices, 185
Rice, M.F., 162
Rich, M.D., 164
Richard B. Russell Library, 203
Ripon College, 203
ripple mapping, 105
Rittel, H.W.J., 22, 275
Roadside Theater, 132, 134, 185
Roberts & Kay, Inc., 101
Robin, V., 221
Robinson, V., 188
Rockenbach, A., 49
Roger Williams University, 115
Rogers, E.B., 238
Ronan, B., 275, 276
Rosenberg, B., 210
Ross, E.D., 275
Ross, J., 238
ross, j.m., 134
Rourke, B., 23, 24, 98
Rous, P., 186
RSVP Cycles, 239
RUCore, 202
Russell, V., 177
Rutgers-Newark Collaboratory for Pedagogy, Professional Development and Publicly-Engaged Scholarship, 204
Rutgers University, 8, 201, 206
Rutgers University Libraries, 200, 202, 204

safe spaces, 47, 70
Salaam, K.y., 133
Saltmarsh, J., 1, 17, 26, 27, 63, 188
sanctuary discussions, 148–49
Sandel, M.J., 58
Santa Fe College, 277
Sarracino, F., 92

Sarrouf, J., 93
Saunders, H., 110, 111
Schechner, R., 131
Schenck-Hamlin, D., 246
scholarship of engagement, 62
Schram, S., 293
Scully, P.L., 101, 107
seed story, 129, 135
self-interest, 251
Selznick, B., 49
Semester in Dialogue Program, 7, 168–69
   assignments during, 172–74
   description of, 171–74
   impact of, 174–75
   purpose of, 169–71
   student description of, 170
   three tenets of, 171–72
service learning, 62–64, 199–206
Shaffer, T.J., 2, 17, 18, 19, 27, 66, 73, 166, 246, 259, 276, 290
Sherman, A., 44
Shor, I., 19
silence, 75–77, 79
Simon Fraser University, 7, 168
skinheads, 44
Sklar, G., 73
slacktivism, 202
Slim, R., 111
small-group communication, 27
Smith Hill Annex. *See* Providence College
Smith Hill Block Party, 225
Smith Hill Community Development Corporation, 219
Smith Hill Jam, 223
Smith Hill Partners Initiative, 225
snowball sample, 242
Snyder, T., 184
social cohesion, 92
social infrastructure, 15
social justice, 122
Social Justice Scholars, 8, 196, 197
social media algorithms, 184

Sojourner House, 223
Somerville, M.M., 240
South Dakota State University (SDSU) Extension, 98, 103, 105
Southern Illinois University, 132
Southern Poverty Law Center, 269
Southern Rural Development Center (SRDC), 105, 107
Soviet Union, 62
Spangler, T., 92
Spelman College, 13
Spirit of the Laws, 293
Sprain, L., 27, 73, 164
Springer, A., 69
Stains, R., 87
St. Bernard's Elementary (St. Paul, MN), 251
St. Edwards University, 161
Stand Up for Androscoggin Valley, 265
Start Talking, 271, 274
Start Talking: A Handbook for Engaging Difficult Dialogues in Higher Education, 272
Staunton, M., 266
Stern, J., 147, 148
St. John Fisher College, 115
Stevenson, E., 246
Steward, H., 134
Stewart, B., 185
Stillwater Public Library, 203
Stillwater Speaks, 204
Stoecker, R., 19
Stop Talking, 272, 274
Stop Talking: Indigenous Ways of Teaching and Learning with Difficult Dialogues in Higher Education, 272
story circles, 6, 128–29, 185
 contemporary use of, 133–35
 guidelines of, 135–37
 in university settings, 134–35
St. Paul Community and Technical College, 277
streams of engagement, 163
structure, 222

structured dialogue, 98
structured speaking and listening, 88
Strum, S., 1
Strunk, K.K., 70
Student Nonviolent Coordinating Committee (SNCC), 130, 255
Students at the Center, 133
Students for a Democratic Society, 287
study circles, 5, 98, 101, 104, 260
Study Circles Resource Center, 97–99
Sturm, S., 188
Sublette, N., 130
Sun, W., 241, 242, 243, 246
Sustained Dialogue, 5, 20, 210
 examples of, 113–16
 five stages of, 112–13
 origins of, 110–11
 primary audience for, 113–16
 settings for, 113–16
 strengths and challenges of, 116–18
Sustained Dialogue Campus Network (SDCN), 4, 5, 111, 112, 113, 117
Sustained Dialogue Institute, 110, 111, 223, 234
Sustained Dialogue Network, 28
Sutherland, E., 132
Sweatt v. Painter, 229
Sweezy v. New Hampshire, 53
systems theory, 221

Tagg, J., 15, 16
Take Part, 239
talk to action, 262
Talking Democracy, 7, 184–85
 examples of initiatives, 187
 fostering a humane civic culture, 185–87
 new platforms and resources, 187–89
Talloires Network, 65
Tang, E., 229, 230
Tannen, D., 177
Tarrant County Community College-Southeast, 277

Task Force on Regional Conflicts, 111
task monopoly, 286
Tatum, B., 13
Teachers College, 120
Teachout, W., 104
Tedin, K., 43
Templeton Foundation, 93
Texas Library Association, 203
Theis, J.J., 276, 278, 280
theories of change, 291–94
theory of change, 188
Thiel, S.G., 202
third space, 8, 15, 33
Thomas, M., 1, 17
Thomas, M.S., 2, 17, 66, 166, 276
Thomas, N., 42, 49
Thomas, N.L., 18
Thompson, M., 120
Those Who Stayed, 230
Thriving Communities, 98
To, H., 92
Tocqueville, A. de, 209, 216, 293
Toxic Friday, 272, 274
Toxic Friday: Resources for Addressing Faculty Bullying in Higher Education, 272
TransLink, 174
Troester, R.R., 221
trolling, 184
Truman Commission on Higher Education, 52
Trump, D., 43
Tryon, E.A., 19
Tufts University, 41, 91, 93, 94
Tumblr, 76
Turner, C., 133, 134, 136
Turner, R.B., 130
Turner, V., 222
Turning the Tide on Poverty (Tide), 105
Turning to One Another, 221
Twill, S., 205
Twitter, 196
Tyee, 174

Ubuntu, 181
United Way, 164, 223
University of Alabama, 116
University of Alaska at Anchorage, 9, 270, 271
University of California Irvine, 271
University of Chicago, 70, 71
University of Georgia, 203
University of Houston-Downtown, 161
University of Iowa, 161
University of Kansas, 202
University of Maryland, Baltimore County (UMBC), 7, 184, 186
University of Michigan, 119, 124, 126, 271
University of Missouri, 271
University of New Hampshire, 9, 41, 102, 259, 262
University of North Carolina (UNC) at Greensboro, 7, 178
University of Notre Dame, 115
University of Texas, 203,
University of Texas at Austin, 8, 228, 236, 271
University of Texas at El Paso Library, 200
University of the Free State of Blomfontein, 273
University of Utah, 161
University of Virginia, 111
Upper Ohio Valley Self-Help Organization, 147
Urban Bush Women, 130
U.S.D.A. Cooperative Extension Service, 106
U.S. Department of Agriculture, 103
U.S. Department of Arts and Culture, 134
U.S. Tenth Circuit, 49

Vancouver Courier, 174
Vancouver Sun, 172
Varieties of Democracy Institute, 16
viral deception, 75

virtue ethics, 60
Vision and Values, 209
Vogt, E., 24
voting, 41

Wabash College, 71, 74, 76
Wabash College Chapel Talk, 69
Wabash Democracy and Public Discourse (WDPD), 73
Wagner, South Dakota, 97
Wall Street Journal, The, 76
Walzer, M., 14
Ward, E., 26
Washington State University, 161
Wasserman, J., 239
Webber, M.M., 22, 275
Wedge, M., 185
Weiksner, G.M., 26
Weinberg, A., 8, 209, 216
Welborn, R., 105
Wesleyan College, 151–55, 157
Western Living, 174
Wheatley, M., 22, 221
White, B., 107
white nationalism, 44
white supremacy, 71
Whitney v. California, 74

Why Are All the Black Kids Sitting Together in the Cafeteria?, 13
wicked problems, 22–25, 150, 275, 276, 278
Wigfall, L.B.J., 243, 246
Wilkinson, Z., 200
William Paterson University, 203
Willingham, T., 200
Wingspread Declaration on the Civic Responsibilities of Research Universities, 63
Winston, M., 168
WISe 101, 151–55
Wichita, KS, 241, 245
Wichita Parks and Recreation, 240
Woessner, M., 49
Wright Community College, 277

Yale University, 271
Yankelovich, D., 22, 142
Yankton Indian Reservation, 97
Young, I.M., 60, 77, 101
Young Turks, 241

Zagorsky, J., 49
Zollar, W.W.J., 129, 136
Zúñiga, X., 20, 119, 120, 121, 122

Association
of American
Colleges and
Universities

About AAC&U

AAC&U is the leading national association concerned with the quality, vitality, and public standing of undergraduate liberal education. Its members are committed to extending the advantages of a liberal education to all students, regardless of academic specialization or intended career. Founded in 1915, AAC&U now comprises nearly 1,400 member institutions—including accredited public and private colleges, community colleges, research universities, and comprehensive universities of every type and size.

AAC&U functions as a catalyst and facilitator, forging links among presidents, administrators, and faculty members who are engaged in institutional and curricular planning. Its mission is to reinforce the collective commitment to liberal education and inclusive excellence at both the national and local levels, and to help individual institutions keep the quality of student learning at the core of their work as they evolve to meet new economic and social challenges.

Information about AAC&U membership, programs, and publications can be found at www.aacu.org

Campus Compact

About Campus Compact

Campus Compact is a national coalition of colleges and universities committed to the public purposes of higher education. We build democracy through civic education and community partnership.

In 1985, Campus Compact was founded by higher education leaders who hypothesized that participatory campuses with robust support structures would be the building blocks of a stronger, more sustainable democracy. They forged a shared commitment—a compact—to focus their own institutions on fulfilling the public purposes of higher education and to cooperate to work toward broad positive change.

Campus Compact envisions colleges and universities as vital agents and architects of a diverse democracy, committed to educating students for responsible citizenship in ways that both deepen their education and improve the quality of community life. We challenge all of higher education to make civic and community engagement an institutional priority.

We support this work locally and nationally by sharing what we know from research and practice to provide our members with the best tools, programming, resources, and hands-on support.

Learn more at compact.org.

For Product Safety Concerns and Information please contact our EU
representative GPSR@taylorandfrancis.com
Taylor & Francis Verlag GmbH, Kaufingerstraße 24, 80331 München, Germany

www.ingramcontent.com/pod-product-compliance
Lightning Source LLC
Chambersburg PA
CBHW070745020526
44116CB00032B/1977